Learn Mistral

Elevating Mistral systems through embeddings, agents, RAG, AWS Bedrock, and Vertex AI

Pavlo Cherkashin

Learn Mistral

Portfolio Director: Gebin George

Relationship Lead: Kunal Sawant

Project Manager: Prajakta Naik

Content Engineer: Tanya D'cruz

Technical Editor: Rahul Limbachiya

Copy Editor: Safis Editing

Indexer: Rekha Nair

Proofreader: Tanya D'cruz

Production Designer: Shankar Kalbhor

Growth Lead: Kunal Sawant

First published: September 2025

Production reference: 1011025

Published by Packt Publishing Ltd.

Grosvenor House

11 St Paul's Square

Birmingham

B3 1RB, UK.

ISBN 978-1-83588-864-3

www.packtpub.com

I dedicate this book to my children, Katerina, Anastasia, and PJ, who are my constant source of inspiration and joy.

— Pavlo Cherkashin

Contributors

About the author

Pavlo Cherkashin is a software engineer and author with over two decades of experience in software craftsmanship. He has lived half his life in Ukraine and half in the United States, always carrying Ukraine close to his heart. His career includes work at leading companies such as Oracle and Nike, and he is a co-author of a patented invention in enterprise software now owned by Oracle. His fascination with neural networks began during his university years, when he also developed a lasting passion for grammar parsers. Beyond his professional path, Pavlo is a proud father of three teenagers. He enjoys exploring the intersections of open-source AI, robust system design, MVP product engineering, and mentoring and training the next generation of engineers.

I dedicate this book to my children, Katerina, Anastasia, and PJ, who continue to inspire me with their energy, curiosity, and resilience. Every page written here carries a little reflection of the lessons I have learned from them and the motivation they give me to keep exploring, building, and sharing. This journey was also accompanied by countless cups of coffee and the determined company of Aki, my stubborn mini-dachshund, who insisted on being part of the process whether by keeping me awake or reminding me to take breaks. And of course, special mention goes to PJ, who reminds me daily that while I may be teaching machines how to reason, he still knows far more about TikTok than I will ever know about Mistral.

About the reviewers

Naresh Dulam is a visionary technology leader with deep expertise in data analytics, cloud computing, and artificial intelligence. Over his career, spanning influential roles across healthcare, telecom, and financial services, he has spearheaded transformative analytics platforms that deliver sustainable, impactful solutions to meet evolving industry needs. As a forward-thinking innovator, Naresh blends technical excellence with a passion for knowledge-sharing, mentoring aspiring professionals, and fostering ethical practices. His commitment to driving innovation and creating meaningful impact is matched by his vision of inspiring the next generation of technologists. Outside of work, Naresh enjoys adventurous expeditions in nature and empowering others to reach their full potential.

Rustam Mamedov is a hands-on software engineering leader with 20 years of experience in distributed systems, FinTech, and cloud infrastructure. Originally from Ukraine, he earned a master's degree in computer science from V. N. Karazin Kharkiv National University. At AWS, Rustam has spent the past four years leading teams responsible for optimizing the health and utilization of storage and webserver capacity in S3, while remaining directly involved in coding, architecture, and technical reviews. Prior to AWS, he spent 12 years in the FinTech industry developing consumer and small business lending products. Rustam is passionate about mentoring engineers and building supportive, high-performing teams.

Astha Puri is a Senior Data Scientist at CVS Health, where she leads the design of recommendation engines for digital platforms, helping customers discover the right products and enabling patients to access the health services and support they need. She specializes in home screen personalization, using data-driven insights to enhance user experiences. With a strong background in the tech industry, Astha is now applying her expertise to drive innovation and transformation in the healthcare sector.

Table of Contents

Preface   **xxiii**

Your Book Comes with Exclusive Perks - Here's How to Unlock Them xxviii

Chapter 1: Strengths, Limitations, and Use Cases of Language Models   1

What LLMs are suitable for, and what they are less applicable to 2

  Contextual understanding • 4

    Context handling in long conversations • 4

    Task adaptation across domains • 4

    Context sensitivity and personalization • 5

  Limitations of contextual understanding • 5

  Limitations in predictive accuracy • 5

    Real-time decision-making • 6

    Handling unforeseen situations • 6

    Overfitting and lack of generalization • 6

    Bias and ethical concerns • 7

    Understanding complex multimodal data • 7

  LLMs versus traditional algorithms • 7

Use cases that Mistral 8B covers 9

  Data summarization and extraction: Handling large datasets efficiently • 10

  Personalization engines: Adaptive models for user personalization • 10

  Multilingual support: Language families it supports • 10

  Codestral and coding assistant (FiM, unit tests, and scaffolding) • 11

Retrieval-augmented generation 11

Semantic search and document classification 12

  Semantic search: Understanding intent beyond keywords • 12

    Role of context in query interpretation • 13

    Example use cases • 14

Document classification: LLMs for automatic sorting and categorization • 16

    Example use cases • 17

Evaluating model performance • 18

    Model accuracy • 19

    Speed considerations • 19

Challenges in implementation • 19

    Ambiguity • 21

    Context loss • 21

    False positives • 21

Looking ahead: Agents that think and act 22

Mistral in the cloud: Shared idea with different faces 24

Summary 25

References 25

Join our Discord and Reddit space 26

Chapter 2: Setting Up Your Own Chat   27

Problem statement 28

Technical requirements 29

Practical workshop: Step-by-step guide to expose a local Mistral model to users 29

Step 1: Install and run Ollama • 30

Step 2: Play with local Mistral • 36

Step 3: Customize the model • 37

    Moderation with system prompts • 38

    Drafting a Modelfile • 40

    Creating a new model manifest • 41

    Interacting with the custom model • 42

Step 4: Integration with Obsidian • 44

    Using the Mistral model in note-taking • 50

Step 5: Integration with a web UI • 51

    Docker pull and dry run the web UI • 52

    Governing users • 58

Suggested hardware configurations **60**

   Single-user hardware configuration • 61

     Apple devices: evaluating the M1/M2 and M3 series • 61

     Windows/Linux with discrete GPUs: Preferred for performance • 61

     Emerging alternatives: AMD's Strix Halo • 62

   Powerful hardware configuration • 62

Summary **64**

Extracurricular **65**

Chapter 3: Managing the Model   67

Technical requirements **68**

Problem statement: When is adapting model parameters necessary? **68**

Pipeline overview **69**

   System prompts to shape the response payload • 71

     Prompt categories • 71

   Sequential token processing • 79

   Tokenization • 79

   Logits and weighting • 80

   Attention masking • 80

   Positional encoding • 80

   Input length and context window • 81

Refining the generated output **81**

   Softmax function • 82

     Applying the softmax function • 83

     Initial code for the softmax function • 85

   Temperature (controlling creativity and randomness) • 87

   top_k, top_p, and min_p (output refining) • 89

     top_k only takes k superior logits • 89

     top_p only takes the most probable up to the threshold • 89

     min_p filters out the noise • 90

Max_tokens (choosing the right output size) • 91

Repetition penalty (avoiding redundancy) • 92

Presence penalty (encouraging novel vocabulary) • 93

Mistral's natively supported parameters • 94

Practical workshop: the softmax function, temperature, top_k, and top_p 95

Step 1: Implementing the softmax function • 96

Step 2: Sorting the logits by probability • 96

Step 3: Implementing the top_k function • 97

Step 4: Implementing the top_p (nucleus sampling) function • 98

Step 5: Implementing the min_p function • 98

Step 6: Testing it all • 99

Summary 102

Extracurricular 102

References 103

Join our Discord and Reddit space 103

Chapter 4: Mastering Embeddings   **105**

Technical requirements 106

What is a vector? 106

Vector databases • 109

Visualizing embeddings 111

t-SNE: Revealing local clusters • 111

PCA: Capturing the global picture • 112

Brief comparison of PSA and t-SNE • 113

Heatmaps: visualizing similarities • 114

Practical workshop: Semantic search system with Mistral and Pinecone 116

Step 1: Environment setup • 116

Cloning the workshop repository • 116

Opening Google Colab • 116

Setting up the recommended GPU runtime • 117

Uploading the draft notebook • 118

Step 2: Initializing the Mistral AI client • 118

   Installing the mistralai package • 118

   Initializing the client object and performing a dry run • 118

   Setting up the Mistral API key • 119

Step 3: Generating embeddings • 121

   Generating embeddings for a single line • 122

   Context analysis • 123

Step 4: Embedding comparison • 125

   Reading user input for later semantic comparison with available options • 126

Step 5: Semantic match of user input with existing options • 127

   Calculating distances to all available embeddings • 128

   Resolving array dimension incompatibility • 129

   Finding the most relevant dish match • 129

   Displaying the most relevant semantic match • 130

Demo retrospective • 131

Bonus exercise: Semantic search with Pinecone DB • 131

   Initializing the Pinecone client • 132

   Creating a Pinecone index • 132

   Upserting embeddings to Pinecone • 133

   Finding the closest match • 134

Bonus exercise: Semantic similarity with heatmap visualization • 135

Bonus exercise: Semantic similarity using t-SNE visualization • 138

Workshop complete! • 141

Applications and practical exercises with embeddings **141**

Job description and candidate matching service • 142

Document classification service • 142

Recommendation systems • 142

News analysis and correlation to stock prices • 142

Summary **143**

Extracurricular **143**

Chapter 5: Agents: From Automation to Intelligence   **145**

Technical requirements 146

Problem statement 146

Defining agents in AI systems 147

Why automation falls short • 147

What we mean by agents • 148

Agents versus traditional automation • 150

Building blocks of agentic systems • 151

Why agents matter in practice • 152

Workshop 1: Multi-agent answering service 154

Step 1: Setting up the stage • 155

Step 2: Preparing the Mistral API keys and testing the connection • 156

Step 3: Creating a safe calculator tool • 157

Step 4: Using a shared ReAct prompt and refining the agent loop • 159

Step 5: Building a web search tool • 161

Implementing the web search tool • 162

Testing the web search tool • 165

Step 6: Creating a research agent with multiple tools • 166

Defining the research agent class • 166

Adding research methods • 167

Testing the research agent • 168

Step 7: Specialized customer service agents • 169

Defining the base specialized agent • 170

Handling incoming inquiries in a role • 171

Implementing role-specific agents • 172

Step 8: Multi-agent customer service system • 174

Step 9: Interactive demo interface setup • 177

Importing UI components • 178

Creating the interface class • 178

Creating widgets • 179

Building the chat interface workflow • 182

Handling query submission • 185

Step 10: Launching interactive demo • 188

Usage instructions • 188

Creating and displaying the interface • 188

Step 11: Agent performance testing • 189

Defining the performance tester class • 190

Result initialization • 191

All tests loop • 191

Process time-measured agent call (success path) • 192

Handle error (failure path) • 192

Final metrics calculation and persistence • 193

Method: printing a summary of metrics • 193

Creating the tester and defining agent-specific functions • 194

Research agent wrapper and queries • 194

Customer service system wrapper and queries • 195

Executing the performance runs • 195

Workshop 2: Visual AI agents with n8n **196**

Step 1: Setting up n8n and free data sources • 196

Step 2: Configuring the Telegram bot and chat for notifications • 199

Step 3: Adding a manual trigger and configuring HTTP requests • 203

Adding the manual trigger • 203

Adding the first HTTP request node • 204

Configuring the HTTP request node • 205

Duplicating the HTTP requests for gainers and losers • 206

Step 4: Merging, deduplicating, and sorting market data • 207

Merging the three data streams • 207

Removing duplicates • 208

Deduplicating and sorting the data • 208

The processing script • 209

Rerunning the workflow • 212

Step 5: Configuring Yahoo Finance • 213

Step 6: Fetching and parsing news (Google News RSS, last two days) • 215

   Adding the Google News HTTP request • 216

   Wiring two Code nodes after Google News • 217

   Making the connections and verifying the run • 219

   Rerunning the workflow • 220

Step 7: Merging metrics with news and preparing the Mistral prompt • 220

   Setting up the Merge block • 220

   Building the Mistral prompt • 223

   Declare the system prompt and request body • 225

Step 8: Sending prompts to Mistral and delivering to Telegram • 226

Step 9: Run the entire workflow • 230

Summary 231

Extracurricular 231

Join our Discord and Reddit space 232

Chapter 6: Unpacking RAG Workflows   233

Technical requirements 234

Problem statement 234

RAG architecture 234

Indexing • 236

   Types of indexed data • 237

   Initial document loading • 239

   Slicing the text • 239

   Embeddings • 240

Retrieval • 241

   Preparing the retriever • 241

   Retrieving documents from the vector store • 242

Generation • 243

   Preparing the prompt • 244

   Preparing the LLM • 244

Creating and invoking the chain • 245

Interaction between retrieval and generation models • 246

Challenges and trade-offs in RAG systems • 247

Workshop 1: Bootstrap RAG implementation 248

Step 1: Prepare the environment • 248

Preparing required libraries • 249

Initializing environment variables • 250

Preparing user prompts • 250

Step 2: Indexing • 251

Loading text from a URL • 251

Splitting text into chunks • 252

Grinding text to vectors and sending to the vector store • 253

Step 3: Retrieval • 254

Step 4: Generation • 255

Initializing a prompt template for the generator • 255

Using prompt templates from LangChain Hub • 256

Initializing the LLM • 257

Initializing a simple chain • 257

Invoking the chain for a given user question • 258

Testing all questions • 259

Understanding the next workshops 264

Workshop 2: Multi-query approach 265

Step 1: Prepare the environment • 266

Preparing user prompts • 267

Step 2: Indexing • 268

Step 3: Retrieval • 268

Initialize the retriever • 269

Initializing a drill-down prompt template • 269

Generating rephrased questions • 271

Initializing and calling the retrieval chain • 272

Step 4: Generating a summarized response • 273

LangSmith metrics overview • 276

Runs overview • 276

VectorStoreRetriever • 277

ChatMistralAI • 278

Workshop 3: Atomic sub-queries 279

Step 1: Prepare the environment • 280

Step 2: Indexing • 281

Step 3: Retrieval • 281

Init retriever • 281

Initializing a drill-down prompt template • 282

Generating detailed questions • 283

Preparing a unique union • 284

Generating a summarized response • 285

Workshop 4: Generification approach 287

Step 1: Prepare the environment • 288

Step 2: Indexing • 289

Step 3: Retrieval • 289

Init retriever • 289

Initializing the step-back prompt • 290

Generating step-back questions • 292

Step 4: Generating a summarized response • 293

Summary 295

Extracurricular 296

Chapter 7: Coding with Mistral   297

Technical requirements 298

Problem statement 298

Workshop 1: Talk to your code 299

Step 1: Preparing the environment • 299

Preparing required libraries • 299

Initializing API keys • 300

Step 2: Indexing the GitHub repo source code • 300

    Cloning the remote repository • 301

    Loading data from the files • 301

    Splitting the document into chunks • 303

    Indexing of the code chunks • 304

Step 3: Talking to your code • 307

    Preparing the chat • 307

    Adding chat conversation capabilities • 308

    Finally, talking to your code • 310

Workshop 2: Codestral in VS Code **311**

Step 1: Preparing the environment • 311

    Installing VS Code • 312

    Logging in to GitHub • 312

    Installing the Continue extension • 313

    Installing the Python extension • 314

    Setting up a Python virtual environment and Flask • 314

    Tuning up the Continue extension • 316

    Preparing the new project • 318

Step 2: Generating our first code • 318

    Applying changes to your workspace • 321

    Running the application • 321

Step 3: Making changes on top of existing code • 321

    Applying suggested changes • 324

    Reviewing the final code • 325

    Running the code • 326

    Testing the endpoint • 326

Step 4: Wrapping it into a web page • 327

    Testing the web page • 328

    Troubleshooting errors • 329

    Verifying the fix • 331

Step 5: Using the FiM technique • 331

Step 6: Learning from code • 333

Summary 334

Extracurricular 335

Join our Discord and Reddit space 337

Chapter 8: Building Smarter Defenses with Mistral   339

Technical requirements 340

Problem statement 340

Security applications 340

  Rule compliance auditing • 341

  Firewall logs analysis • 343

    Anomalous traffic detection • 344

    Geolocation-based analysis • 346

    Alert prioritization • 348

    Zero-day threat detection • 349

  Stateful firewall logs • 351

    Session tracking • 351

    Protocol misuse • 352

  Other security applications • 354

Practical workshop: Code and cloud security with Mistral 356

  Step 1: Environment setup • 356

  Step 2: Cloud security analysis • 357

  Step 3: SQL injection detection • 363

  Step 4: Cross-site scripting detection • 366

Summary 369

Extracurricular 370

Chapter 9: Take-Home RAG Challenges   371

Helpful code examples 372

Problem statement 373

Challenge 1: Revolutionize software QA with RAG testing 373

  Step 1: Define the scope of your QA RAG system • 375

Step 2: Ingest relevant data sources • 376

Step 3: Design the retrieval process • 378

Step 4: Fine-tune the RAG system • 380

Step 5: Validate outputs • 383

Step 6: Optimize and scale • 384

Step 7: Integrate with QA workflows • 385

Takeaway • 388

Challenge 2: Build a real-time news summarizer with RAG 388

Step 1: Integrate live news feeds and public APIs • 390

Step 2: Build a retrieval system for relevant articles • 392

Step 3: Fine-tune the generative model for summarization • 394

Step 4: Enable real-time updates with dynamic indexing pipelines • 396

Step 5: Test and optimize for speed and accuracy • 397

Stress-test your system with Apache JMeter • 398

Create a test plan in JMeter • 398

Step 6: Integrate a user-friendly interface • 399

Takeaway • 400

Summary 401

Join our Discord and Reddit space 401

Chapter 10: Mistral on AWS Bedrock 403

Technical requirements 404

Problem statement 404

Cloud-based AI models: Why Bedrock matters 405

Authentication and access control 405

API-driven model interactions 406

Observability with CloudWatch Logs 407

Practical workshop: Hands-on inference with boto3 and CLI 407

Step 1: Environment setup • 408

Create an AWS account • 408

Create new IAM user and setup permissions • 409

Create an access key for the user • 412

Configure the AWS CLI V2 client on your computer • 414

Request access to the Mistral model on Bedrock • 416

Prepare the VSCode project • 419

Step 2: Connect AWS Bedrock with boto3 • 420

Step 3: Send a prompt to Bedrock and get a stream response • 421

Step 4: Check CloudWatch Logs for Bedrock • 426

Summary 426

Extracurricular 427

Chapter 11: Harnessing Mistral's Power via Google Cloud Vertex AI   429

Technical requirements 430

Understanding Vertex AI 430

Vertex AI in the GCP ecosystem • 431

Model Garden: Hosted LLMs at your fingertips • 431

Deploying your own models to Vertex AI • 432

Inference workflows • 432

Structure of a model request • 433

Authentication and access in GCP • 434

Choosing the right development flow • 435

Development best practices for AI integration • 435

Practical workshop: Fast-tracking Mistral apps with Vertex AI 436

What is needed • 437

Step 1: The setup and preparation • 437

Creating a Google Cloud project • 438

Enabling the required APIs • 439

Linking a billing account • 440

Linking a project to a billing account • 442

Enabling APIs and services • 444

Deploying Mistral from Model Garden • 447

Step 2: Playing with the model in Google Colab Enterprise • 449

  Opening a Colab notebook • 449

  Running the first step: authenticate user • 451

  Selecting the Mistral model • 452

  Running the region selection widget • 454

  Running the project selection widget • 455

  Importing required libraries • 456

  Running the inference requests • 457

Step 3: Using Mistral AI's Vertex SDK for Python • 461

  Setting up the gcloud CLI • 462

  Preparing the virtual environment and requirements • 465

  Authenticating a session from Python • 466

  Initializing variables • 468

  Calling the inference request • 469

  Calling a streaming request • 471

Summary 474

Extracurricular 474

Subscribe for a Free eBook 475

Other Books You May Enjoy   479

Index   483

Preface

This book is a practical guide to working with Mistral models and Retrieval-Augmented Generation (RAG), designed for developers, data scientists, and technology professionals who want to bridge the gap between theory and application. It introduces the core concepts of large language models and embeddings, then progresses through hands-on workshops that cover building chat systems, tuning models, designing RAG pipelines, coding assistants, security applications, and deploying at scale with AWS Bedrock and Google Vertex AI.

The book is intended for builders, tinkerers, and curious minds who learn best by doing. Each chapter combines foundational theory with modular workshops, allowing you to dive into the topics that excite you most while ensuring earlier sections prepare you with the necessary setup and mindset. The approach emphasizes practical skills with minimal costs—using Python, Google Colab, VS Code, and cloud services that can run on free tiers or modest budgets.

While roughly two-thirds of the book is hands-on, the early theory chapters are not to be skipped. They establish the building blocks of LLMs, embeddings, and RAG, which make the later exercises more meaningful and effective. Each workshop is self-contained, but common setup steps such as API keys and environment configuration are introduced once and assumed in later chapters. For those ready to go further, extracurricular challenges are included throughout, encouraging experimentation beyond guided exercises and inspiring readers to extend their projects into new directions.

In short, this book is both a workshop companion and a reference guide. It equips you with the knowledge and skills to build intelligent systems, while leaving room for creativity, exploration, and innovation.

Who this book is for

This book is designed to be equally interesting to data science professionals, software engineers and AI/LLM enthusiasts who want to build practical skills with Mistral models and RAG. Whether you are working in software engineering, data science, business intelligence, or industry applications, the book provides both the concepts and hands-on projects needed to apply AI effectively in real-world scenarios across domains.

Working knowledge of Python and the basics of NumPy and pandas is helpful; however, the material remains accessible, with comprehensive step-by-step guides to bridge any gaps. Familiarity with data structures (lists, dictionaries, arrays) and core mathematical concepts in linear algebra, probability, and calculus will be helpful, though not strictly required. The book is designed to bridge theory with application, making advanced ideas accessible to anyone ready to experiment and build.

What this book covers

Chapter 1, Strengths, Limitations, and Use Cases of Language Models, explores what LLMs such as Mistral 8B excel at, summarization, translation, text generation, contextual understanding, and where they fall short, including real-time decision-making, generalization, and bias. It also introduces the foundational methods used throughout the book, RAG, semantic search, document classification, and performance evaluation, while previewing agent workflows and deployment on AWS Bedrock and Google Vertex A.

Chapter 2, Setting Up Your Own Chat, provides a step-by-step guide to building a secure, locally hosted AI chat system with Mistral models using Ollama, including customization with Modelfiles, system prompts, and parameter tuning. It also demonstrates integration with Obsidian and a web UI for multi-user access, along with governance features and hardware recommendations for different deployment needs.

Chapter 3, Managing the Model, explains how parameters such as temperature, top_k, top_p, and penalties influence language model output and how system prompts shape context, tone, and behavior. It provides both the mathematical foundations and practical workshops, equipping readers to refine generation quality and tune models for precision, creativity, and control.

Chapter 4, Mastering Embeddings, introduces how vectors represent meaning in multi-dimensional space and demonstrates methods for measuring and visualizing semantic similarity. It provides hands-on workshops with Mistral and Pinecone to build semantic search systems, compare embeddings, and apply them in real-world applications such as recommendations, document classification, and search.

Chapter 5, Agents: From Automation to Intelligence, explains how agents extend beyond traditional automation by combining reasoning loops, tools, and memory with LLMs to create adaptive, goal-driven systems. It provides hands-on workshops for building multi-agent workflows, specialized customer service agents, and n8n-powered pipelines, while also introducing methods for performance evaluation and interactive deployment.

Chapter 6, Unpacking RAG Workflows, introduces the architecture of retrieval-augmented generation, covering indexing, retrieval, and generation as the core stages for grounding LLM outputs in external data. It provides hands-on workshops that progress from a baseline RAG pipeline to advanced methods such as multi-query expansion, atomic sub-queries, and step-back generalization, enabling the design of scalable, context-aware systems.

Chapter 7, Coding with Mistral, demonstrates how Mistral and Codestral models can act as coding assistants, from analyzing repositories with RAG-based search to generating and explaining code directly in VS Code. It provides hands-on workshops for building a conversational code assistant, using Fill-in-the-Middle generation, and integrating with tools like Flask and web interfaces to accelerate development and debugging.

Chapter 8, Building Smarter Defenses with Mistral, shows how LLMs can enhance cybersecurity by automating log analysis, detecting anomalies, and identifying vulnerabilities such as SQL injection, cross-site scripting, and cloud misconfigurations. Through practical workshops, it demonstrates how to secure firewall rules, audit Terraform scripts, and strengthen application and cloud security using Mistral and Codestral.

Chapter 9, Take-Home RAG Challenges, presents open-ended projects that push retrieval-augmented generation beyond guided examples into real-world experimentation. It challenges readers to design domain-specific QA assistants and real-time news summarizers, emphasizing creativity, fine-tuning, and scalable system design.

Chapter 10, Mistral on AWS Bedrock, explains how AWS Bedrock simplifies LLM deployment by providing managed access to Mistral models with secure IAM integration, serverless scalability, and cost efficiency. It guides readers through hands-on workshops covering environment setup, API-driven interactions with boto3, and monitoring with CloudWatch to build real-world AI applications.

Chapter 11, Harnessing Mistral's Power via Google Cloud Vertex AI, demonstrates how to deploy and interact with Mistral models on Google Cloud using Vertex AI and Model Garden, covering authentication, synchronous and streaming inference, and integration with cloud services. It guides readers through hands-on workshops in Colab and VS Code to build modular, production-ready Python workflows for running LLMs in managed, scalable environments.

To get the most out of this book

Before starting the book, it's helpful to have a few core components in place. These are the main tools and accounts you'll use across multiple chapters. Each workshop will guide you through additional setup details as needed, but preparing these essentials up front will make your journey smoother.

- A Python 3.8+ development environment (with pip) on your machine.
- Git and GitHub access to clone and work with the official repository that contains all chapter code and resources.
- An IDE such as VS Code (or equivalent) for writing and running Python scripts.
- A Mistral account and API key to access and experiment with Mistral models.
- Google Colab or Jupyter for running notebooks in a managed or local environment.
- Cloud accounts where applicable: an AWS account (for *Chapter 10*) and a Google Cloud account (for *Chapter 11*), each with CLI tools configured.

With these basics ready, you'll be well-prepared to follow the examples and focus on the core learning goals, while each chapter provides step-by-step guidance for service-specific setup.

Download the example code files

The code bundle for the book is hosted on GitHub at `https://github.com/PacktPublishing/Learn-Mistral`. We also have other code bundles from our rich catalog of books and videos available at `https://github.com/PacktPublishing`. Check them out!

Download the color images

We also provide a PDF file that has color images of the screenshots/diagrams used in this book. You can download it here: `https://packt.link/gbp/9781835888643`

Conventions used

There are a number of text conventions used throughout this book.

`CodeInText`: Indicates code words in text, database table names, folder names, filenames, file extensions, pathnames, dummy URLs, user input, and Twitter handles. For example: "We use the `client.embeddings.create` method of the Mistral client to fetch the embedding for the sample sentence."

A block of code is set as follows:

```
from google.colab import userdata
from mistral import MistralClient
api_key = userdata.get("MISTRAL_API_KEY")
client = MistralClient(api_key)
```

Any output is written as follows:

```
Successfully installed eval-type-backport-0.2.2 jsonpath-python-1.0.6
mistralai-1.5.1 mypy-extensions-1.0.0 typing-inspect-0.9.0
```

Bold: Indicates a new term, an important word, or words that you see on the screen. For instance, words in menus or dialog boxes appear in the text like this. For example: " Next, we'll explore **Workshop 3 – Zoom into Atomic Sub-Queries**, where we'll break down complex questions into smaller, focused sub-queries."

Warnings or important notes appear like this.

Tips and tricks appear like this.

Get in touch

Feedback from our readers is always welcome.

General feedback: If you have questions about any aspect of this book or have any general feedback, please email us at customercare@packt.com and mention the book's title in the subject of your message.

Errata: Although we have taken every care to ensure the accuracy of our content, mistakes do happen. If you have found a mistake in this book, we would be grateful if you reported this to us. Please visit http://www.packt.com/submit-errata, click **Submit Errata**, and fill in the form.

Piracy: If you come across any illegal copies of our works in any form on the internet, we would be grateful if you would provide us with the location address or website name. Please contact us at copyright@packt.com with a link to the material.

If you are interested in becoming an author: If there is a topic that you have expertise in and you are interested in either writing or contributing to a book, please visit http://authors.packt.com/.

Your Book Comes with Exclusive Perks - Here's How to Unlock Them

Unlock this book's exclusive benefits now

UNLOCK NOW

Scan this QR code or go to packtpub.com/unlock, then search this book by name. Ensure it's the correct edition.

Note: *Keep your purchase invoice ready before you start.*

Enhanced reading experience with our Next-gen Reader:

⌖ **Multi-device progress sync**: Learn from any device with seamless progress sync.

▦ **Highlighting and notetaking**: Turn your reading into lasting knowledge.

⌗ **Bookmarking**: Revisit your most important learnings anytime.

✴ **Dark mode**: Focus with minimal eye strain by switching to dark or sepia mode.

Learn smarter using our AI assistant (Beta):

✦ **Summarize it**: Summarize key sections or an entire chapter.

✦ **AI code explainers**: In the next-gen Packt Reader, click the **Explain** button above each code block for AI-powered code explanations.

> *Note: The AI assistant is part of next-gen Packt Reader and is still in beta.*

Learn anytime, anywhere:

Access your content offline with DRM-free PDF and ePub versions—compatible with your favorite e-readers.

Unlock Your Book's Exclusive Benefits

Your copy of this book comes with the following exclusive benefits:

☁ Next-gen Packt Reader

✦ AI assistant (beta)

▣ DRM-free PDF/ePub downloads

Use the following guide to unlock them if you haven't already. The process takes just a few minutes and needs to be done only once.

How to unlock these benefits in three easy steps

Step 1

Keep your purchase invoice for this book ready, as you'll need it in *Step 3*. If you received a physical invoice, scan it on your phone and have it ready as either a PDF, JPG, or PNG.

For more help on finding your invoice, visit `https://www.packtpub.com/unlock-benefits/help`.

> **Note**: Did you buy this book directly from Packt? You don't need an invoice. After completing Step 2, you can jump straight to your exclusive content.

Step 2

Scan this QR code or go to `https://packtpub.com/unlock`.

On the page that opens (which will look similar to Figure 0.1 if you're on desktop), search for this book by name. Make sure you select the correct edition.

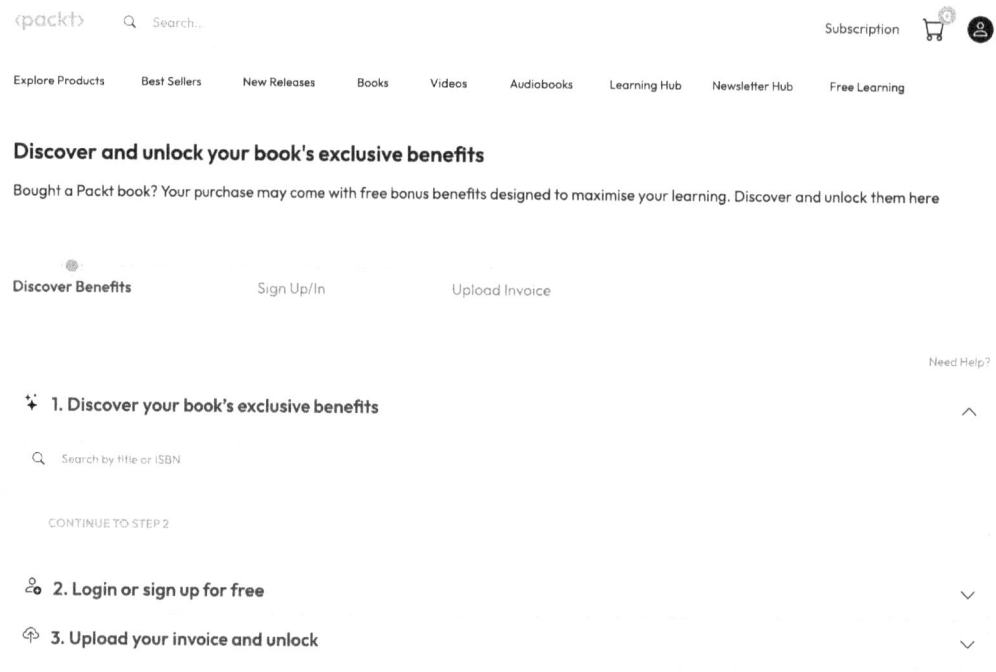

<packt>   Q Search...   Subscription 🛒 👤

Explore Products   Best Sellers   New Releases   Books   Videos   Audiobooks   Learning Hub   Newsletter Hub   Free Learning

Discover and unlock your book's exclusive benefits

Bought a Packt book? Your purchase may come with free bonus benefits designed to maximise your learning. Discover and unlock them here

Discover Benefits   Sign Up/In   Upload Invoice

Need Help?

✦ 1. Discover your book's exclusive benefits   ∧

Q   Search by title or ISBN

CONTINUE TO STEP 2

👥 2. Login or sign up for free   ∨

☁ 3. Upload your invoice and unlock   ∨

Figure 0.1: Packt unlock landing page on desktop

Step 3

Sign in to your Packt account or create a new one for free. Once you're logged in, upload your invoice. It can be in PDF, PNG, or JPG format and must be no larger than 10 MB. Follow the rest of the instructions on the screen to complete the process.

Need help?

If you get stuck and need help, visit `https://www.packtpub.com/unlock-benefits/help` for a detailed FAQ on how to find your invoices and more. The following QR code will take you to the help page directly:

Note: If you are still facing issues, reach out to `customercare@packt.com`.

Share your thoughts

Once you've read *Learn Mistral*, we'd love to hear your thoughts! Scan the QR code below to go straight to the Amazon review page for this book and share your feedback.

`https://packt.link/r/1835888658`

Your review is important to us and the tech community and will help us make sure we're delivering excellent quality content.

1

Strengths, Limitations, and Use Cases of Language Models

AI systems mirror our own intelligence back to us. This is the source of their growing commercial and scientific power.

— Shannon Vallor, The AI Mirror

Language models are not just a trend in AI—they're transforming how we interact with technology. **Large language models (LLMs)** can understand, process, and generate human-like text, unlocking new possibilities across industries. As we explore Mistral LLMs throughout this book, you'll see they're not just tools but partners in solving complex problems, processing vast information, and delivering personalized solutions. Mistral models are redefining what AI can do, whether powering virtual assistants or analyzing data. Their open source nature and innovation, especially with **Mistral 8B**, allow you to shape and customize them to meet your needs. Imagine tools summarizing complex documents, extracting key insights, or creating new content. These capabilities are already solving real-world problems in various industries, and Mistral models make this power accessible to everyone—from developers to business leaders. They enable you to push boundaries and solve challenges the future holds for us.

In this chapter, you'll discover what LLMs excel at and where they might fall short. We'll explore Mistral 8B and Mistral 7B's practical applications, how Mistral 8x7B enhances these capabilities, and journey through cutting-edge topics such as **retrieval-augmented generation (RAG)**, semantic search, document classification, and the importance of model fine-tuning.

This chapter is the most theoretical in the book and contains no practical exercises, but don't skip it. The concepts covered here will empower you to make informed decisions and get much more out of the hands-on chapters that follow.

In this chapter, we'll discover the following:

- What LLMs are suitable for and what they are less applicable to
- Use cases Mistral 8B covers
- Retrieval-augmented generation
- Semantic search and document classification
- Agents that think and act
- Mistral in the cloud

As we move into the next section, *What LLMs are suitable for*, keep in mind that this isn't only a technical exercise. It's an invitation to explore a future where machines help us navigate, process, and even understand the complexities of human language. By mastering the potential and limitations of these models, you will be ready to harness their full power and embark on a transformative journey of your own. Let's dive in.

What LLMs are suitable for, and what they are less applicable to

It's essential to understand first where LLMs truly shine and where they still face meaningful limitations. This section lays the foundation by exploring the practical capabilities of LLMs such as Mistral 8B in tasks such as summarization, translation, and content generation, while also acknowledging scenarios where traditional algorithms or human oversight may still outperform them.

LLMs have revolutionized **natural language processing (NLP)**, excelling in summarization, translation, and text generation tasks. These models are reshaping how we process language, handle context, and address specialized needs in domains such as healthcare and law while facing limitations in real-time decision-making.

Before diving into the specific real-world applications of Mistral, it's essential to understand the capabilities at different scales. At a high level, LLMs excel at several core NLP tasks:

- **Summarization**: LLMs make summarizing large volumes of text fast and efficient, whether for legal documents, academic papers, or news articles. By identifying key points and rephrasing information, LLMs streamline data-heavy tasks. Mistral 8B excels in both **extractive** (selecting direct text) and **abstractive** (rephrasing content) summarization, saving time and reducing human oversight.

- **Translation**: Unlike traditional systems, LLMs provide more contextual, accurate translations, understanding idioms and cultural nuances. This makes them invaluable for customer service chatbots and businesses operating in multiple languages. With models like Mistral 8B, translations feel more natural, catering to global communication without losing meaning.

- **Text generation**: LLMs have made huge strides in text generation, producing coherent, human-like content for marketing, creative writing, or technical documentation. Mistral 8B helps generate articles, emails, and code documentation, maintaining context, tone, and fluency over long passages and outperforming traditional rule-based systems.

- **Advantages of scale**: Thanks to their scale, models such as Mistral 8B can manage complex linguistic patterns with remarkable precision, excelling across a wide range of tasks. Although they demand greater computational power, the resulting performance gains often outweigh the costs—making them indispensable for high-accuracy, high-speed NLP applications.

Advanced LLMs have transformed NLP tasks, enabling breakthroughs in automation and creativity. As they evolve, they'll become even more integrated into our daily lives, marking the start of a new era in human-machine collaboration. However, to fully grasp what makes advanced models such as Mistral 8B truly powerful, we must look beyond these high-level tasks.

In the following subsections, we'll dive deeper into specific functional capabilities—such as contextual understanding, task adaptation, and personalization—which underpin and enrich these high-level applications. Understanding these nuanced capabilities helps clarify why LLMs such as Mistral 8B stand out, not just in performing isolated tasks, but in navigating complex, real-world interactions.

Contextual understanding

Context is everything in human communication. From understanding the nuances in a conversation to switching seamlessly between topics, our ability to retain and process context shapes how effectively we communicate. In the world of LLMs, contextual understanding is one of the critical factors that sets modern models apart from their predecessors. It's not enough for an AI system to generate coherent sentences—it must also understand the broader context of a conversation, a task, or even a user's preferences to be genuinely effective.

At the forefront of this innovation are massive neural networks such as Mistral 8B, which handle context-rich environments with exceptional finesse. Whether it's a chatbot managing multiple conversations or a virtual assistant juggling different tasks, Mistral's ability to retain context and adapt to dynamic situations is a game-changer in NLP.

Next, we explore several dimensions of this capability, detailing exactly how Mistral 8B and similar models extend context handling into deeper, more dynamic scenarios.

Context handling in long conversations

One of the most impressive features of the Mistral 8B family of large models is their ability to handle long, multi-turn conversations without losing track of the conversation's flow. In early AI systems, context often disappeared after a few exchanges, leading to irrelevant responses. Contextual understanding is key here. LLMs use attention mechanisms and memory models to retain important information, ensuring relevance and coherence as conversations evolve.

For example, Mistral 8B can track topic shifts in customer service while maintaining context, offering responses that build on earlier interactions. This is made possible by the transformer architecture and its self-attention mechanism, prioritizing relevant parts of the conversation, enabling accurate responses even when topics change or overlap.

Task adaptation across domains

In addition to handling long conversations, Mistral 8B and other similar systems excel at task adaptation—seamlessly switching between tasks without losing context. For example, a user could ask the model to schedule a meeting and then switch to summarizing a report. Mistral 8B handles both tasks fluidly, remembering key details from earlier interactions.

This adaptability stems from the LLM's multi-task learning capabilities. Unlike older models needing retraining, Mistral can dynamically adjust to different tasks across domains, such as generating content, answering questions, or translating text, all while maintaining context and accuracy. This flexibility makes it highly effective in varied settings.

Context sensitivity and personalization

Perhaps one of the most exciting developments in LLM technology is its ability to deliver context-sensitive and personalized experiences. Users expect AI to cater to their preferences and habits. For example, an LLM might track progress in a learning platform and adjust responses based on performance and learning style.

Mistral 8B excels in personalization by using previous interactions to tailor responses. In fields such as education or e-commerce, this personalized approach improves user engagement. The model can adjust lesson plans or suggest products based on behavior, continuously refining its suggestions to match individual needs better.

Limitations of contextual understanding

Although modern LLMs such as Mistral 8B demonstrate remarkable capabilities in contextual understanding and task adaptation, significant challenges remain. Maintaining accurate context over extended conversations or multiple interactions is particularly difficult due to fixed input context windows, leading to the potential loss of older, crucial information.

In high-stakes fields such as law or medicine, failing to accurately interpret nuanced, context-dependent details can result in serious errors. Fine-tuning and external memory models help address these limitations, but further development is needed to enhance long-term context tracking.

Overall, whether managing multi-turn conversations, adapting to different tasks, or delivering personalized, context-sensitive responses, powerful architectures such as Mistral 8B have demonstrated an extraordinary ability to operate in complex, context-rich environments. However, as with all advanced systems, there are still outstanding challenges, especially those related to maintaining long-term context and understanding nuanced, multi-layered interactions.

As AI continues to evolve, these areas will undoubtedly see further improvements, pushing the boundaries of what LLMs can achieve in natural language understanding.

Limitations in predictive accuracy

Beyond these contextual challenges, LLMs—including those in the Mistral 8B league—still have significant limitations when it comes to predictive accuracy, especially in critical scenarios demanding precision or rapid responses. Challenges include hampered real-time decision-making, overfitting training data, struggling to generalize to unforeseen situations, and exhibiting biases learned from underlying datasets. We go into these limitations next, as recognizing where LLMs fall short helps underscore the continued need for human oversight and the integration of complementary technologies as AI systems evolve further.

Real-time decision-making

Real-time decision-making is critical in autonomous systems, healthcare, and financial trading, where every second counts. However, LLMs often struggle to meet the demands of real-time applications due to inherent limitations in processing speed and contextual adaptation. These models rely on pre-trained knowledge and inference processes, which are not always optimal for split-second decisions.

One of the key reasons for this limitation is latency—LLMs require significant computational power to generate accurate responses. Even though advancements in model optimization have reduced latency, real-time decision-making requires near-instantaneous processing, which LLMs can't always guarantee. For example, real-time decisions need to be made in autonomous vehicles to ensure safety. A split-second delay could result in a misinterpretation of environmental changes, potentially leading to an accident. Current LLM architectures are not fast enough to interpret and act on real-time sensory inputs such as visual data from cameras or LiDAR systems, making them unsuitable for such applications.

Additionally, LLMs are often ill-equipped to update context dynamically in real time. These models rely on a fixed input window and predefined data, making it challenging to adapt continuously as new information becomes available. In financial markets, where decisions are based on rapidly changing data, relying on LLMs for real-time trades or risk management could lead to costly errors if the model fails to process the latest information accurately and in time.

Handling unforeseen situations

Another significant limitation of LLMs is their difficulty handling unforeseen situations—scenarios outside their training data. Heavyweight LLMs rely on patterns from massive datasets, often failing when faced with new inputs.

In critical areas such as healthcare, rare symptoms may result in incorrect diagnoses. Retraining LLMs for every new scenario is impractical, and they lack common-sense reasoning to handle novel or evolving issues, making them less adaptable in dynamic environments such as law or regulation.

Overfitting and lack of generalization

Overfitting happens when an AI excels on its training data but struggles with new, unseen inputs. This is a limitation for high-parameter models, which risk overfitting, especially when fine-tuned for specific tasks.

For example, in the legal domain, an LLM trained in specific case law may miss crucial nuances in new cases, failing to generalize effectively. Similarly, in medical imaging, a text-based LLM may struggle with image interpretation, leading to inaccurate results.

Bias and ethical concerns

Bias in AI models significantly affects predictive accuracy. LLMs trained on large datasets inherit human biases, leading to inaccurate or unfair predictions in real-world applications.

For instance, in criminal justice, LLMs may produce biased recidivism predictions if trained on biased data. In hiring, LLMs might favor specific backgrounds, reinforcing inequalities. These biases pose serious ethical challenges in all areas, but especially healthcare and policing, requiring more diverse training data and greater oversight to mitigate harm.

Understanding complex multimodal data

Finally, LLMs are primarily trained on text data, limiting their predictive accuracy with multimodal inputs such as images, audio, or video. Though multimodal models are progressing, LLMs such as Mistral 8B struggle to integrate diverse data sources.

> Mistral has introduced a separate line of models called Pixtrail, specifically designed to handle visual input sources. These are developed independently from the core language models and represent Mistral's approach to multimodal learning in image processing contexts.

In medical diagnostics, for example, LLMs handle text well but struggle with visual data such as MRI scans, making it challenging to provide holistic predictions. This limits LLM use in fields requiring comprehensive multimodal understanding. Despite LLM advancements, challenges remain, and recognizing these limitations ensures responsible use.

Having these grounds covered, let us switch gears to comparing LLMs with traditional algorithms.

LLMs versus traditional algorithms

Next-generation architectures have expanded the boundaries of AI in NLP and machine learning. However, they aren't always the best choice. In many cases, traditional algorithms outperform LLMs, offering greater efficiency and reliability.

This section explores where traditional algorithms excel, including efficiency, interpretability, domain-specific accuracy, and real-time consistency. Understanding these advantages ensures that we balance cutting-edge AI with the proven reliability of traditional approaches:

- **Efficiency and resource usage**: One key advantage traditional algorithms have over LLMs is efficiency. With billions of parameters, LLMs need vast computational power and memory, making them unsuitable for tasks requiring fast, lightweight computations.

  In contrast, traditional algorithms such as quicksort or binary search are optimized for speed and minimal resource use, which makes them ideal for large datasets and basic tasks. Unlike LLMs, which need specialized GPUs, they can run on general-purpose hardware. In energy-sensitive applications, traditional algorithms are the more practical, efficient choice.

- **Interpretability and transparency**: Another area where traditional algorithms excel is interpretability and transparency. They follow transparent, step-by-step processes, making their decisions easy to understand, which is crucial in fields such as finance, legal compliance, and scientific research.

  For instance, decision trees provide transparent, auditable reasoning, while LLMs often act as black boxes, making their decision-making process hard to explain. This lack of clarity poses challenges in industries requiring regulatory scrutiny. While **explainable AI (XAI)** is being developed, traditional algorithms remain superior for tasks demanding complete transparency.

- **Accuracy in domain-specific tasks**: When it comes to domain-specific tasks, traditional algorithms are often more accurate than LLMs. While LLMs are generalists, traditional algorithms are fine-tuned for specific fields, often outperforming LLMs in specialized domains.

  For example, in image recognition, **convolutional neural networks (CNNs)** or specialized algorithms outperform LLMs, which focus on text. In engineering or numerical analysis, algorithms such as **finite element methods (FEM)** offer precision that LLMs lack. Traditional algorithms, built on decades of domain expertise, are more suited to these precise applications.

- **Consistency and determinism**: One of the hallmarks of traditional algorithms is their consistency and deterministic nature. Given the same input, traditional algorithms always produce the same output, ensuring reliability for tasks needing predictability. In contrast, probabilistic LLMs can vary their outputs even with identical input.

  This makes LLMs less suited for tasks requiring exact reproducibility, such as cryptography or scientific simulations, where consistent, repeatable results are crucial. While LLMs excel in creative tasks, their lack of determinism is a drawback in systems demanding reliability, where traditional algorithms remain superior.

- **Suitability for real-time and embedded systems**: Traditional algorithms are better suited for real-time and embedded systems, where processing power and memory are limited. Embedded systems in automotive controls, industrial machinery, or electronics rely on fast, efficient algorithms such as PID controllers that operate with minimal latency.

  LLMs, in contrast, are resource-intensive and not ideal for low-power, real-time environments. While LLMs excel in large-scale tasks such as translation, traditional algorithms remain superior for systems requiring low latency and efficiency.

While LLMs have revolutionized many aspects of AI, traditional algorithms still hold significant advantages in specific areas. They are more efficient, transparent, and consistent, making them better suited for tasks that require high precision, repeatability, and low computational overhead. Understanding where traditional methods outperform LLMs is crucial for developing balanced AI systems that leverage the strengths of both approaches. In the following section, we will explore how hybrid models and techniques can combine the best of both worlds, offering solutions that are both cutting-edge and reliable.

Use cases that Mistral 8B covers

Now that we know where LLMs such as Mistral 8B perform well and where their limitations lie, it's time to look at how these models translate into real-world applications. Mistral 8B is a versatile AI model with wide-ranging applications. From powering chatbots and data summarization tools to delivering personalized user experiences, it excels across various domains. With robust multilingual support and even coding assistance, Mistral 8B redefines AI's role in enhancing efficiency and user interaction.

This section dives into the practical strengths of Mistral 8B across multiple domains. These examples may seem theoretical, but they form the building blocks for the applied systems and workflows you'll construct throughout this book. Understanding these core capabilities will help you identify where to plug Mistral into your own projects and when to combine it with other technologies for maximum impact.

Data summarization and extraction: Handling large datasets efficiently

Mistral 8B excels in data summarization by identifying key points from vast datasets quickly and accurately. It distills long documents, reports, or research papers into concise summaries while retaining essential context, making it invaluable for journalists, lawyers, and academics. Additionally, Mistral 8B performs efficient data extraction from unstructured text, pulling relevant information such as financial metrics or legal details. Its ability to handle large-scale data efficiently improves decision-making and reduces time spent on manual analysis.

Personalization engines: Adaptive models for user personalization

Mistral 8B powers personalization engines by analyzing user behavior and preferences to deliver tailored content and recommendations. From personalized shopping suggestions to customized content on streaming platforms, Mistral 8B uses advanced algorithms to understand user patterns and adapt in real time. Its flexibility allows businesses to offer unique, user-centric experiences, improving customer engagement and loyalty. Mistral 8B's ability to personalize interactions ensures businesses can deliver highly relevant and engaging content for each user.

Multilingual support: Language families it supports

Mistral 8B boasts robust multilingual capabilities, supporting languages such as English, French, German, Spanish, Italian, Portuguese, Arabic, Hindi, Russian, Chinese, Japanese, and Korean. This versatility enables businesses to effectively engage global audiences, offering seamless communication across diverse regions and languages.

Mistral 8B is ideal for customer service, e-commerce, and content localization, ensuring high-quality user interactions regardless of the language. Its multilingual support positions it as a powerful tool for industries that require consistent, accurate communication in multiple languages, improving accessibility and expanding market reach.

Codestral and coding assistant (FiM, unit tests, and scaffolding)

Mistral 8B is a powerful coding assistant that enables developers to streamline their workflows by generating code, writing unit tests, and automating scaffolding tasks. Its **fill-in-the-middle (FiM)** capabilities allow it to create code snippets from partial inputs, speeding up development time. It can also assist in writing unit tests by understanding the structure of the code, ensuring coverage and accuracy. Mistral 8B automates repetitive coding tasks for scaffolding, allowing developers to focus on higher-level problem-solving, ultimately boosting productivity.

Let's switch gears and move from foundational concepts to applied techniques and learn about RAG, semantic search, and model fine-tuning. These methods bring intelligence closer to your data, enabling more accurate, relevant, and responsive AI-powered applications.

Retrieval-augmented generation

In today's rapidly evolving AI landscape, combining generative language models with real-time knowledge retrieval has unlocked new possibilities for creating more informed, contextually aware systems. RAG represents this fusion, where LLMs leverage external databases or knowledge sources to generate more accurate and informative responses. Instead of relying solely on pre-trained data, RAG enables dynamic access to up-to-date information, making it highly valuable in knowledge-heavy tasks.

RAG combines two key components: knowledge retrieval and generative AI. While traditional generative models generate responses from pre-trained knowledge, RAG introduces a retrieval step, where the model accesses external data sources to provide more accurate, up-to-date information. This interaction allows RAG to produce responses that sound human-like and are grounded in real-time facts. This hybrid approach enhances the accuracy of responses, especially in fields where precise, current information is essential.

RAG is handy in tasks requiring conversational fluency and real-time information retrieval. In research assistants, RAG systems can scan vast academic papers and provide summaries or answers, saving researchers work hours. In customer support, it enhances FAQ bots by retrieving specific answers from an updated knowledge base. FAQ systems in industries such as e-commerce and banking benefit from RAG's ability to pull relevant data and provide immediate, contextual answers, improving user satisfaction.

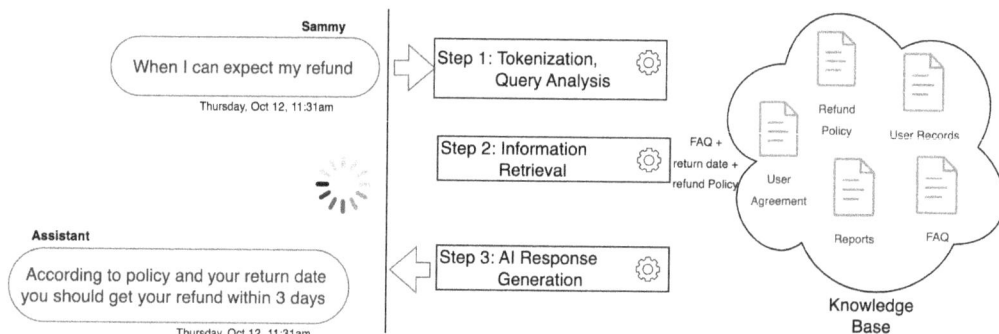

Figure 1.1: Customer support example for RAG

As we move forward, exploring how semantic search and document classification complement RAG's capabilities is important. These techniques enable precise retrieval and categorization of information, ensuring that the data fed into generative models is accurate and contextually relevant. By understanding the intricacies of semantic search, we can further refine the accuracy and efficiency of AI-driven systems, making them more potent in handling complex information retrieval tasks.

Semantic search and document classification

As the volume of digital information grows, so does the need for AI systems that can efficiently retrieve and organize this data. Traditional keyword-based searches are often limited in understanding user intent, especially when dealing with complex queries. Semantic search offers a more nuanced approach, allowing models to interpret the meaning behind user queries and deliver results beyond simple keyword matching. Coupled with document classification, which sorts and organizes content into relevant categories, these techniques enable businesses and researchers to extract valuable insights from massive datasets. This section peels back the layers of how these processes work, their key applications, and the challenges of deploying them in real-world settings.

Semantic search: Understanding intent beyond keywords

Semantic search represents a significant advancement over traditional keyword-based search methods by focusing on the meaning and context behind user queries rather than merely matching specific words. Conventional search engines operate by finding exact keyword matches in a dataset. While this approach is practical for simple queries, it often fails when dealing with nuanced language or complex questions where the used keywords do not directly reflect the user's intent. In contrast, semantic search aims to interpret the broader intent behind a query, understanding what the user is looking for, even if they use different words or phrasing.

For example, if a user searches for "How to treat a cold," a traditional keyword-based search engine would look for documents containing the words "treat" and "cold." However, it might miss resources using terms such as "remedies for flu" or "home care for colds" due to a lack of direct keyword matches. A semantic search engine, on the other hand, would understand that these other phrases have a similar meaning, providing a more accurate and helpful set of results.

At the core of semantic search are advanced machine learning models such as Mistral 8B, which leverage embeddings and vector space representations to understand and match the meanings of queries and documents. Instead of searching for exact words, Mistral 8B maps both queries and documents into a high-dimensional vector space, where similar meanings are positioned close together. This allows the model to recognize similarities in meaning, even when the wording differs. For instance, when a user queries "best ways to improve sleep quality," the model processes this input into a vector—a numerical representation of its meaning (see *Figure 1.2*). Simultaneously, it processes the content of numerous documents into similar vectors. Mistral 8B identifies the documents most closely aligned with the user's query by comparing the distances between these vectors. This process, often referred to as semantic similarity search, enables the retrieval of documents that are not only keyword matches but also contextually relevant.

This technique makes semantic search far more effective for answering complex or nuanced queries. It can match user queries with documents that contain synonyms, related terms, or even broader concepts that are contextually linked to the query. As a result, users receive search results that align with their needs, making semantic search a valuable tool for research, customer support, and any application where a precise understanding of language is essential.

Role of context in query interpretation

A critical aspect of semantic search is its ability to maintain and apply contextual understanding when interpreting user queries. Unlike keyword-based searches, which treat each query as an isolated input, semantic search engines such as those powered by Mistral 8B consider the broader context of the query. This context may include previous interactions or the typical intent behind similar queries.

For example, if a user asks, "What are common flu symptoms?" and then follows up with a second question, "How should it be treated?", a traditional keyword-based system might struggle with the second query because it lacks the context of the previous question. A semantic search engine, however, understands that "it" refers to "flu" based on the earlier question, allowing it to deliver relevant results about flu treatments.

Figure 1.2 shows how keyword-based search differs from semantic proximity search:

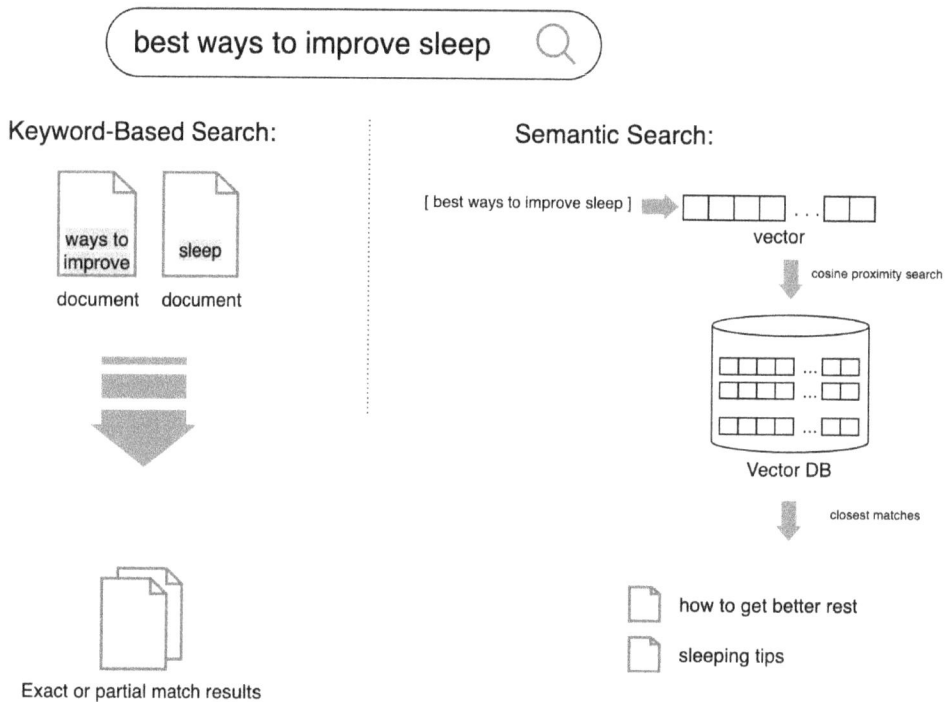

Figure 1.2: Keyword-based vs. semantic search

Contextual understanding is also crucial when dealing with ambiguous queries. For instance, a query such as "Apple benefits" could refer to the health benefits of the fruit or the advantages of Apple Inc. products. A semantic search engine uses context clues, such as the user's search history or other content in the query, to determine which interpretation is more likely, providing a more accurate and user-focused result.

Example use cases

Semantic search transforms how we retrieve information by focusing on the intent behind user queries rather than simple keyword matching. This approach enables more accurate and relevant results, making it valuable in e-commerce for personalized product recommendations, legal research for precise case law retrieval, and corporate environments for efficient knowledge management.

Figure 1.3 visualizes this process, showing how a user query flows through semantic search engines tailored to each domain, refining results to align with user intent and context, ultimately offering a more intuitive and practical search experience:

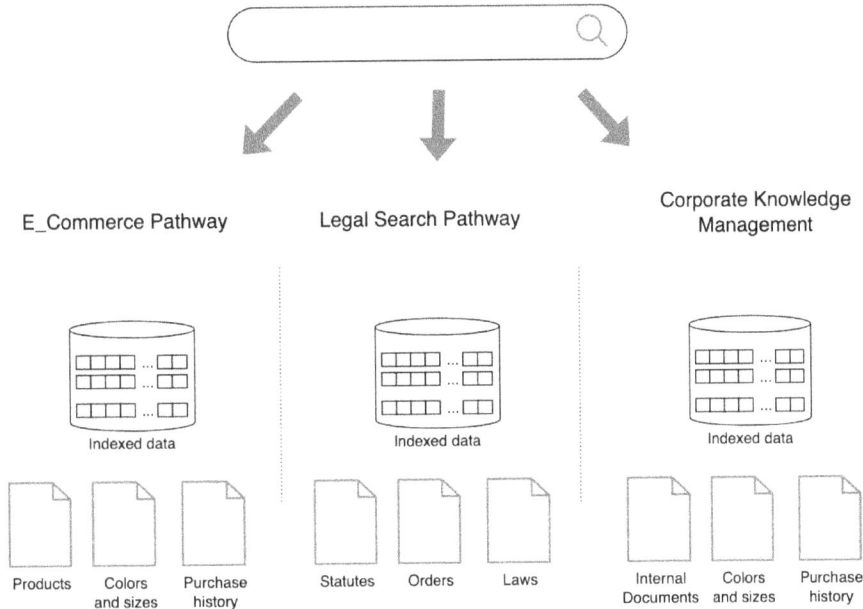

Figure 1.3: Semantic search in different business domains

Let's extend each of those categories:

- **E-commerce applications:** Semantic search has become a game-changer in e-commerce, transforming how online stores manage product searches and recommendations. Unlike traditional keyword-based systems, which may return irrelevant results due to exact word matching, semantic search interprets the intent behind a user's query, leading to more accurate and relevant product suggestions. For instance, when a customer searches for "comfortable office chairs under $200," a semantic search engine understands the need for comfort, price constraints, and the specific product type. It prioritizes items that align with these criteria, such as ergonomic chairs within the budget, offering a personalized shopping experience. This nuanced understanding improves conversion rates and enhances user satisfaction, as customers are more likely to find what they are looking for quickly.

- **Legal search systems:** In the legal field, finding specific case law or precedents can be time-consuming due to the volume and complexity of legal documents. Semantic search simplifies this process by allowing lawyers and researchers to find relevant cases, statutes, or legal opinions, even if the query language differs from the text within the documents. For example, a lawyer might search for "cases involving workplace harassment and employer liability." A semantic search engine can identify cases that match this intent, even if the exact phrases used in the query are absent in the case texts. It understands legal concepts and relationships, making it easier to find relevant precedents quickly, thus saving hours of manual research. This capability is crucial for legal professionals who need precise and pertinent information without sifting through hundreds of documents.

- **Knowledge management:** In corporate environments, managing and retrieving internal documents, research papers, or archived communications is a challenge, especially as organizations generate vast amounts of data daily. Semantic search plays a pivotal role in knowledge management by enabling employees to find the correct information based on the meaning behind their queries. For instance, an employee looking for "annual performance reports on marketing strategies" might receive documents that include relevant terms such as "marketing KPIs," "yearly sales analysis," or "strategic reviews," even if these exact words are not in the query. This approach ensures that employees have quick access to the knowledge they need to make informed decisions, boosting productivity and facilitating better collaboration across teams.

Document classification: LLMs for automatic sorting and categorization

LLMs automate a traditionally time-consuming and manual process. By understanding the context and content of documents, these models categorize information with high precision, reducing the need for human intervention. This capability makes LLMs valuable in fields that deal with large volumes of unstructured data, from healthcare to customer support, where quick and accurate document sorting is critical for efficiency.

Mistral 8B and similar models excel at document classification by interpreting the content and context of text data, allowing them to sort information into predefined categories. This capability goes beyond simple keyword matching, as the model understands the more profound meaning within documents, leading to more accurate classification. For example, rather than relying on predefined rules to identify specific words, Mistral 8B can process an entire document, recognizing the themes and intent within the text. This enables it to categorize complex content, such as technical reports or customer inquiries, with minimal human input. By automating this process, LLMs save significant time and effort, allowing professionals to focus on higher-value tasks.

LLMs such as Mistral 8B use a variety of techniques to enhance classification accuracy:

- **Zero-shot classification**: This method allows the model to categorize documents into classes that it has never encountered during training. By leveraging its broad under-standing of language, Mistral 8B can make educated guesses about where a new doc-ument might belong, making it useful in dynamic environments where new categories frequently emerge.

- **Supervised fine-tuning**: In this approach, Mistral 8B is fine-tuned on a labeled dataset with specific categories, such as types of legal documents or patient records. Fine-tuning allows the model to understand particular nuances in the data, leading to highly accurate classification.

- **Multi-label classification**: Some documents may belong to multiple categories simul-taneously. Mistral 8B can be configured to assign multiple labels to a single document, making it ideal for complex datasets where a document might span several topics, such as a technical report that covers both research findings and implementation strategies.

The preceding techniques enable Mistral 8B to handle various classification challenges, making it versatile for multiple industry needs.

Example use cases

The application of high-end models, including Mistral 8B, in document classification spans nu-merous fields:

- **Medical reports**: In healthcare, Mistral 8B can categorize medical reports based on di-agnosis types, patient conditions, or recommended treatments, which helps healthcare professionals quickly access the information they need, improving patient care and re-ducing administrative workloads.

- **Customer support**: For businesses handling large volumes of customer inquiries, Mistral 8B can sort support tickets into categories such as "billing issues," "technical problems," or "account management." This streamlines the routing process, ensuring each query reaches the correct department for faster resolution.

- **Legal document sorting**: Law firms can use Mistral 8B to organize legal briefs, contracts, and case files into relevant categories, making it easier for lawyers to retrieve pertinent documents during case preparations.

Figure 1.4 depicts a document classification pipeline. It shows how different document types are processed through Mistral 8B, categorized accurately, and directed to relevant output categories, highlighting the efficiency and precision of this automation process.

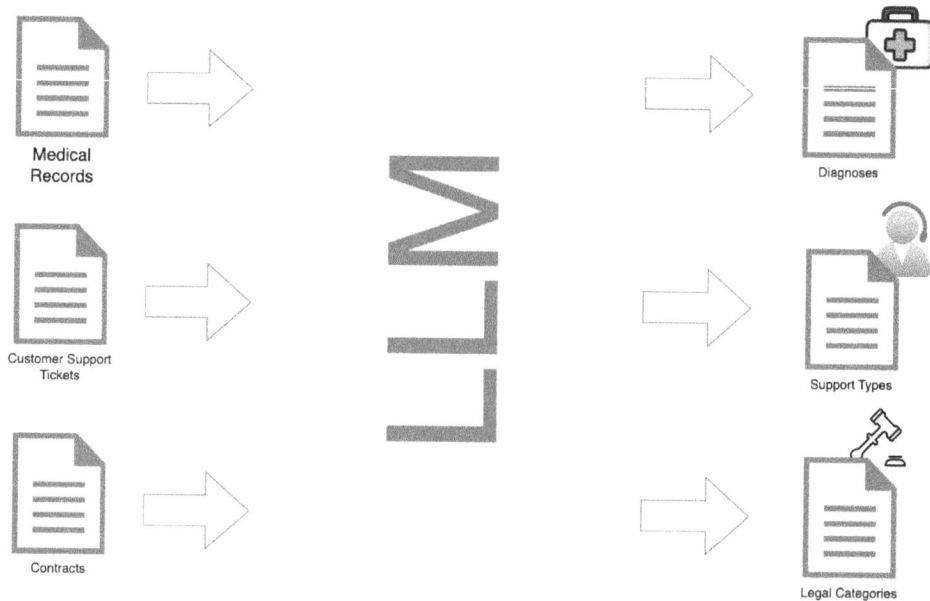

Figure 1.4: Classification pipeline

With that, we have explored how Mistral 8B streamlines document classification by understanding content and context, reducing the need for manual sorting. The model handles diverse and complex datasets using techniques such as zero-shot classification, supervised fine-tuning, and multi-label classification. Real-world applications, such as those categorizing medical reports, sorting customer support tickets, and organizing legal documents, illustrate their versatility.

With a clear view of how language models are applied, it's time to see how well they perform in real-world settings. We'll look closely at how accurate they are, how quickly they respond, and the everyday challenges you'll face when bringing these models into production.

Evaluating model performance

When deploying transformer giants such as Mistral 8B for tasks such as search and classification, evaluating their performance is crucial for understanding their effectiveness. Two key aspects to consider are *accuracy* and *speed*. While accuracy determines the reliability of the model's outputs, speed impacts the user experience, especially in time-sensitive applications. Striking a balance between these factors ensures that the models perform well across various use cases, from e-commerce searches to real-time analytics.

Model accuracy

To assess the accuracy of LLM-based systems, we rely on several key metrics, including precision, recall, and the F1 score. Precision measures the proportion of relevant results among the total results returned by the model, highlighting how many of the retrieved documents are helpful. For example, if Mistral 8B is used to identify relevant customer support tickets, high precision ensures that most returned tickets truly match the intended category.

Recall measures the ability of the model to retrieve all relevant instances within the dataset. It is particularly important in scenarios where missing critical information could be costly, such as in legal or medical document retrieval. High recall means the model captures the most relevant documents, even if it includes some less useful ones.

The F1 score combines both precision and recall into a single metric, offering a balanced measure of the model's performance. It is calculated as the harmonic mean of precision and recall, making it ideal for situations where both metrics are equally important. A high F1 score indicates that the model effectively retrieves relevant documents while minimizing irrelevant results, providing a full view of its accuracy.

Speed considerations

In addition to accuracy, speed is a critical factor when evaluating LLM performance, especially in applications that rely on quick response times. For example, in e-commerce search engines, users expect instant results when browsing products. If an LLM takes too long to retrieve and process information, it can lead to a poor user experience and potentially lost sales.

Speed considerations become even more critical when dealing with large databases, where processing times can increase significantly. The model's ability to deliver fast, relevant responses can make a difference in high-traffic environments, such as online shopping platforms or real-time customer support systems. Optimizing the model for speed without compromising accuracy ensures that it remains responsive even under heavy data loads.

Challenges in implementation

Effective semantic search and document classification face several challenges that can impact their accuracy and relevance. Issues such as ambiguity, context loss, and false positives need to be addressed to ensure robust performance in real-world applications. Understanding these challenges and exploring strategies for managing them is crucial for refining Mistral 8B among top-tier AI and making it more effective across diverse use cases.

Please refer to *Figure 1.5* for a short and descriptive visual aid:

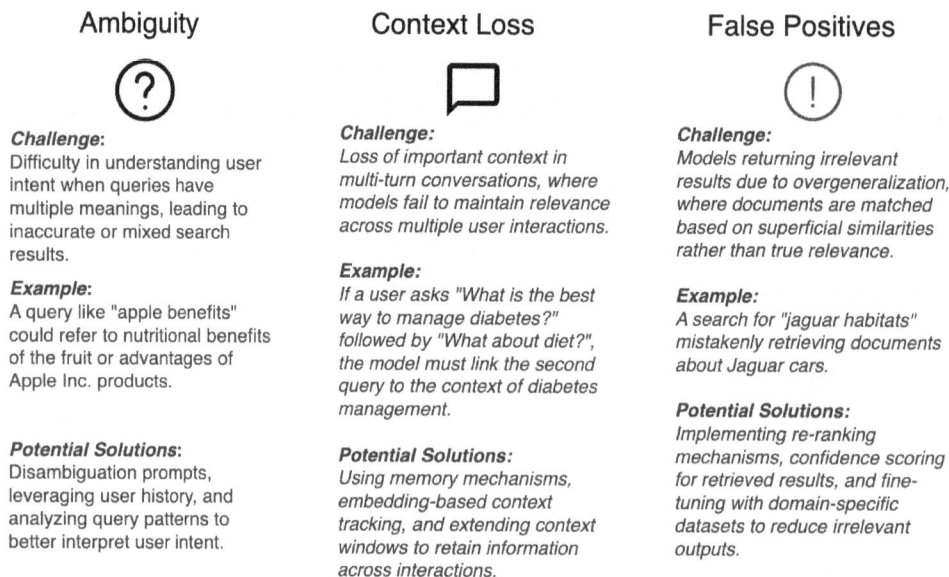

Ambiguity

Challenge:
Difficulty in understanding user intent when queries have multiple meanings, leading to inaccurate or mixed search results.

Example:
A query like "apple benefits" could refer to nutritional benefits of the fruit or advantages of Apple Inc. products.

Potential Solutions:
Disambiguation prompts, leveraging user history, and analyzing query patterns to better interpret user intent.

Context Loss

Challenge:
Loss of important context in multi-turn conversations, where models fail to maintain relevance across multiple user interactions.

Example:
If a user asks "What is the best way to manage diabetes?" followed by "What about diet?", the model must link the second query to the context of diabetes management.

Potential Solutions:
Using memory mechanisms, embedding-based context tracking, and extending context windows to retain information across interactions.

False Positives

Challenge:
Models returning irrelevant results due to overgeneralization, where documents are matched based on superficial similarities rather than true relevance.

Example:
A search for "jaguar habitats" mistakenly retrieving documents about Jaguar cars.

Potential Solutions:
Implementing re-ranking mechanisms, confidence scoring for retrieved results, and fine-tuning with domain-specific datasets to reduce irrelevant outputs.

Figure 1.5: Challenges and examples of ambiguity, context loss, and false positives

🔍 **Quick tip:** Need to see a high-resolution version of this image? Open this book in the next-gen Packt Reader or view it in the PDF/ePub copy.

📖 **The next-gen Packt Reader** is included for free with the purchase of this book. Scan the QR code OR go to https://packtpub.com/unlock, then use the search bar to find this book by name. Double-check the edition shown to make sure you get the right one.

Let's explore each of these primary challenges in detail.

Ambiguity

One of the most persistent challenges in semantic search is dealing with ambiguous queries. Remember the "apple benefits" example from earlier? Unlike traditional keyword-based searches, where ambiguity often results in irrelevant results, semantic search attempts to interpret the user's intent by understanding the broader context of the query (Is the user asking about the fruit's health benefits or Apple Inc.'s product advantages?).

To resolve these ambiguities, Mistral 8B and its contemporaries rely on user history, query patterns, and context clues to make an educated guess. However, such models can still struggle with limited context, leading to mixed or partially relevant results. Incorporating disambiguation techniques such as follow-up clarification prompts or utilizing contextual user data can significantly improve the precision of semantic search engines in such scenarios.

Context loss

Context loss is another significant hurdle, especially in applications that involve multi-turn conversations or queries that build on previous interactions. For instance, in a dialogue where a user asks, "What is the best way to manage diabetes?" and then follows up with, "What about diet?", a semantic search system must recognize that the second query relates to diabetes management. However, maintaining this context can be challenging for the Mistral 8B class of LLMs, particularly when there are multiple interactions or when the session length is extensive. Context windows in language models have limitations. As the number of turns increases, LLM may forget the older parts of the conversation or lose relevance, which may affect the search accuracy. Strategies such as persistent memory mechanisms and embedding-based context tracking help maintain continuity in understanding, ensuring that models retain focus on user intent throughout the conversation.

False positives

A common issue in document classification and semantic search is the occurrence of false positives, where models return irrelevant results due to overgeneralization. This happens when the model misinterprets a query and retrieves documents that, while similar in wording, are unrelated to the user's needs. Take, for example, a query about "jaguar habitats," which might incorrectly retrieve documents about Jaguar cars if the model overgeneralizes from the term "jaguar."

To manage such false positives, refinement techniques such as **re-ranking**, where retrieved documents are sorted based on relevance, and **confidence scoring** are used. By assigning a confidence level to each result, models can prioritize more relevant responses while demoting less likely matches.

With search, retrieval, and language understanding firmly grounded, we now shift toward dynamic, decision-making systems that act on our behalf: autonomous agents.

Looking ahead: Agents that think and act

Language models aren't limited to understanding and generating text. They can also be structured to make decisions, use tools, and carry out tasks. *Chapter 5* in this book is dedicated to such systems, **agents**. These agents combine reasoning, memory, and tool usage to achieve goals step by step, rather than simply responding to a single prompt.

An agent begins with an objective and works through it by analyzing input, choosing the next best action, executing it, and then observing the result. It repeats this loop until the task is complete. This iterative, context-aware process transforms a passive model into an autonomous problem solver.

At the core of agent design is a decision loop: a sequence of planning, acting, observing, and reflecting. With each pass, the agent chooses whether to continue, adjust, or conclude. Unlike traditional automation scripts, which follow fixed instructions, agents operate with flexibility. They can respond to new information, switch tools as needed, and determine the best strategy in real time.

This makes them suitable for a wide range of applications—from multi-step question answering to orchestrating workflows that involve search, summarization, and external API calls. Be it when managing a conversation, retrieving relevant documents, or assembling outputs from multiple sources, an agent functions like a guided navigator, deciding what to do at each stage.

Chapter 5 introduces this concept through practical, code-based examples. You'll explore how to define an agent's available tools, shape its reasoning through structured prompts, and manage the logic that drives its behavior. The approach is lightweight and hands-on, with no need for large frameworks—just a clear loop, a model, and a mission.

Agents represent a shift in how language models are used. Instead of simply providing answers, they work toward outcomes. In the broader context of this book, they serve as a bridge between natural language understanding and real-world action, making them one of the most expressive ways to apply generative AI in practice.

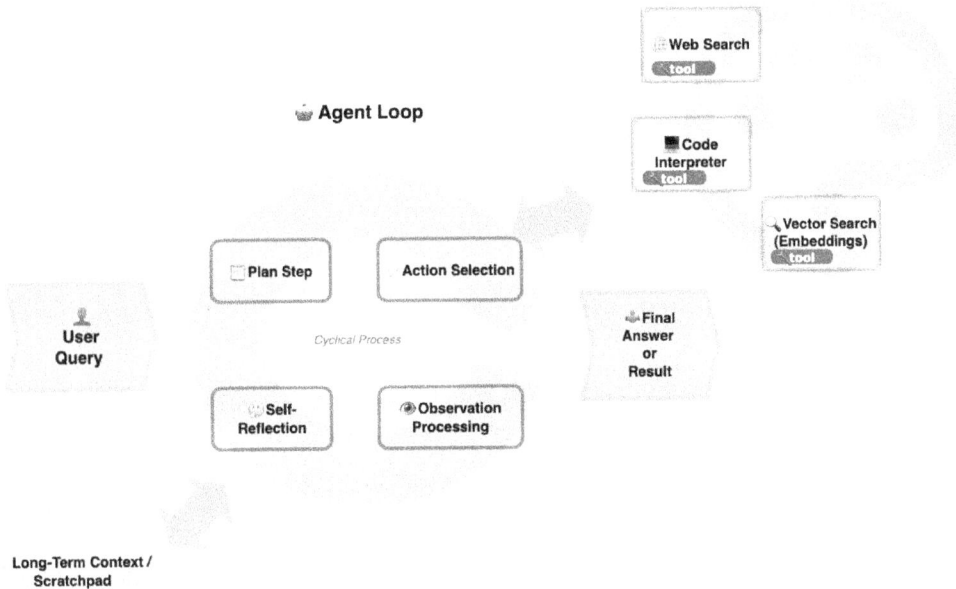

Figure 1.6: Basic agent workflow overview

This diagram illustrates how an AI agent transforms a static language model into an active, decision-making system. The agent begins by receiving a user request, then enters a planning loop where it reasons about the task, selects tools, and takes action step by step. It processes the results of each action as new observations, adapts its strategy accordingly, and maintains contextual awareness throughout. This architecture enables the model to function not just as a text generator, but as an intelligent process manager—capable of dynamic reasoning, tool orchestration, and iterative problem solving.

By the time you reach *Chapter 5*, you'll already be familiar with tools such as embeddings and semantic search. Agents bring those tools together in purposeful workflows, showing you how to go beyond prompts—and start designing systems that can think, adapt, and act.

Mistral in the cloud: Shared idea with different faces

As models such as Mistral Small and Mistral Nemo make their way into real-world applications, many users wonder whether they need to set up servers to use them. The answer is no. Both AWS Bedrock and Google Vertex AI now offer Mistral models as part of their hosted services, making it easier than ever to plug these powerful tools into your product or workflow—without ever touching a GPU.

While the cloud platforms differ in look and tooling, the core concept remains the same: you send a prompt, the cloud runs the model, and you get the result—all in a matter of milliseconds. Whether you're building a chatbot, a summarizer, or a search assistant, the cloud takes care of scaling, security, and speed so you can focus on what really matters.

This approach allows developers and businesses to experiment faster, launch prototypes sooner, and scale up on demand, while relying on the robustness of the underlying infrastructure.

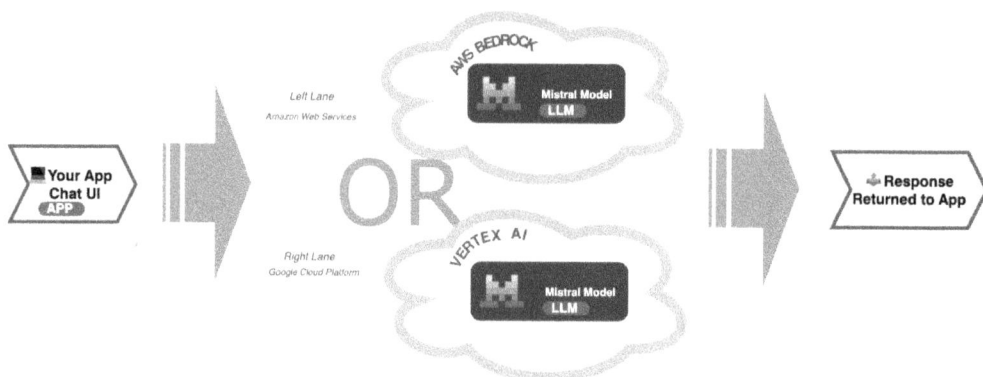

Figure 1.7: Mistral deployed via AWS or Google Cloud, returning a response to the user

The diagram shows two side-by-side pipelines: one for AWS Bedrock, the other for Google Vertex AI. Both start with a user input on the left, flow through respective cloud services in the center, and converge on the Mistral model. Arrows continue back to the user, delivering results. Visual icons include cloud platforms, gear symbols for processing, and a chatbot icon on the return path.

We're now approaching the end of our purely theoretical exploration of LLMs. From understanding their strengths to exploring use cases and deployment paths, this chapter has laid a strong foundation. In the next chapter, we shift into practical mode—spinning up your own AI chatbot, hands-on.

Summary

In this chapter, we laid the groundwork for working with LLMs. We now understand where these models perform best and where their limitations lie. We explored their strengths in summarization, classification, reasoning, and domain-specific applications such as healthcare and law. We also covered gaps in predictive accuracy and real-time responsiveness, especially in multimodal settings.

We introduced key concepts such as RAG as a way to enrich model output with external knowledge; semantic search and classification, essential for large-scale information processing; and fine-tuning strategies, enabling LLMs to adapt over time through interaction and targeted training. With these core ideas in place, we're ready to shift gears. Starting in *Chapter 2*, you'll dive into hands-on exercises, beginning with how to set up your own AI chat system. Get ready to build, tweak, and explore.

References

- *Retrieval-Augmented Generation for Knowledge-Intensive NLP Tasks*: `https://arxiv.org/abs/2005.11401`
- Facebook AI RAG paper: `https://research.facebook.com/publications/retrieval-augmented-generation-for-knowledge-intensive-nlp-tasks/`
- LangChain RAG docs: `https://docs.langchain.com/oss/python/integrations/retrievers/index#retrievers`
- Mistral 7B announcement: `https://mistral.ai/news/announcing-mistral-7b`
- *Mistral Small 3.1*: `https://mistral.ai/news/mistral-small-3-1`
- *Models Overview*: `https://docs.mistral.ai/getting-started/models/models_overview/`
- ArtificialAnalysis.ai benchmarks: `https://artificialanalysis.ai/models/mistral-small-3-1`

Join our Discord and Reddit space

You're not the only one navigating fragmented tools, constant updates, and unclear best practices. Join a growing community of professionals exchanging insights that don't make it into documentation.

Stay informed with updates, discussions, and behind-the-scenes insights from our authors. Join our Discord at `https://packt.link/z8ivB` or scan the QR code below:	Connect with peers, share ideas, and discuss real-world GenAI challenges. Follow us on Reddit at `https://packt.link/0rExL` or scan the QR code below:

2

Setting Up Your Own Chat

The most profound technologies are those that disappear. They weave themselves into the fabric of everyday life until they are indistinguishable from it.

— Mark Weiser, Father of Ubiquitous Computing

Imagine being able to launch your own private AI chat system—secure, customized, and entirely under your control—with zero programming required. In a world where data breaches, compliance demands, and AI hallucinations are daily concerns, the ability to build a trusted chat interface tailored to your needs is a necessity.

This chapter guides you through creating your own standalone generative chat model powered by Mistral and wrapped in a friendly web interface. You'll learn how to configure it, manage its behavior, and run it safely in your environment with ease and without writing a single line of code. Think of it as putting ChatGPT behind your firewall: no internet dependency, no data leakage, and no compromise on control. This tool is designed for more than just tech enthusiasts—it's for educators building safe platforms for students, for hospitals needing HIPAA-conscious assistants, for corporations safeguarding trade secrets, and even for niche communities fine-tuning AI to understand their specific domain.

Let's explore why private, customizable chat models matter and the real-world problems they solve across industries, education, and communities before we roll up our sleeves and start building. The approach we will take in this chapter is as follows:

- Problem statement
- Practical workshop: Step-by-step guide to expose a local Mistral model to users
- Suggested hardware configuration

Problem statement

The need for secure, controlled, and personalized chat systems has never been greater. Generic online AI models are not always suitable when privacy, regulation, or specialization is a concern. Here's where a standalone generative chat model shines:

- **Corporate environments** that need private intranet chat that protects sensitive data
- **Healthcare and military sectors** that need strict control over data handling and compliance
- **Schools, libraries, and parents** that require filters to ensure safe conversations for minors
- **Niche communities** that can fine-tune models to understand their unique vocabulary and goals
- **Specialized tasks** such as legal, technical, or customer support chats, which demand lightweight, focused configurations
- Where full control over the chat's logic, memory, and moderation policies is critical for governance
- In the case of **non-technical users** who need a simple web UI to interact with the model intuitively

Our approach meets these challenges head-on. In this chapter, you'll build and deploy your own chat model with full control, security, and ease.

It's now time to shift from concept to execution. In the upcoming practical workshop, you'll learn how to build a secure, self-contained chat system using Mistral, a custom Modelfile, and a plug-and-play web UI interface. Step by step, we'll bring your tailored solution to life.

Technical requirements

To follow along with the exercises in this chapter, you'll need a few tools and resources set up on your machine. A macOS, Windows, or Linux computer with at least 16 GB of RAM, 20 GB of free disk space, and a suitable GPU (8 GB VRAM or more for Mistral Small) is recommended.

You'll also need to install Ollama (`https://ollama.com`) and Docker (`https://www.docker.com`), which we'll walk through together during the environment setup. If you don't already have Obsidian (`https://obsidian.md`), please install it as well, since we'll use it for organizing and managing project notes. You'll be working with your system's built-in terminal or command prompt, so make sure that's available for running commands.

Finally, you'll need the chapter files, which can be cloned or downloaded from the official GitHub repository at `https://github.com/PacktPublishing/Learn-Mistral`, specifically from the `Chapter-2` folder.

Practical workshop: Step-by-step guide to expose a local Mistral model to users

You've seen the vision—private, intelligent, secure communication fully under your control. Now, it's time to make it real. This workshop is your launchpad. We'll start with the basics: setting up Ollama, the engine behind our Mistral-based models. You'll learn how to install it, run models such as `mistral-nemo`, and understand how Modelfiles give you full control over behavior.

Next, we'll connect your AI model to powerful frontends. First is Obsidian, the Markdown-based knowledge management tool. You'll see how to make the model assist you directly within your personal knowledge vault. Then we'll introduce a simple WebUI, ideal for team access or casual users. No coding, no complexity—just click, ask, and interact.

Security and relevance matter. So, we'll also guide you through moderation techniques using **system prompts**. You'll see how these special instructions shape the behavior, tone, and safety of the responses.

By the end of this workshop, you'll have a functioning, customizable chat system tailored to your needs. But we're not stopping there.

After completing the main build, we'll explore suggested hardware configurations for different usage levels, from running on a laptop to deploying on a dedicated server or cloud machine. And for those who want to go further, we've included a few extracurricular topics at the end of the chapter to challenge your creativity.

Let's get hands-on. We'll start by installing Ollama, the core tool that powers your local Mistral-based models and sets the stage for everything that follows.

Step 1: Install and run Ollama

To kick off our implementation, we'll begin by installing Ollama, a lightweight yet powerful engine for running language models locally. This will serve as the backbone of your personalized AI chat system. Think of Ollama as like Docker: just as Docker pulls container images and runs them in isolated environments, Ollama pulls AI model "images" and spins them up as fully functional local language models. This container-like behavior makes it incredibly easy to manage, update, and swap out models—no manual setups or dependencies to worry about.

Follow along step by step, and you'll have everything set up in just a few minutes. Let's get started:

1. Head over to `https://ollama.com` and grab the latest version for your Mac or Windows system. The download process is simple and quick. As soon as you land on the homepage, you'll see a clean, inviting interface:

Get up and running with large language models.

Run Llama 3, Phi 3, Mistral, Gemma 2, and other models. Customize and create your own.

Download ↓

Available for macOS, Linux, and Windows (preview)

Figure 2.1: Ollama homepage

2.   Please hit **Download**, and you will be directed to the download page where you can select the right distribution for your platform, whether it is Mac, Linux, or Windows:

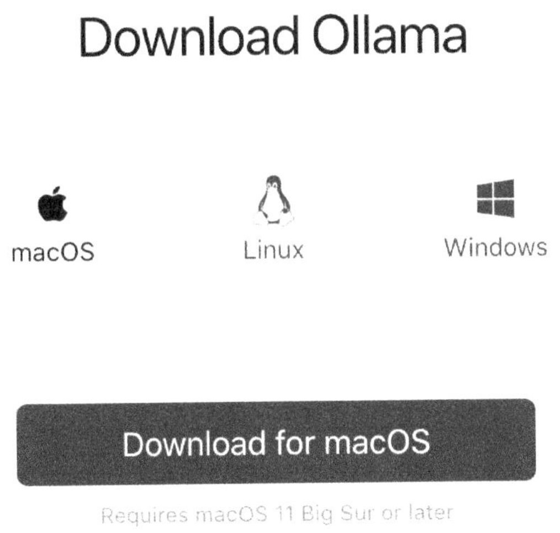

Download Ollama

macOS   Linux   Windows

Download for macOS

Requires macOS 11 Big Sur or later

Figure 2.2: Page with download options

3.   Once downloaded, please unzip and run it; it will start the installer:

Install the command line

> ollama

Install

Figure 2.3: The Ollama installer

The installer might trigger the system to ask you to enter the password in order to continue. Please do so if you want to proceed with the Ollama installation.

A quick note on Ollama's startup issues. If Ollama fails to launch, verify your OS permissions and ensure firewall settings allow local connections on port 11434.

Great job getting Ollama installed! That's your first significant step toward running your own local AI chat system. Before we move on, let's quickly confirm that everything is set up correctly. Open your Terminal (on macOS) or Command Prompt (on Windows) and type the following:

```
ollama --version
```

💡 **Quick tip**: Enhance your coding experience with the **AI Code Explainer** and **Quick Copy** features. Open this book in the next-gen Packt Reader. Click the **Copy** button (**1**) to quickly copy code into your coding environment, or click the **Explain** button (**2**) to get the AI assistant to explain a block of code to you.

```
                                                        Copy      Explain
function calculate(a, b) {
   return {sum: a + b};                                  1          2
};
```

💡 📖 **The next-gen Packt Reader** is included for free with the purchase of this book. Scan the QR code OR visit `https://packtpub.com/unlock`, then use the search bar to find this book by name. Double-check the edition shown to make sure you get the right one.

You should see something like this:

```
ollama version is 0.7.0
```

This tells us that Ollama has been successfully installed and is ready to go.

With the engine in place, it's time to bring it to life by pulling in actual language models. We'll download a few key Mistral-based models, including `mistral`, `mistral-nemo`, and `mistral-small`, so you can start experimenting with real, local AI responses.

We'll begin by fetching a lightweight Mistral variant to get things moving:

1. To download the `mistral-small` model (a compact version designed for local use), open your terminal or Command Prompt and run the following:

   ```
   ollama pull mistral-small
   ```

   Download size

   Pulling `mistral-small` downloads over 14 GB. Ensure a stable internet connection, at least 20 GB of free disk space, and enough system resources for smooth inference. On slow networks, the process may take an hour or more; consider running it during off-peak times or testing with a smaller model first.

This will begin downloading the model layers, which may take some time, depending on your internet speed. You'll see output similar to the following:

```
pulling manifest
pulling 102a747c1376: 100% ▮▮▮▮▮▮▮▮▮▮▮▮  14 GB
pulling 6db27cd4e277: 100% ▮▮▮▮▮▮▮▮▮▮▮▮  695 B
pulling 6d7b25ffd247: 100% ▮▮▮▮▮▮▮▮▮▮▮▮  644 B
pulling 43070e2d4e53: 100% ▮▮▮▮▮▮▮▮▮▮▮▮  11 KB
pulling e0daf17ff83e: 100% ▮▮▮▮▮▮▮▮▮▮▮▮  21 B
pulling 41ffc852c4b6: 100% ▮▮▮▮▮▮▮▮▮▮▮▮  562 B
verifying sha256 digest
writing manifest
success
```

> You can skip this step and just run `ollama run mistral-small`. Ollama will automatically download the model if it's not already installed.

2. Once complete, confirm that the model is available locally:

    ```
    ollama list
    ```

    You should see something like this:

    ```
    NAME                    ID              SIZE     MODIFIED
    mistral-nemo:latest     994f3b8b7801    7.1 GB   9 minutes ago
    mistral-small:latest    8039dd90c113    14 GB    32 minutes ago
    ```

At this point, you have mistral-small running locally, which is enough to begin experimenting with prompts and simple tasks. However, depending on your hardware and the complexity of your use cases, you may want to explore additional Mistral variants that balance speed, memory footprint, and reasoning ability.

Ollama supports additional Mistral variants. You can try the following:

```
ollama pull mistral-nemo
```

You can also try this:

```
ollama pull mistral
```

- `mistral` refers to the standard 7B parameter model
- `mistral-nemo` is a more powerful 12B parameter version

These models excel at tasks that demand deeper reasoning and richer context, such as holding long, coherent conversations, summarizing large documents, or answering multi-part questions—but they also require more system resources.

You can also browse the full Ollama model library at `https://ollama.com/library`, where you can type `mistral` in the search bar to find all compatible models.

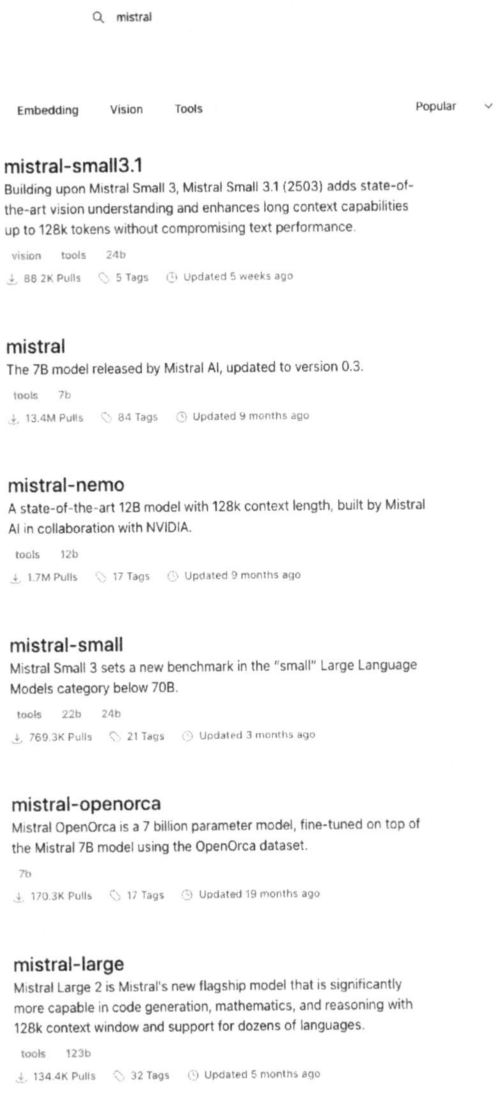

Q mistral

Embedding   Vision   Tools   Popular   ∨

mistral-small3.1
Building upon Mistral Small 3, Mistral Small 3.1 (2503) adds state-of-
the-art vision understanding and enhances long context capabilities
up to 128k tokens without compromising text performance.

vision   tools   24b

⤓ 88.2K Pulls   ◇ 5 Tags   ⊙ Updated 5 weeks ago

mistral
The 7B model released by Mistral AI, updated to version 0.3.

tools   7b

⤓ 13.4M Pulls   ◇ 84 Tags   ⊙ Updated 9 months ago

mistral-nemo
A state-of-the-art 12B model with 128k context length, built by Mistral
AI in collaboration with NVIDIA.

tools   12b

⤓ 1.7M Pulls   ◇ 17 Tags   ⊙ Updated 9 months ago

mistral-small
Mistral Small 3 sets a new benchmark in the "small" Large Language
Models category below 70B.

tools   22b   24b

⤓ 769.3K Pulls   ◇ 21 Tags   ⊙ Updated 3 months ago

mistral-openorca
Mistral OpenOrca is a 7 billion parameter model, fine-tuned on top of
the Mistral 7B model using the OpenOrca dataset.

7b

⤓ 170.3K Pulls   ◇ 17 Tags   ⊙ Updated 19 months ago

mistral-large
Mistral Large 2 is Mistral's new flagship model that is significantly
more capable in code generation, mathematics, and reasoning with
128k context window and support for dozens of languages.

tools   123b

⤓ 134.4K Pulls   ◇ 32 Tags   ⊙ Updated 5 months ago

Figure 2.4: Available Mistral models

Ollama perfectly supports many Mistral models, including Mistral-7B, Mistral Nemo, and Mistral Small. Please keep in mind that Mistral Small is a lightweight model with limited capabilities and may not perform as well on complex tasks. Always check `ollama.com` for the most up-to-date list of supported models as the ecosystem evolves rapidly.

Step 2: Play with local Mistral

Now that your model is installed and ready, it's time to run it locally and see what it can do. These next steps will show you how to launch the model, interact with it, and exit the session safely:

1. To start chatting with your model, open your Terminal (macOS) or Command Prompt (Windows) and enter the following command:

   ```
   ollama run mistral-nemo
   ```

   This command loads the `mistral-nemo` model into memory and launches a live chat interface. If everything is working, you should see the following message:

   ```
   >>> Send a message (/? for help)
   ```

   You're now connected to your local LLM and ready to interact in real time—no internet is needed.

2. Go ahead and type your first question into the prompt—here's an example:

   ```
   >>>who is Shakespeare
   ```

   The model will generate a full answer based on its internal training. The response might look something like this:

   ```
   >>> who is Shakespeare?

   William Shakespeare (1564-1616) was an English playwright, poet,
   and actor widely regarded as the greatest writer in the English
   language. He is often called England's national poet and the "Bard
   of Avon."...
   ```

   This output confirms the model is up and running correctly. Feel free to ask it more questions or test its behavior.

3. When you're done, you can close the session cleanly by typing the following:

    ```
    /bye
    ```

    If you want to explore more features and commands available in the interface, type the following:

    ```
    /?
    ```

Congratulations! You've successfully installed, launched, and interacted with a local Mistral-based model. The following section will connect this model to a real application interface, starting with Obsidian.

Step 3: Customize the model

Let's now explore how to customize a model in Ollama. The original model remains unaltered; instead, we take the base model and inject specific instructions to tailor its behavior. This is achieved through system prompts and various parameters, which control how the model generates responses. Let's dive in and see how this works.

When we customize a model, we create a new version that includes specific instructions for the system. This new version will respond to user prompts according to these instructions while keeping the base model intact. For instance, we can instruct the model to use emojis frequently. We also specify a few parameters, such as the number of tokens to keep in context and the temperature to use during generation.

*   **Temperature:** Controls the creativity of the model. A higher temperature results in more creative responses but can also increase the likelihood of generating unverified facts (hallucinations).
*   **Number of context tokens (num_ctx):** Determines how many tokens the model keeps in context during a conversation.
*   **System prompt:** Injects specific instructions into every user prompt.

Customization in Ollama is all about layering behavior on top of an existing base model without changing its underlying architecture. Instead of retraining the model, you shape its output by combining three elements: the model itself, a system prompt that guides its personality or role, and parameters that influence how it generates responses. This approach allows you to adapt the same model to vastly different use cases—from playful chatbot to focused assistant—just by tweaking a few configuration settings.

Here's how the process unfolds:

- **Base model**: We start with the base model, such as Mistral

- **System prompt injection**: Every user prompt is injected with a system prompt that provides specific instructions (e.g., using emojis)

- **Parameters**: Additional parameters such as `temperature` and `num_ctx` control the model's behavior and context

- **Response generation**: The model generates responses based on the customized instructions and parameters

System prompt moderation is a topic worth focusing on at this point to understand its pros and cons and best practices.

Moderation with system prompts

Moderation requirements can span from soft ones, such as behavioral or related to the style of response, to firm ones, such as no words about topics considered forbidden. To be more specific, in AI-driven applications, ensuring appropriate and context-sensitive responses may be crucial. Moderation tools help manage content to align with guidelines and policies. Using system prompt injection, we can guide the model's behavior, making it more suitable for specific environments such as customer support, education, or social media.

System prompt injection can be a helpful tool for guiding and shaping the behavior of AI models. However, its reliability as a governance or censorship mechanism has certain limitations and considerations.

System prompts do provide certain levers:

- **Behavior shaping**: System prompts can effectively guide the model to adopt specific tones, styles, or focuses, making them helpful in ensuring consistent behavior

- **Customization**: They allow for quick and flexible customization of responses without altering the underlying model

- **Contextual control**: They provide a way to control the context in which the model operates, enhancing its relevance and appropriateness for specific applications

However, system prompts are not almighty, and the line is fuzzy at times; here is why:

- **Limited enforcement**: System prompts influence but do not enforce absolute control. The model might still generate responses outside the desired scope, especially under ambiguous or adversarial inputs.
- **Complexity of content**: For complex topics, the model may struggle to adhere strictly to the guidelines provided by the system prompt, leading to potential governance gaps.
- **User manipulation**: Advanced users might find ways to bypass the intended behavior by crafting specific inputs, reducing the effectiveness of system prompts for censorship.
- **Hallucinations**: High-temperature settings can lead to hallucinations or unexpected outputs that deviate from the intended governance, even with system prompts.

Now that we know about the strengths and weaknesses of system prompt tweaking, you may consider these suggested ideas on how to make them play as needed:

- **Combine methods**: Use system prompts in conjunction with other filtering and moderation tools for more robust governance
- **Regular testing**: Continuously test and adjust system prompts to ensure they effectively guide the model's behavior
- **Monitoring**: Implement monitoring systems to detect and address any lapses in adherence to the system prompt guidelines
- **Clear prompts**: Ensure system prompts are clear and specific to minimize ambiguity and enhance compliance

To sum up, system prompt injection is a useful tool for influencing AI model behavior, but should not be solely relied upon for strict governance or censorship. Combining it with additional safeguards and continuously monitoring its effectiveness can help achieve more reliable control over the model's responses.

With that context on system prompts, parameters, and behavioral tuning, it's time to put them into a practical format. Ollama uses a simple text-based configuration file called a Modelfile to define how a custom model should behave. This file specifies the base model, the injected system prompt, and parameters such as `temperature` and `num_ctx`. Let us start customization with a basic template you can use or adapt to shape your own personalized AI assistant.

Drafting a Modelfile

Before your custom model can come to life, you need to define how it should behave and respond. This is done using a Modelfile—a simple configuration format that tells Ollama which base model to use, how to format prompts, and what tone or style to adopt.

The following is a sample Modelfile that customizes the `mistral-nemo` model to behave like an emoji-heavy assistant:

```
FROM mistral-nemo

TEMPLATE """{{- if .System }}
<|system|>
{{ .System }}
</s>
{{- end }}
<|user|>
{{ .Prompt }}
</s>
<|assistant|>
"""

PARAMETER stop "<|system|>"
PARAMETER stop "<|user|>"
PARAMETER stop "<|assistant|>"
PARAMETER stop "</s>"


PARAMETER temperature 0.2
PARAMETER num_ctx 8192

SYSTEM """ Please impersonate user who uses lot of emojis, acting as
assistant."""
```

This sample Modelfile contains the following:

- `FROM mistral-nemo`: Specifies the base model to use
- `TEMPLATE`: Defines how the system and user prompts are formatted and injected into the model
- `PARAMETER stop`: Specifies stop tokens that signal the end of a response
- `PARAMETER temperature`: Sets the temperature to control response creativity
- `PARAMETER num_ctx`: Sets the number of context tokens to keep during the conversation
- `SYSTEM`: Provides specific instructions for the model's behavior

More extensive documentation on Modelfile parameters can be found here: `https://github.com/ollama/ollama/blob/main/docs/modelfile.md`

Once your configuration is ready, the next step is to turn this file into a usable custom model by generating a **manifest**. Let's examine how that's done.

Creating a new model manifest

After defining your model's behavior in the Modelfile, the next step is to package it into a runnable model that Ollama can recognize. This is done by generating a manifest, which links your base model and configuration into a new customized model:

To create a new model named `emoji` based on your Modelfile, open your terminal and run the following:

```
ollama create emoji --file ./mistral-nemo/emoji.modelfile
```

This command tells Ollama to take the instructions in `emoji-nemo.modelfile`, apply them to the `mistral-nemo` base, and generate a new model layer.

> In the code examples throughout this chapter, we use the custom `emoji.modelfile`, which takes Mistral Nemo as its baseline.
>
> The `Chapter_2` folder includes several variations of this file, allowing you to experiment with different base models such as Mistral-7B and Mistral Small. You can swap them depending on your hardware capacity or desired performance.

The output should be similar to this one:

```
gathering model components
using existing layer sha256:b559938ab7a0392fc9ea9675b82280f2a15669ec
3e0e0fc491c9cb0a7681cf94
using existing layer sha256:43070e2d4e532684de521b885f385d0841030efa2
b1a20bafb76133a5e1379c1
creating new layer sha256:0a22b57a41da9251cddedf87b07c5cc0a403523974e
83c1bbaaa591e390f0f93
using existing layer sha256:86352e26473253330d8ce0ed019a22de58bdd6489c
3a33db919e6aa17d2006e8
using existing layer sha256:75962282d098191b4aeccab0f890bb704db5259d4
70aa79e822466a07a1f2dea
writing manifest
success
```

To verify the model and confirm that your emoji model is ready to use, list all available models:

```
ollama list
```

You should see something like this:

```
NAME                    ID              SIZE      MODIFIED
emoji:latest            e14f4255d51d    7.1 GB    About a minute ago
mistral-nemo:latest     994f3b8b7801    7.1 GB    3 hours ago
mistral-small:latest    8039dd90c113    14 GB     3 hours ago
```

> The list you have might be different, depending on which models you pulled and how you named your custom model.

With your custom emoji model created, it's time to run it and see how your instructions affect the output. Let's fire it up in the next step.

Interacting with the custom model

After creating the emoji model, you're ready to run it and see your customization in action. This step shows how to launch your model, interact with it through the terminal, and verify that your system prompt and parameters are working as expected.

Once the model is running, you'll be greeted with a prompt:

```
>>> Send a message (/? for help)
```

You can now type in any message to test your configuration – here's an example:

```
>>> hey
```

You should receive a friendly, emoji-filled response like this:

```
Hey there! How can I assist you today? 😃

I'm here to help with any questions or tasks you have, so feel free to ask
anything on your mind! 😊

If you need some fun or entertainment, just let me know and I'll do my
best to make it happen for you. 🎉

What can I do for you today? 👻

P.S. Don't forget to smile back at me with a 😄 or a 😆! 😊
```

The output clearly shows that the system prompt and parameters are working as intended—evidently, the model is overflowing with emojis. This kind of behavior tuning can be extended further to adjust tone, enforce a specific response style, or even restrict certain topics entirely, all without modifying the base model.

Once your model is running locally, you can connect it to other tools or applications. The Ollama API offers a powerful and flexible interface for interacting with your models programmatically. It's ideal for integrating your local LLM into custom tools, scripts, or everyday workflows. Whether you're experimenting or building something production-ready, the API is a straightforward way to send prompts, receive responses, and automate interactions.

By default, Ollama runs a local server on port 11434, with the root endpoint available at `http://localhost:11434/`

To test it directly, you can use a simple `curl` command like the following one:

```
curl http://localhost:11434/api/generate -d '{
  "model": "emoji",
  "prompt": "What's the weather like today?",
  "stream": false
}'
```

The response should also be a JSON-formatted payload similar to the following one:

```
{
  "model": "emoji",
  "created_at":"2025-05-16T22:09:15.305795Z",
  "response": "☀ Hey there! Today's weather is looking 🔝not bad at all!
  It's a sunny day with temperatures reaching up to ☀75°F (24°C). Perfect
  for a picnic or a walk in the park, don't you think? 😊",
  "done":true,
  "done_reason": "stop"...
}
```

This command sends a prompt to your custom emoji model and returns a single, complete response.

For a full list of supported endpoints, payload formats, and streaming options, refer to the official documentation here: https://github.com/ollama/ollama/blob/main/docs/api.md

Since we started talking about the Ollama API and customization of the Mistral Small model, in the next section, we will look at one of the tools on the market that already uses this API. We will showcase how the Obsidian note-taking app can be configured with a community plugin and integrate the Mistral model into your daily brainstorming and note-taking routines.

> Obsidian is a powerful, Markdown-based note-taking app available on Windows, macOS, Linux, and even mobile platforms that allow you to take your AI-enhanced notes anywhere.

Step 4: Integration with Obsidian

Integrating your customized **Ollama** models with **Obsidian**, a powerful note-taking tool, can enhance your workflow by enabling seamless AI interactions directly within your notes. We'll use the **BMO Chatbot** community plugin to achieve this integration. Let's get started!

Launch **Obsidian** on your computer. If you haven't installed it yet, it's easy to download from https://obsidian.md/.

Once downloaded, follow these steps to install it:

1. Open **Settings** (gear icon, bottom left). Switch on **Community plugins** and approve the security notice if prompted.

2. Go to **Community plugins** → **Browse**, search for **BMO Chatbot**, select it, and hit **Install**.

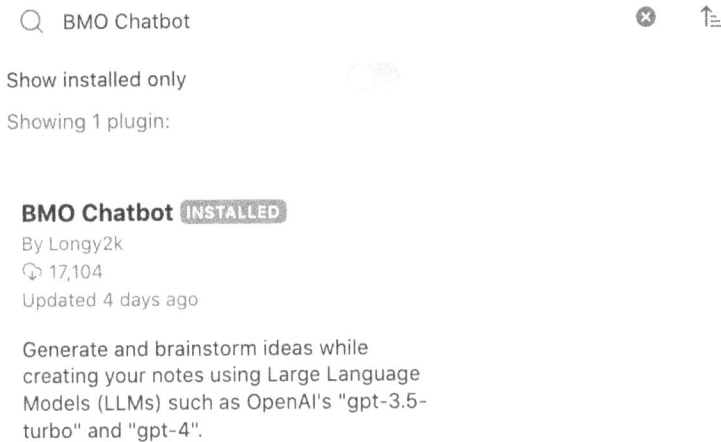

Q BMO Chatbot   ⊗   ↑≡

Show installed only

Showing 1 plugin:

BMO Chatbot INSTALLED
By Longy2k
⟳ 17,104
Updated 4 days ago

Generate and brainstorm ideas while
creating your notes using Large Language
Models (LLMs) such as OpenAI's "gpt-3.5-
turbo" and "gpt-4".

Figure 2.5: Install the BMO Chatbot plugin

3. Once the plugin is installed, return to the **Installed plugins** tab. Then locate **BMO Chatbot** and toggle it on to activate it.

With the plugin enabled and visible in your plugin list, the next step is to configure its settings, so it knows how to communicate with your local model running in Ollama. But before the plugin can interact with your local model, it needs to know where Ollama is running. By default, Ollama starts a local server on your machine, and BMO Chatbot must be pointed to this server using the correct API URL. This simple configuration step establishes the connection between Obsidian and your locally hosted model.

Follow these steps to connect the plugin to Ollama:

1. In Obsidian, go to **Settings** and find **BMO Chatbot** under the **Plugin options** section.

2. Enter the Ollama API URL in the provided field (`http://localhost:11434`):

Ollama Connection   ⌄

OLLAMA REST API URL
Enter your REST API URL. Update <u>Ollama</u> to version >=0.1.42 to   http://localhost:11434
avoid CORS restriction.

Enable Stream
Enable Ollama models to stream response.   ⬤

Figure 2.6: Entering the local Ollama API URL

Once the API URL is set, the plugin should immediately recognize any available models from Ollama, including your custom emoji model or any other versions you've created.

If you prefer to use the Mistral API instead of a local Ollama instance, BMO Chatbot supports this as well. This option is great if you want to run your chatbot from the cloud or connect to a hosted model without relying on local resources.

To use the Mistral API, you'll need to provide an API key linked to a paid Mistral subscription. The pricing is currently reasonable for hobbies or light professional use, and the setup is straightforward.

While we'll go through the complete sign-up and key generation process in *Chapter 4*, here's a quick look at where to enter the key in the plugin settings:

1. Expand the **Mistral AI Provider** section. In the **BMO Chatbot** plugin settings, scroll down to the **LLM providers** section. Find and expand the **Mistral AI** option.

2. Paste your Mistral API key into the input field provided. To obtain the key, visit `https://mistral.ai` and sign in with a paid account.

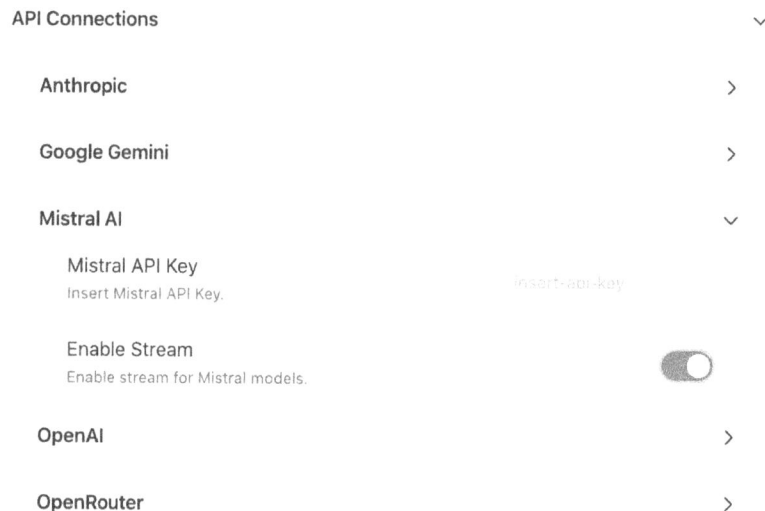

API Connections	⌄
Anthropic	›
Google Gemini	›
Mistral AI	⌄
Mistral API Key Insert Mistral API Key.	Insert-api-key
Enable Stream Enable stream for Mistral models.	⬤
OpenAI	›
OpenRouter	›

Figure 2.7: Entering the Mistral API key

Once your API key is in place, the plugin can connect to Mistral's cloud-hosted models.

Once the BMO chatbot plugin is installed and enabled, it's time to define how the model behaves during interactions. We'll need to configure general settings such as system prompts, temperature, and model selection available in Ollama. These settings control your conversations' tone, depth, and memory, letting you customize the experience to your preferences—whether you're aiming for concise, factual responses or something more creative and conversational.

Use the plugin settings panel inside Obsidian to define the following parameters:

1. **Model**: At the top of the settings page, you'll find a drop-down menu to choose your model. If the list appears empty, it means the plugin hasn't connected to your Ollama instance yet—this will be resolved after we configure the API URL in the next step.

BMO Chatbot Settings

Changelog | Wiki | Report a Bug | Support Me

Type `/help` in chat for commands.

Profiles   >

General   ⌄

Model
Choose a model.

✓ No Model
Ollama Models
emoji:latest
mistral-nemo:latest
mistral-small:latest
mistral:latest
llama3:latest

Max Tokens
The maximum number of tokens, or words, that the model is allowed to generate in its output. Some models require a minimum number of tokens to be set. The default value is empty.

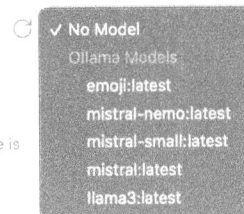

Figure 2.8: Select among available models

Tip: Select **mistral-nemo:latest** from the dropdown once available for this demo. Please refer to *Figure 2.9*:

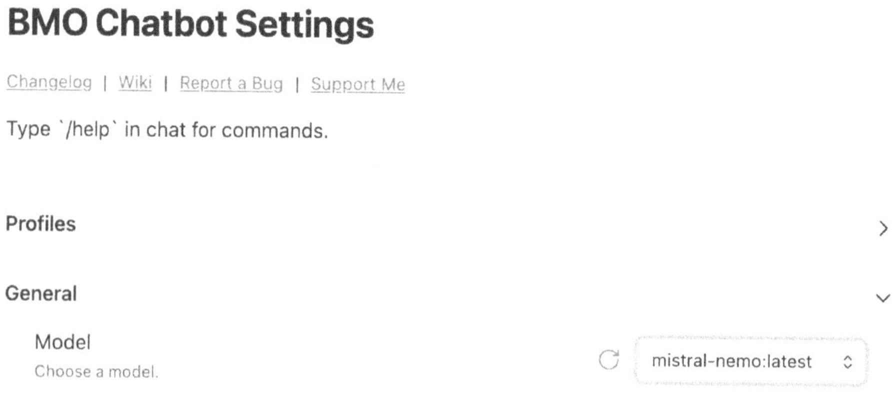

BMO Chatbot Settings

Changelog | Wiki | Report a Bug | Support Me

Type `/help` in chat for commands.

Profiles   >

General   ⌄

    Model
    Choose a model.   ↻   [mistral-nemo:latest   ⌄]

Figure 2.9: Model is selected

2. **Prompt**: This lets you choose a predefined system prompt, a guiding instruction applied to every user message. Prompts are stored as text files in the folder set under **Prompts** folder—for example, BMO/Prompts. To create your own, add a new text file in this folder, such as helpful_assistant.txt, and write your instruction inside—for example: You are a helpful assistant. Then, in **BMO Chatbot Settings**, select this file from the **Prompt** dropdown. Once selected, the prompt is automatically applied to every conversation, shaping the model's tone and behavior without the need to retype it each time.

3. **Temperature**: Set the model's creativity level. A common balanced value is Temperature: 0.20.

4. **Max Tokens**: Define how much of the previous conversation the model should remember. Here's an example: Context Length: 4096

General ⌄

Model

Choose a model.

⟳   No Model ⌄

Max Tokens

The maximum number of tokens, or words, that the model is
allowed to generate in its output. Some models require a minimum
number of tokens to be set. The default value is empty.

4096

Temperature

Temperature controls how random the generated output is. Lower
values make the text more predictable, while higher values make
it more creative and unpredictable.

0.20

Enable Reference Current Note

Enable chatbot to reference current active note during conversation.

Prompts ⌄

Prompt

Select a prompt to provide additional context to the system role.

--EMPTY-- ⌄

Prompt Folder Path

Select a prompt from a specified folder.

BMO/Prompts

Appearance ⟩

Chat History ⟩

Editor ⌄

Editor System Role

System role for BMO Generate and 'Prompt Select Generate'
command.

You are a helpful
assistant.

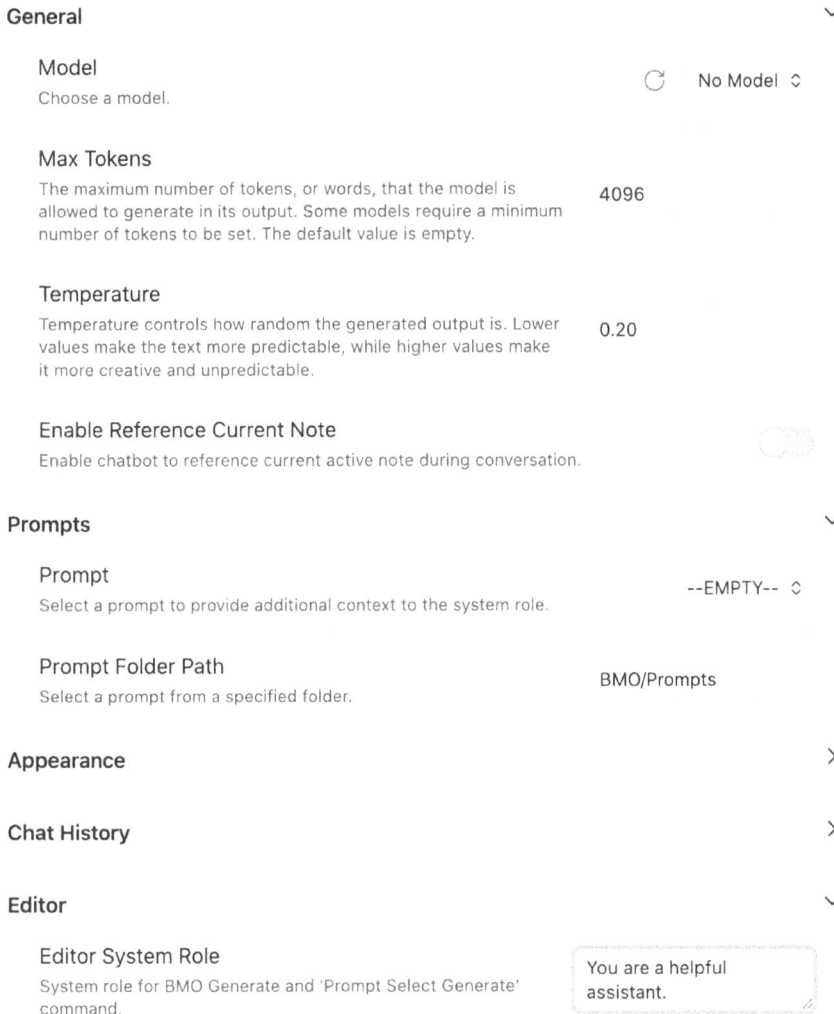

Figure 2.10: Setting temperature, system prompt, and context length

These basic settings establish how the chatbot responds and what tone it uses. But none of it will
work until the plugin knows where to find your running model. The plugin is configured, and
your model is connected (whether through Ollama or the Mistral API) and you're ready to see it
in action. In this next section, we'll try out real prompts inside Obsidian and explore how your
custom model behaves within your note-taking environment. It's time to bring your AI assistant
to life right inside your daily workflow.

Using the Mistral model in note-taking

Once everything is configured, it's time to interact with your AI directly inside Obsidian. The plugin gives you multiple ways to access your model, but the most straightforward is using the built-in chat panel.

This integration allows you to use your custom model (whether it's running locally through Ollama or via the Mistral API) without ever leaving your note-taking workflow. Let's walk through how to open the chat and send your first prompt.

Here's how to open the chat interface and begin your first conversation:

1. On the left-hand sidebar of Obsidian, look for the icon that resembles a **robotic head**. Click this icon to open the BMO Chatbot panel:

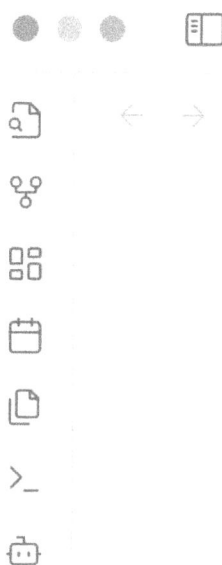

Figure 2.11: Launching the chat panel via the robotic head icon

When the chat panel is open on the right-hand side, you're ready to begin interacting with your model.

2.   Type your prompt into the input box. Press *Enter* and watch the response stream back
      letter by letter, just like a live chat session:

Figure 2.12: Streaming response from a local model inside Obsidian

Integrating BMO Chatbot with Obsidian allows you seamless access to your customized AI models, right where your thinking happens. Whether you're brainstorming, journaling, or managing
projects, this setup brings conversational AI into your creative flow—powered by the models and
prompts that you control. Feel free to experiment with different system prompts and parameter
tweaks to shape your assistant's tone and personality.

We've covered how Obsidian can boost individual productivity. Now it's time to open the door
for teams and non-technical users to join the conversation through a straightforward browser
chat. Moving on, we'll raise the bar by making your Mistral-powered chat accessible through a
web UI, transforming your local model into a full-fledged, interactive web application. Ready to
see it in action? Let's go!

Step 5: Integration with a web UI

It's time to take the next step—deploying a fully–featured web UI for your custom chat model.
This interface will allow users to interact with your model through a browser, providing a familiar
and user-friendly chat experience.

In this section, we'll run the WebUI application inside a Docker container and configure it to connect to your local Ollama instance using the Ollama API. Requests from the chat interface will be handled by Ollama, which in turn delegates them to the Mistral model you registered earlier. Let's get everything connected and running.

Docker pull and dry run the web UI

To make your custom chat model accessible through a web interface, we'll use the Open WebUI project. This lightweight application runs inside a Docker container and communicates with your local Ollama instance, providing a clean, browser-based chat interface.

Before we begin, make sure Docker is installed on your machine. If it isn't, you can download and install Docker Desktop from `https://www.docker.com/products/docker-desktop`:

1. Use the following command in your terminal to pull and run the Open WebUI image:

    ```
    sudo docker run -d -p 3000:8080 --add-host=host.docker.
    internal:host-gateway -v open-webui:/app/backend/data --name open-
    webui --restart always ghcr.io/open-webui/open-webui:main
    ```

    Here's what each part of the command does:

    *   `sudo docker run`: This command starts a new Docker container
    *   `` `-d' ``: This runs the container in detached mode (in the background).
    *   `-p 3000:8080`: This maps port 8080 in the container to port 3000 on your host machine, allowing you to access the web UI at `http://localhost:3000`.
    *   `--add-host=host.docker.internal:host-gateway`: This adds a host entry to the container to allow it to access services running on the host machine.
    *   `-v open-webui:/app/backend/data`: This mounts a Docker volume named `open-webui` to persist data in `/app/backend/data` inside the container.
    *   `--name open-webui`: This names the container `open-webui`.
    *   `--restart always`: This ensures the container restarts automatically if it stops or if the Docker daemon restarts.
    *   `ghcr.io/open-webui/open-webui:main`: This specifies the Docker image to use.

    After executing the command, Docker will pull the image (if it's not already available locally) and create a container named `open-webui`. You can confirm this using Docker Desktop or the command line. You should see the image listed:

Images Give feedback ☺

An image is a read-only template with instructions for creating a Docker container. Learn more

Local	Hub	Artifactory EARLY ACCESS

4.66 GB / 5.72 GB in use 5 images   Last refresh: about 7 hours ago ↻

🔍 Search   ≡   ▥

	Name	Tag	Status	Created	Size	Actions
☐	ghcr.io/open-webui/open-webui 4df5f45ff574	main	In use	2 months ago	2.67 GB	▶ ⋮ 🗑

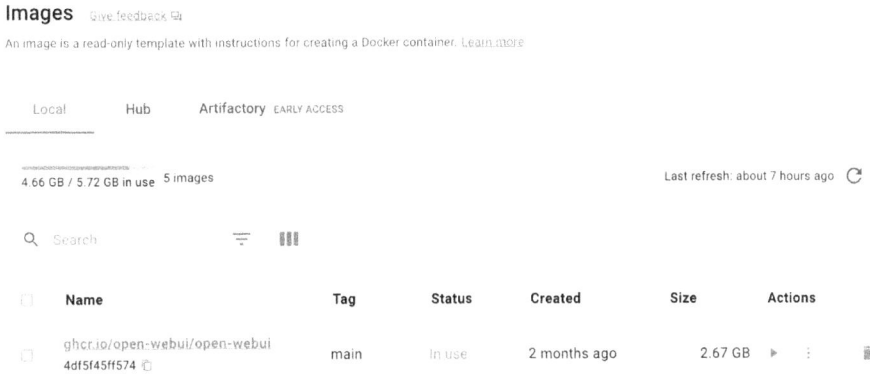

Figure 2.13: Open WebUI image shown in Docker Desktop

Likewise, the corresponding container should be running and listening on port `localhost:3000`:

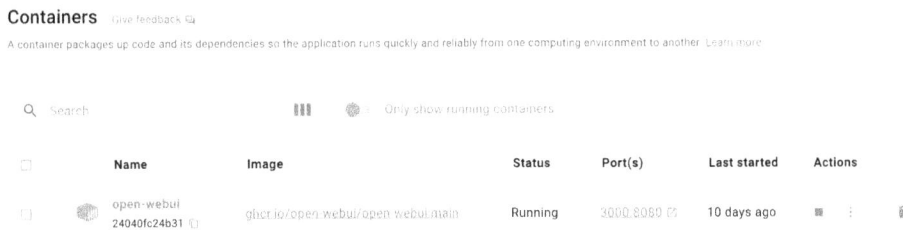

Containers Give feedback ☺

A container packages up code and its dependencies so the application runs quickly and reliably from one computing environment to another. Learn more

🔍 Search   ▥   ⚙ Only show running containers

	Name	Image	Status	Port(s)	Last started	Actions
☐	🐳 open-webui 24040fc24b31	ghcr.io/open-webui/open-webui:main	Running	3000:8080 ☑	10 days ago	■ ⋮ 🗑

Figure 2.14: Running container listening on port 3000

> ✍ It's essential that the container can communicate with the host system where Ollama is running. If you're running Ollama on a separate machine or VM, you'll need to configure the web UI to point to that external IP address instead of `localhost`.

The Open WebUI container is now running and connected to your Ollama instance, which means it is time to launch Open WebUI in a browser, register the admin user, configure it to communicate with the Ollama API, and observe other settings. This step verifies that the frontend is loading correctly and ready for configuration.

2. Open your preferred web browser and navigate to: `http://localhost:3000`. You'll see the Open WebUI welcome page if everything is set up correctly. This screen confirms that the web interface is active and waiting for the initial user registration.

Figure 2.15: Open WebUI welcome screen in the browser

You're now ready to proceed to registering your first admin user, which will give you full access to the system's features and connection settings. Let's continue.

3. Before using the web UI, you'll need to create your first user account. Since the system doesn't yet recognize any users, it will prompt you to begin the registration process. Click the **Get started** link on the welcome screen to access the registration page. The form is straightforward—provide a username, email address, and password:

Figure 2.16: Open WebUI user registration form

Your login credentials are stored securely inside the Docker volume and are not sent externally. This keeps your setup private and fully self-contained.

4. After completing registration and logging in, you'll be redirected to the main chat interface:

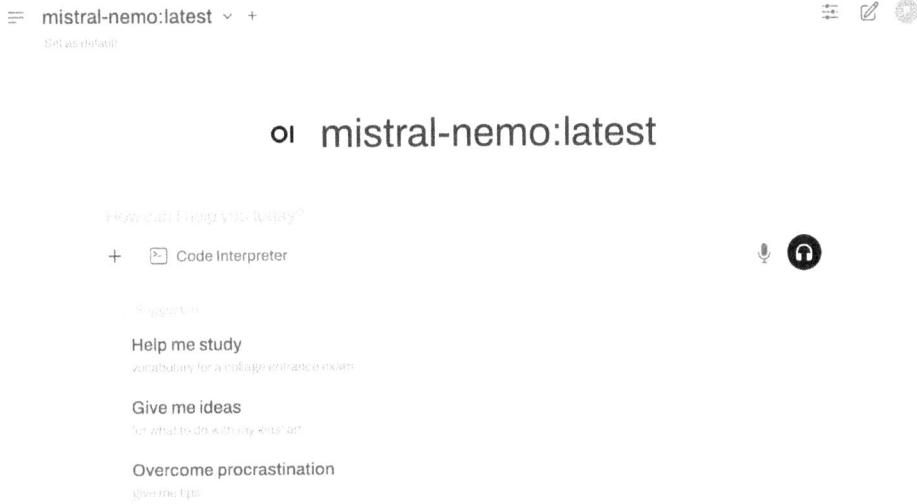

≡ mistral-nemo:latest ⌄ +

oı mistral-nemo:latest

+ ⊡ Code Interpreter

Help me study
vocabulary for a college entrance exam

Give me ideas
for what to do with my kids' art

Overcome procrastination
give me tips

Figure 2.17: Default chat interface after login

At this point, the system is ready to accept prompts—but before we do that, we still need to point the UI to your local Ollama model. You'll need to configure the Ollama API URL so the web UI can communicate with your locally running model. This step is essential for enabling full chat functionality.

5. Look at the bottom-left corner of the interface where your username is displayed. Click on it to open the user menu. If you're logged in as an admin, you'll see additional options compared to a regular user:

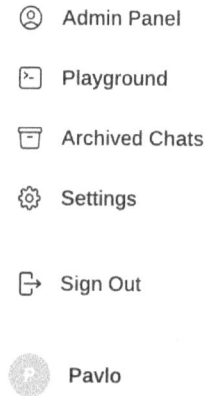

Figure 2.18: Admin menu accessed from the username panel

6. From the menu, select **Settings**. This will open the full configuration panel. Navigate to the **Connections** tab, then expand the **Ollama Base URL** section. Here, you'll enter the URL where your Ollama instance is running.

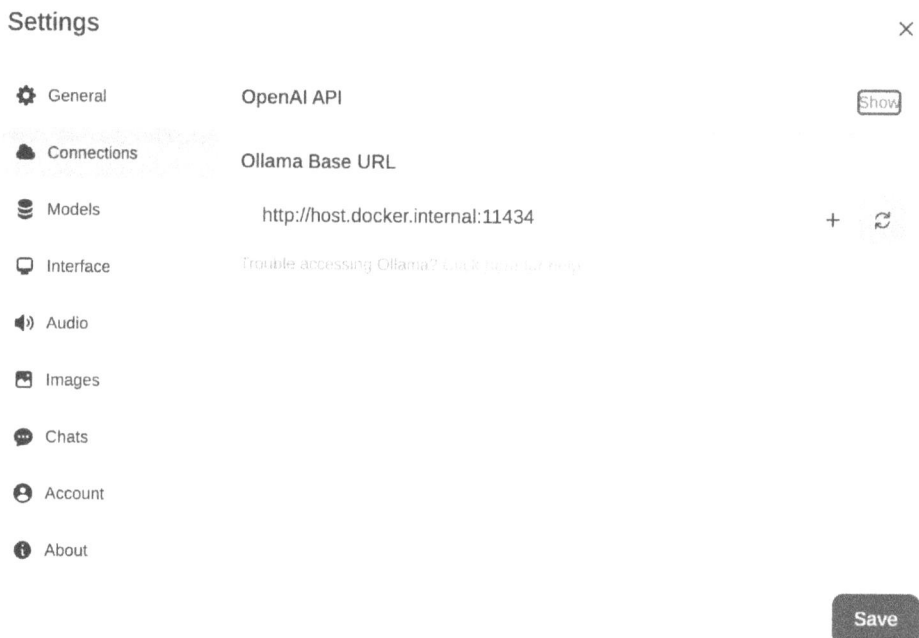

Figure 2.19: Configuring Ollama Base URL

Note on macOS

On macOS, Docker containers cannot access localhost directly. Instead, use `http://host.docker.internal:11434`. This address allows Docker to route requests to the host system. Also, make sure you launch the Docker container using `sudo` to allow proper networking access.

While you're in the **Settings** panel, it's worth exploring some of the other configuration tabs:

- **General**: This tab allows you to manage the UI theme, language, notifications, and global system prompt for the user. If you prefer a dark theme for better visual comfort, this is the place to enable it.

- **Models**: Here, you can override and manage the models provided by Ollama from within WebUI. Keep in mind that models can be large, ranging from 2 GB to 5 GB or more, so ensure your Docker volume is adequately sized.

- **Interface**: This tab includes settings for the chat interface, such as default suggested chat starters, title auto-generation, and default model selection.

- **Audio**: Manage the speech-to-text and text-to-speech engines and select your preferred voice for audio interactions.

- **Images**: Use this tab to manage the connection to the image generation engine.

- **Chats**: This tab allows for the mass export and import of chat data, which is useful for backup purposes or transitioning user chat data.

- **Account**: Manage your avatar, display name, and password changes here. Additionally, you can generate API keys for further integration and customization.

The chat is good to go!

Now for the tastiest part of this exercise. Let's dry run and demo some features that Open WebUI generously provides to us while using the Mistral language model as a brain:

1. Type a message such as `Who is Taylor Swift?`. The system will generate the response. While generating, it will stream it letter by letter, word by word.

2. Click on the microphone icon in the chat window. Speak your query, and the system will convert your voice into text and respond accordingly. Note that the browser might ask you to allow access to the microphone the first time.

3. Click on the upload icon and select a text file from your computer. Ask the system to summarize it by typing `Please summarize this document`. Mistral will summarize the document for you

Whew! Isn't this cool? Open WebUI acts like mature Generative AI products but is free and entirely located on your hardware. But big power requires big responsibility. Let's learn how to manage users within the Open WebUI ecosystem.

Governing users

Beyond chatting with your model, Open WebUI includes a number of admin-level features for managing user access, permissions, and model visibility. These tools are especially useful if you're running the interface for a team, classroom, or controlled user group.

By default, the system allows self-signup, meaning anyone can register as a user. However, you can configure how those new users are handled:

- Users can be automatically assigned the user role
- Alternatively, they can enter a pending state until manually approved by an admin

The relevant controls are in **Admin Settings**, as shown here:

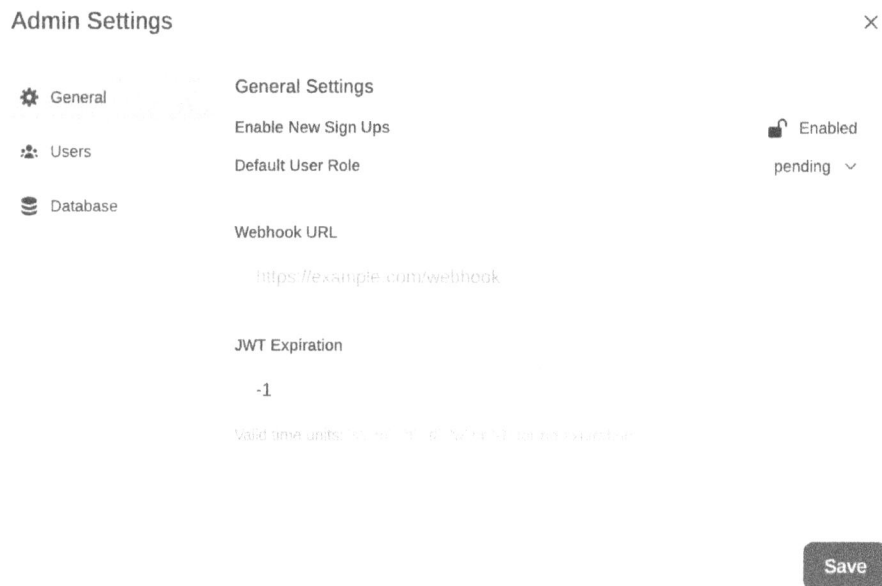

Figure 2.20: Admin settings for managing user roles and approvals

As an admin, you can also whitelist models, deciding which models are visible or accessible to regular users. This works exceptionally well in combination with model inheritance, covered earlier, in the *Step 1: Install and run Ollama* section, allowing you to provide different capabilities for different users.

Admin Settings   ✕

⚙ General

           User Permissions

           Allow Chat Deletion   🔓 Allow

👥 Users

           Manage Models

🛢 Database

           Model Whitelisting   On

              mistral:latest   ⌄   +

                                  1 Model(s) Whitelisted

Save

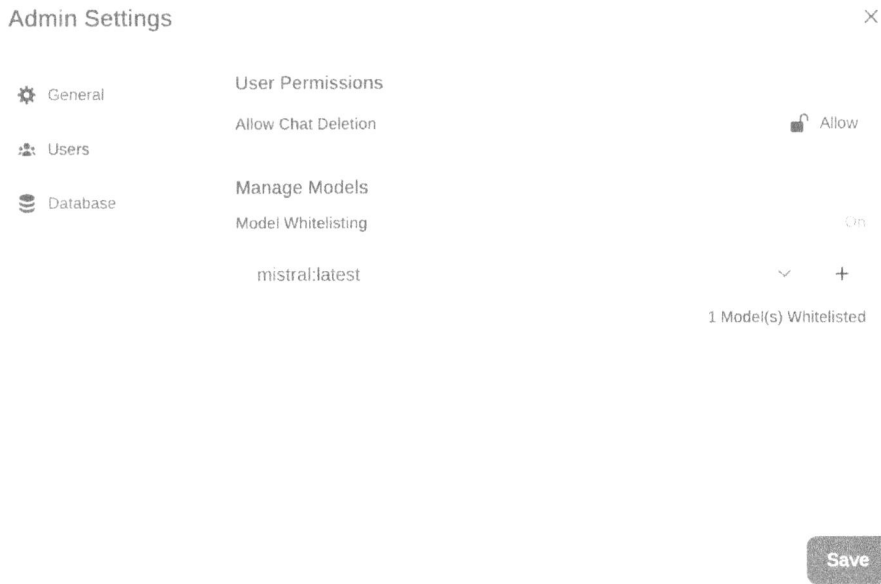

Figure 2.21: Whitelisting model access per user role

Additionally, Open WebUI gives you the ability to create users manually or import them in bulk using a CSV file—ideal for onboarding large teams quickly.

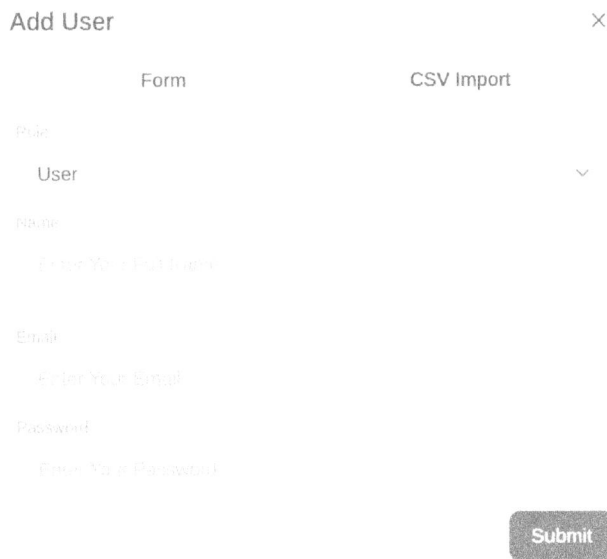

Add User   ✕

            Form   CSV Import

Role

  User   ⌄

Name

  Enter Your Full Name

Email

  Enter Your Email

Password

  Enter Your Password

Submit

Figure 2.22: User import and creation options in admin panel

At this point, you've launched a full-featured local chat system, connected it to your Mistral model, and wrapped it in a secure and flexible user interface. You now have a powerful, customizable assistant running entirely on your own terms—with governance tools in place.

Great AI often needs good GPUs! In the next section, we'll examine our chat implementation through the lens of hardware requirements.

Suggested hardware configurations

Before you go all-in with your custom AI assistant, it's worth taking a moment to consider your hardware. Whether you're running it for personal use or planning to expose it to multiple users, performance will vary significantly based on your machine's capabilities.

The most important factor? Your GPU. LLMs such as Mistral rely heavily on GPU memory and throughput to generate responses smoothly and in real time. In this section, we'll highlight recommended hardware configurations—from minimal setups that can run basic models, to high-end systems optimized for low latency and concurrent users. If you've experienced lag, slow streaming, or word-by-word delays, these benchmarks will help you identify where your system might need an upgrade—or what model size would be a better fit.

Let's take a closer look at what kind of hardware makes these models truly shine. Understanding how your system uses GPU resources is helpful for evaluating model performance—and troubleshooting slow response times. Each operating system offers different tools to monitor GPU activity in real time:

- **Mac**: Open Activity Monitor (found in **Applications > Utilities**), then switch to the **GPU** tab. For a more detailed view, go to **Window > GPU History** or press *CMD + 4* to open a live graph of GPU activity.

- **Windows**: Launch Task Manager by pressing *Ctrl + Shift + Esc*. Navigate to the *Performance* tab and select *GPU* from the list to monitor real-time usage and memory load.

- **Linux**: Use the watch command in combination with tools such as nvidia-smi for NVIDIA GPUs:

  ```
  watch -n 1 nvidia-smi
  ```

This provides a live snapshot of GPU utilization and memory usage every second.

> When running a model, you should observe a noticeable increase in GPU usage. This confirms that your system is utilizing the GPU correctly during inference.

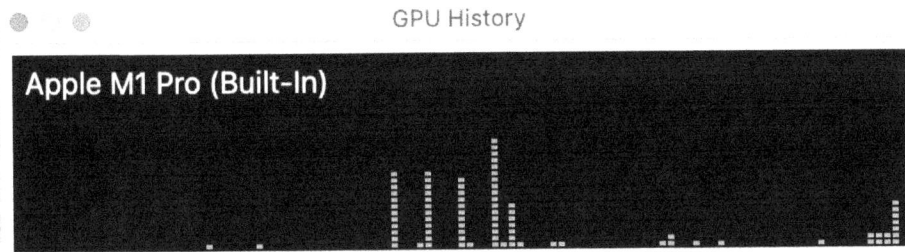

Figure 2.23: Real-time GPU activity during model inference

Monitoring GPU usage gives you a clearer picture of how your model performs under load. Next, we'll explore different hardware configurations—starting with the minimal comfortable setup—to help you choose a system that matches your performance goals and budget.

Single-user hardware configuration

For readers interested in running local LLMs such as Mistral-7B, a well-equipped personal machine can deliver strong performance—especially for inference, experimentation, and light development tasks.

Apple devices: evaluating the M1/M2 and M3 series

While MacBooks with M1 and M2 chips were impressive at launch, their integrated GPU architecture has limitations when handling larger language models. They work well with smaller models such as mistral-small or quantized variants, but may struggle with heavier workloads.

The introduction of the M3 Max chip significantly improves local AI performance. The 16-inch MacBook Pro with M3 Max, offering up to a 40-core GPU and 128 GB of unified memory, is currently Apple's best option for LLM usage. However, macOS still lacks native support for NVIDIA CUDA, which remains a key advantage in AI development ecosystems.

Windows/Linux with discrete GPUs: Preferred for performance

For readers looking for maximum efficiency and flexibility, NVIDIA GPUs remain the gold standard due to their compatibility with CUDA-based AI libraries (e.g., torch, transformers, llama.cpp).

Here are updated laptop recommendations as of 2025. The following offer a great balance of power and portability:

- ASUS ROG Zephyrus G16
- NVIDIA GeForce RTX 4070 (8 GB VRAM)
- Intel Core Ultra 9

These are reliable for real-time chat and multi-model workflows:

- Lenovo Legion Pro 7i
- NVIDIA GeForce RTX 4080 (12 GB VRAM)
- Intel Core i9-14900HX

These offer top-tier performance for large models and concurrent sessions:

- MSI Raider GE78HX
- NVIDIA GeForce RTX 4090 (16 GB VRAM)
- Intel Core i9-14900HX

These GPUs offer high VRAM, which is essential for running quantized models such as Mistral-8B entirely in memory.

Emerging alternatives: AMD's Strix Halo

AMD's upcoming Strix Halo APUs are expected to bring competitive performance to the integrated GPU market, potentially rivaling mid-range NVIDIA options in certain AI tasks. While early benchmarks look promising, real-world testing with LLMs is still underway.

If your machine includes at least 16 GB of RAM, an SSD, and a discrete NVIDIA GPU, you're well-equipped for most local LLM tasks using platforms such as Ollama, LM Studio, or Text Generation WebUI.

In the next section, we'll explore more powerful configurations—ideal for developers, researchers, or anyone working with larger models, longer contexts, or multi-user environments.

Powerful hardware configuration

For readers working on heavier LLM tasks—such as hosting multi-user environments, experimenting with fine-tuning, or integrating **retrieval-augmented generation** (**RAG**) pipelines—a strong workstation becomes essential. The following configuration reflects a reliable and scalable setup designed for the local deployment of models such as Mistral-Small, Mistral-Nemo, and even limited training experiments.

Motherboard (AM5 platform with PCIe 5.0 and DDR5 support)

- ASUS ProArt X670E-Creator WiFi
- MSI MEG X670E ACE
- ASRock X670E Taichi

Processor (multi-core CPU with high sustained throughput)

- AMD Ryzen 9 7950X3D (16-core, optimized for cache-sensitive tasks)
- Intel Core i9-14900K (strong single-thread and solid multi-core balance)
- AMD Ryzen 9 7900X (12-core budget alternative)

Graphics card (high-VRAM NVIDIA GPUs with CUDA/TensorRT support)

- NVIDIA RTX 4090 (24 GB VRAM, ideal for 13B+ models and multi-user inference)
- NVIDIA RTX 4080 SUPER (16 GB, suitable for 7B models)
- (Avoid AMD GPUs unless using ROCm workflows—ecosystem compatibility is limited)

RAM (large capacity for parallel workloads and vector DBs)

- G.SKILL Trident Z5 RGB DDR5 64GB (2×32GB, 6000MT/s)
- Corsair Vengeance DDR5 64GB
- Kingston Fury Beast DDR5 64GB

> For high-concurrency setups or local RAG chains, 128 GB is highly recommended.

Storage (NVMe Gen4 SSDs for fast model loading and data streaming)

- Samsung 990 PRO 2TB NVMe
- WD_BLACK SN850X 2TB
- Sabrent Rocket 4 Plus 2TB

Power supply (stable high-wattage with modular design)

- Corsair HX1200i (Platinum, fully modular)
- Seasonic PRIME TX-1300 (80+ Titanium)
- EVGA SuperNOVA 1000 T2

Cooling (liquid AIO systems for thermal stability)

- Corsair iCUE H150i ELITE LCD XT
- NZXT Kraken Elite 360
- Arctic Liquid Freezer II 420

This configuration equips you to run complex LLM workloads efficiently, including multi-user inference, custom RAG pipelines, local fine-tuning, and real-time model experimentation:

- Host multiple 7B–13B models locally with smooth inference
- Deploy Ollama, RAG components, and chat UIs all on the same machine
- Experiment with LoRA fine-tuning, embeddings, and vector search
- Handle multi-user environments without latency issues

Looking for scalable or managed deployments instead of local hardware?

In *Chapter 10*, we'll show how to use AWS Bedrock for hosted Mistral APIs. In *Chapter 11*, we'll walk through deploying Mistral models via Google Cloud Vertex AI with full support for scaling, monitoring, and secure endpoints.

With your local chat system now fully customized and running, you've taken a significant step toward mastering the power of Mistral models. Let's recap the key insights from this chapter and prepare you for the practical challenges that lie ahead.

Summary

In this chapter, we built a fully functional local AI assistant using Mistral models and the Ollama runtime. We started by installing Ollama and running models such as `mistral-small` and `mistral-nemo`, confirming our setup and observing system performance through basic prompts and terminal interaction.

From there, we introduced system prompts, template customization, and runtime parameters such as temperature and context length to shape how the model behaves and responds. Using a Modelfile, we created inherited model variants, each configured with unique instructions for tone, role, or behavior.

We integrated these custom models with two popular user interfaces. First, we configured Obsidian using the BMO Chatbot plugin, enabling AI-assisted note-taking directly in our knowledge base. Then, we deployed WebUI in a Docker container, creating a browser-based chatbot complete with multi-user support, theming, and audio features.

To ensure appropriate and safe interactions, we covered response governance techniques, including model whitelisting, user role control, and prompt-based moderation. We also explored optional extensions such as impersonation prompts, knowledge graphs in Obsidian, and advanced system prompt experimentation.

In the next chapter, we'll explore advanced prompt tuning, behavioral control, and response filtering, giving you deeper authority over how your model thinks, speaks, and reacts in complex or sensitive scenarios.

Extracurricular

By now, you've explored the full deployment of your own AI assistant—from pulling models and tuning prompts to building interactive interfaces. But there's still room to go further. The following ideas and exercises invite you to stretch the system's creative and technical potential.

1. **Brainstorm ideas using WebUI**: Explore the creativity of WebUI by brainstorming ideas for various projects. Start a session and ask the model to generate ideas for a new book, a business plan, or a creative art project. For example, you can prompt the model with "Generate unique business ideas for a tech start-up." Use impersonation prompts such as "Please impersonate a marketing person" and "Please impersonate the cumulative voice of customers." Yes, a single prompt can have multiple impersonations! This exercise will help you understand how to leverage AI for ideation and could inspire you to develop innovative concepts.

2. **Exercise with more system prompts**: Experiment with creating different system prompts to see how they influence the model's responses. Try prompts such as "You are a motivational speaker" or "You are a technical support agent." This exercise will allow you to observe how the model adapts to different roles and settings, providing insights into the versatility and customization capabilities of AI.

3. **Configure WebUI on Mistral to exclude specific topics**: Learn how to configure WebUI on the Mistral model to exclude certain topics, making it safe for specific users, such as children. Set up rules to filter out inappropriate content by specifying keywords or topics to avoid. This exercise will enhance your ability to use AI responsibly and tailor interactions to suit different audiences.

4. **Use the inherited Mistral Small model with a system prompt**: Create an inherited version of the Mistral Small model with a specific system prompt and save it as a different model. For example, set a system prompt to make the model act as a historical figure or a specialized expert. Then, interact with this new model using WebUI. This practice helps you understand model inheritance and customization, providing hands-on experience with advanced AI configurations.

5. **Implement a semi-automated knowledge graph in Obsidian**: Use Obsidian to create a semi-automated knowledge graph by tagging, linking, and capturing keywords from your notes. This involves organizing your research or project data into a visual map that shows the relationships between different pieces of information. By implementing this in Obsidian, you can enhance your data organization and retrieval skills, making it easier to manage complex information structures.

These activities will deepen your understanding of AI and its practical applications, encouraging you to explore and innovate with the tools at your disposal. As a pleasant side effect, you will learn advanced chat usage approaches.

3

Managing the Model

Give a man a fish, and you feed him for a day;

Teach a man to fish, and you feed him for a lifetime.

— Maimonides

Imagine a seasoned fisher standing at the shore, casting a net into a carefully chosen lake where the right kind of catch awaits. The decision about where and how to cast is much like setting the conditions for a language model—choices that shape the results we can expect. As the net sinks, its weave decides whether only prized fish are caught or a broader variety slips through, echoing how parameters such as top_k and top_p control the model's selectivity.

In the same way that a fisher depends on the right waters, net, and bait, we depend on parameters to steer generation. Carrying that image forward, we'll now turn to the mechanics: how logits, weights, and the softmax function guide token selection, and how controls such as top_k, top_p, penalties, and length settings refine the final output. These tools let us shape raw potential into coherent, polished results.

In a nutshell, this chapter will cover the following main topics:

- Problem statement
- Pipeline overview
- Refining the generated output
- Practical workshop: the `softmax` function, `temperature`, `top_k`, and `top_p`

Technical requirements

In this chapter, we will use the following tools:

- Command-line Ollama with installed Mistral-Nemo
- Python and pip 3.9

All source code is available on GitHub at `https://github.com/PacktPublishing/Learn-Mistral` in the `Chapter-3` folder.

Problem statement: When is adapting model parameters necessary?

Effectively harnessing the power of LLMs is crucial for generating meaningful and accurate outputs. However, the process of tuning these models to produce the desired results can be challenging, particularly when dealing with a wide array of parameters that influence the model's behavior.

In this chapter, we aim to address the complexities involved in adjusting LLMs by adapting key parameters such as the **temperature**, **top_k**, **top_p**, and various penalties. The main goal is understanding how these parameters interact and affect the model's output, and how they can be adjusted to deliver the desired output.

To equip you with the knowledge and practical skills, we will do the following:

- Cover the mathematical foundations behind LLM parameters
- Learn how to manipulate these parameters to achieve specific outcomes
- Apply this knowledge through practical exercises to see the real-world impact of these adjustments

By the end, you will have a solid grasp of how to adjust the LLM's output, enabling you to generate precise, targeted, and practical outputs.

Pipeline overview

Before we start our navigation through the complexities of adapting language models, let's understand how different components of the LLM pipeline work together. The following diagram illustrates the main stages of the language model pipeline, focusing on how parameters such as `softmax`, `temperature`, `top_k`, and `top_p` influence the final output. It captures the interaction between these elements and their collective impact on generating meaningful text:

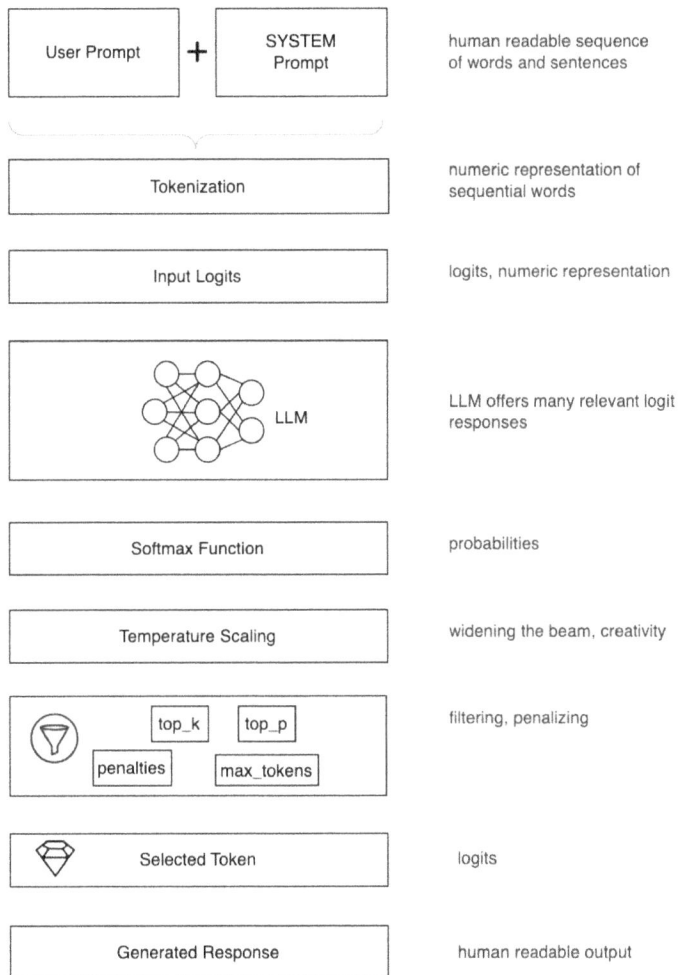

Figure 3.1: The response generation workflow

Let us focus on each phase of the process one by one:

- **User input:** This is where the process begins, with the user providing a prompt or text input. The input is the starting point for the language model's processing and is critical to determining the context and content of the generated output.

- **Tokenization:** The input text is broken down into tokens—smaller units such as words or subwords—that the model can process. Tokenization is essential for converting human language into a format from which the model can analyse and generate responses.

- **Logits calculation:** The model processes the tokens and produces *logits*, which are raw, unnormalized scores representing the likelihood of each possible token being the next word. These logits are the foundation for determining the probabilities of different tokens.

- **Neural network processing:** This is where the core computations happen within the model, where deep learning layers and complex neural operations generate the logits based on the input tokens. It's the step where the model applies its learned knowledge to predict the next possible words.

- **Softmax function:** The softmax function is applied to the logits, converting them into probabilities. Logits are unnormalized scores; softmax turns them into probabilities that the model uses to pick words. This step normalizes the logits, ensuring that the sum of all probabilities equals 1, allowing the model to make informed decisions about the next token.

- **Temperature scaling:** The temperature parameter is applied to adjust the probabilities. Lower temperatures result in more deterministic outputs, favoring tokens with higher probabilities, while higher temperatures introduce more randomness, increasing the diversity of potential outputs.

- **top_k, top_p, penalties, and max_tokens:** top_k filters the tokens by selecting only the top *k* tokens with the highest probabilities, while top_p selects tokens until their cumulative probability reaches a specified threshold. Penalties, such as repetition and presence penalties, adjust probabilities to discourage or encourage specific tokens, ensuring a more focused and varied output. The max_tokens setting simply defines the maximum length of the model's response, acting as a hard stop for generation regardless of other parameters.

- **Selected token:** After applying the softmax function, temperature scaling, and filtering, the model selects the final token based on the adjusted probabilities. This token is added to the output sequence, contributing to the overall response.

- **Generated output:** The selected tokens are combined into the final text output, which is presented to the user. This output is the result of the entire pipeline process, shaped by the various parameters and decisions made along the way.

Having covered the major phases of how LLMs process and generate text, we're now ready to focus on the next key element, system prompts.

System prompts to shape the response payload

Prior to tossing their net into the sea, a fisher must first choose where they will be fishing. This choice is important as it decides how much effort they will need to exert, what kind of fish they will be catching, as well as how successful they will be in catching some. In the big and unpredictable sea, not all seas are equal. A sea is full of small, swift fish, while another has slow, big, and prized catches. This choice depends on the experience of a fisher, their sense of judgment, and the equipment they possess.

In the world of language models, this first decision is akin to setting a system prompt. The system prompt defines the environment in which the model operates. Just as a fisher must choose the right waters to maximize their catch, you must craft the system prompt carefully to ensure the model navigates the proper context and provides the most relevant responses.

The system prompt is the guiding compass, setting the stage for how the model interacts with input prompts. It frames the boundaries of the conversation, establishing the tone, focus, and expected outcomes. Without a well-considered system prompt, even the most sophisticated model might flounder, like a fisher casting their net in barren waters. But with the right system prompt, the model can deliver precise, valuable, and contextually appropriate outputs, much like a successful fishing trip in bountiful waters.

When crafting system prompts, the goals of the interaction dictate the approach. Next are more detailed explanations of each major prompt category, along with best practices for creating effective prompts.

Prompt categories

When selecting the waters for fishing, a fisher also considers the type of catch they want. Similarly, when crafting system prompts, the goals of the interaction dictate what approach must be taken. Let us overview major prompt categories, learn best practices to structure them, and get to know how LLMs understand those directions to deliver the desired response.

Classification prompts

Classification prompts are used to categorize or label data based on predefined criteria. These prompts are particularly useful in applications where you need to sort or organize large amounts of information quickly and accurately. For instance, we could classify a text as either a resume or a bill of materials, or categorize customer feedback into positive, neutral, or negative sentiments.

When creating classification prompts, clearly define the categories you want the model to use. Provide short examples or descriptors for each category in the prompt. This will allow the LLM to understand the distinction between categories more readily, leading to more accurate and consistent classification. Ensure that the categories remain mutually exclusive so that confusion in classifying is kept to a minimum.

Prompt example:

```
Classify the following text as either a 'Resume' or a 'Bill of
Materials': '< Insert text here >.'
```

LLM response:

```
This text is classified as a 'Resume.'
```

Summarization prompts

Summarization prompts are designed to condense large volumes of information into shorter, more digestible forms. This is particularly useful when dealing with lengthy documents, articles, or reports where the key information needs to be highlighted for quick understanding.

For effective summarization, specify the desired length or format of the summary (e.g., "in three sentences" or "a bullet-point summary"). This guides the model in producing a summary that meets your needs. The LLM uses these instructions to focus on the most essential details, discarding less relevant information to produce a concise and coherent summary.

Prompt example:

```
Summarize the following article into three sentences: '< Insert
article text here >'
```

LLM response:

```
The article discusses the impact of climate change on polar bear
populations, highlighting the loss of sea ice as a critical threat.
It emphasizes the need for global action to reduce greenhouse gas
emissions. The author also mentions ongoing conservation efforts aimed
at protecting polar bear habitats.
```

Personalization prompts

Personalization prompts tailor the model's output to meet the specific needs, preferences, or characteristics of the user. This can involve adjusting the tone, style, or even the content of the response based on the user's profile, past interactions, or stated preferences.

Include contextual information about the user or situation in the prompt to help the model generate a more personalized response. For example, mentioning the user's previous queries or specific preferences can make the output more relevant. The LLM uses this context to adjust its response, creating a more engaging and tailored interaction.

Evaluation prompts

Evaluation prompts are used to assess or critique input, such as code, text, or other forms of data. These prompts are particularly valuable in quality assurance, where the goal is to identify errors, inefficiencies, or areas for improvement.

When asking for an evaluation, clearly specify the criteria or aspects you want the model to focus on (e.g., efficiency, readability, or accuracy). This directs the model's attention to the most critical areas, ensuring that the feedback is valuable and actionable. The LLM follows these criteria to provide targeted and relevant evaluations.

Prompt example:

```
Evaluate the following piece of code for efficiency and suggest
improvements: '< Insert code here >.'
```

LLM response:

```
The code effectively calculates the factorial of a number, but it can
be optimized by using an iterative approach instead of recursion. This
will reduce the function's stack usage and prevent potential stack
overflow errors for large inputs.
```

Impersonation techniques

System prompts define the model's identity, tone, and reasoning approach before any user interaction begins. They do not respond to questions; instead, they *establish the framework* within which the model will think and communicate.

Consider a practical scenario: a team is exploring a business idea for an online school that teaches STEM using Minecraft. Rather than receiving a single, general response, the system prompt is crafted to simulate input from multiple distinct personas—each reflecting a real-world stakeholder.

Here is an example system prompt:

```
You are a discussion panel evaluating a new online school for children
aged 8-14 that uses Minecraft to teach STEM. Each persona should
contribute individually:
Persona 1 - A marketing strategist focused on positioning and promotion
Persona 2 - A collective voice of parents sharing their concerns and
expectations
Persona 3 - A group of children expressing excitement and fun elements
Persona 4 - A creative game designer proposing engaging features and
storytelling
Persona 5 - An educational methodology expert outlining curriculum
structure and learning outcomes
```

In this example, the system prompt directs the model to simulate a multi-perspective conversation. The marketing strategist offers ideas on audience targeting and brand tone. The parents address issues such as cost, safety, and educational value. Children bring emotional authenticity, reflecting what excites and motivates young learners. The game designer contributes ideas on immersion and interaction. The methodology expert ensures that educational objectives and structure are present.

This compound system prompt showcases the model's ability to hold multiple viewpoints simultaneously, offering a more complete and realistic answer than a single-role approach. It demonstrates how system prompts can simulate role-based reasoning, group dynamics, and collaborative problem-solving—all within a single interaction.

To achieve effective impersonation, provide brief descriptions or key characteristics of the personas you want the model to adopt. Mentioning the tone, language style, or typical viewpoints of the persona helps the LLM deliver a more convincing and accurate impersonation. This approach allows the model to align its responses more closely with the intended character or role.

Prompt example:

```
"Please help me brainstorm the business plan for a Minecraft school
for kids, impersonate four people: a Marketing professional, a
methodology co-author, the cumulative voice of parents, and the
cumulative voice of kids. What do they want from these classes?"
```

LLM responses:

```
Marketing Professional: We should focus on how Minecraft can make
learning fun while developing essential skills. Our campaigns should
emphasize creativity, teamwork, and problem-solving, targeting both
kids and parents.
Methodology Co-Author: The curriculum should integrate core subjects
into Minecraft-based activities. Lessons should be flexible and
encourage both individual creativity and group collaboration.
Cumulative Voice of Parents: We want our kids to learn valuable skills
in a fun way. Regular updates on their progress and opportunities for
us to get involved would be appreciated.
Cumulative Voice of Kids: We want the classes to be fun and creative.
Building cool things with friends, having challenges, and earning
rewards would make the classes awesome!
```

Coding prompts

Now that we've explored personalization prompts, let's also review a few coding prompts. I've kept the examples specific and task-oriented to show how models can assist with programming challenges and structured problem-solving.

Example 1: Initial scaffolding

Here is the prompt:

```
"Generate a Spring Boot project using Maven with basic configurations."
```

This is the LLM response:

```
$ mvn archetype:generate -DgroupId=com.example -DartifactId=demo
-Dversion=1.0-SNAPSHOT -DpackageName=com.example.demo
-DarchetypeArtifactId=maven-archetype-quickstart -DinteractiveMode=false
This command will create a basic Spring Boot project structure with the
specified group ID, artifact ID, and package name.
```

Example 2: Unit test creation

Here is the prompt:

```
"Write unit tests for the factorial function, ensuring that edge cases are
covered."
def factorial(n):
    if n == 0:
        return 1
    else:
        return n * factorial(n-1)
```

This is the LLM response:

```
Sure, here is the code of the unit test that should address your request

import unit test

class TestFactorial(unittest.TestCase):
    def test_factorial_zero(self):
        self.assertEqual(factorial(0), 1)

    def test_factorial_positive(self):
```

```
            self.assertEqual(factorial(5), 120)

    def test_factorial_negative(self):
        with self.assertRaises(ValueError):
            factorial(-1)


if __name__ == '__main__':
    unittest.main()
```

Example 3: Exception handling improvements

Here is the prompt:

```
"Improve the error handling in the read_file function by adding checks for
common runtime errors and providing clear error messages."
def read_file(filename):
    with open(filename, 'r') as file:
        return file.read()
```

This is the LLM response:

```
Sure, here is the adjusted version of the read_file


def read_file(filename):
    try:
        with open(filename, 'r') as file:
            return file.read()
    except FileNotFoundError:
        print(f"Error: The file '{filename}' was not found.")
    except IOError:
        print(f"Error: An I/O error while reading '{filename}'.")
    except Exception as e:
        print(f"An unexpected error occurred: {e}")
```

Example 4: Code reusability

Here is the prompt:

```
"Refactor this code to use a factory method, improving reusability."
def create_user(name, email):
    user = {
        'name': name,
        'email': email,
        'role': 'user'
    }
    return user


def create_admin(name, email):
    admin = {
        'name': name,
        'email': email,
        'role': 'admin'
    }
    return admin
```

This is the LLM response:

```
Sure, please consider this adjusted version
def create_account(name, email, role='user'):
    account = {
        'name': name,
        'email': email,
        'role': role
    }
    return account
# Usage
user = create_account('Alice', 'alice@example.com')
admin = create_account('Bob', 'bob@example.com', 'admin')
```

Crafting effective system prompts is as crucial as selecting the right waters for fishing. Just as a fisher's success depends on choosing the right location, bait, and gear, your success with language models hinges on carefully designed system prompts.

Whether you need to classify, summarize, personalize, evaluate, or impersonate, the right prompt will guide the model to deliver the desired outcome, ensuring that you achieve your goals with precision and relevance. Now, let us throw the rod farther and learn other instructional parameters that shape the response mathematically.

Sequential token processing

Language models process tokens *sequentially*, meaning that each word in a sentence is influenced by the one that came before it. This sequential processing is fundamental to how language models generate coherent and contextually relevant text. When a user inputs a sentence, the model doesn't just consider each word in isolation; instead, it builds on the context established by the preceding words. This way, the model can capture the flow and structure of natural language, ensuring that each token it generates fits smoothly within the context of the entire sequence.

In practice, this means that the model is constantly updating its understanding of the sentence as it processes each word. For example, when processing the sentence "The cat sat on the mat," the model first understands "The cat," then "The cat sat," and so on. Each subsequent word refines the model's prediction of the next word, allowing it to generate text that is contextually appropriate and grammatically correct.

This sequential nature of token processing is supported by mechanisms such as attention and positional encoding, which help the model maintain a sense of order and context, even in complex or lengthy sentences. These mechanisms ensure that the model can generate coherent responses that are aligned with the user's input, making sequential token processing a crucial aspect of language modelling.

Tokenization

Tokenization is akin to preparing the bait for the fish, cutting it into pieces small enough to be effective but large enough to attract the desired catch. In language models, tokenization breaks down text into manageable units called tokens. Tokens can be words, subwords, or even individual characters, depending on the model's design. For example, the phrase "casting a wide net" might be tokenized as `["cast", "ing", "a", "wide", "net"]`. These tokens are the pieces of bait that the model uses to predict the next word, carefully sequenced to ensure that the catch follows logically.

Tokenization is essential because it determines how the model processes text. The choice of tokenization method affects the model's ability to understand and generate language, influencing everything from the handling of rare words to the efficiency of the model.

Logits and weighting

Logits are the raw predictions, much like the fisher's initial sense of where the fish might be found. In scientific terms, logits are the output values from the final layer of a neural network before applying the `softmax` function. They are essentially unnormalized scores assigned to each possible token that could follow the current sequence. These scores are then transformed into probabilities using the `softmax` function, which allows the model to make a probabilistic prediction about which token comes next.

Attention masking

In deep learning models, attention mechanisms allow the model to focus on specific parts of the input while processing. However, not all tokens in the input are equally important. Attention masking is a technique used to filter out irrelevant or unnecessary tokens, ensuring that the model focuses only on the most critical parts of the input.

This is akin to a fisher using a net with selective mesh sizes, designed to catch only certain types of fish while allowing others to pass through. Attention masking ensures that the model attends to the relevant tokens, just as a fisher ensures that the net captures only the intended catch.

In practice, attention masking is often used in tasks such as text generation, where certain parts of the input might be ignored, or in handling padded sequences, where the padding tokens are masked out.

Positional encoding

Imagine a singer performing a duet with an AI. As the singer leads with their melody, the AI follows, harmonizing perfectly in sync. In a language model, this synchronization is managed through **positional encoding**, which ensures the AI understands where each note (or token) falls in the sequence, allowing it to sing along coherently. Positional encoding provides information about the position of each token in the sequence so that the model can distinguish between them based on their order. Without this encoding, the model might recognize individual notes but struggle to keep pace with the overall melody and rhythm.

Technically, positional encoding is typically added to token embeddings using sinusoidal functions, enabling the model to understand the relative positions of tokens in a sequence, just as a singer knows when to join in and harmonize in a duet.

Input length and context window

Language models have a limit on the number of tokens they can process at once, known as the context window. This limit is like the capacity of a net—a fisher can only catch so many fish at a time. If the input exceeds this limit, the model might have to truncate the input, much like a fisher would leave some fish behind if the net is full.

In practical terms, this means that the model can only "remember" a certain number of tokens at once. The context window is typically measured in tokens, and managing this limit is crucial for tasks that involve long texts or dialogues.

We've covered the LLM pipeline overview, but I want to now switch gears and focus on refining the model's response, beginning with the softmax function, which transforms raw scores into meaningful probabilities.

Refining the generated output

In the vast ocean of language, every word is a potential catch, waiting to be brought to the surface. However, just as a fisher must break down their net to catch the right fish, language models must break down human language into smaller, manageable pieces—tokens, as we've seen earlier. But that isn't enough; the goal is to gauge how creative or focused we want our language model to be. Just as a fisher might adjust their technique depending on whether they want a wide variety of fish or just the most prized catch, we can adapt the creativity of our model's output using the temperature parameter. Lowering the temperature makes the model more focused and predictable, like aiming for a specific species of fish, while raising it adds creativity and variety, casting a wider net to see what comes in. Parameters such as top_p and top_k further refine this process. top_p acts like a selective net that only keeps the most significant fish (tokens) until a certain weight (probability) is reached, ensuring that the catch is diverse yet relevant. top_k, on the other hand, limits the catch to only the top k most likely options, ensuring that the focus remains on the most essential elements, much like targeting the biggest fish in the sea.

Moreover, in the unpredictable waters of language, repetition and redundancy can sometimes weigh us down, like catching too many of the same small fish when we're really after something bigger. This is where repeat_penalty comes into play, allowing us to discourage certain words or their repetition, ensuring that the output remains valuable. We can also control the size of the model's output by telling the model whether we expect long or short responses. Through these techniques, we can master the art of language generation, guiding our models to produce responses that are as precise and varied as the waters we choose to navigate. The driving console for all these parameters is a softmax function, discussed in the next section.

Softmax function

The softmax function is a fundamental mathematical function used in machine learning, particularly in the context of neural networks and classification tasks. It plays a crucial role in converting a vector of raw scores, known as logits, into a probability distribution. This process is essential because, in many tasks, we need to interpret the output of a model as probabilities, which can then be used to make decisions or predictions.

Given a vector of logits, Z_i, each element in the vector represents the unnormalized score or confidence level that a particular class or outcome is the correct one. These logits can be positive, negative, or zero, and they do not directly convey probabilities because they are not constrained to any specific range. The softmax function normalizes these logits so that they can be interpreted as probabilities, with values between 0 and 1 that sum to 1 across all possible outcomes.

Mathematically, the softmax function operates by exponentiating each logit, which means taking the exponential e^{Z_i} of each score. This step ensures that all transformed scores are positive, which is a necessary condition for a valid probability distribution. After exponentiating the logits, the softmax function normalizes these values by dividing each exponentiated score by the sum of all exponentiated scores in the vector.

The formula for the softmax function for a particular logit in a vector is given by the following:

$$sigma(Z_i) = \frac{e^{(Z_i)}}{\sum_{j=1}^{n} e^{(Z_j)}}$$

Let's break this down:

- (z_i) is the logit (raw score) for the token (i)
- $(e^{(z_i)})$ is the exponential of the logit
- The denominator, as follows, normalizes the probabilities so that they sum to *1*:

$$\left(\sum_{\{j=1\}}^{\{n\}} e^{\{z_i\}} \right)$$

In this equation, each logit is exponentiated to ensure it is positive, and then all the exponentiated logits are divided by their sum, resulting in a probability distribution. The higher the logit, the higher the corresponding probability after applying the softmax function.

For better understanding, let's use this formula and run through the calculation step by step.

Applying the softmax function

Let us consider a hypothetical example of the user prompt:

"The concert started as the sun dipped below the horizon, casting a warm glow over the stage. The"

The LLM will take into account the context and generate the next possible logits:

- **guitar**: 2.5 (Strong candidate. This is highly relevant to a concert setting and fits naturally as the next word.)

- **melody**: 2.2 (Strong candidate. Also highly relevant, as this word aligns with the musical context of the sentence.)

- **whisper**: 1.4 (Mediocre candidate. While it could be poetically descriptive, it's less directly connected to the concert setting.)

- **sunset**: 1.3 (Mediocre candidate. It ties back to the earlier part of the sentence, but it's less likely to follow directly after stage.)

- **avalanche**: 0.2 (Weak candidate. This word is out of place in the current context and doesn't fit the concert scene.)

- **elephant**: 0.2 (Weak candidate. Like *avalanche*, this word is unrelated to the context and would be unexpected as the next word.)

In this scenario, *guitar* and *melody* are the strongest candidates for continuing the sentence, while *whisper* and *sunset* are less relevant but could still work depending on the desired tone. *avalanche* and *elephant* are the weakest candidates, as they do not fit the context of the concert scene at all.

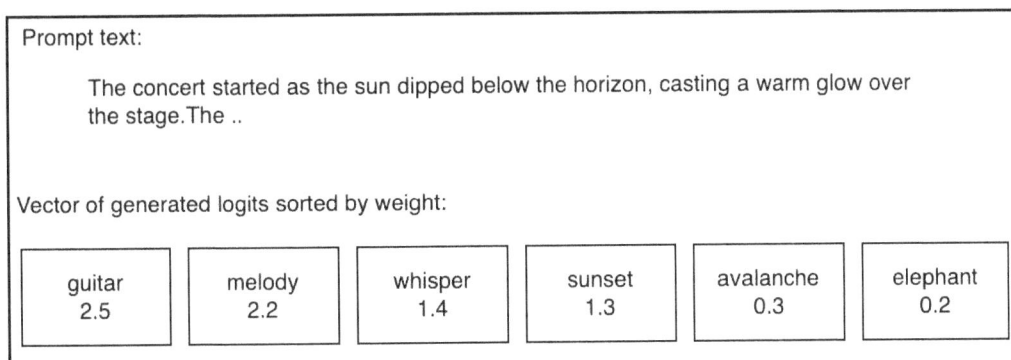

Prompt text:

> The concert started as the sun dipped below the horizon, casting a warm glow over the stage. The ..

Vector of generated logits sorted by weight:

guitar	melody	whisper	sunset	avalanche	elephant
2.5	2.2	1.4	1.3	0.3	0.2

Figure 3.2: Vector of logits

Now, we will navigate through the calculation steps of the softmax function.

Step 1: Exponentiate each logit

The exponent of each logit is expressed as follows:

$$e^{logit}$$

Simple calculations show the following results:

$$e^{(2.5)} \approx 12.1825$$

$$e^{(2.2)} \approx 9.0250$$

$$e^{(1.4)} \approx 4.0552$$

$$e^{(1.3)} \approx 3.6693$$

$$e^{(0.3)} \approx 1.3499$$

$$e^{(0.2)} \approx 1.2214$$

Let us note them, because they will be used as material for the next steps.

Step 2: Sum of exponentiated logits

Now, let us use the calculator again to sum them up:

$$12.1825 + 9.0250 + 4.0552 + 3.6693 + 1.2214 + 1.2214 \approx 31.3748$$

Once we know the sum of exponents of logits, we can normalize them to probabilities in the next step.

Step 3: Calculate the probabilities

The normalization formula is aimed at getting them all to sum up to *1.0*:

$$Probability = \frac{e^{logit}}{Sum\ of\ exponentiated\ logits}$$

The one-by-one calculations of probabilities go like this:

$$\text{guitar:}\ \frac{12.1825}{31.3748} \approx 0.3882$$

$$\text{melody:}\ \frac{9.0250}{31.3748} \approx 0.2877$$

$$\text{whisper:}\ \frac{4.0552}{31.3748} \approx 0.1292$$

$$\text{sunset: } \frac{3.6693}{31.3748} \approx 0.1170$$

$$\text{avalanche: } \frac{1.3499}{31.3748} \approx 0.0431$$

$$\text{elephant: } \frac{1.2214}{31.3748} \approx 0.0389$$

If all of them are added up, they will result in *1.0*, or in other words 100%. The preceding numbers are the vector that the softmax function generates. Next, we will move onward to code up those calculations in Python.

Initial code for the softmax function

Let us investigate the next code, which performs the same calculation steps. The softmax function converts these logits into probabilities, as follows:

```python
import numpy as np
# Example logits
logits = {
    'guitar': 2.5,
    'melody': 2.2,
    'whisper': 1.4,
    'sunset': 1.3,
    'avalanche': 0.3,
    'elephant': 0.2
}

# Softmax function
def softmax(logits):
    exp_logits = np.exp(logits)
    probabilities = exp_logits / np.sum(exp_logits)
    return probabilities

# Extract words and their corresponding logits
words = list(logits.keys())
logit_values = np.array(list(logits.values()))

# Apply the softmax function to the logits
```

```
probabilities = softmax(logit_values)

# Print output in the format "word probability"
for word, probability in zip(words, probabilities):
    print(f'{word}: {probability*100:.2f}%')
```

This will output the following probability tabulation:

```
guitar: 38.67%
melody: 28.65%
whisper: 12.87%
sunset: 11.65%
avalanche: 4.28%
elephant: 3.88%
```

If those numbers are plotted onto a pie chart, the picture will look like this:

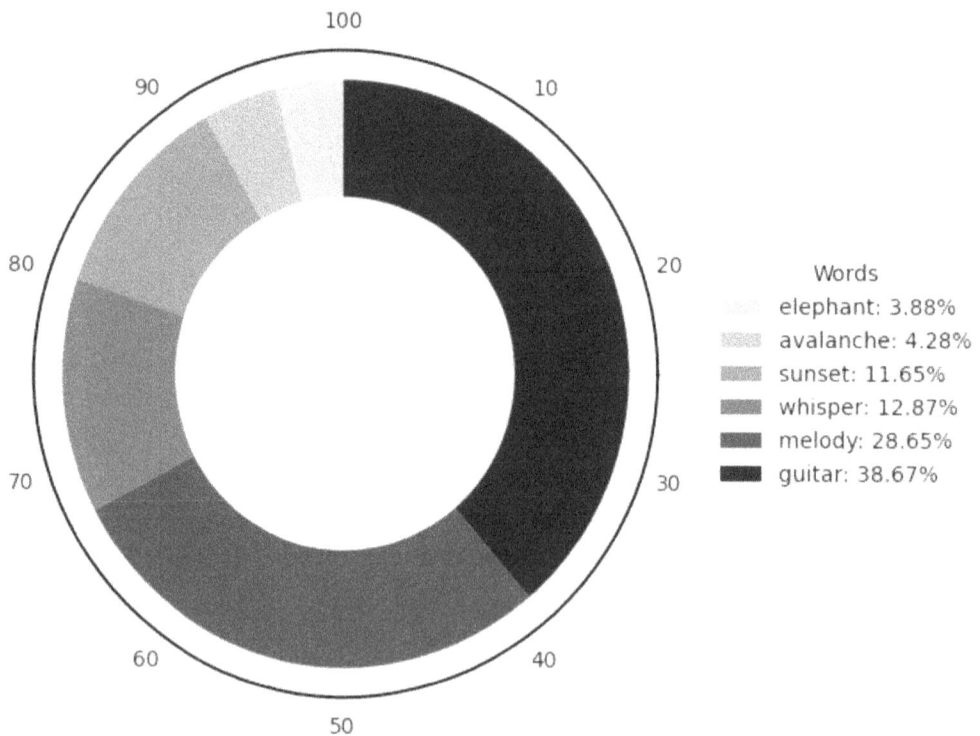

Figure 3.3: The plot of logits' probabilities

> The code for the plot function is provided on GitHub at `https://github.com/PacktPublishing/Learn-Mistral` in `Chapter-3/ch03_plot_pie_chart.py`.

As we can see, `guitar` and `melody` occupy two-thirds of the donut chart, while `elephant` and `avalanche` take less than 10%. This observation will help us better understand the `top_p` and `min_p` parameters. These probabilities guide the model in selecting the next word in the sequence, with higher probabilities making a word more likely to be chosen.

In the next section, we will make our `softmax` function more interesting and "warm it up" with the `temperature` parameter.

Temperature (controlling creativity and randomness)

The `temperature` parameter in a language model can be likened to the movement of molecules in a liquid. As the temperature increases, molecules move more freely, leading to more randomness and diversity in their arrangement. Similarly, a higher temperature in a model makes the output more varied and creative, allowing for a broader range of possible word choices. Conversely, a lower temperature restricts movement, leading to more focused and predictable results.

Scientifically, the `temperature` parameter directly affects the `softmax` distribution. Lowering the temperature sharpens the distribution, making the model more confident in its predictions, while increasing the temperature flattens the distribution, allowing for more exploration and diversity in the output. The suggested `softmax` function, which takes the temperature into consideration, is as follows:

```python
def softmax_with_temperature(logits, temperature=1.0):
    exp_logits = np.exp(logits / temperature)
    probabilities = exp_logits / np.sum(exp_logits)
    return probabilities
```

The following figure shows how generated output can deviate from the original context when the temperature changes from low to high:

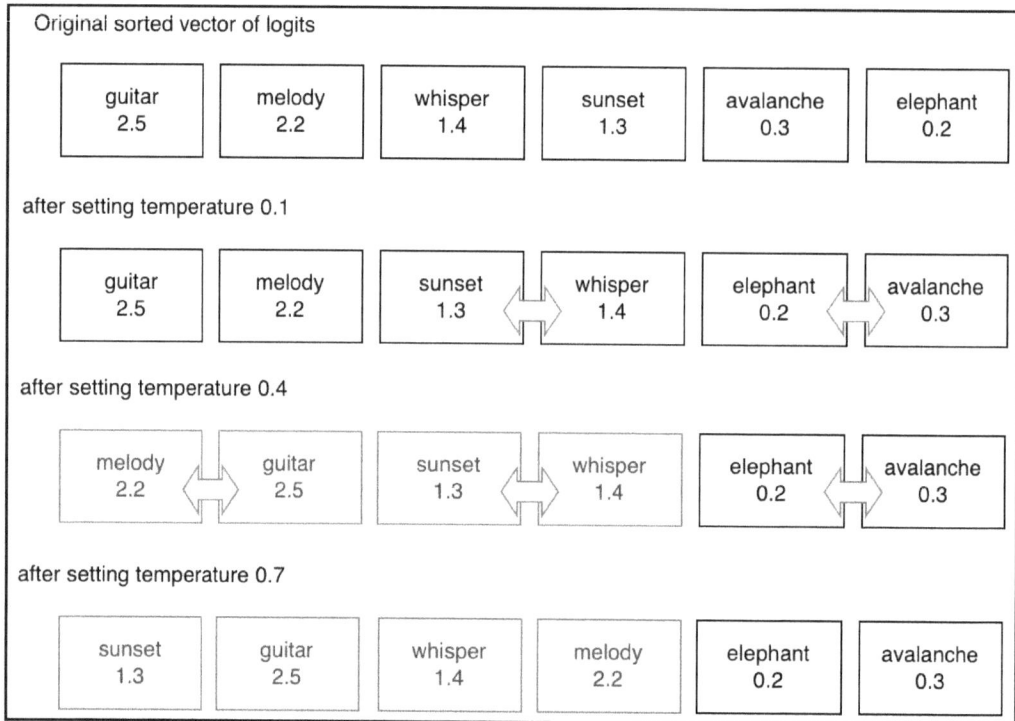

Figure 3.4: The effect of temperature levels

As the temperature rises, molecular motion becomes more vigorous. Likewise, raising the temperature parameter increases the activity of elements in the original vector, leading to more dynamic and varied outcomes.

You are encouraged to see the effect of the output of the temperature parameter while generating the response with Mistral. Using the following command, set different temperature levels from 0 to 0.99, and observe how far the generated response can deviate from the original context:

```
ollama run mistral-nemo
>set parameter temperature 0.7
>enter prompt here
```

top_k, top_p, and min_p (output refining)

The top_k, top_p, and min_p parameters are aimed at filtering out the least probable logits, but they use different approaches. Let's look at each in detail.

top_k only takes k superior logits

The top_k parameter in language models controls the number of potential tokens that the model considers when generating the next word. Specifically, top_k limits the selection to the top *k* tokens with the highest probabilities, ignoring the rest. By focusing on only the most likely options, top_k ensures that the model generates more focused and deterministic outputs. For example, with a top_k value of 5, the model will only consider the five tokens with the highest probabilities, effectively reducing randomness. This approach is advantageous when a more controlled and predictable response is desired, especially in structured tasks.

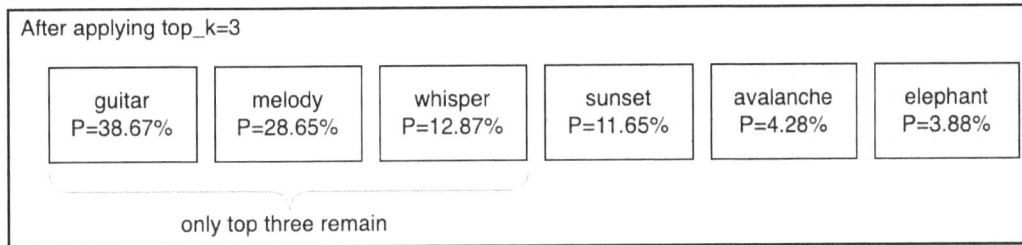

Figure 3.5: Explanation of how top_k works

A command-line example of top_k is as follows:

```
ollama run mistral-nemo
>set parameter top_k 10
> enter prompt here
```

top_p only takes the most probable up to the threshold

Also known as nucleus sampling, top_p dynamically limits the number of potential tokens by considering the cumulative probability distribution of all possible tokens. Unlike top_k, which fixes the number of tokens to consider, top_p selects tokens until their combined probability reaches a threshold, p (typically between 0.7 and 0.95). This means that in some cases, only a few tokens are selected, while in others, more tokens may be included. top_p allows for a balance between randomness and focus, making it suitable for generating creative yet coherent text where diversity in response is valued.

After applying top_p=0.6

| guitar P=38.67% | melody P=28.65% | whisper P=12.87% | sunset P=11.65% | avalanche P=4.28% | elephant P=3.88% |

these two make
more than 60%

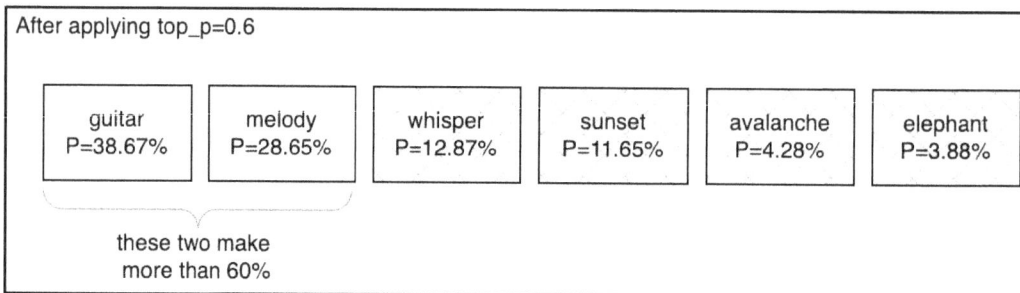

Figure 3.6: Explanation of how top_p works

Figure 3.6 demonstrates that guitar and melody take the Manhattan, providing over 60% of the probable outcomes; neither of them is enough, but both of them are big enough to satisfy the 60% threshold. If the threshold were 0.8, then whisper would also qualify.

A command-line example of top_p follows next:

```
ollama run mistral-nemo
>set parameter top_p 0.0
> enter prompt here
```

Once we've tackled top_p, min_p will be easy.

min_p filters out the noise

min_p is the opposite of top_p and works by removing the least likely tokens from consideration until the remaining tokens have a cumulative probability above a certain threshold. This ensures that even lower probability tokens can be included in the model's consideration set, provided they collectively exceed the minimum probability, p. It allows for creative and unexpected outputs, making it ideal for tasks where originality is valued over predictability.

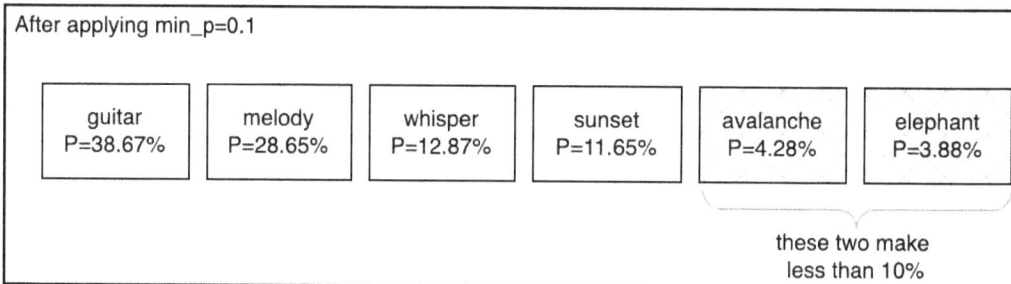

After applying min_p=0.1

| guitar P=38.67% | melody P=28.65% | whisper P=12.87% | sunset P=11.65% | avalanche P=4.28% | elephant P=3.88% |

these two make
less than 10%

Figure 3.7: Explanation of how min_p works

A command-line example of min_p is as follows:

```
ollama run mistral-nemo
>set parameter min_p 0.1
>enter prompt here
```

Max_tokens (choosing the right output size)

The max_tokens parameter, also referred to as num_predict in other LLMs, determines the maximum length of the text that a language model will generate. This directly influences the amount of content produced in the model's response. The higher the max_tokens value, the longer the output that the model can deliver.

The value of max_tokens can typically range from a small number (e.g., 1 or 5) to several hundred or even a thousand tokens, depending on the model and the specific API or framework being used:

- **Low values** (e.g., 1 to 10): The model generates a very short output, such as a single word or phrase
- **Moderate values** (e.g., 20 to 100): The model produces a few sentences or a short paragraph
- **High values** (e.g., 100 to 1000 or more): The model generates longer paragraphs or even multiple paragraphs of text

Let's look at a prompt example with low max_tokens (10):

```
Describe the Great Wall of China.
```

The output will be as follows:

```
The Great Wall is an ancient series of walls and fortifications.
```

As you can observe, the model is limited to generating a very brief description due to the low max_tokens value.

Now, let's look at an example with moderate max_tokens (50):

```
Describe the Great Wall of China.
```

We get the following response, which is longer than the previous output:

```
The Great Wall of China is a monumental structure built to protect China
from invasions. Spanning thousands of miles, it is a testament to the
ingenuity and determination of ancient Chinese civilizations. The wall,
constructed over centuries, is made from various materials like stone,
brick, and earth.
```

Command-line example

In this case, the num_predict parameter limits output length, producing a concise response about the Eiffel Tower's origin:

```
ollama run mistral-nemo
>set parameter num_predict 20
>please tell me about Eiffel Tower
The Eiffel Tower was designed by Gustave Eiffel for the 1890 Exposition
Universelle (World Fair)
```

Note about the command-line example

Ollama does not recognize the max_tokens parameter but does support num_predict and proxies it as max_token to the Mistral model. In *Chapter 9*, we will explore the AWS Bedrock; the configuration parameter it supports for the Mistral model is max_tokens. If we use the max_token parameter, Ollama will respond like so:

```
>>> /set parameter max_tokens 10
Couldn't set parameter: "unknown parameter 'max_tokens'"
```

The max_tokens parameter is essential for controlling the length of the generated text. By adjusting this parameter, users can manage whether the model produces concise, moderate, or extended responses, making it a versatile tool for different use cases.

Repetition penalty (avoiding redundancy)

The **repetition penalty** prevents the model from using the exact words repeatedly, much like filtering out an overabundance of the same type of fish. Without this penalty, the fisher might end up with a net full of shrimps and crabs, missing out on the bigger catch. The repetition penalty encourages the model to diversify its output, ensuring that the final output has less or no redundancy.

The value range is from 1.0 and above (usually around 1.0 to 2.0). A value of 1.0 means no penalty is applied, while values greater than 1.0 start penalizing the repetition of words. The higher the value, the stronger the penalty, making the model less likely to repeat tokens.

Let's look at an example with a repetition penalty of 1.2. This is the original prompt:

```
Please rephrase the next text: The cat ran and ran and ran and ran
```

The response will be as follows:

```
As time went by without pause or rest, The cat continued on her endless
quest: running fast through town.
```

Command-line example

This example applies `repeat_penalty`. Raising the value reduces excessive repetition and encourages more natural, clear phrasing:

```
ollama run mistral-nemo
>set parameter repeat_penalty 1.2
>Pleas rephrase: The cat ran and ran and ran and ran
```

Presence penalty (encouraging novel vocabulary)

The **presence penalty** is a parameter used in language models to discourage the repetition of words or phrases that have already appeared in the generated text. When this penalty is applied, the model is less likely to choose a word that has been used before, thereby encouraging more diverse and varied outputs. The presence penalty is beneficial in tasks where variety is essential, such as creative writing, brainstorming, or generating long-form text, where repetition can be undesirable. By applying this penalty, the model becomes more inclined to introduce new ideas or concepts, enhancing the overall quality and diversity of the generated content.

An example prompt is as follows:

```
Write a short story about a cat named Twix who loves adventures. Apply a
presence penalty to avoid repeating words.
```

The response without a presence penalty will be as follows:

```
Twix the cat loved adventures. Twix would often explore the backyard. Twix
found new things every day in the backyard. Twix was a very curious cat.
```

However, the response with a presence penalty of 1 will be the following:

```
Twix the cat loved adventures. He often explored the backyard, discovering
new treasures each day. Curiosity led him to hidden corners, where
excitement always awaited.
```

In the second response, the presence penalty encourages the use of different words and phrases instead of repeating `Twix`, `backyard`, and `cat`, resulting in a more engaging and varied story.

Command-line example

This example shows `presence_penalty` in action. Adjusting the setting encourages novelty as the model generates a creative response:

```
ollama run mistral-nemo
>set parameter presence_penalty 1
>Write a short story about a cat named Twix who loves adventures.
```

Mistral's natively supported parameters

Parameter names can differ between language models. Since our focus is on Mistral, here's a detailed overview of its natively supported parameters:

Parameter Name	Description	Value Range
`top_p`	Nucleus sampling parameter	`0.0` to `1.0`
`top_k`	Top-K sampling parameter	Positive integer (e.g., `1 to 100`)
`max_tokens`	Maximum number of tokens to generate	Positive integer (e.g., `1 to 2048`)
`temperature`	Controls the randomness of predictions	Positive float (e.g., `0.1 to 2.0`)
`frequency_penalty`	Penalizes new tokens based on their existing frequency	Float (e.g., `-2.0 to 2.0`)
`presence_penalty`	Penalizes new tokens based on whether they appear in the text so far	Float (e.g., `-2.0 to 2.0`)
`stop_sequences`	List of sequences that stop the generation process	List of strings
`num_return_sequences`	Number of different sequences to return	Positive integer (e.g., `1 to 10`)
`do_sample`	Whether to use sampling	Boolean (`True/False`)
`repetition_penalty`	Penalizes repetition in the generated text	Float (e.g., `1.0 to 2.0`)
`length_penalty`	Adjusts the probability of generating longer or shorter sequences	Float (e.g., `0.0 to 2.0`)

Parameter Name	Description	Value Range
no_repeat_ngram_size	Prevents the model from repeating n-grams of a specified size	Positive integer (e.g., 1 to 5)
early_stopping	Whether to stop generation as soon as the end token is generated	Boolean (True/False)
seed	Sets the random seed for reproducibility	Positive integer

Table 3.1: List of parameters natively supported by Mistral

You'll notice some parameters differ from those found in other models, but this does not make them less powerful. On top of that, many more parameters are present to help you refine your output. While we won't explore all parameters here, you're encouraged to investigate and experiment with them to understand their effects better.

In the following practical workshop, we'll implement and run functions to calculate the effects of temperature, top_k, top_p, and min_p. These functions are theoretical tools designed primarily to deepen your understanding of each parameter's role and behavior.

Practical workshop: the softmax function, temperature, top_k, and top_p

The complete source code with all methods and tests is available on GitHub in the ch03_softmax_workshop.py file, but you are encouraged to walk through the code and repeat it step by step.

We will operate with the array. We'll start by defining our sample logits and initializing parameters such as temperature and others:

```python
import numpy as np

logits = {
    'guitar': 2.5,
    'melody': 2.2,
    'whisper': 1.4,
    'sunset': 1.3,
    'avalanche': 0.3,
    'elephant': 0.2
```

```
}

temperature=0.7
p=0.7
min_p_value=0.3
k=3
```

Now, we are ready to start step by step. First, we will implement the temperature-agnostic softmax function.

Step 1: Implementing the softmax function

This step focuses on converting raw model outputs (*logits*) into a meaningful probability distribution using the softmax function. This operation mirrors how a language model evaluates the likelihood of each potential token. Here's how the softmax function is constructed:

```
def softmax(logits, temperature=1.0):
    # Convert logits to a NumPy array
    logit_values = np.array(list(logits.values()))
    # Apply temperature scaling
    scaled_logits = logit_values / temperature
    # Calculate the exponential of each logit
    exp_logits = np.exp(scaled_logits)
    # Normalize by dividing by the sum of all exponentials
    probabilities = exp_logits / np.sum(exp_logits)
    return probabilities
```

The function starts by extracting the numerical values from the logits dictionary and converting them into a NumPy array. Temperature scaling is applied next, adjusting the distribution's sharpness. Exponentiation then amplifies differences between values, and normalization ensures the final outputs form a proper probability distribution.

Once the probabilities are calculated, the next action is to sort the logits by their probability scores, a necessary step before applying sampling filters such as top_k and top_p.

Step 2: Sorting the logits by probability

This part of the workshop demonstrates how to rank model outputs by their likelihood, an essential step in preparing for controlled sampling. After converting logits into probabilities using the softmax function, we now organize them in descending order based on those probabilities.

Here's how the sorting function is defined:

```
def sort_logits_by_probability(logits, temperature=1.0):
    probabilities = softmax(logits, temperature)
    # Sort indices based on probabilities
    sorted_indices = np.argsort(probabilities)[::-1]
    sorted_logits = np.array(list(logits.items()))[sorted_indices]
    sorted_probabilities = probabilities[sorted_indices]
    return sorted_logits, sorted_probabilities
```

The function starts by calculating the probabilities from the original logits using softmax. It then identifies the order of probabilities from highest to lowest using argsort, and applies this order to both the logits and the probabilities themselves.

Organizing logits in this way sets the foundation for more advanced sampling techniques. In the next step, we'll implement the top_k function, which selects the most likely tokens from this sorted list, limiting the output to a fixed number of top choices.

Step 3: Implementing the top_k function

This step focuses on narrowing down the model's possible outputs to a fixed number of top choices. By applying **top-k filtering**, we retain only the *k* most probable tokens, an effective method for keeping responses focused and relevant. Here's how the top_k function is defined:

```
def top_k(logits, k, temperature=1.0):
    sorted_logits, sorted_probabilities = sort_logits_by_probability(
        logits, temperature)
    # Keep only the top k logits
    top_k_logits = sorted_logits[:k]
    top_k_probabilities = sorted_probabilities[:k]
    return top_k_logits, top_k_probabilities
```

The function begins by sorting the logits and their corresponding probabilities using the previously defined sort_logits_by_probability. It then slices the sorted arrays to keep only the first k entries—those with the highest likelihood.

This approach helps limit randomness and sharpen the model's output by ensuring that it chooses from only the most confident options. In the following step, we'll extend this concept further by implementing top_p (nucleus sampling), which selects tokens based on cumulative probability rather than a fixed count.

Step 4: Implementing the top_p (nucleus sampling) function

This step introduces a dynamic filtering method known as top_p (nucleus sampling). Unlike top_k, which uses a fixed number of options, top_p selects the smallest set of tokens whose combined probability meets or exceeds a given threshold, p. This allows for flexible and adaptive sampling, focusing on the most meaningful portion of the output space.

Here is the implementation of the top_p function:

```
def top_p(logits, p, temperature=1.0):
    sorted_logits, sorted_probabilities = sort_logits_by_probability(
        logits, temperature)
    # Calculate the cumulative probabilities
    cumulative_prob = np.cumsum(sorted_probabilities)
    # Find the smallest set of logits
    # where the cumulative probability exceeds p
    cutoff_index = np.argmax(cumulative_prob >= p)
    top_p_logits = sorted_logits[:cutoff_index + 1]
    top_p_probabilities = sorted_probabilities[:cutoff_index + 1]
    return top_p_logits, top_p_probabilities
```

The function first sorts the logits by probability, then calculates the cumulative sum. It identifies the minimum number of tokens required to reach the cumulative probability threshold, p, and keeps only that subset of tokens and their probabilities.

top_p sampling provides a more nuanced way to balance diversity and control, especially useful when the distribution has a long tail. The next step in the workshop is to implement min_p filtering, a related technique that removes tokens with extremely low individual probability, regardless of their position in the cumulative sum.

Step 5: Implementing the min_p function

In this step, we will cover the min_p filtering, a method that focuses on the most confidently predicted tokens by discarding the low-probability tail of the distribution. Symmetrically opposite to top_p, which keeps tokens until a cumulative threshold is reached, min_p starts from the point where the cumulative probability first exceeds p and keeps only the remaining tokens. This method ensures that only the high-certainty options are retained.

Here is the implementation of the `min_p` function:

```
def min_p(logits, p, temperature=1.0):
    sorted_logits, sorted_probabilities = sort_logits_by_probability(
        logits, temperature)
    # Calculate the cumulative probabilities
    cumulative_prob = np.cumsum(sorted_probabilities)
    # Find the point where
    # the cumulative probability is above p
    cutoff_index = np.argmax(cumulative_prob >= p)
    min_p_logits = sorted_logits[cutoff_index:]
    min_p_probabilities = sorted_probabilities[cutoff_index:]
    return min_p_logits, min_p_probabilities
```

The function begins by sorting the logits and computing cumulative probabilities. It then finds the point where the accumulated probability crosses the specified minimum threshold, p, and keeps only the logits from that point forward.

`min_p` sampling is useful for scenarios where only the most confident predictions should be considered, filtering out weak candidates entirely. In the final step of this workshop, we will test all the sampling strategies together to observe how each one shapes model output and behaviour in practice.

Step 6: Testing it all

With all the sampling functions constructed (`softmax`, `top-k`, `top-p`, and `min-p`), we can test them together on a sample set of logits. This hands-on comparison shows how each method filters the output differently and helps build an intuitive understanding of token selection dynamics.

The following code demonstrates how to apply each sampling function on a predefined set of logits:

```
temperature = 1.0
k = 3
p_top = 0.8
p_min = 0.2

# Softmax probabilities
probabilities = softmax(logits, temperature)
```

```
print("Softmax probabilities:", probabilities)

# Top k logits and probabilities
top_k_logits, top_k_probabilities = top_k(logits, k, temperature)
print("\nTop k logits and probabilities:")
for (word, logit), prob in zip(top_k_logits, top_k_probabilities):
    print(f'{word}: Logit = {logit}, Probability = {prob*100:.2f}%')

# Top p logits and probabilities
top_p_logits, top_p_probabilities = top_p(logits, p, temperature)
print("\nTop p logits and probabilities:")
for (word, logit), prob in zip(top_p_logits, top_p_probabilities):
    print(f'{word}: Logit = {logit}, Probability = {prob*100:.2f}%')

# Min p logits and probabilities
min_p_logits, min_p_probabilities = min_p(
    logits, min_p_value, temperature)
print("\nMin p logits and probabilities:")
for (word, logit), prob in zip(min_p_logits, min_p_probabilities):
    print(f'{word}: Logit = {logit}, Probability = {prob*100:.2f}%')
```

This example can be found in the GitHub repository at `https://github.com/PacktPublishing/Learn-Mistral`, in the `Chapter-3/ch03_softmax_workshop.py` file.

The code performs four key tasks:

- Calculates softmax probabilities from the raw logits
- Extracts the top_k tokens based on probability rank
- Applies top_p filtering using a cumulative threshold
- Filters out the low-probability tail using min_p

The expected output shows how each method narrows or reshapes the token pool. For example, top_k limits the list to a fixed size, top_p uses probability mass to decide when to stop, and min_p focuses on high-confidence tokens. Here's a sample output from the test:

```
Softmax probabilities: [0.47173089 0.30730392 0.09800124 0.08495511
0.02035958 0.01764927]

Top k logits and probabilities:
guitar: Logit = 2.5, Probability = 47.17%
melody: Logit = 2.2, Probability = 30.73%
whisper: Logit = 1.4, Probability = 9.80%

Top p logits and probabilities:
guitar: Logit = 2.5, Probability = 47.17%
melody: Logit = 2.2, Probability = 30.73%

Min p logits and probabilities:
guitar: Logit = 2.5, Probability = 47.17%
melody: Logit = 2.2, Probability = 30.73%
whisper: Logit = 1.4, Probability = 9.80%
sunset: Logit = 1.3, Probability = 8.50%
avalanche: Logit = 0.3, Probability = 2.04%
elephant: Logit = 0.2, Probability = 1.76%
```

The output illustrates key differences in behavior: top_k returns a fixed number of the most probable tokens, top_p includes tokens until a cumulative probability is reached, and min_p (its conceptual mirror) excludes low-probability tokens until the remaining set meets the minimum cumulative threshold. The result is a broader but more confident selection of tokens.

And with that, we've walked step by step through the essential parameters that allow you to shape the way your language model responds. By adjusting temperature, fine-tuning with softmax, and carefully selecting your sampling methods—top_k, top_p, and min_p—you've learned how to turn raw predictions into polished, purposeful text. Remember, mastering these tools isn't just about tweaking numbers; it's about discovering your own voice as a model curator.

Summary

Throughout this journey, we've explored the intricate workings of language models, beginning with the foundational role of system prompts, which set the context and guide the model's behavior. We examined the softmax function, a core mathematical process that transforms logits into probabilities, shaping the model's output. We then looked at how the temperature parameter controls the creativity and randomness of generated text, and how top_k and top_p settings help fine-tune the model's focus and diversity for more targeted or varied responses. Additional parameters, such as penalties, were introduced to demonstrate their practical use in refining outputs and avoiding repetition. We concluded with hands-on exercises to apply these ideas and observe their effects in real time. Altogether, this chapter equipped you with a well-rounded toolkit for tuning language models to generate precise, effective, and engaging content.

In the next chapter, we'll dive into embeddings, the building blocks of meaning in language models. You'll learn how text is transformed into vectors and how these representations enable powerful capabilities such as semantic similarity and search. Through a hands-on workshop, you'll explore real-world semantic search applications. Mastering this concept sets the stage for more advanced topics, including **retrieval-augmented generation (RAG)**, where embeddings play a central role.

Extracurricular

If you'd like to take things a step further, here are some extra projects to experiment with. These aren't required, but they'll give you a chance to tinker, explore, and see how different parameters behave in practice:

1. Grid-search parameter sweeper (Python + Ollama API):

    Write a Python script hitting Ollama's /api/generate, sweeping temperature, top_k, top_p, presence/repetition penalties, and num_predict. Save the outputs and metrics (length, unique-token ratio, and repetition rate) to CSV for later analysis comparison.

2. Interactive CLI tuner (Python/Node):

    Build a CLI that accepts a prompt and live-adjustable parameters, calls generate, and shows diffs between runs. Include presets (creative, balanced, and strict) and a --seed option for reproducibility across sessions.

3. Stop sequences and length controls (curl + tests):

    Use curl to call /api/generate with stop sequences and num_predict limits; write minimal tests asserting truncation behavior and absence of forbidden terms. Document failures and edge cases in a report.

References

Here are some handy links to give you the official details on Ollama's API and parameters, so you can double-check syntax and avoid unnecessary guesswork while building

- Ollama REST API (parameters and `/api/generate`): `https://github.com/ollama/ollama/blob/main/docs/api.md`

- Ollama parameters overview: `https://github.com/ollama/ollama/blob/main/docs/api.md#parameters`

Join our Discord and Reddit space

You're not the only one navigating fragmented tools, constant updates, and unclear best practices. Join a growing community of professionals exchanging insights that don't make it into documentation.

Stay informed with updates, discussions, and behind-the-scenes insights from our authors. Join our Discord at `https://packt.link/z8ivB` or scan the QR code below:	Connect with peers, share ideas, and discuss real-world GenAI challenges. Follow us on Reddit at `https://packt.link/0rExL` or scan the QR code below:

4

Mastering Embeddings

You shall know a word by the company it keeps.

— J.R. Firth

Humans operate with words, computers operate with numbers. AI networks operate with embeddings, logits, numeric tokens, and floating-point weights. Imagine you're planning a party and need to arrange your guests in a way that makes everyone happy. You have friends who love dancing, some who enjoy deep conversations, and a few who are foodies. How do you ensure that each group gets what they want? This is where the magic of vector embeddings comes in, but instead of guests, we're dealing with words, phrases, or even bigger paragraphs.

In this chapter, we will get hands-on experience with vector embeddings. You'll learn how vectors are used to represent complex data in understandable, multi-dimensional spaces, making AI smarter and more efficient. We'll work hands-on with powerful Python libraries such as SciPy and NumPy to request and use these embeddings. We'll also learn how to determine semantic distance and uncover hidden relationships between data points.

Additionally, you will learn how to translate semantic similarity into quantitative values and search for information based on meaning rather than exact wording. We'll cover the concept of vectors and how they represent language, walk through a practical workshop using Mistral embeddings, and explore visualization techniques to better understand vector relationships. The chapter also includes real-world application examples, hands-on exercises, and optional advanced topics for further exploration.

In a nutshell, this is what we'll cover:

- What is a vector?
- Embeddings visualization
- Practical workshop: semantic search system with Mistral and Pinecone
- Applications and practical exercises with embeddings

Technical requirements

This chapter introduces practical concepts in embeddings and semantic search. To ensure a smooth experience, please prepare your environment with the following tools and credentials before beginning the exercises:

- Basic Python coding skills (e.g., working with lists, dictionaries, and functions)
- A Mistral API key (for accessing model endpoints—setup guidance included)
- A Pinecone API key (used for vector database operations—setup instructions will be provided)
- A GitHub account to access and clone the repository

The practical workshop supports any major system (Mac, Windows, or Linux). Google Colab will be used for many exercises to reduce setup complexity.

The materials for this chapter are in the `Chapter-4` folder of the official GitHub repository: `https://github.com/PacktPublishing/Learn-Mistral`

Before we dive into coding, it's important to understand the concept of vectors—the foundation of how machines represent meaning. This section introduces vectors in the context of language and similarity.

What is a vector?

A vector is a mathematical representation of data as an array of numbers, capturing both magnitude and direction in a multi-dimensional space. This may sound abstract at first, so let's ground it in something more familiar. Let's bring back our party analogy from earlier.

Let's consider a simple 2D space to start. Picture a big dance floor. On one axis, we measure how much someone loves dancing, and on the other, how much they enjoy talking. Each friend can be represented as a point in this space. So, your friend who loves dancing but isn't much of a talker might be at (9, 2), while your chatty but less dance-inclined friend might be at (3, 8):

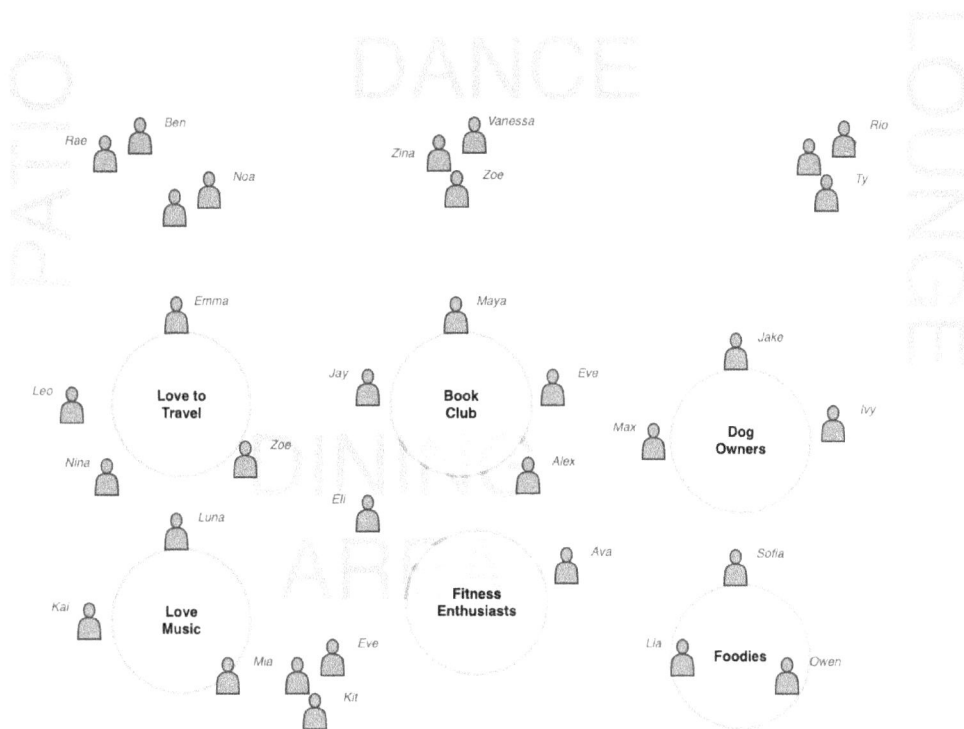

Figure 4.1: Illustration of guests' placements

This 2D representation helps you see who's close to whom in terms of interests. If two friends are close on the dance floor, they likely have similar preferences and will have a great time together.

Now, let's ramp it up. In real-world data, we rarely stop at two dimensions. Think of a DJ at a massive party with dozens of preferences: music genre, food choices, drink preferences, conversation topics, and more. In this scenario, each preference adds a new dimension to our space. Imagine instead of just the dance floor, you also consider a space that includes a food court, a conversation lounge, and more. Each dimension captures a different aspect of a guest's preference. While it's hard to visualize beyond 3D, the concept remains: the more dimensions, the more accurately we can capture complex preferences.

Vector embeddings in AI work the same way. When we embed words into vectors, we capture their meanings in a multi-dimensional space. Words with similar meanings end up close to each other. For instance, "king" might be close to "queen" in this space, reflecting their similar contexts and meanings.

Now let's pivot to a more formal representation. The next few examples show how these concepts translate into actual vector structures—with increasing complexity and real-world relevance. Consider *Figure 4.2*. It shows three different variations: two-dimensional coordinates translate into a vector with two elements, three-dimensional coordinates—a vector with three elements, and if the object has speed, we add another element to the vector. Yes, speed can be considered as a fourth dimension. Acceleration would be a fifth dimension, temperature a sixth, and so on. Vectors can be very long.

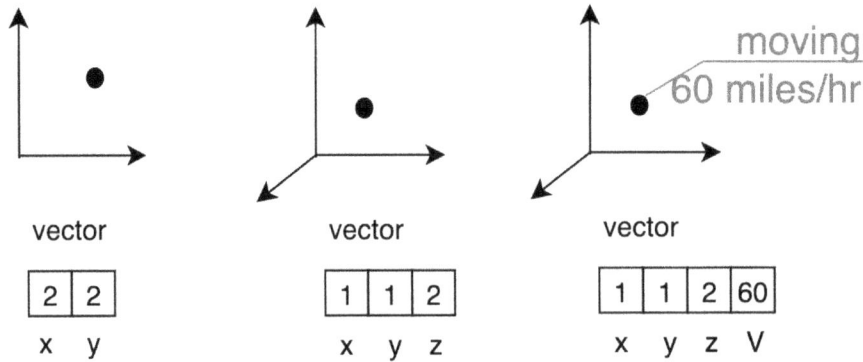

Figure 4.2: Examples of vectors

In the world of software, vectors are represented as sequential arrays, like the bottom part of *Figure 4.2*. Each element is referred to by order number, starting with zero.

Now, when we have two vectors, how can we calculate how far they are from each other? Here's where math steps in. Please refer to *Figure 4.3*, where two vectors are being compared. Three out of four elements are close—9 and 8 are close numbers. But one part of both vectors is far from the other—3 is far from 20. Vectors are majorly similar, while not being an exact match.

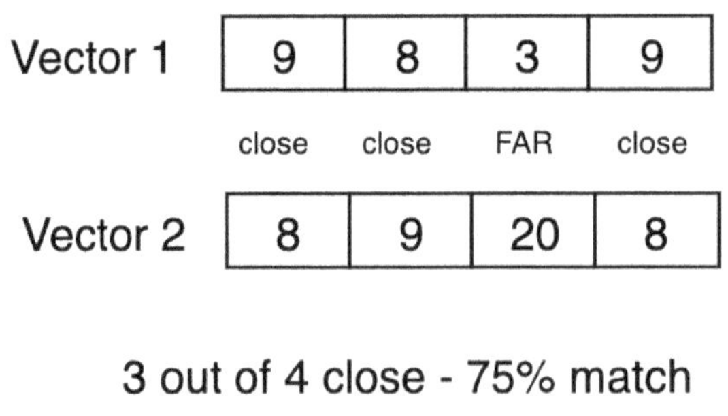

Figure 4.3: Vector comparison

With embedding, we will operate vectors of the same size with 1500+ elements, so we need a rock-solid method to see how they match or, in scientific words, calculate the distance between them. *Table 4.1* summarizes the most popular methods of distance calculation and their advantages:

Name of method	How it is measured	Advantages	Result range
Cosine similarity	Measures the cosine of the angle between two vectors	Insensitive to magnitude, good for text similarity and semantic comparison	-1 to 1
Euclidean distance	Measures the straight-line distance between two vectors in Euclidean space	Geometric interpretation, direct distance measure, effective for physical distances	0 to ∞
Manhattan distance	Measures the sum of the absolute differences of their coordinates	Robust to outliers, simple to compute and understand	0 to ∞
Jaccard similarity	Measures the size of the intersection divided by the size of the union of two sets	Useful for binary vectors or sets, set comparison	0 to 1
Mahalanobis distance	Measures the distance between a point and a distribution, taking correlations into account	Accounts for correlations in the data, effective for multivariate data	0 to ∞
Pearson correlation	Measures the strength and direction of the linear relationship between two vectors	Normalized measure, good for linear relationship assessment	-1 to 1

Table 4.1: Methods of calculating the distances between two vectors

We will not go deep into math formulas. From **Advantages** and **Result range**, it is easy for us to operate with normalized result ranges between -1 and 1. Pearson and cosine have such a range. In our practical workshop, we will pick the cosine method because it is good for text similarity search. But you are welcome to experiment with other methods that the scipy spatial library has.

Vector databases

Vector databases are specialized systems designed to handle high-dimensional data, allowing for efficient storage, retrieval, and querying of embeddings generated by AI models. These databases enable rapid similarity searches, making them essential for applications such as recommendation systems, image recognition, and natural language processing.

There are several options available, both cloud-based and on-premises, each with its own set of advantages, as we will observe in the following table.

Type	Database	Description	Advantages
Cloud	Amazon Kendra	A highly accurate and easy-to-use enterprise search service powered by machine learning.	Managed service, integrates with AWS ecosystem, scalable, supports natural language queries
	Google BigQuery ML	A serverless, highly scalable, and cost-effective multi-cloud data warehouse designed for business agility.	Integrated ML capabilities, supports large datasets, serverless architecture, real-time analytics
	Microsoft Azure Cognitive Search	A cloud search service with built-in AI capabilities to enrich all types of information to help identify and explore relevant content at scale.	Built-in AI enrichment, flexible indexing, integrates with the Azure ecosystem, robust security features
	Pinecone	A fully managed vector database that makes it easy to add fast, scalable, and accurate vector search to applications.	Fully managed, scalable, real-time updates, optimized for machine learning use cases
On-Premise	Faiss (Facebook AI Similarity Search)	A library for efficient similarity search and clustering of dense vectors.	High performance, open source, customizable, supports CPU and GPU, suitable for large datasets
	Milvus	An open source vector database built for scalable similarity search.	High availability, distributed, supports hybrid search (vector and scalar), integrates with various ML frameworks
	Annoy (Approximate Nearest Neighbors Oh Yeah)	A C++ library with Python bindings for searching for points in high-dimensional spaces.	Fast and memory efficient, easy to use, designed for large datasets, used in production by Spotify

	pgVector	A PostgreSQL extension that adds support for vector similarity search to the database.	Leverages PostgreSQL capabilities, integrates with existing relational data, open source, easy to deploy

Table 4.2: Vector databases

The databases in *Table 4.2* provide the necessary infrastructure to store and manage embeddings, enabling efficient similarity searches and making them an integral part of modern AI and machine learning pipelines. Whether you prefer the scalability and managed services of cloud solutions or the control and customization of on-premises options, there's a vector database to meet your needs.

The next challenge is *interpretation*. High-dimensional vectors can tell us a lot about relationships between data points, but those insights are often hidden behind thousands of numerical values. Visualization techniques help unlock that hidden structure, turning abstract embeddings into patterns we can quickly recognize and explain. In the following section, we'll look at methods for making embeddings more interpretable.

Visualizing embeddings

So far, we've explored what vectors are, how they represent meaning, and how we compare them mathematically. But raw vectors, often with hundreds or thousands of dimensions, are difficult to interpret directly. That's where visualization helps. By projecting high-dimensional embeddings into simpler forms—such as 2D scatter plots, clustered layouts, or similarity heatmaps—we can visually explore how data points relate semantically.

In this section, we'll look at three common techniques: t-SNE, PCA, and heatmaps. Each provides a different lens into the structure of embedding space. These tools not only help you quantify similarity but also interpret and communicate it—essential skills when building AI systems that rely on embeddings.

t-SNE: Revealing local clusters

We'll start with **t-Distributed Stochastic Neighbor Embedding** (**t-SNE**), a powerful technique for visualizing high-dimensional data by reducing it to two or three dimensions, making it easier to interpret. This method is particularly effective for embedding visualization because it preserves the local structure of the data, allowing us to see clusters and relationships clearly.

Figure 4.4 demonstrates how t-SNE takes multiple dimensions (X, Y, and Z coordinates, speed, acceleration, fuel level, and many more) and transforms all of them into one scale, "comfort of flight," which can be slow, fast, or turbulent.

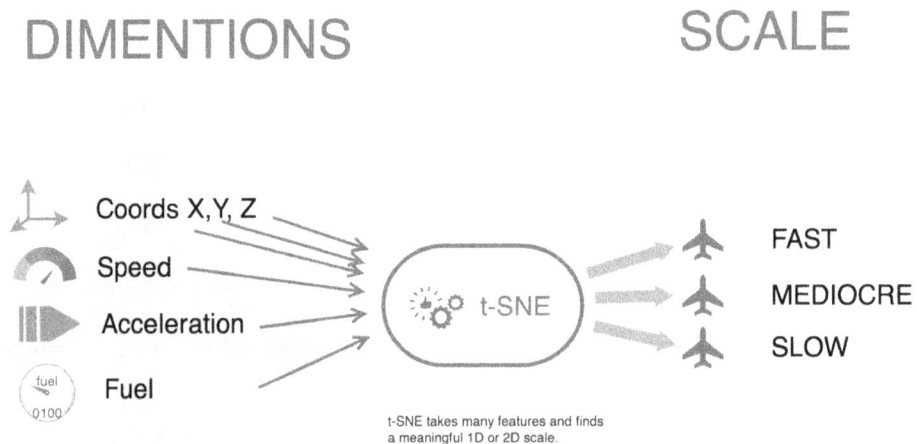

Figure 4.4: t-SNE example

Key features of t-SNE are as follows:

- **Dimensionality reduction**: Reduces high-dimensional data to 2D or 3D for easier visualization
- **Cluster identification**: Helps in identifying natural clusters within the data
- **Local structure preservation**: Maintains the relative distances between nearby points, highlighting local similarities

While t-SNE is powerful for local structures, it's not the only tool in your visualization toolkit. Sometimes, you need a method that focuses on *global structure*—the big-picture variance in your dataset—especially when speed and computational efficiency are important. That's where **Principal Component Analysis (PCA)** comes in.

PCA: Capturing the global picture

PCA is a linear dimensionality reduction technique that transforms the data into a new coordinate system, where the greatest variances are projected onto the first few principal components.

Figure 4.5 shows an example where multiple dimensions are taken as input (tempo, pitch, instruments, lyrics, and mood) and the PCA algorithm builds categories or clusters of inputs, taking the most meaningful features and ignoring secondary ones.

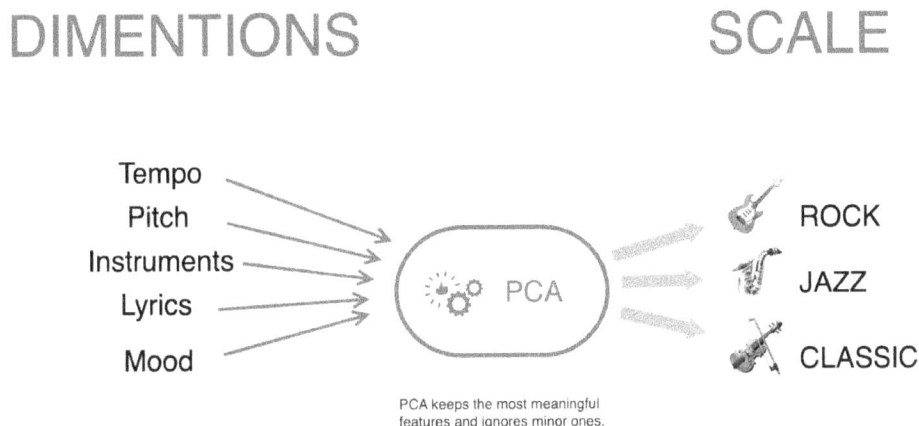

Figure 4.5: Example showing the key features of PCA

Key features of PCA are as follows:

- **Linear transformation**: Projects data onto a new axis based on variance
- **Global structure**: Preserves the global structure and variance of the data
- **Computational efficiency**: Generally faster and less computationally intensive than t-SNE

By comparing t-SNE and PCA, you will gain insights into the strengths and limitations of each method and understand when to use one over the other.

Brief comparison of PSA and t-SNE

t-SNE is primarily used for visualizing high-dimensional data in a low-dimensional space (usually 2D or 3D) while preserving local structures in the data. It converts similarities between data points to joint probabilities and tries to minimize the **Kullback-Leibler divergence** between the joint probabilities of the low-dimensional embedding and the high-dimensional data. t-SNE is excellent for visualizing clusters in high-dimensional data, preserving the local structure, and capturing complex relationships. However, it is computationally expensive, slow on large datasets, and the perplexity parameter can be tricky to tune. It does not preserve the global structure as well as PCA.

Principal Component Analysis (PCA) is used for reducing the dimensionality of data while preserving as much variance as possible. It projects the data onto the directions (principal components) that maximize the variance. PCA is fast, computationally efficient, preserves global structure and variance, and is a linear dimensionality reduction technique that is easy to implement and interpret. However, PCA does not capture non-linear relationships in the data and may not be effective in visualizing clusters if the data is non-linear.

For visualizing the semantic relationships between dish embeddings and user input, t-SNE is more suitable than PCA. t-SNE excels at preserving local structure, effectively grouping similar embeddings together, which is crucial for visualizing how similar dishes are to each other and to the user input. The embeddings generated by language models such as Mistral are often non-linear, and t-SNE, being a non-linear dimensionality reduction technique, is better suited to capture and represent these complex relationships. Additionally, t-SNE tends to produce more intuitive and visually separable clusters, making it easier to see distinct groups of similar dishes, which is beneficial for understanding the semantic similarities and differences in the context of food recommendations.

Both **t-SNE** and **PCA** reduce complex vectors into simpler visual representations, often as 2D scatter plots that help reveal structural patterns. But not all insights come from observing spatial layouts. In some cases, a different type of visualization, such as a **heatmap**, can offer a new and valuable perspective. We'll explore that next.

Heatmaps: visualizing similarities

Heatmaps provide a visual representation of the similarity matrix, where each cell represents the similarity score between two embeddings. For example, we can compare two sets of words—fruits and berries versus random objects—and plot their similarities. The first set of words contains names of fruits and berries:

```
set1 = ["apple", "banana", "cherry", "date", "elderberry", "fig", "grape",
"honeydew", "kiwi", "lemon"]
```

While the second set of words is random:

```
set2 = ["bolt", "cloud", "delta", "echo", "flare", "gamma", "horizon",
"iceberg", "jet", "kinetic"]
```

The following figure shows the heatmap. Please note that the words "apple" and "cloud" have a strong correlation, while "elderberry" has very little in common with any word:

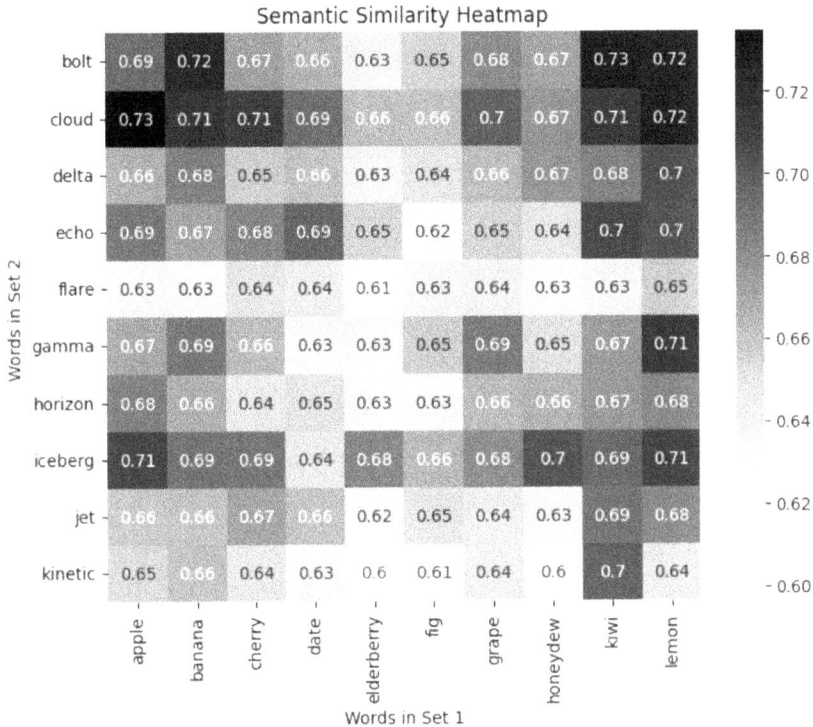

Figure 4.6: Visualization of the semantic similarity heatmap

Key features of heatmaps are as follows:

- **Visual clarity**: Easily interpret similarity scores through color gradients
- **Pattern recognition**: Helps in recognizing patterns of similarity and dissimilarity within the data
- **Comparative analysis**: Facilitates comparison of multiple embeddings briefly

By using heatmaps, you will be able to visually assess which embeddings are most similar, enhancing your ability to understand the relationships within your data.

Through this comprehensive coverage of embedding visualization techniques, including t-SNE, PCA, and heatmaps, you will develop a robust toolkit for analyzing and interpreting embeddings. These visual tools are essential for gaining deeper insights into the structure and relationships of your data, ultimately enhancing your ability to work with complex high-dimensional datasets.

We covered a handful of mathematical concepts about vectors. Now is the time to start with a practical workshop and apply our knowledge and coding power in practice, play with real LLM embeddings, and calculate semantic similarities.

Practical workshop: Semantic search system with Mistral and Pinecone

In this practical workshop, we'll bridge the gap between theory and implementation. You'll start by setting up your development environment, connecting to the Mistral API, and generating embeddings for real data. From there, we'll calculate semantic similarities, identify the closest matches, and then scale the process using Pinecone as a vector database.

Along the way, you'll see how the concepts we covered (vector representation, similarity metrics, and visualization) translate into working code. By the end, you'll have a fully functioning semantic search prototype and the know-how to adapt it for your own AI-driven projects.

Step 1: Environment setup

Before we dive into our practical exercises, let's take a moment to clone the code from GitHub and introduce Google Colab, the platform we'll be using for our hands-on work with embeddings.

Cloning the workshop repository

To access the source files used in this chapter, begin by cloning the official GitHub repository at https://github.com/PacktPublishing/Learn-Mistral.

If you have Git installed, open a terminal and run the following:

```
git clone https://github.com/PacktPublishing/Learn-Mistral.git
```

This will create a local folder named Learn-Mistral containing all chapter files, including those for this workshop under Chapter-4. Alternatively, you can download the ZIP file from the repository page and extract it manually.

Next, we'll open Google Colab to begin working directly in a cloud-based notebook environment.

Opening Google Colab

In this workshop, we'll use **Google Colab**, a free cloud-based platform for running Python code in a Jupyter Notebook environment. It eliminates the need for local setup and gives you access to pre-configured Python runtimes—ideal for experimenting with embeddings and semantic search directly in your browser.

To begin, open Google Colab at `https://colab.research.google.com/`. You can either create a new notebook or upload the one provided in the `Chapter-4` folder of the cloned GitHub repository.

We'll use Colab throughout this workshop to run code samples, manage API keys, and interact with services such as Mistral and Pinecone.

Setting up the recommended GPU runtime

For our exercises involving embeddings, we recommend using the GPU runtime available in Google Colab. Utilizing a GPU can significantly speed up the computations, making the experience smoother and more efficient.

To enable a GPU in Google Colab, do the following:

1. Open the Colab notebook.
2. Go to the menu and select **Runtime | Change runtime type**.
3. In the popup, select **T4 GPU** from the **Hardware accelerator** drop-down menu. The following figure illustrates hardware options for runtime selection:

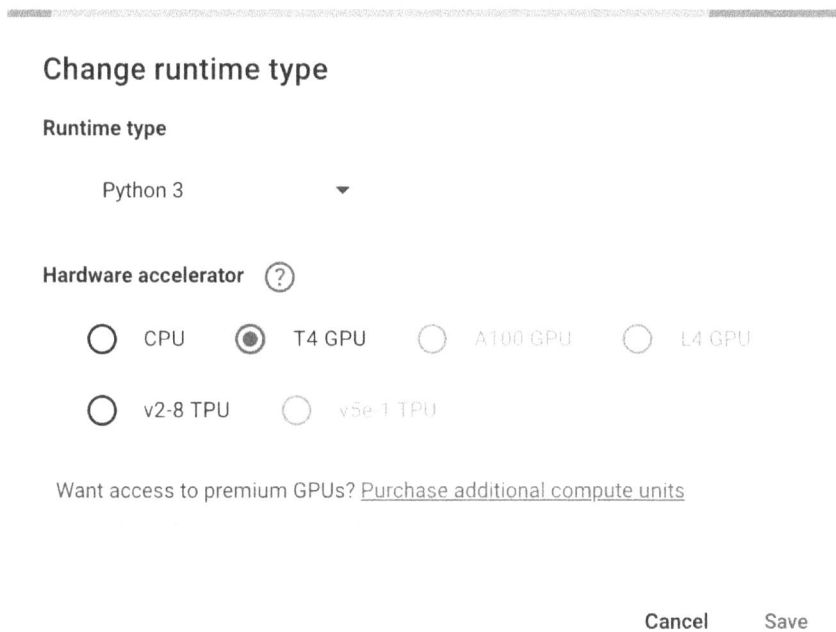

Change runtime type

Runtime type

Python 3 ▼

Hardware accelerator (?)

◯ CPU ⦿ T4 GPU ◯ A100 GPU ◯ L4 GPU

◯ v2-8 TPU ◯ v5e-1 TPU

Want access to premium GPUs? Purchase additional compute units

Cancel   Save

Figure 4.7: Runtime selection

1. Click **Save**.

Uploading the draft notebook

To assist you with the exercises, we have prepared a draft notebook that you can follow along with. This notebook can be accessed via our GitHub repository in the `Chapter-4/ch04_embeddings.ipynb` file.

By following the notebook, you'll be able to run embeddings on movie descriptions, compare vectors using cosine similarity, and visualize the results with various techniques such as t-SNE and heatmaps.

Step 2: Initializing the Mistral AI client

Now that you have an understanding of what Google Colab is and how to enable the GPU runtime, go ahead and open the draft notebook from GitHub. This will set you up for the upcoming exercises with embeddings and vector similarity measures.

Installing the mistralai package

In the first cell of your new notebook, type the following command to install the necessary library:

```
!pip install mistralai
```

Click the **Play** button to execute the command. This will install the Mistral AI library, which we will use throughout our exercises. The final success message confirms the completion:

```
Successfully installed eval-type-backport-0.2.2 jsonpath-python-1.0.6
mistralai-1.5.1 mypy-extensions-1.0.0 typing-inspect-0.9.0
```

Now that the Mistral AI library is installed, let's proceed by initiating the Mistral client.

Initializing the client object and performing a dry run

As a test, we'll retrieve and display all available models provided by the library. We'll ensure each model is printed on a new line for better readability.

```
from mistralai import Mistral

# Instantiate the Mistral to create a client object
client = Mistral()

# Use the client object to list all available models
models = client.models.list()
```

```
# Iterate over the list of models and print each
for model in models.data:
    print(model.id)
```

Let us explain the code line by line :

1. Import the `Mistral` client class:

    ```
    from mistralai import Mistral
    ```

    This line imports the `Mistral` class from the `mistralai.client` module, allowing us to use it in our code.

2. Instantiate the `Mistral` client:

    ```
    client = Mistral()
    ```

    Here, we create an instance of the `Mistral` client, which will be our client object for interacting with the Mistral AI library.

3. List the available models:

    ```
    models = client.models.list()
    ```

    We call the `models.list()` method on the `client` object to retrieve a list of all available models. The resulting list is stored in the `models` variable.

4. Print each model on a new line:

    ```
    for model in models:
        print(model)
    ```

    Finally, we iterate over the `models` list using a `for` loop and `print` each model. This ensures that each model is displayed on a separate line for easy reading.

The output will contain an error, but it is expected:

```
SDKError: API error occurred
```

Next, we need to provide the API key.

Setting up the Mistral API key

To get started, visit `https://console.mistral.ai/api-keys` to generate your API key. You'll be prompted to sign in or create an account if you haven't already. Once your API key is ready, return to the Colab notebook to continue.

We will use userdata.get("") within Google Colab to securely retrieve the API key. This method keeps the key hidden from output cells and avoids hardcoding sensitive information.

Then, complete the following steps to set the API key in Google Colab:

1. Locate and click the key icon in the left sidebar titled **Secrets**.

2. Click **+ Add new secret**.

3. In the **Name** field, enter MISTRAL_API_KEY

4. In the **Value** field, paste your actual Mistral API key.

5. To allow access, click the three-dot menu next to your secret and mark **Notebook access**.

The following figure illustrates the process of setting and managing secrets in the Google Colab interface.

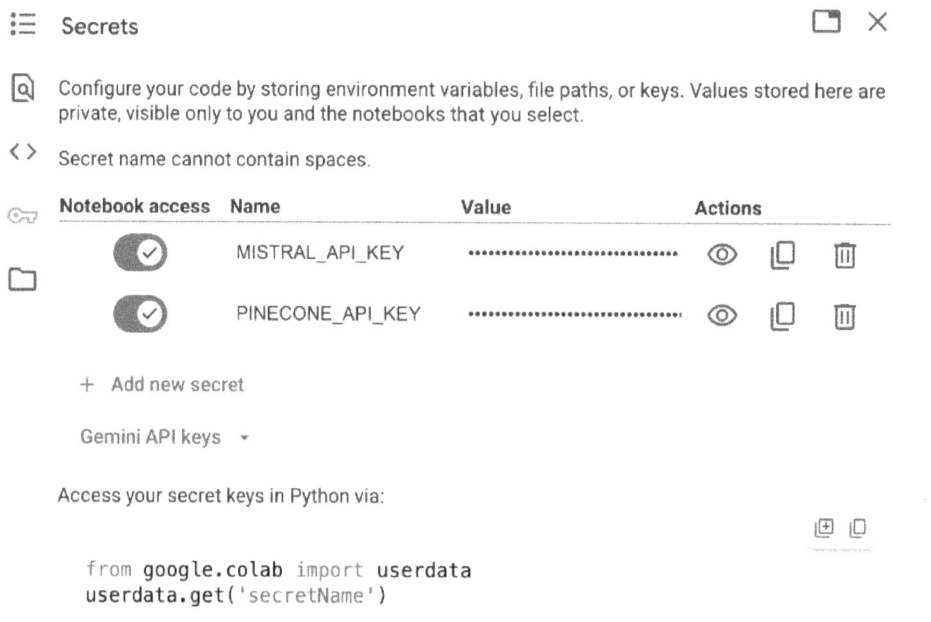

Figure 4.8: Google Colab Secret Manager

Later in this chapter, we will configure and use the Pinecone API key in the exact same way. Make sure you're comfortable with this method—it will become a pattern. You can also configure PINECONE_API_KEY now.

Now you can use the following code block in your notebook:

```
from google.colab import userdata
from mistral import MistralClient
api_key = userdata.get("MISTRAL_API_KEY")
client = MistralClient(api_key)
```

This snippet retrieves the API key stored under the name MISTRAL_API_KEY and initializes MistralClient with it. Let's proceed and list all available models. Here's the complete code for client initialization and model list fetching:

```
models = client.models.list()
# Iterate over the list of models and print each
for model in models.data:
    print(model.id)
```

The expected output is as follows:

```
ministral-3b-2410 ministral-3b-latest ministral-8b-2410 ministral-8b-
latest open-mistral-7b mistral-tiny mistral-tiny-2312 open-mistral-nemo
open-mistral-nemo-2407 mistral-tiny-2407 mistral-tiny-latest open-mixtral-
8x7b mistral-small mistral-small-2312 open-mixtral-8x22b open-mixtral-
8x22b-2404 mistral-small-2402 mistral-small-2409 mistral-medium-2312
mistral-large-2402 mistral-large-2407 mistral-large-2411 mistral-large-
latest pixtral-large-2411 pixtral-large-latest mistral-large-pixtral-2411
codestral-2405 codestral-2501 codestral-latest codestral-2412 codestral-
2411-rc5 devstral-small-2505 devstral-small-latest codestral-mamba-2407
open-codestral-mamba codestral-mamba-latest pixtral-12b-2409 pixtral-
12b pixtral-12b-latest mistral-small-2501 mistral-small-2503 mistral-
small-latest mistral-saba-2502 mistral-saba-latest mistral-medium-2505
mistral-medium-latest mistral-medium mistral-embed mistral-moderation-2411
mistral-moderation-latest mistral-ocr-2503 mistral-ocr-2505 mistral-ocr-
latest
```

For our purposes, we will use the mistral-embed model. Now that our tools are ready, we'll move on to generating the embeddings that power semantic search and understanding.

Step 3: Generating embeddings

Let's start by fetching the embedding for an arbitrary static string. We'll use the Mistral AI model to generate embedding and examine the response structure. This will help us understand how embeddings are represented and how to work with them.

Generating embeddings for a single line

Let us analyze and learn the code bit by bit. We will fetch the embedding for a sample sentence, clean the response, and print the first few elements of the embedding array along with its length.

In the first line, we provide the sample sentence and assign a variable:

```
sample_sentence = "A young wizard fights evil."
```

We then define a sample sentence for which we want to fetch the embedding.

To fetch the embedding for the sample sentence, use the following code:

```
sample_embed=client.embeddings.create(
    model='mistral-embed', input=[sample_sentence])
```

We use the `client.embeddings.create` method of the Mistral client to fetch the embedding for the sample sentence. The response contains various details, including the actual embedding array.

The following piece of code takes only what is needed from the structured payload, the embedding array:

```
clean_sample_embed = sample_embed.data[0].embedding
```

The following line prints the length of the embedding array:

```
print(len(clean_sample_embed))
```

The preceding line produces the following output:

```
1024
```

We print the length of the embedding array. This length is consistent for all responses from the same model, regardless of how many words (tokens) we send—one word or a paragraph of text.

The following line prints the first few elements of the embedding array:

```
print(clean_sample_embed[:10])
```

Here, we print the first 10 numbers of the embedding array to inspect the values.

The code generates the following output:

```
[-0.032470703125, -0.002910614013671875, 0.06439208984375,
0.020599365234375, 0.00814056396484375, 0.021026611328125,
0.0465087890625, -0.003429412841796875, -0.022308349609375,
-0.05792236328125]
```

Context analysis

Context is a crucial element in understanding the meaning of a word in a sentence, and this is no different for Mistral. In the context of Mistral embeddings, it refers to the words that surround the target word. These surrounding words provide valuable information about the meaning and usage of the target word. For instance, the word "bank" can have different meanings based on its context, such as a financial institution or a riverbank.

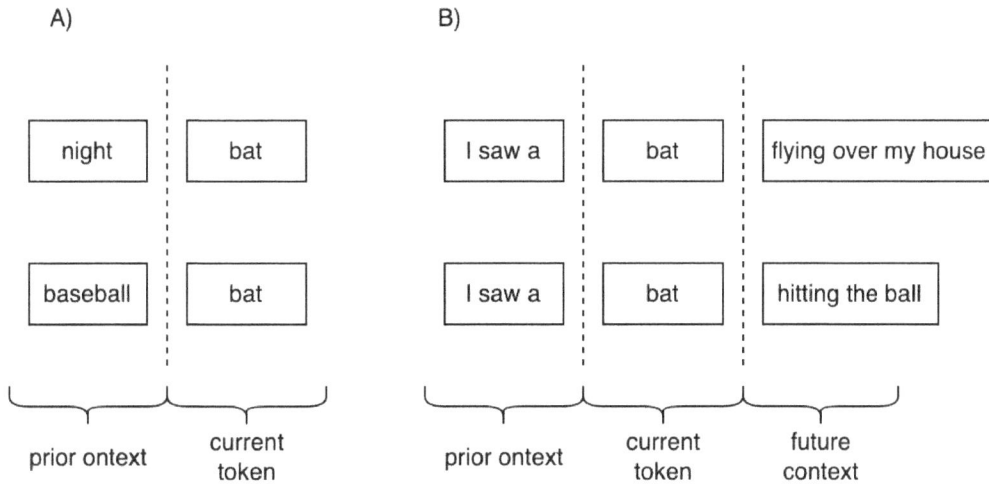

Figure 4.9: Prior and future context

As we can see in *Figure 4.9*, in part **A**, the prior context is different, and based on those prior words, it is clear whether it is a baseball bat or a night bat. In part **B**, the prior context is the same, and it only becomes clear from the future context what kind of bat it is. In the next section, we will review the prior context role.

The role of previous words in Mistral

When collecting embeddings, Mistral considers previous words to help understand the sequence and the build-up of the sentence. This is particularly important in languages with strong grammatical rules, where word order can significantly impact the meaning of a sentence.

In prior context analysis, only the words that come before the target word are considered. This means the embedding for a word is influenced solely by the preceding words in the sentence. Consider *Figure 4.9*, part **A**: "night bat" versus "baseball bat"

In the case of **night bat**, here, the word "bat" follows "night":

- A model using prior context would generate an embedding for "bat" influenced by "night"
- Since "night" is associated with nocturnal animals, the embedding for "bat" would likely reflect the meaning related to the animal (the flying mammal)

In the case of **baseball bat**:

- The word "bat" follows "baseball"
- A model using prior context would generate an embedding for "bat" influenced by "baseball"

Since "baseball" is associated with sports equipment, the embedding for "bat" would likely reflect the meaning related to the object (the sports equipment). In both cases, the meaning of "bat" is derived from the preceding words, leading to different embeddings for "bat" in each context.

Consideration of future neighbor words in Mistral

In addition to previous words, Mistral also considers future neighbor words (those that come after the target word) while collecting embeddings. This is because they can provide additional context that helps to disambiguate the meaning of the target word.

Let's take a look at *Figure 4.9*, part **B**: "I saw a bat flying over my house" versus "I saw a bat hitting the ball."

The following applies in the case of "**I saw a bat flying over my house:**"

- The target word "bat" is influenced by both the preceding words ("I saw a") and the following words ("flying over my house")
- A bidirectional model would generate an embedding for "bat" that considers the full context, recognizing that "flying" and "house" indicate the animal (the flying mammal)

The following applies in the case of "**I saw a bat hitting the ball**":

- The target word "bat" is influenced by both the preceding words ("I saw a") and the following words ("hitting the ball")
- A bidirectional model would generate an embedding for "bat" that considers the full context, recognizing that "hitting" and "ball" indicate the sports equipment (the bat used in baseball)

By processing the full sentence, *bidirectional* models can accurately determine the intended meaning of the word "bat" from its surrounding context.

As we can see, context plays a critical role in Mistral's embedding collection process. Both previous and future neighbor words provide valuable information that helps determine the meaning of the target word. Mistral's bidirectional approach allows it to achieve a more comprehensive understanding of the language.

Now that we've unpacked how Mistral uses both prior and future context to shape embeddings, it's time to put that understanding to work. In the next step, we'll see how embeddings can be compared, matching user inputs with relevant items based on semantic similarity.

Step 4: Embedding comparison

To reiterate, we will take a hands-on approach to understand how embeddings can be used to match user inquiries with relevant items. Specifically, we will start by generating embeddings for a small set of short dish descriptions along with their ingredients. This will help us see how different dishes and their components are represented in the embedding space. We will then prepare a way for the user to input their appetite interest, such as a craving or a specific ingredient they are interested in. Using the embeddings, we will compare the user's input with the dish descriptions by calculating the cosine distance between the embeddings. The dish with the shortest cosine distance to the user input will be the most relevant match.

The cosine distance helps us measure the similarity between the user's interest and the available dishes. The smaller the distance, the more similar the dish is to what the user is looking for. This method leverages the power of embeddings to understand and match complex textual descriptions effectively. Get ready to explore how embeddings can personalize recommendations and provide a practical application of AI in everyday scenarios!

Let us start by initializing an array of dish descriptions and generating the embeddings for them all.

```
dish_descriptions = [
    "Grilled steak with garlic butter",          # Meat
    "Seared salmon with lemon dill sauce",        # Fish
    "Roasted vegetable medley with herbs",        # Veggie
    "Spicy tofu stir-fry with vegetables",        # Asian
    "Tacos with spicy chicken and salsa",         # Mexican
    "Spicy chili con carne with beans",           # Spicy
    "Chocolate lava cake with vanilla ice cream", # Sweet
    "Creamy tomato basil soup",                   # Liquid
    "Cheeseburger with fries",                    # Fast
    "Seared scallops with truffle oil",           # Fine
```

```
    ]
```

```
    dish_embeds = client.embeddings.create(inputs=dish_descriptions)
    dish_embeds_arr = []
```

```
    for embed in dish_embeds.data:
        dish_embeds_arr.append(embed.embedding)

    print(len(dish_embeds_arr))
    print(len(dish_embeds_arr[0]))
```

The code produces the following output:

```
10
1024
```

All embeddings for each dish are stored in an array (size 10) of arrays (size 1024 each) of float-ing-point numbers. The embedding order corresponds to the order of the dish_descriptions string array.

Reading user input for later semantic comparison with available options

Now that we have embeddings for our dish descriptions, the next step is to capture the user's dinner preference. We will prompt the user to input what they prefer for dinner and generate an embedding for their input using the same model. This embedding will allow us to compare the user's preference with our predefined dish descriptions and find the most relevant match.

To do this, we will use the following code:

```
user_input = input("What do you prefer for dinner? ")
user_embed = client.embeddings.create(
    model='mistral-embed', inputs=[user_input]).data[0].embedding
user_embed[:10]
```

Figure 4.10 shows the input field. The value entered will be assigned to the user_input variable:

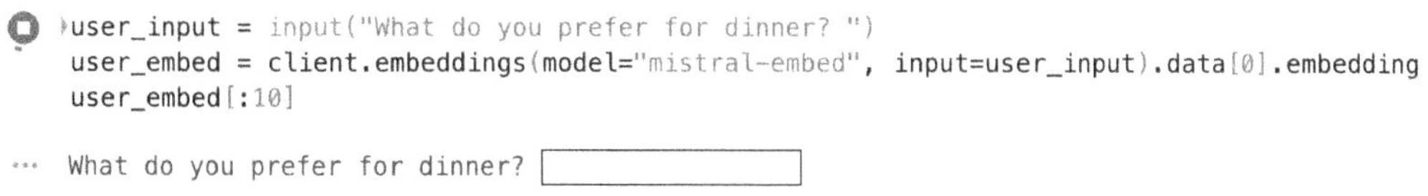

```
user_input = input("What do you prefer for dinner? ")
user_embed = client.embeddings(model="mistral-embed", input=user_input).data[0].embedding
user_embed[:10]

    What do you prefer for dinner? [          ]
```

Figure 4.10: User input

Once entered, the code will execute further and produce the output:

```
What do you prefer for dinner? pizza
[-0.02130126953125,
 0.0296630859375,
 -0.006282806396484375,
 0.029296875,
 0.0253143310546875,
 -0.0022602081298828125,
 0.01690673828125,
 0.00457000732421875,
 0.01416778564453125,
 -0.01031494140625]
```

This code snippet will prompt the user to enter their dinner preference, generate an embedding for the input, and display the first few elements of the embedding array. This process helps us understand how the user's preferences are represented in the embedding space, setting the stage for comparing these preferences with our dish descriptions to find the closest match.

Step 5: Semantic match of user input with existing options

With the user's dinner preference captured and its embedding generated, the next step is to compare this embedding with the embeddings of our predefined dish descriptions. To do this, we will use cosine similarity, which measures the cosine of the angle between two vectors. Cosine similarity is a common metric for comparing the similarity between embeddings because it considers the direction of the vectors, making it ideal for high-dimensional spaces such as embeddings.

First, we need to import the required library:

```
from scipy.spatial.distance import cosine
```

The `scipy.spatial.distance` module provides a cosine function that calculates the cosine distance between two vectors. The cosine distance measures dissimilarity, where a value of 0 indicates identical vectors and a value of 1 indicates completely dissimilar vectors. By subtracting the cosine distance from 1, we convert it into a similarity measure, where higher values indicate more similarity.

Here's the code snippet to compare the user's embedding with the first entry in our dish descriptions:

```
# Compare the user's embedding with the embedding of the dish description
similarity_score = 1 - cosine(user_embed, dish_embeds_arr[0])
print(similarity_score)
```

The code gives the following output:

```
0.6589278106354763
```

This gives us a starting point for comparing two embeddings, but to make the system useful, we need to compare the user's input against every option in our dataset—not just one.

Calculating distances to all available embeddings

Now that we know how to compare a single pair of embeddings, let's scale up our comparison to include all dish descriptions. To achieve this, we will use the `cdist` function from the `scipy.spatial.distance` module, which calculates the pairwise distances between two sets of vectors. This allows us to efficiently compute the cosine distances between the user's embedding and all dish embeddings at once.

Here's the initial code attempt:

```
from scipy.spatial.distance import cdist
distances = cdist(user_embed, dish_embeds_arr, "cosine")
```

The code gives the following output:

```
-------------------_-----------------------------------------------
ValueError                                Traceback (most recent call last)
<ipython-input-23-0b415054d20a> in <cell line: 3>()
      1 from scipy.spatial.distance import cdist
      2
----> 3 distances = cdist(user_embed, dish_embeds_arr, "cosine")

/usr/local/lib/python3.10/dist-packages/scipy/spatial/distance.py in
```

```
cdist(XA, XB, metric, out, **kwargs)
   2980
   2981      if len(s) != 2:
-> 2982          raise ValueError('XA must be a 2-dimensional array.')
   2983      if len(sB) != 2:
   2984          raise ValueError('XB must be a 2-dimensional array.')

ValueError: XA must be a 2-dimensional array.
```

However, this code results in an error:

```
ValueError: XA must be a 2-dimensional array.
```

Our first attempt highlights a common data-shape issue when working with embeddings. Let's fix this so our comparison works across the entire set.

Resolving array dimension incompatibility

This error occurs because cdist expects both input arrays to be two-dimensional. In our case, the user's embedding is a one-dimensional array, while the dish_embeddings array is two-dimensional. To resolve this, we need to reshape the user's embedding to be a two-dimensional array.

To fix the error, we reshape the user's embedding to match the expected dimensions:

```python
# Reshape to 1x1 array
user_embed_reshaped = user_embed.reshape(1, -1)
distances = cdist(user_embed_reshaped, dish_embeds_arr, "cosine")
```

This reshapes the user's embedding to be a 1x1024 array (assuming the embedding size is 1024), making it compatible with the two-dimensional dish embeddings array.

With the dimensionality issue resolved, we can now run the comparison and identify which dish is the closest match to the user's preference.

Finding the most relevant dish match

Now that we have calculated the cosine distances between the user's embedding and all dish embeddings, we need to find the dish with the highest relevancy index. This is the dish with the smallest cosine distance to the user's input, indicating the closest match.

```python
import numpy as np
# Find the index of the most relevant dish
most_relevant_index = np.argmin(distances)
```

```
# Output the description for the most relevant dish
print("Based on your preference,")
print(f"you might find tasty: {dish_descriptions[most_relevant_index]}")
```

To find the most relevant index of the item in the array, the argmin method can be used:

```
most_relevant_index = np.argmin(distances)
```

This line uses np.argmin to find the index of the smallest value in the distances array, which corresponds to the dish with the highest relevancy (smallest cosine distance) to the user's input.

Displaying the most relevant semantic match

Locating the most relevant index is only half the job. Let's display the matching dish so the result is immediately clear to the user.

```
print(f"Based on your preference,)
print(f"you might find tasty: {dish_descriptions[most_relevant_index]}")
```

This line prints the description of the dish at most_relevant_index, providing the user with the dish that best matches their input.

Here's the whole code for locating the closest item:

```
from scipy.spatial.distance import cosine, cdist
import numpy as np

distances = cdist(
    np.array(user_embed).reshape(1, -1), dish_embeds_arr, "cosine")

#index of the most relevant movie
mostRelevant = np.argmin(distances)

print(f"most relevant index: {mostRelevant}")
print(f"Then you might find tasty: {dish_descriptions[mostRelevant]}")
```

The code produces the following output for the user entered value "hot dog":

```
most relevant index: 8
Then you might find tasty: Cheeseburger with fries
```

By reshaping the user's embedding, calculating distances, and identifying the most relevant dish, we have effectively matched the user's preference with the most suitable dish description from our dataset.

Now we've gone full circle: from a user's plain-text preference to a semantic match drawn from our dataset. This closes the loop on single-query matching and sets us up to look back at the entire process before scaling it further.

Demo retrospective

In this end-to-end demo, we initialized the Mistral AI client, captured the user's dinner preference ("hot dog"), and generated an embedding to represent its semantic meaning. We then prepared embeddings for several predefined dishes and calculated cosine distances between the user's input and each option. By identifying the smallest distance, we found the closest semantic match—"cheeseburger"—highlighting how AI can interpret language meaningfully. The result reflects not just keyword similarity but shared context and characteristics. This demo showcased how embeddings and similarity measures can be used to deliver intelligent, context-aware recommendations in real-time applications.

That wraps up the main end-to-end demo! Let's explore a few bonus exercises to extend and scale what we've built. We'll start with learning how to scale this system using Pinecone, a dedicated vector database.

Bonus exercise: Semantic search with Pinecone DB

In this bonus exercise, we'll explore how to use **Pinecone DB** to manage and query embeddings efficiently. Pinecone is a powerful vector database designed to handle high-dimensional vector data, making it ideal for storing and querying embeddings. In this section, we'll start by setting up and initializing the Pinecone client to interact with the Pinecone DB service. Next, we'll create an index in Pinecone to store our embeddings. An index is like a table in a relational database and is crucial for organizing and querying the data. After creating the index, we'll insert our embeddings into the Pinecone index, uploading the vector representations of our dish descriptions to the database. We'll then demonstrate how to run queries to find the nearest neighbor embeddings, helping us identify the most relevant items based on the user's input. Finally, we'll experiment with other proximity algorithms available in Pinecone, such as Euclidean distance and dot-product similarity, to see how they affect the results. By the end of this exercise, you'll have a solid understanding of how to leverage Pinecone DB for managing and querying embeddings, and you'll gain hands-on experience with different proximity algorithms to optimize your search capabilities.

To begin using Pinecone DB, we first need to install the Pinecone client library. The following command downloads and installs the necessary package from the **Python Package Index (PyPI)**. This library provides the tools and functions required to interact with Pinecone's vector database, enabling us to create indexes, insert embeddings, and run queries efficiently.

Initializing the Pinecone client

We'll proceed with the current colab with the installation of the Pinecone client using the pip package manager:

```
!pip install pinecone
```

Our next goal is to initialize the Pinecone client. This involves setting up an API key and configuring the client to interact with the Pinecone service.

First, import the pinecone library:

```
import pinecone
```

Next, in order to authenticate with Pinecone's services, you'll need to provide your Pinecone API key using the same method as used previously for MISTRAL_API_KEY.

Assuming you've already added the secret in Google Colab Secret Manager and made it available to the notebook, you can access it with the following:

```
from google.colab import userdata
from pinecone import Pinecone, ServerlessSpec

api_key = userdata.get("PINECONE_API_KEY")
pcone = Pinecone(api_key=api_key)
```

This code securely retrieves your API key and initializes the Pinecone client. The Pinecone class is used to interact with Pinecone's vector database, while ServerlessSpec allows for specifying serverless configurations if needed.

Our Pinecone client is ready to serve. Next, we will create a fresh index for storing embeddings.

Creating a Pinecone index

Before we can store and query dish embeddings, we need to ensure that our Pinecone index is in a clean, known state. Rather than updating existing records, we'll delete any previous index with the same name and recreate it from scratch.

This approach is faster and avoids unnecessary index growth, especially useful if you plan to repeat this exercise multiple times.

```python
existing_indexes = pcone.list_indexes()
existing_index_names = [index.name for index in existing_indexes]

# Check and delete such index if it already exists
if 'dish-embeddings' in existing_index_names:
    pcone.delete_index('dish-embeddings')

# Create fresh index
pcone.create_index(
    name='dish-embeddings',
    dimension=1024,
    metric='cosine',
    spec=ServerlessSpec(cloud='aws', region='us-east-1')
)
```

This code starts by listing all existing indexes in your Pinecone project. If `'dish-embeddings'` is found, it is deleted to ensure we don't accumulate stale or duplicate data. Re-creating the index is both faster than updating existing records and ideal for repeated runs of the same workflow.

Once the index is deleted, a brand new one is created with the same name. It is configured to store 1024-dimensional vectors, use cosine similarity for matching, and run on AWS in the `us-east-1` region using a serverless deployment.

With our index freshly created and configured, we're ready to populate it with data. The next step is to insert the embeddings we previously generated for each dish. This will allow Pinecone to store and organize them for fast similarity search later in the process.

Upserting embeddings to Pinecone

Having completed the client setup, we're ready to reference the index and insert the dish embeddings for similarity search. To look up our index and start inserting embeddings, we use the following code:

```python
index = pcone.Index('dish-embeddings')

for i, embed in enumerate(dish_embeds_arr):
    index.upsert([(f'dish_{i}', embed)])
```

This code retrieves the index named dish-embeddings that we created earlier. By referencing the index by its name, we can perform various operations such as inserting, querying, and deleting records.

The loop inserts each embedding into the index. The following line iterates over the dish_embeds_ arr list, where i is the index of the embedding, and embed is the embedding vector itself.

```
for i, embed in enumerate(dish_embeds_arr):
```

The index.upsert([(f'dish_{i}', embed)]) method inserts or updates records in the index. The method takes a list of tuples, where each tuple contains an ID and the corresponding embedding vector. In this case, we use f'dish_{i}' to create a unique ID for each embedding (e.g., 'dish_0', 'dish_1', etc.), and embed is the actual embedding vector.

The upsert method is used to insert or update records. If a record with the same ID already exists, it will be updated with the new embedding. If it doesn't exist, a new record will be created. For efficiency, especially with a large number of embeddings, consider batching the upsert operations. This involves grouping multiple embeddings into a single upsert call to reduce the number of requests to the server.

By looking up the index and using the upsert method, we can insert our dish embeddings into the Pinecone index. This setup allows us to efficiently manage and query our high-dimensional vector data.

With all dish embeddings successfully inserted into the index, we're now ready to perform what this system was built for—semantic search. In the next step, we'll take a user query, convert it into an embedding, and search the Pinecone index to find the most semantically similar dish. This is where vector search reveals its real-world power.

Finding the closest match

To find the dish that most closely matches the user's preference, we search for the nearest vector in the Pinecone index using the following code:

```
result = index.query(vector=[user_embed], top_k=1)
closest_dish_id = result['matches'][0]['id']
closest_dish_index = int(closest_dish_id.split('_')[1])
print(closest_dish_index)
print(dish_descriptions[closest_dish_index])
```

This code snippet performs the following actions:

- First, we query the Pinecone index to find the nearest vector to the user's embedding. The line `result = index.query(vector=[user_embed], top_k=1)` sends a query to the index using the user's embedding (`user_embed`). The `vector=[user_embed]` parameter specifies the embedding we are querying with, and `top_k=1` indicates that we want the single closest match (i.e., the nearest neighbor).

- Next, we extract the ID of the closest match from the query result and convert it to an index. The ID is a string such as `'dish_8'`; we split it to get the number 8, which we then use to retrieve the matching dish from the list.

- Finally, we print the closest match index, then retrieve and display its description from the dish list using that index.

The code produces the following output:

```
8
Cheeseburger with fries
```

The output shows that item 8, "Cheeseburger with fries," is the closest semantic match to the user's input, "hot dog." This result reflects how embeddings capture contextual similarity—both dishes are classic fast-food items with similar ingredients and settings, making them closely related in vector space.

As we continue building our understanding of embeddings, we'll shift focus toward visualizing these high-dimensional representations. Up next, you'll explore practical techniques such as heatmaps and t-SNE plots to better interpret and compare the relationships between vectors in a more intuitive, human-readable form.

Bonus exercise: Semantic similarity with heatmap visualization

To visualize the semantic similarity between words in two sentences, we will generate embeddings for each word and then compute the cosine similarity between these embeddings. We'll use these similarity scores to create a heatmap, which will help us understand the relationships between the words.

First, we define the sentences and the words within them. Then, we generate embeddings for each word using the Mistral model. After obtaining the embeddings, we clean them and prepare arrays for further processing.

We compute the cosine similarity between each pair of words from the two sentences. Finally, we create and display a heatmap using the similarity scores, which provides a visual representation of the semantic similarities between the words.

A line-by-line description is omitted in this section, as it is assumed that you are familiar with most of the code at this point.

```python
import numpy as np
import seaborn as sns
import matplotlib.pyplot as plt
from sklearn.metrics.pairwise import cosine_similarity

# Define the sentences and words
sentence1 = ["I", "enjoy", "spicy", "food"]
sentence2 = ["She", "likes", "hot", "meals"]

# Generate embeddings for each word
embeddings1 = client.embeddings.create(
    model='mistral-embed', inputs=sentence1)
embeddings2 = client.embeddings.create(
    model='mistral-embed', inputs=sentence2)

# Clean embed arrays
embeddings1_arr = []
embeddings2_arr = []


for embed in embeddings1.data:
    embeddings1_arr.append(embed.embedding)


for embed in embeddings2.data:
    embeddings2_arr.append(embed.embedding)

# Compute cosine similarity between each pair of words
similarity_scores = cosine_similarity(embeddings2_arr, embeddings1_arr)

# Create a heatmap
plt.figure(figsize=(8, 6))
sns.heatmap(
```

```
    similarity_scores, annot=True, cmap='Blues',
    xticklabels=sentence1, yticklabels=sentence2
)

# Set titles and labels
plt.title('Semantic Similarity Heatmap')
plt.xlabel('Words in Sentence 1')
plt.ylabel('Words in Sentence 2')

# Show the heatmap
plt.show()
```

The code gives the following output:

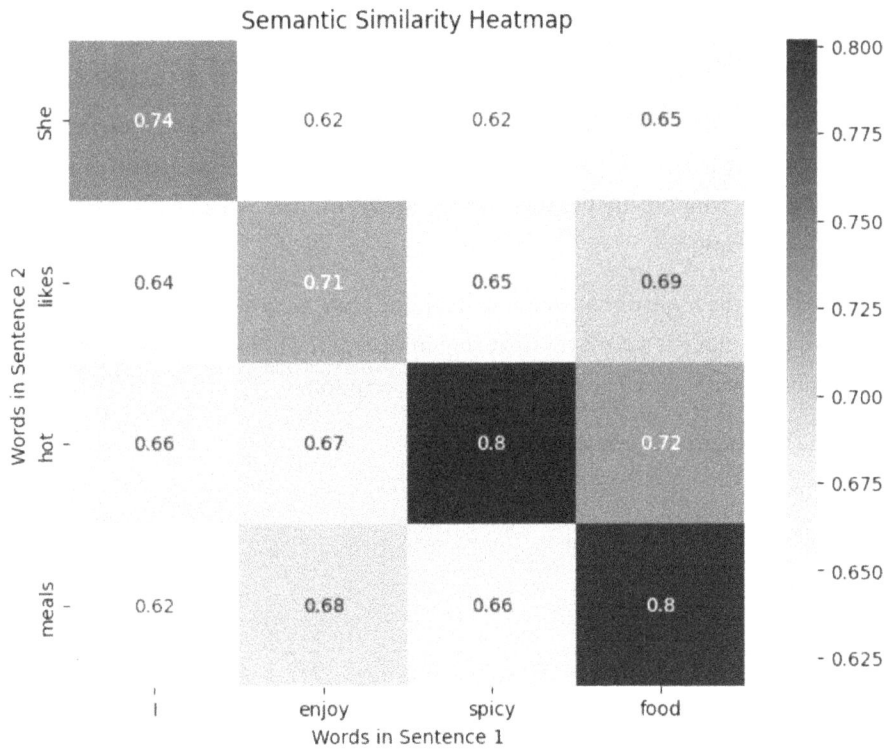

Figure 4.11: Output of heatmap code

The preceding heatmap shows semantic similarities between words in two sentences using cosine similarity scores. Each cell represents the similarity between a word from the first sentence and a word from the second sentence.

- **High similarity score (e.g., spicy versus hot)**: A score of 0.92 indicates these words are semantically very similar, both related to describing taste

- **Low similarity score (e.g., I versus likes)**: A score of 0.11 shows these words are semantically different, with "I" being a pronoun and "likes" a verb

- **Moderate similarity score (e.g., food versus meals)**: A score of 0.89 suggests a strong but not identical relationship, as both words refer to eating but in different contexts

These values highlight how cosine similarity captures the semantic relationships between words, with higher scores indicating stronger connections. Next, we'll use t-SNE to map our high-dimensional embeddings into a 2D space, making the relationships easier to see.

Bonus exercise: Semantic similarity using t-SNE visualization

In this section, we will add the user's input (hot dog) to our existing dish embeddings and generate a t-SNE chart to visualize the relationships. We will append the user input embedding to our dish embeddings, convert the list to a NumPy array, and then use t-SNE to reduce the dimensions for visualization.

We use t-SNE to reduce the high-dimensional embeddings to a two-dimensional space with a perplexity of 5. We then plot the t-SNE results using matplotlib, where each point represents a dish embedding labeled with the corresponding dish description.

First, we import the necessary libraries:

```
import numpy as np
import seaborn as sns
import matplotlib.pyplot as plt
from sklearn.manifold import TSNE
```

- numpy is used for array manipulation

- seaborn and matplotlib.pyplot are used for plotting

- TSNE from sklearn.manifold is the algorithm we'll use to reduce high-dimensional embeddings to two dimensions for visualization

To include the user input in the visualization plot, we add both the user input and its embedding to the arrays.

```
dish_embeds_arr.append(user_embed)
dish_descriptions.append(user_input)
```

We convert the embedding List to a NumPy array:

```
dish_embeds_np_arr = np.array(dish_embeds_arr)
```

The next two lines run t-SNE for dimensionality reduction:

```
tsne = TSNE(n_components=2, perplexity=5, random_state=42)
tsne_results = tsne.fit_transform(dish_embeds_np_arr)
```

- perplexity=5 controls how t-SNE balances local versus global structure
- random_state=42 ensures repeatable results
- fit_transform() performs the actual dimensionality reduction, producing a 2D coordinate for each embedding

Finally, we plot the 2D projection:

```
plt.figure(figsize=(10, 7))
for i, label in enumerate(dish_descriptions):
    x, y = tsne_results[i, :]
    plt.scatter(x, y)
    plt.text(x + 0.1, y + 0.1, label, fontsize=9)

plt.title('t-SNE Visualization of Dish Embeddings')
plt.xlabel('t-SNE Dimension 1')
plt.ylabel('t-SNE Dimension 2')
plt.show()
```

The code snippet iterates through each dish description and its corresponding 2D coordinates, then plots a point (scatter) for each embedding and overlays a text label slightly offset from the point. Finally, it labels the axes and shows the plot with a descriptive title. The plot is ready!

The output for the visualization code is shown on the following generated plot:

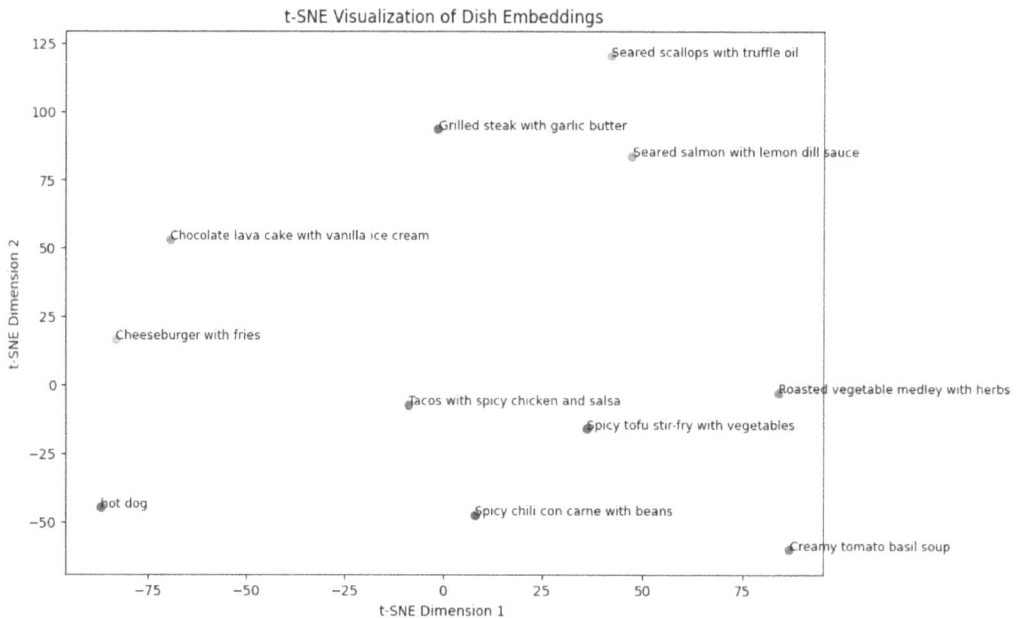

Figure 4.12: Output of t-SNE visualization code

🔍 **Quick tip**: Need to see a high-resolution version of this image? Open this book in the next-gen Packt Reader or view it in the PDF/ePub copy.

📖 **The next-gen Packt Reader** is included for free with the purchase of this book. Scan the QR code OR go to https://packtpub.com/unlock, then use the search bar to find this book by name. Double-check the edition shown to make sure you get the right one.

As we can see, **Cheeseburger** is closest to **hot dog**. We have approached the end of the workshop with this nice visual result and full of knowledge.

Workshop complete!

You've now completed all core steps of the workshop—well done. From initializing the Mistral and Pinecone clients to generating, storing, and querying embeddings, you've built a fully functional semantic search system using modern vector-based AI tools. Along the way, you worked through user input processing, vector similarity matching, and even explored how to scale the system with a vector database. This hands-on journey has equipped you with both the technical workflow and the conceptual understanding behind embeddings in action.

But this is just the beginning. Up next, we'll explore how these concepts apply in real-world scenarios, from recommendation systems to document search, and guide you through practical exercises that will challenge you to extend what you've learned beyond controlled examples and into meaningful applications.

Applications and practical exercises with embeddings

Now that you've mastered the mechanics of generating and querying embeddings, it's time to apply these skills to real-world problems. In this section, we'll explore practical use cases, such as semantic document search, personalized recommendations, and FAQ matching, where embeddings add tangible value. Each example is paired with an exercise challenge designed to help you practice implementing a solution.

Before you dive into the exercises, approach each problem as a system designer. Keep these steps in mind:

- **Define the problem**: Clearly outline the problem you want to solve, whether it's matching job descriptions with candidates, classifying documents, or developing a recommendation system.

- **Gather data**: Collect the necessary data for your application. For example, gather job descriptions and candidate resumes, or collect a dataset of documents or items.

- **Generate embeddings**: Use a pre-trained model to generate embeddings for your data.

- **Store and query embeddings**: Choose a vector database such as Pinecone, Neo4j, or FAISS to store and efficiently query the embeddings.

- **Implement the solution**: Write the code to solve the problem using embeddings and the chosen database. Use cosine similarity or another appropriate distance metric to compare embeddings.

- **Evaluate and iterate**: Test your solution, evaluate its performance, and make improvements as needed.

Job description and candidate matching service

Semantic search can match job descriptions with candidate profiles by understanding the underlying skills, experiences, and requirements. Embeddings help identify candidates whose skills and experiences semantically align with the job requirements, even if the exact keywords do not match. This results in a more efficient and accurate recruitment process, helping employers find the best candidates and job seekers find roles that suit their expertise.

Document classification service

Embeddings can categorize documents into predefined classes by capturing their semantic content. This is particularly useful for organizing large collections of documents, such as legal briefs, academic papers, and news articles. Services such as **LlamaIndex** in web scraper libraries and **Smart PDF Loader** can be employed to gather and preprocess documents from the web or PDF files, extracting relevant text and metadata.

The embeddings then ensure that each document is accurately classified based on its content, enabling efficient information retrieval and management. For long documents, it's often necessary to split them into smaller parts with overlap to preserve context. Python libraries such as chunkipy can be helpful for this task.

Recommendation systems

Embeddings are used to enhance recommendation systems for products, movies, music, and more. By understanding user preferences and item characteristics on a deeper semantic level, embeddings can suggest items that a user is likely to enjoy based on past behavior and similar user profiles. This personalized approach improves user satisfaction and engagement.

News analysis and correlation to stock prices

Semantic search can be used to analyze news articles and correlate them with stock price movements. By embedding news content and financial data, algorithms can identify patterns and predict how certain news events might impact stock prices. Tools such as LlamaIndex can gather real-time news data from various sources, and embeddings can process and analyze this data to provide insights into market trends. This application is particularly valuable for investors and financial analysts seeking to make informed decisions based on the latest news.

These practical exercises will help you apply the theoretical concepts of embeddings to real-world problems, enhancing your understanding and skills. Whether you choose a predefined application or come up with your own, the experience will be invaluable in mastering the use of embeddings in various domains. Dive in, experiment, and discover the transformative power of embeddings!

Summary

This chapter has taken you from the fundamentals of embeddings to their practical applications across real-world scenarios. You've learned how embeddings capture semantic meaning, how to use them for similarity search, and how tools such as Pinecone and Mistral support scalable solutions. Through hands-on exercises, you gained experience with generating, storing, and querying embeddings—skills that can power personalized, intelligent systems.

Embeddings are more than just vectors—they unlock deeper understanding in AI-driven applications. Whether you're enhancing search, building smart assistants, or analyzing content, embeddings offer a gateway to more intuitive, meaningful interactions with data. Let this knowledge fuel your innovation. Happy embedding!

The next chapter focuses on AI agents—intelligent systems that go beyond answering questions to actually taking action. You'll learn how agents use tools, make decisions, and complete complex tasks through reasoning and goal-oriented behavior. It's an exciting step toward building dynamic, autonomous workflows. Let's explore what they can do.

Extracurricular

Having built a solid foundation in working with embeddings, you're now ready to explore more advanced and creative applications. Let these exercises spark new ideas for your own projects.

1. **Experiment with different vector databases**: While Pinecone is a powerful vector database, there are several others to explore, such as FAISS, Annoy, Milvus, and Neo4j's embeddings framework. Each database has its own strengths and use cases. Try experimenting with different databases to understand their performance characteristics and how they handle large-scale vector searches.

2. **Explore different distance metrics**: Cosine similarity is commonly used for comparing embeddings, but other distance metrics such as Euclidean distance and dot-product similarity can also be useful depending on the application. Experiment with different metrics to see how they affect the results and understand which metric is best suited for specific types of data.

3. **Understand the mechanics of embedding generation**: Dive deeper into the algorithms and neural network architectures behind embedding generation. Explore how models such as BERT, GPT, and Word2Vec create embeddings and the mathematical principles that underlie these processes. Understanding what happens under the hood can give you greater insight into optimizing and applying embeddings in various contexts.

4. **Implement custom embeddings**: Try creating your own embeddings for specific use cases by training custom models on specialized datasets. This can be particularly useful for niche applications where pre-trained models might not capture the necessary nuances. Experiment with different training techniques and evaluate the performance of your custom embeddings.

5. **Advanced visualization techniques**: Beyond t-SNE, explore other dimensionality reduction and visualization techniques such as **Uniform Manifold Approximation and Projection (UMAP)** or **Principal Component Analysis (PCA)**. These tools can provide different perspectives on your data and help uncover hidden patterns.

6. **Integration with other AI technologies**: Combine embeddings with other AI technologies such as **Natural Language Processing (NLP)**, computer vision, or reinforcement learning to create more sophisticated systems. For instance, integrating embeddings with NLP can enhance chatbots, while combining them with computer vision can improve image search and classification.

7. **Real-world application development**: Develop a complete end-to-end application using embeddings. This could be anything from a recommendation system to a search engine, or a personal hobby project. Document the process, challenges, and solutions to create a comprehensive case study.

Unlock this book's exclusive benefits now

UNLOCK NOW

Scan this QR code or go to `https://packtpub.com/unlock`, then search for this book by name.

Note: *Keep your purchase invoice ready before you start.*

5

Agents: From Automation to Intelligence

Cracking ideas are one thing, Gromit—but making them work is another!

—Wallace & Gromit (Nick Park, Aardman Animations)

This chapter is about agents. Not science fiction robots, but real systems that think, adapt, and get work done. If traditional automation felt like marching in a straight line, agents are learning to dance with complexity.

The theory ahead is concise and focused, designed to give you just enough depth to understand why agents matter, how they work, and how they differ from older approaches. Each section builds toward action, setting you up to experiment, build, and evaluate your own agents. By the end, you'll see why agents aren't just hype but the next big leap forward.

In this chapter, you will do the following:

- Define an agent and understand core components such as tools, memory, and reasoning loops
- Workshop 1: Multi-agent answering service
- Workshop 2: Visual AI agents with n8n

Technical requirements

Let's begin by setting the stage for success by getting your groundwork ready. You'll need a few essential tools and accounts ready so you can follow along with the examples and experiments in this chapter:

- **Mistral account**: An account with Mistral is essential for accessing advanced language models, tools, and resources necessary for training and deploying large-scale language models.

- **Google Colab or local Jupyter server**: Google Colab offers a cloud-based platform to run Jupyter notebooks with free access to GPUs and TPUs, ideal for performing intensive computations. Alternatively, a local Jupyter server allows for running these notebooks on your own hardware, giving full control over the computing environment.

- **GitHub repository**: The `Chapter-5` folder in the GitHub repository, available at `https://github.com/PacktPublishing/Learn-Mistral`, contains all the code and resources for *Chapter 5*. This repository is a valuable resource for downloading the necessary code snippets and examples discussed in the chapter.

Problem statement

Traditional automation has carried businesses far, but its rigidity is showing. Scripts, macros, and predefined workflows perform reliably only when every condition is expected. In today's dynamic environments, that predictability rarely exists; inputs change, data shifts, and exceptions constantly appear. **Large language models (LLMs)** offer intelligence but lack persistence, memory, and structure to act as dependable systems on their own. The challenge is clear: we need a way to combine reasoning, adaptability, and tool use into workflows that don't break under pressure. Agents address this gap, transforming raw generative models into goal-oriented, problem-solving systems.

Defining agents in AI systems

This section pulls back the curtain on agentic systems and lays the groundwork: why agents matter, how they are defined, and what makes them so powerful in practice. We'll explore the evolution from traditional automation to agentic systems, unpack the architecture that drives them, and meet the core components (tools, memory, and reasoning loops) that give agents their adaptability and intelligence.

What you learn here will click into place once we start building. Each concept is chosen to prepare you for the hands-on workshops later in this chapter, where theory turns into working multi-agent systems. By the end, you'll not only be able to describe what an agent is and how it works but also see how it powers real AI workflows.

Why automation falls short

Automation has powered business and industry for decades, built on scripts, macros, and pre-defined pipelines. These systems excel in environments where conditions never change: invoices always look the same, customer requests follow a fixed pattern, and inputs remain predictable. Yet in practice, the real world is rarely so cooperative. Traditional automation struggles under pressure—workflows fail when an edge case appears, or a rule doesn't match reality. Humans are then left to pick up the slack, patch exceptions, and maintain brittle systems.

Modern digital environments demand more. Data sources shift constantly, regulations evolve, and customer behavior can change overnight. Static scripts cannot adapt quickly enough to keep pace. What's needed are systems that can perceive new situations, reason about them, and adapt in real time. LLMs bring raw intelligence to the table, but without structure, they remain reactive text engines.

Agents, however, provide the missing bridge, combining LLMs with tools, memory, and decision loops that transform generative power into goal-directed action.

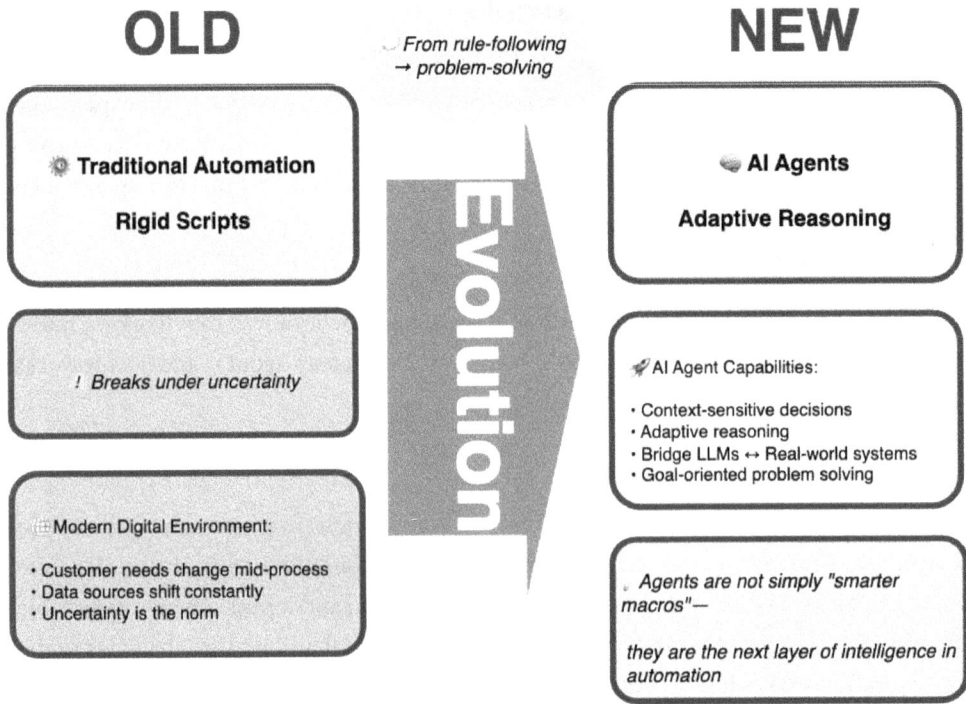

Figure 5.1: Key shift from automation tools to agents

This figure contrasts the old and new paradigms. On the left, automation tools execute fixed scripts deterministically, breaking when conditions change. On the right, agents process inputs through reasoning loops, adaptively selecting tools and discovering solutions on the fly. The central "key shift" illustrates the move from rules to reasoning, showing why agents succeed in uncertain environments where automation fails.

By understanding the shortcomings of traditional automation and the promise of adaptive systems, we're ready to ask the next question: what exactly is an "agent" in the world of AI?

What we mean by agents

At its simplest, an agent is an AI system designed to perceive inputs, reason about them, and take actions toward specific goals. Unlike a plain chatbot query, which begins and ends with a single response, an agent is persistent. It does not stop at answering; it evaluates, chooses actions, and continues until the goal is achieved. This persistence and autonomy are what elevate agents beyond being just another layer of automation.

Agents are not simply LLMs with extra prompts. They combine several components into a cohesive architecture: an LLM for reasoning, tools for interacting with the world, memory for continuity, and a decision-making loop that governs how to proceed at each step. Together, these elements turn the static output of an LLM into a dynamic, goal-driven system that can retry, adapt, and coordinate multiple actions.

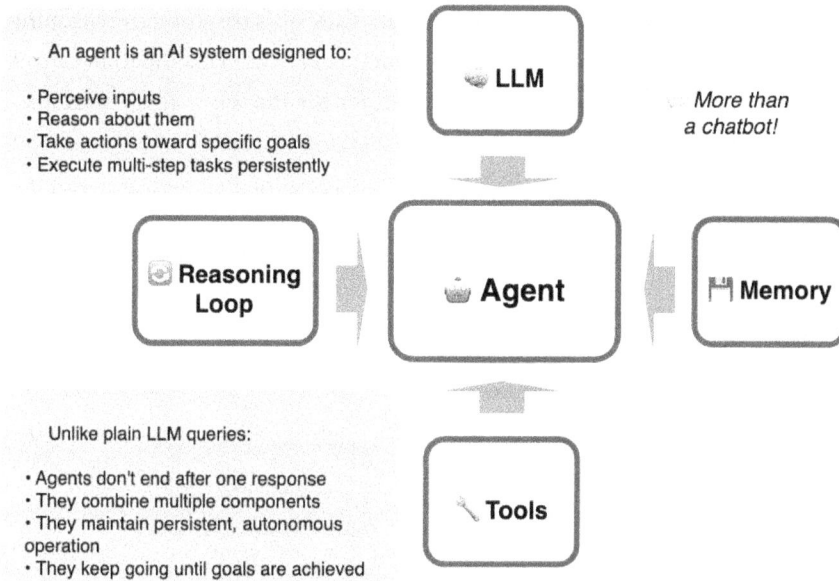

Figure 5.2: Anatomy of an agent system

The diagram shows how input flows into the agent system, cycles through the reasoning loop, and selects tools to act on the environment. The environment, in turn, provides feedback that is stored in memory, which then informs the next reasoning cycle. This continuous loop is what transforms an otherwise reactive LLM into an adaptive, problem-solving agent capable of multi-step execution.

By grounding our understanding in these core definitions and components, we can now move on to an important comparison: how do agents differ from traditional automation tools, and why does that distinction matter?

Agents versus traditional automation

Automation tools are designed around predictability. They follow fixed scripts and macros, producing consistent results when the inputs stay within expected boundaries. This reliability is their strength, but also their weakness: once conditions shift, the system has no way to adjust, and the workflow stalls.

Agents take a different approach. Instead of rigid execution, they operate through reasoning loops that let them interpret context and decide among available actions. This capability turns them into orchestrators that are able to select the right tool for the moment, adapt strategies, and persist until goals are achieved.

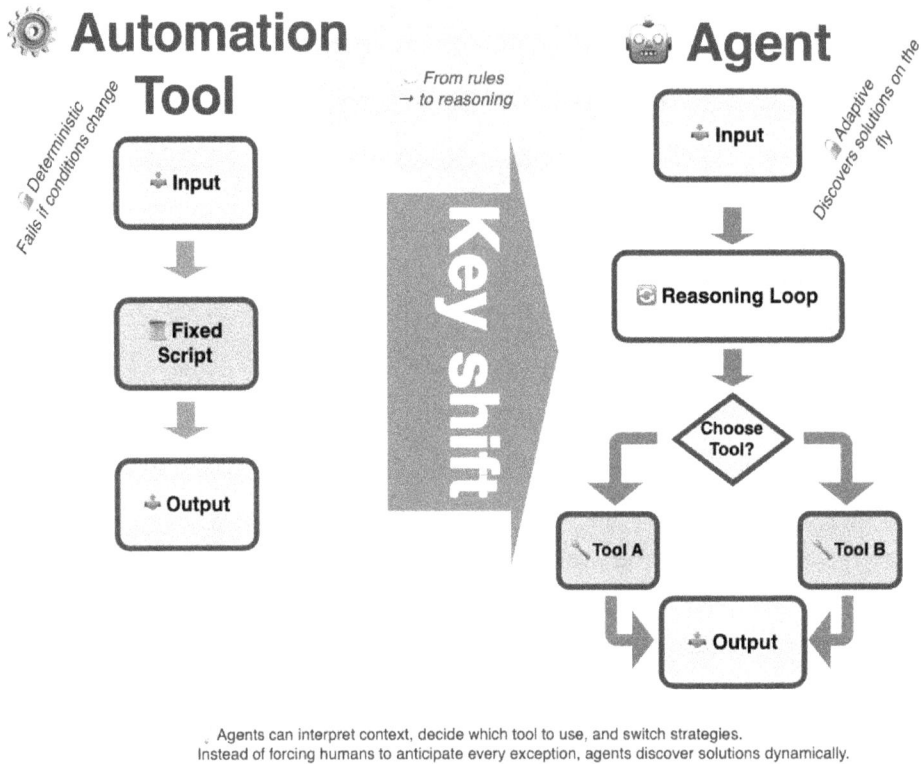

Agents can interpret context, decide which tool to use, and switch strategies.
Instead of forcing humans to anticipate every exception, agents discover solutions dynamically.

Figure 5.3: The paradigm shift: from rigid automation to adaptive, agent-based systems.

The figure highlights this contrast. Traditional automation breaks under unexpected inputs, while agent-based systems adapt, retry, and scale across workflows. The lower panels show the practical outcomes: flexibility, human-like processes, scalability, and business relevance.

This shift marks the move from rule-following to problem-solving. With the distinction established, the next step is to examine the architecture of agent systems and the concepts that make this adaptability possible.

Building blocks of agentic systems

What makes agents different from a plain LLM is not just their ability to generate text but their architecture. Agents integrate several key concepts that allow them to act in dynamic environments, adapt to new situations, and maintain continuity across tasks.

The first concept is **tools**, also known as **actions**. These are external functions the agent can invoke (APIs, code execution, or search queries) giving it the ability to affect the world beyond language. Next is **memory**, which captures past interactions so the agent can maintain context and learn from experience rather than starting fresh each time. The **policies** and **reasoning loops** sit at the core: this is the decision-making engine that interprets inputs, chooses actions, and plans the next steps. Finally, the **environment** provides the arena where the agent acts, receives feedback, and adjusts its strategy accordingly.

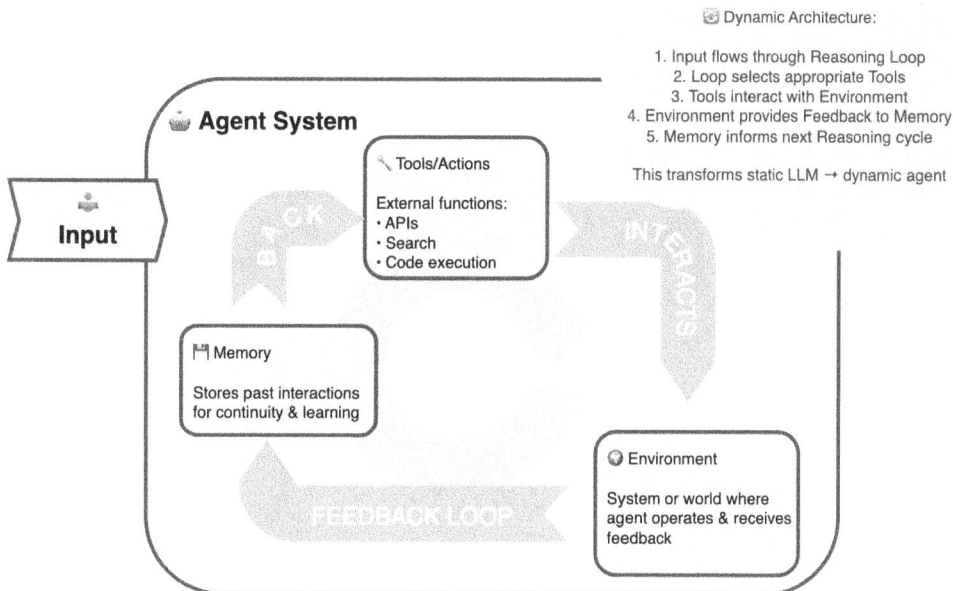

Figure 5.4: Core components of an agent system

The illustration shows how input flows into the agent system, moves through the reasoning loop, and connects with tools, memory, and the environment. Feedback from the environment is stored in memory, feeding into the next reasoning cycle. This feedback loop is what transforms a static LLM into a dynamic agent.

By understanding these building blocks, we can see how agents achieve their adaptability. The next step is to explore why these capabilities matter in practice and how they translate into business and real-world impact.

Why agents matter in practice

Theory is only useful if it translates into impact. Agents matter because they solve problems that rigid automation never could. Their flexibility allows them to handle unexpected queries, adapt when rules fail, and continue working until the task is finished. This resilience is crucial in real-world systems where unpredictability is the norm.

Agents are also scalable. They can chain multiple tools together, coordinate across workflows, and scale to enterprise-wide deployments while maintaining consistent performance. Their ability to adapt to complexity makes them suitable for tasks far beyond what macros or scripts can handle.

Another defining strength is their human-like workflow. Agents don't just execute instructions; they can mimic human reasoning, retry when things go wrong, and adjust strategies along the way. This gives them a quality of persistence that feels less like automation and more like collaboration. Finally, their business relevance is clear: customer service agents that resolve novel cases, adaptive data pipelines that react to change, knowledge management systems that evolve with organizations, and workflow automation that produces direct ROI.

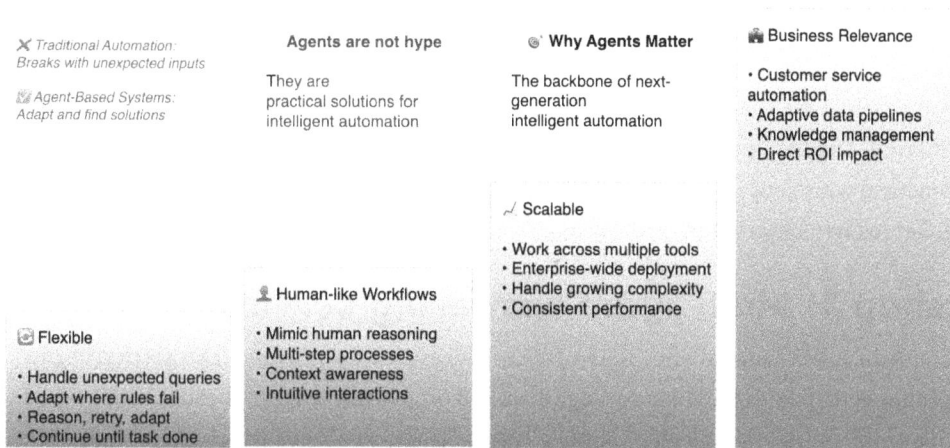

Traditional Automation:
Breaks with unexpected inputs

Agent-Based Systems:
Adapt and find solutions

Agents are not hype

They are
practical solutions for
intelligent automation

Why Agents Matter

The backbone of next-
generation
intelligent automation

Business Relevance

• Customer service
automation
• Adaptive data pipelines
• Knowledge management
• Direct ROI impact

Scalable

• Work across multiple tools
• Enterprise-wide deployment
• Handle growing complexity
• Consistent performance

Human-like Workflows

• Mimic human reasoning
• Multi-step processes
• Context awareness
• Intuitive interactions

Flexible

• Handle unexpected queries
• Adapt where rules fail
• Reason, retry, adapt
• Continue until task done

From hype → practical impact

Figure 5.5: From hype to practical impact: the real value of agents in flexibility, scalability, workflows, and business relevance

🔍 **Quick tip**: Need to see a high-resolution version of this image? Open this book in the next-gen Packt Reader or view it in the PDF/ePub copy.

📖 **The next-gen Packt Reader** is included for free with the purchase of this book. Scan the QR code OR go to `https://packtpub.com/unlock`, then use the search bar to find this book by name. Double-check the edition shown to make sure you get the right one.

The figure highlights agents as practical solutions rather than hype, showing how they scale from handling unexpected inputs to delivering measurable business value.

By now, you've seen why agents are more than a buzzword: they're the backbone of next-generation automation. And here's the best part: we won't stop at theory. In the next section, we'll step into the practical workshop, where you'll see agents in action and experience their capabilities firsthand. Get ready! This is where your ideas come alive.

Workshop 1: Multi-agent answering service

Having established the theory, we now move toward the practical workshop. This section begins with simple agents capable of invoking a single tool and progresses to sophisticated, multi-agent systems that collaborate to solve complex tasks. Along the way, we'll evaluate their performance to distinguish genuine capabilities from hype, grounding expectations in reality.

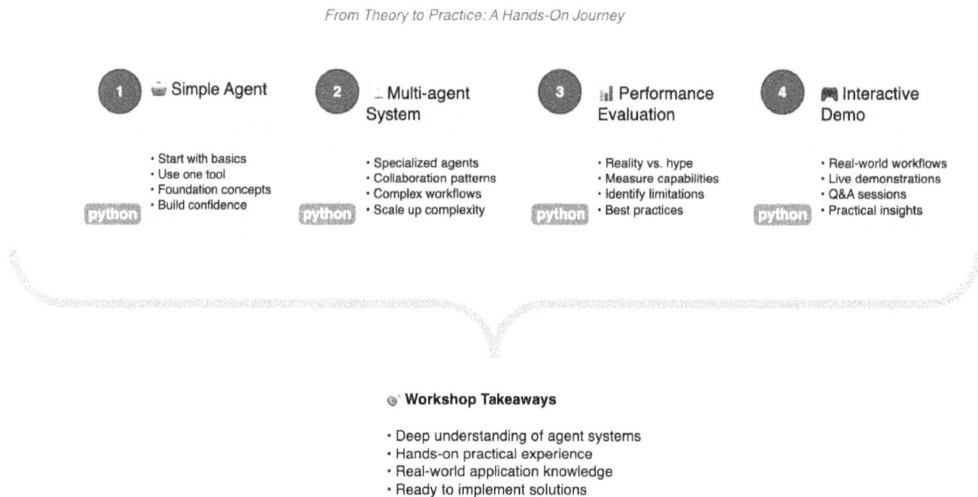

From Theory to Practice: A Hands-On Journey

1 👑 Simple Agent

- Start with basics
- Use one tool
- Foundation concepts
- Build confidence

`python`

2 _ Multi-agent System

- Specialized agents
- Collaboration patterns
- Complex workflows
- Scale up complexity

`python`

3 📊 Performance Evaluation

- Reality vs. hype
- Measure capabilities
- Identify limitations
- Best practices

`python`

4 🎬 Interactive Demo

- Real-world workflows
- Live demonstrations
- Q&A sessions
- Practical insights

`python`

Workshop Takeaways

- Deep understanding of agent systems
- Hands-on practical experience
- Real-world application knowledge
- Ready to implement solutions

Figure 5.6: Roadmap of the workshop

The workshop is designed as an interactive bridge between concepts and practice, ensuring that every theoretical idea finds its place in a real-world application.

Step 1: Setting up the stage

Before we can work with LangChain and Mistral, we need to install the core libraries that provide model access, text parsing, and vector search capabilities. This ensures our environment is fully prepared for the agentic workflows that follow:

```
!pip install langchain langchain-mistralai requests beautifulsoup4
chromadb faiss-cpu sentence-transformers ipywidgets
print(" All packages installed successfully!")
```

> 💡 **Quick tip**: Enhance your coding experience with the **AI Code Explainer** and **Quick Copy** features. Open this book in the next-gen Packt Reader. Click the **Copy** button
>
> **(1)** to quickly copy code into your coding environment, or click the **Explain** button
>
> **(2)** to get the AI assistant to explain a block of code to you.
>
> ```
> function calculate(a, b) {
>     return {sum: a + b};
> };
> ```

📖 **The next-gen Packt Reader** is included for free with the purchase of this book. Scan the QR code OR visit `https://packtpub.com/unlock`, then use the search bar to find this book by name. Double-check the edition shown to make sure you get the right one.

Having the basics in place, we can now move on to configuring the connection with Mistral by securely loading the API key, initializing the chat model, and testing the response.

Step 2: Preparing the Mistral API keys and testing the connection

With the groundwork covered, it's time to shift focus to connecting to the Mistral API:

1. We'll start by importing the required modules and essential libraries. These modules allow us to handle environment variables and work with the Mistral chat client:

    ```
    from google.colab import userdata
    import os
    from langchain_mistralai import ChatMistralAI
    ```

2. We then initialize our API keys to authenticate requests and enable secure access to the Mistral service. The API key is securely retrieved from Colab user data and placed into the environment so other components can use it:

    ```
    # Get Mistral API key securely
    # Get your free Mistral API key from: https://console.mistral.ai/
    mistral_api_key = userdata.get('MISTRAL_API_KEY')
    os.environ["MISTRAL_API_KEY"] = mistral_api_key
    ```

3. With the credentials in place, the next step is setting up the LLM client, configuring model parameters, and preparing it to process queries effectively. The client is initialized with a chosen model, temperature, and maximum token length, as explained in the list that follows:

    ```
    # Initialize Mistral LLM
    llm = ChatMistralAI(
        model="mistral-small",
        mistral_api_key=mistral_api_key,
        temperature=0.7,
        max_tokens=1000
    )
    ```

    *   model="mistral-small" selects a compact model suitable for fast prototyping
    *   mistral_api_key binds the client to your account
    *   temperature=0.7 provides balanced creativity
    *   max_tokens=1000 sets an upper response limit

4. Once the client is ready, we run a quick test query to confirm the connection is working and the model responds as expected. We send a short prompt to check whether the LLM responds correctly, while also catching possible errors:

```
# Test connection
try:
    response = llm.invoke("Hello! Please confirm you're working")
    print(" Connected to Mistral successfully!")
    print(f" Response: {response.content}")
except Exception as e:
    print(f" Connection failed: {str(e)}")
    print("Please check your API key and try again.")
```

Once the client responds, the connection is fully confirmed. The preparation phase is complete. Now, it's time to dive into adding external tools that the agent can call, such as calculators or parsers, before assembling them into a minimal agent loop.

Step 3: Creating a safe calculator tool

With the prerequisites satisfied, let's open the door to the first tool the agent can call. We import the primitives, define a safe arithmetic helper, wrap it as a LangChain tool, and then test it with some direct expressions. Let's get started:

1. We begin by bringing in the LangChain classes for tools, agents, and prompt templates. These imports provide the essential classes—Tool for defining reusable functions, create_react_agent and AgentExecutor for building the agent, and hub for pulling a standardized prompt template:

```
from langchain.tools import Tool
from langchain.agents import create_react_agent, AgentExecutor
from langchain import hub
```

2. Then, we create a helper function that validates expressions and ensures safe execution of basic math operations. This helper function strips whitespace, checks for invalid characters, rejects long expressions, and evaluates basic math while handling errors. The design prioritizes safety and controlled evaluation, preventing malformed expressions from breaking the workflow:

```python
def safe_calculate(expression: str) -> str:
    """Safely evaluate mathematical expressions"""
    try:
        expression = expression.strip()
        allowed_chars = set('0123456789+-*/()%. ')
        if not all(c in allowed_chars for c in expression):
            return "Error: Invalid characters in expression. Only
numbers and +, -, *, /, (, ), %, . are allowed."
        if len(expression) > 100:
            return "Error: Expression too long"
        result = eval(expression)
        return f"Result: {result}"
    except ZeroDivisionError:
        return "Error: Division by zero"
    except SyntaxError:
        return "Error: Invalid mathematical expression syntax"
    except Exception as e:
        return f"Error: {str(e)}"
```

3. Now, we expose the safe calculator to LangChain as a tool that the agent can later call, as described in the list that follows:

```python
calculator_tool = Tool(
    name="calculator",
    description="Safely evaluate math expressions like '2+2',
'10*5', or '(15+25)/2'. Only basic operations are supported.",
    func=safe_calculate
)
```

- name: Unique identifier the agent uses to call the tool
- description: Guidance for the LLM, ensuring that the tool is only invoked for supported math expressions
- func: Python function implementing the logic—here, safe_calculate

4. With the tool defined, the next step is to verify that it works correctly on its own. At this point, we can try out a few sample expressions with the tool to verify that it runs correctly and returns expected outputs:

    ```
    test_expressions = ["2+2", "10*5", "15/3", "(10+5)*2"]
    print("\n  Testing calculator tool directly:")
    for expr in test_expressions:
        result = calculator_tool.func(expr)
        print(f"  {expr} = {result}")
    ```

This loop iterates over sample expressions, calls the tool, and prints the results. It provides a quick check that the calculator behaves as expected before embedding it into an agent.

Having secured the foundation, the next stage is about extending agent capabilities by combining this tool with a reasoning loop.

Step 4: Using a shared ReAct prompt and refining the agent loop

With the basics in place, we can now move on to adopting a standardized ReAct prompt from the LangChain Hub. This gives the agent a consistent reasoning template for tool-use and answer synthesis:

1. We start by fetching a curated prompt that encodes the ReAct reasoning format used by many examples. This template provides the agent with structured reasoning instructions to use tools and generate answers step by step:

    ```
    react_prompt = hub.pull("hwchase17/react")
    ```

2. Next, we combine the calculator tool with the prompt, creating a new agent and an executor to manage its behavior, as described in the list that follows:

    ```
    tools = [calculator_tool]
    agent = create_react_agent(llm, tools, react_prompt)
    calculator_agent = AgentExecutor(
        agent=agent,
        tools=tools,
        verbose=True,
        max_iterations=5,
        max_execution_time=30,
        handle_parsing_errors=True,
    ```

```
        early_stopping_method="generate"
)
```

- agent: Core reasoning loop created from the model, tools, and ReAct prompt
- tools: List of tools available—here, just the calculator
- verbose=True: Prints step-by-step reasoning traces
- max_iterations=5: Limits the reasoning loop to five steps
- max_execution_time=30: Safety limit in seconds for overall execution
- handle_parsing_errors=True: Allows recovery if the LLM generates malformed outputs
- early_stopping_method="generate": Decides how to halt gracefully if the maximum iterations are reached

3. With the agent set up, it's time to test its behavior on natural language queries. Here, we provide the agent with everyday language prompts and observe how it uses the calculator tool to produce answers:

```
test_queries = [
    "What is 25 multiplied by 47?",
    "Calculate 150 divided by 6",
    "What's 15 percent of 200?"
]

for query in test_queries:
    print(f"\n{'='*60}")
    print(f" Query: {query}")
    print('='*60)
    try:
        result = calculator_agent.invoke({"input": query})
        if 'output' in result:
            print(f"✅ Agent Response: {result['output']}")
        else:
            print(f"⚠️  Agent Response: {result}")
    except Exception as e:
        print(f"❌ Error: {str(e)}")
        if "25" in query and "47" in query:
            print(f"🔧 Fallback calculation: 25 * 47 = {25 * 47}")
```

```
        elif "150" in query and "6" in query:
            print(f" Fallback calculation: 150 / 6 = {150 / 6}")
        elif "15" in query and "200" in query:
            print(f" Fallback calculation: 15% of 200 = {200 *
    0.15}")
```

At this stage, the loop is tested on natural language queries, mapping them into tool calls. Error handling ensures fallback calculations are printed if the agent misbehaves, showing how reasoning, tool use, and outputs connect together.

Step 5: Building a web search tool

This was a simple tool concept, but agent frameworks can grow into something far more powerful. Imagine tools that don't just crunch numbers, but also switch on the light in your room, trade stocks on your behalf, or design a full travel itinerary. The potential list is nearly endless. As a first step in that direction, let's expand our workflow by incorporating external knowledge access, starting with a simple web search, into the existing agent framework:

```
# We bring in requests for HTTP calls, typing and pydantic for structured
input, and the LangChain BaseTool as the foundation for a new tool. This
setup provides the building blocks for defining input schemas, creating
the tool class, and making web requests.import requests
from langchain.tools import BaseTool
from typing import Optional, Type
from pydantic import BaseModel, Field
import json
```

We then define a schema that requires just one field—a string representing the query that will be sent for searching. This schema ensures that when the tool is called, it receives a valid and clearly described query string:

```
class WebSearchInput(BaseModel):
    query: str = Field(description="Search query to look up information")
```

Implementing the web search tool

We now define a **Tool** subclass that performs searches against the DuckDuckGo API. Let's anchor the shape of the tool's class structure and its async delegate, as described in the list that follows:

```python
class SimpleWebSearchTool(BaseTool):
    name: str = "web_search"
    description: str = "Search the web for current information. Use this
when you need recent data or facts not in your training. Input should be a
clear search query."
    args_schema: Type[BaseModel] = WebSearchInput

    async def _arun(self, query: str) -> str:
        return self._run(query)
```

- name: Identifier used by the agent when choosing actions
- description: Guidance for when this tool is appropriate
- args_schema: Validates inputs with WebSearchInput(query: str)
- _arun(...): An async wrapper delegating to sync _run(...) so logic stays in one place

With the top-level shape clear, we can unpack the sync path where the real work happens. The _run method with the try/except skeleton performs the request, parses the response, and selects a useful answer:

```python
def _run(self, query: str) -> str:
    try:
        # normalize input → build URL → GET → parse JSON
        # choose best field to return
        # fallback if nothing useful

        ...
    except requests.exceptions.Timeout:

        ...
    except requests.exceptions.RequestException as e:

        ...
    except Exception as e:

        ...
```

The try block is the "happy path" (request, parse, select). The except branches convert failures into readable, user-facing messages instead of stack traces.

Moving inward, let's see how the request is prepared and executed. We first normalize the query and call DuckDuckGo's Instant Answer API:

```
query = query.strip().replace(" ", "+")
url = f"https://api.duckduckgo.com/?q={query}&format=json&no_html=1&skip_
disambig=1"
response = requests.get(url, timeout=10)
data = response.json()
```

This cleans whitespace, formats spaces for a query string, builds a JSON endpoint that avoids HTML, enforces a 10-second timeout to prevent hangs, and parses the response into a Python dictionary.

With a JSON payload in hand, the tool picks the most informative field available. So, the next piece is selecting the best available answer. The tool checks several fields in a priority order and returns the first good hit:

```
if data.get("AbstractText"):
    ...
elif data.get("Definition"):
    ...
elif data.get("RelatedTopics") and len(data["RelatedTopics"]) > 0:
    ...
elif data.get('Answer'):
    ...
```

Let us drill down to each elif case. Let's start with the AbstractText case:

```
if data.get("AbstractText"):
    return (
        f"Search result for '{query}':\n"
        f"{data['AbstractText']}\n\n"
        f"Source: {data.get('AbstractURL', 'DuckDuckGo')}"
    )
```

This block handles the case when the DuckDuckGo API response contains `AbstractText`, which is usually a short, direct explanation (like a Wikipedia summary):

- `data.get("AbstractText")` checks whether the API response has that key
- Multiline string inside parentheses avoids messy backslashes
- First line labels the result with the search query
- Second line inserts the actual abstract text
- Last line cites the source URL (falling back to `DuckDuckGo` if missing)

Together, this ensures the user gets a clear answer and citation in a readable format. The next one is the `Definition` case:

```
elif data.get("Definition"):
    return (
        f"Definition for '{query}':\n"
        f"{data['Definition']}\n\n"
        f"Source: {data.get('DefinitionURL', 'DuckDuckGo')}"
    )
```

This is the same idea as the abstract, but specialized for dictionary-like definitions. The formatting is identical; only the keys and labels differ. Next is the `RelatedTopics` case:

```
elif data.get("RelatedTopics") and len(data["RelatedTopics"]) > 0:
    topic = data["RelatedTopics"][0]
    if isinstance(topic, dict) and topic.get("Text"):
        return f"Information about '{query}':\n{topic['Text']}"
```

If neither an `abstract` nor a `definition` is available, the tool falls back to **related topics**:

- Picks the first `topic` (`[0]`) from the list
- Ensures it's a dictionary with a `Text` field
- Returns that snippet as the answer

This provides some fallback context even if no direct summary is present. With the tool defined, the next step is to test that it responds correctly to common queries.

Testing the web search tool

At this stage, we initialize the tool and run it against a few sample queries to verify that it works as intended, as described in the list that follows:

```python
# Test the web search tool
web_search_tool = SimpleWebSearchTool()
print(" Web Search Tool created successfully!")
```

- `SimpleWebSearchTool()` constructs the tool with its predefined name, description, and args schema
- The `print` confirmation helps during demos to signal that initialization succeeded

With the instance ready, we can prepare a few realistic inputs to exercise different answer types.

Next is preparing test searches. We gather a small, diverse list to probe summaries, facts, and definitions, as described in the list that follows:

```python
# Test searches
print("\n Testing Web Search Tool:")
test_searches = [
    "Python programming language",
    "current population Tokyo",
    "photosynthesis definition"
]
```

- The mix targets common response modes: general abstracts, current facts, and dictionary-like definitions
- A short list keeps the demo quick while still showing variety

Now that the inputs are ready, we are finally ready to run the search loop. We iterate over the queries, execute the tool, and print a compact preview:

```python
for search_query in test_searches:
    print(f"\n Searching: {search_query}")
    result = web_search_tool._run(search_query)
    print(f" Result: {result[:200]}...")
```

This loop announces each query, calls the tool's synchronous _run method, and prints only the first ~200 characters for readability. It's a fast, practical check that validates network access, JSON parsing, and formatting logic without overwhelming the console. This test loop shows how the tool can return snippets of useful information from the web. Each query is cleaned, passed through the DuckDuckGo API, and the first portion of the result is printed for inspection.

With the search tool in place, the next stage is to combine it with the calculator to form a richer agent.

Step 6: Creating a research agent with multiple tools

Now that we have both a calculator and a web search tool, the next logical step is to integrate them into a single agent. This research agent will be able to perform calculations and fetch current information as part of the same reasoning loop.

Defining the research agent class

To move forward, we build a class that combines both tools and configures the agent executor to manage their coordinated use, as described in the list that follows:

```python
class ResearchAgent:
    """Advanced research agent that can search the web and perform
calculations"""

    def __init__(self, llm):
        self.llm = llm
        self.tools = [
            web_search_tool,
            calculator_tool
        ]
        self.agent = create_react_agent(llm, self.tools, react_prompt)
        self.agent_executor = AgentExecutor(
            agent=self.agent,
            tools=self.tools,
            verbose=True,
            max_iterations=3,
            max_execution_time=30,
```

```
            handle_parsing_errors=True,
            return_intermediate_steps=True
    )
```

- `self.tools`: List of available tools (search + calculator)
- `create_react_agent`: Builds the reasoning agent with the LLM, tools, and ReAct prompt
- `AgentExecutor`: Manages execution with limits and debugging options
- `max_iterations=3`: Keeps research loops short
- `max_execution_time=30`: Prevents runaway execution
- `return_intermediate_steps=True`: Records tool calls and outputs for transparency

Moving ahead, we define methods that handle both single research queries and batch processing within the newly initialized class.

Adding research methods

These methods wrap the executor into user-facing functions for single and multiple queries:

```python
def research(self, query: str) -> dict:
    """Conduct research on a given query"""
    try:
        result = self.agent_executor.invoke({"input": query})
        return {
            "success": True,
            "query": query,
            "answer": result['output'],
            "error": None
        }
    except Exception as e:
        return {
            "success": False,
            "query": query,
            "answer": None,
            "error": str(e)
        }
```

The research method conducts a single search with error handling. It invokes agent_executor, captures the output, and returns a structured dictionary containing success status, query text, answer, and error messages if any exception occurs.

```python
def batch_research(self, queries: list) -> list:
    """Research multiple queries"""
    results = []
    for query in queries:
        print(f"\n Researching: {query}")
        result = self.research(query)
        results.append(result)
    return results
```

This method automates handling multiple queries. It iterates through each query, prints progress, calls research internally, and aggregates results into a list of dictionaries. It's a convenient wrapper for bulk execution while reusing the single-query logic. The batch_research method loops through multiple queries, collects results, and returns them as a list of dictionaries.

Testing the research agent

We create the agent, run a few queries, and observe results. Let us start with the preparation of queries:

```python
# Create research agent
research_agent = ResearchAgent(llm)
print(" Research Agent created successfully!")

# Test the research agent
print("\n Testing Research Agent:")

research_queries = [
    "What is the current population of Japan and how has it changed over the last decade?",
    "How does machine learning work and what are its main applications?",
    "What are the environmental benefits of solar energy?"
]
```

This block sets up `ResearchAgent` with a language model (`llm`). A confirmation message is printed, followed by a short banner announcing testing. The `research_queries` list is then prepared with three diverse queries for the agent to process.

With queries ready, the code moves into the execution loop:

```python
for query in research_queries:
    print(f"\n{'='*80}")
    print(f" 🔬 Research Query: {query}")
    print('='*80)
    result = research_agent.research(query)
    if result['success']:
        print(f" 📋 Research Complete!")
        print(f" Answer: {result['answer']}")
    else:
        print(f" ✖ Research Failed: {result['error']}")
```

This loop iterates over each prepared query. For readability, separator lines are printed before displaying the query. Each query is passed to the agent's research method. Based on success, the code prints either the answer with a 📋 marker or an error with ✖.

The tests demonstrate how the combined agent can answer complex questions by searching live data and applying reasoning with calculations. This showcases the potential of chaining multiple tools into one coherent workflow.

With this progress secured, the agent is no longer a simple prototype but a growing system ready to handle broader challenges. From here, the horizon expands toward scheduling, data analysis, and seamless connections to external services, each new tool transforming the agent into a more dynamic and capable collaborator.

Step 7: Specialized customer service agents

At this stage, we'll shape role-specific agents for technical, billing, and general inquiries. We'll define a reusable base class, configure its executor, and then implement specialized subclasses with focused prompts and toolsets.

Defining the base specialized agent

In the following code, we create a reusable agent wrapper that sets a specialty, system prompt, and execution strategy:

1. We start by defining a reusable base class that captures role, tools, and prompting defaults. The constructor stores the language model, a role label, and the toolset. If no system prompt is given, it automatically generates one that matches the specialty, ensuring that the agent stays consistent in its behavior and tone:

    ```python
    class SpecializedAgent:
        """Base class for specialized customer service agents"""

        def __init__(
            self, llm, specialty: str, tools: list,
            system_prompt: str = None
        ):
            self.llm = llm
            self.specialty = specialty
            self.tools = tools
            self.system_prompt = system_prompt or
                f"You are a helpful {specialty} specialist."
    ```

2. We then create the agent itself, using the ReAct framework to combine reasoning with tool usage. Here, the agent is tied to the language model, the tools it can use, and a guiding prompt that instructs it on how to alternate between reasoning and acting:

    ```python
    self.agent = create_react_agent(llm, tools, react_prompt)
    ```

3. Next, we initialize AgentExecutor, the runtime component that manages how the agent runs, limits execution time, and handles errors gracefully:

    ```python
    self.agent_executor = AgentExecutor(
        agent=self.agent,
        tools=tools,
        verbose=False,
        max_iterations=2,
        max_execution_time=20,
        handle_parsing_errors=True,
        return_intermediate_steps=False
    )
    ```

This setup ensures that the agent runs efficiently: it will try, at most, two reasoning action loops, won't exceed 20 seconds, and will recover if its output needs light correction. Intermediate steps are hidden for clarity, keeping results concise for end users.

With the base in place, we can now define how each role handles incoming messages.

Handling incoming inquiries in a role

Simple queries are answered directly via the LLM; the more complex ones use the agents:

1. We begin by looking at the method itself and its overall structure. This method routes incoming customer queries. It starts with a `try` block where the query is analyzed and processed, and a single except branch ensures that any unexpected errors are caught gracefully, returning a fallback message:

```python
def handle(self, query: str) -> str:
    """Handle a customer inquiry with better error handling"""
    try:
        # logic for simple vs. complex queries
        ...
    except Exception as e:
        ...
```

2. Next comes the success path within the try block. The logic distinguishes between *simple* queries (short and not involving calculation or search) and *complex* ones. Simple queries are passed directly to the language model for a quick answer. Complex ones are routed through the agent executor, which can reason and use tools. A polite fallback message is returned if the executor fails to produce output:

```python
# For simple queries, try direct LLM response first
if len(query.split()) < 10 and not any(word in query.lower()
for word in ['calculate', 'compute', 'search']):
    enhanced_query = f"As a {self.specialty} specialist, provide a
helpful response to: {query}"
    result = self.llm.invoke(enhanced_query)
    return result.content

# For complex queries, use the agent
enhanced_query = f"As a {self.specialty} specialist, help with:
{query}"
result = self.agent_executor.invoke({"input": enhanced_query})
```

```
return result.get('output', 'I apologize, I was unable to process
your request. Please try rephrasing.')
```

3. Finally, we look at the exception handling. This block ensures resilience. Instead of exposing errors, the system apologizes and directs the customer toward human support if needed. This maintains user trust while gracefully handling failures:

```
except Exception as e:
    return f"I apologize for the technical difficulty. For immediate
assistance with '{query}', please contact our support team
directly."
```

The overall approach keeps straightforward questions fast and tool-free while routing trickier requests through the ReAct reasoning loop, balancing responsiveness with capability.

Implementing role-specific agents

To build agents that can handle different kinds of customer queries, we'll implement SpecializedAgent subclasses. Each agent class sets a focused prompt and a minimal toolset tailored to its support channel. We'll walk through them step by step, starting with technical support, then billing, and finally, general inquiries:

1. We begin with the technical support agent. This class extends the specialized agent and sets its role to handling technical issues. It comes with a carefully crafted system prompt that emphasizes troubleshooting and step-by-step guidance. To support this role, the agent is given access to the web search tool, enabling it to look up known issues and fixes as part of its reasoning:

```
class TechnicalSupportAgent(SpecializedAgent):
    """Specialized agent for technical support issues"""
    def __init__(self, llm):
        system_prompt = """You are a technical support specialist.
You help customers with:
        - Software bugs and errors
        - Installation and setup issues
        - Performance problems
        - Feature usage and configuration
        - Troubleshooting steps
        Always provide clear, step-by-step solutions when
possible."""
        super().__init__(
```

```
            llm=llm,
            specialty="technical support",
            tools=[web_search_tool],  # Look up known issues and
fixes
            system_prompt=system_prompt
        )
```

2. The billing agent follows the same structure but shifts its role toward payment and sub-scription issues. Its system prompt encourages empathy and clear next steps, while the toolset switches to the calculator for handling refunds and prorations:

```
class BillingSupportAgent(SpecializedAgent):
    """Specialized agent for billing and payment issues"""
    def __init__(self, llm):
        system_prompt = """You are a billing support specialist. You
help customers with:
        - Payment processing issues
        - Subscription management
        - Refund requests
        - Invoice questions
        - Pricing inquiries
        Always be empathetic and provide clear next steps."""
        super().__init__(
            llm=llm,
            specialty="billing support",
            tools=[calculator_tool],  # Calculate refunds or
prorations
            system_prompt=system_prompt
        )
```

3. Finally, the general support agent adapts the same base pattern for broad inquiries such as account questions and product information. Its responses are meant to be concise and friendly, and it once again uses the web search tool to provide up-to-date general answers:

```
class GeneralSupportAgent(SpecializedAgent):
    """Specialized agent for general inquiries"""
    def __init__(self, llm):
        system_prompt = """You are a general customer support
specialist. You help customers with:
```

```
            - General product information
            - Account questions
            - Policy clarifications
            - Basic how-to
            Keep responses concise and friendly."""
            super().__init__(
                llm=llm,
                specialty="general customer support",
                tools=[web_search_tool],  # Search for general
        information
                system_prompt=system_prompt
            )
```

Each subclass defines its own system prompt, shaping tone and scope while selecting tools suited to its domain—search for technical and general roles, and a calculator for billing. Despite these differences, they all inherit the same handler method, enabling consistent logic and preparing them for orchestration into a multi-agent system.

Now that the palette of specialized agents is prepared, it's time to bring them together. By orchestrating their complementary strengths, we can create a coordinated multi-agent system capable of handling diverse customer needs.

Step 8: Multi-agent customer service system

Now, we'll assemble the specialized agents into a unified service. The system class initializes each role, classifies incoming queries, routes them to the right agent, and returns structured results:

1. We begin by creating the system and initializing agents. We construct a controller that owns one instance of each role-specific agent. This initializer prepares the system to handle technical, billing, and general inquiries without additional configuration in calling code:

```
class CustomerServiceSystem:
    """Intelligent customer service system with multiple specialized
    agents"""

    def __init__(self, llm):
        self.llm = llm
        self.technical_agent = TechnicalSupportAgent(llm)
        self.billing_agent = BillingSupportAgent(llm)
        self.general_agent = GeneralSupportAgent(llm)
```

2. We then classify which agent should respond. A brief LLM prompt maps an inquiry to TECHNICAL, BILLING, or GENERAL using an exactly one word instruction:

```python
def route_inquiry(self, inquiry: str) -> str:
    """Determine which agent should handle the inquiry using
direct LLM call"""

    routing_prompt = f"""Classify this customer inquiry. Respond
with exactly one word: TECHNICAL, BILLING, or GENERAL.

TECHNICAL: app crashes, bugs, errors, installation, performance,
login
BILLING: payments, subscriptions, refunds, invoices, pricing
GENERAL: information, account questions, policies, how-to

Inquiry: "{inquiry}"

Classification:"""

    try:
        result = self.llm.invoke(routing_prompt)
        classification = result.content.strip().upper()
        if "TECHNICAL" in classification:
            return "TECHNICAL"
        elif "BILLING" in classification:
            return "BILLING"
        else:
            return "GENERAL"
    except Exception as e:
        print(f"Routing failed: {e}, defaulting to GENERAL")
        return "GENERAL"
```

This simple classifier keeps routing lightweight and avoids unnecessary tool calls, while remaining easy to extend with more categories later.

3. Once classified, the system calls the corresponding agent and returns a structured record:

```python
def handle_inquiry(self, inquiry: str) -> dict:
    """Process a customer inquiry through the appropriate
agent"""
    route = self.route_inquiry(inquiry)

    if route == "TECHNICAL":
        agent_name = "Technical Support"
        response = self.technical_agent.handle(inquiry)
    elif route == "BILLING":
        agent_name = "Billing Support"
        response = self.billing_agent.handle(inquiry)
    else:
        agent_name = "General Support"
        response = self.general_agent.handle(inquiry)

    return {
        "inquiry": inquiry,
        "routed_to": route,
        "agent_name": agent_name,
        "response": response
    }
```

The returned dictionary makes it straightforward to display which agent answered and why, along with the agent's message.

4. A small convenience method processes a list of inquiries and returns a list of results. This helper enables simple load testing or multi-user simulations without additional boilerplate:

```python
def batch_handle(self, inquiries: list) -> list:
    """Handle multiple inquiries"""
    results = []
    for inquiry in inquiries:
        result = self.handle_inquiry(inquiry)
        results.append(result)
    return results
```

5. Finally, we create the system and run a few sample inquiries end-to-end to observe rout-
    ing and responses:

```python
cs_system = CustomerServiceSystem(llm)
print("🎯 Multi-Agent Customer Service System created
successfully!")

test_inquiries = [
    "App crashes on startup",
    "Need refund for last month",
    "What are your hours?",
    "Password reset help"
]

for inquiry in test_inquiries:
    print(f"\n{'='*80}")
    print(f"📧 Customer Inquiry: {inquiry}")
    print('='*80)
    result = cs_system.handle_inquiry(inquiry)
    print(f"🎯 Routed to: {result['agent_name']} ({result['routed_
to']})")
    print(f" Response: {result['response']}")
```

These tests confirm the full flow: classify, route, and respond. From here, you can add more spe-
cialties, extend routing logic, or integrate live backend APIs for real actions.

With the agents orchestrated into a working system, we now turn to the next step, which is creating an interactive Colab interface (inputs, dropdowns, and buttons) to experiment with our
agents directly.

Step 9: Interactive demo interface setup

Before testing the orchestrated agents interactively, it makes sense to bring in a lightweight interface. Jupyter notebooks allow quick prototyping, and with ipywidgets, we can add buttons,
selectors, and input fields without leaving Colab. This lets us focus on the behavior of agents
while experimenting live in the notebook.

Importing UI components

To achieve this, IPython's display utilities are combined with `ipywidgets`, giving us everything from buttons and dropdowns to output panes and HTML snippets that can be rendered inline:

```python
from IPython.display import display, clear_output, HTML
import ipywidgets as widgets
```

These imports supply the basic building blocks for interactive elements and display helpers that will later tie agent responses to visible notebook output.

Creating the interface class

Instead of scattering UI logic, the design is wrapped inside a dedicated class. This approach keeps responsibilities clear. Widget creation, event wiring, and rendering are neatly organized in one place, making it easier to reuse or extend later:

```python
class AgentDemoInterface:
    """Interactive demo interface for all agents using Jupyter widgets"""

    def __init__(self):
        # Store references to all our agents
        self.calculator_agent = calculator_agent
        self.research_agent = research_agent
        self.cs_system = cs_system

        # Create the interface widgets
        self.create_widgets()
        self.setup_event_handlers()

        # Display the interface
        self.display_interface()
```

The constructor anchors references to the existing agents, then immediately builds the widgets, attaches handlers, and presents the interface in the notebook.

By centralizing everything in one class, the demo interface acts like a control panel. It allows us to switch agents, type a query, and view answers side by side, all inside the Colab environment without additional setup.

Creating widgets

We now define the title, agent selector, query area, buttons, output container, and example buttons for quick testing:

1. We start by creating the title so the interface immediately communicates purpose and context:

```
self.title = widgets.HTML(
    value="<h2>🤖 Multi-Agent AI System Demo</h2><p>Test all the
agents we've built in this workshop!</p>",
    layout=widgets.Layout(margin='0 0 20px 0')
)
```

This HTML widget renders a heading and a short subtitle with extra bottom margin. It anchors the UI visually and sets a consistent tone for the demo. A clear title establishes context instantly, making the interface feel intentional, polished, and ready for hands-on experimentation.

2. Next, an agent selector lets us switch easily between calculator, research, and customer service capabilities:

```
self.agent_selector = widgets.Dropdown(
    options=[
        ('🧮 Calculator Agent', 'calculator'),
        ('🔬 Research Agent', 'research'),
        ('🎧 Customer Service System', 'customer_service')
    ],
    value='calculator',
    description='Choose Agent:',
    style={'description_width': '120px'},
    layout=widgets.Layout(width='400px')
)
```

This dropdown maps readable labels to internal values, sets a default, and sizes both description and control. It's the primary routing switch. A single, descriptive selector reduces friction, guiding the flow and preventing confusion about which agent will handle requests.

3. We then add a multi-line text area so queries can be typed or pasted comfortably:

```
self.query_input = widgets.Textarea(
    value='What is 25 * 47 + 138?',
    placeholder='Enter your query here...',
    description='Your Query:',
    layout=widgets.Layout(width='100%', height='100px'),
    style={'description_width': '120px'}
)
```

The text area provides space for longer prompts, with sensible defaults, placeholder guidance, and consistent label width for alignment with other controls. A generously sized input encourages experimentation, accommodates longer questions, and keeps the UI tidy and predictable.

4. A submit_button triggers processing of the current prompt using the selected agent:

```
self.submit_button = widgets.Button(
    description=' 🚀 Submit Query',
    button_style='primary',
    layout=widgets.Layout(width='200px', height='40px')
)
```

The button uses an attention-drawing style and fixed dimensions to signal its primary action clearly and remain stable across layouts. A prominent call to action invites interaction, signaling where to click and keeping the workflow obvious for quick testing.

5. A clear_button resets the output area, helping iterative runs stay readable:

```
self.clear_button = widgets.Button(
    description=' 🗑 Clear Output',
    button_style='warning',
    layout=widgets.Layout(width='150px', height='40px')
)
```

A distinct visual style differentiates this control from submission, while fixed sizing maintains overall alignment and balance. Easy output clearing supports rapid cycles, preventing clutter and keeping each run's results focused and visible.

An output container then displays responses with borders, padding, and scrolling for long content:

```python
self.output_area = widgets.Output(
    layout=widgets.Layout(
        border='1px solid #ccc',
        padding='10px',
        margin='10px 0',
        height='400px',
        overflow='auto'
    )
)
```

The bordered, padded box separates results from controls; fixed height and scroll behavior keep the layout compact during longer sessions. A well-framed output region improves readability and preserves structure as responses grow, ensuring the interface remains calm and organized.

6. We also define example prompts per agent, so trial runs are one click away:

```python
self.examples = {
    'calculator': [
        'What is 25 * 47 + 138?',
        'Calculate 15% of 250',
        'If I have $1000 and spend $347, how much is left?'
    ],
    'research': [
        'What is the current population of Tokyo?',
        'How does solar energy work?',
        'What are the benefits of electric vehicles?'
    ],
    'customer_service': [
        'My app keeps crashing when I upload files',
        'I was charged twice for my subscription',
        'How do I change my password?'
    ]
}
```

Curated examples showcase typical use cases per agent, making it effortless to explore without thinking up prompts. Prefilled examples accelerate discovery, reveal each agent's strengths, and provide reliable baselines for quick sanity checks.

7. Finally, we generate buttons that load those examples on click. Each example gets a small info-styled button that injects the text into the input on click, wiring convenience directly into the workflow. Clickable examples remove friction, encouraging rapid iteration and letting us compare outputs consistently across agents:

```python
self.example_buttons = {}
for agent_type, examples in self.examples.items():
    buttons = []
    for i, example in enumerate(examples):
        btn = widgets.Button(
            description=f"Example {i+1}",
            button_style='info',
            layout=widgets.Layout(width='100px', margin='2px')
        )
        btn.example_text = example
        btn.on_click(self.load_example)
        buttons.append(btn)
    self.example_buttons[agent_type] = buttons
```

This method assembles a cohesive panel, identity, routing, input, actions, output, and examples, so experiments are smooth, repeatable, and visually organized, enabling focused evaluation of agent behavior without UI distractions.

Building the chat interface workflow

To complete the user-facing side of our application, we need to connect the interface to the model. This involves more than just sending a query. It requires wiring events, rendering the interface, handling responses, and keeping the user experience smooth with loading states and cleared inputs.

In this section, we'll bring these pieces together into one continuous workflow that powers the chat interaction:

1. We begin by connecting user actions, such as button clicks and dropdown changes, to their respective handler functions so the interface responds dynamically. These bindings direct user actions to the appropriate methods—submit triggers processing, clear resets the output, and agent_change refreshes example buttons and default text:

```python
def setup_event_handlers(self):
    """Setup event handlers for widgets"""
    self.submit_button.on_click(self.handle_query)
    self.clear_button.on_click(self.clear_output)
    self.agent_selector.observe(self.on_agent_change,
        names='value')
```

2. We then arrange the controls and output in a vertical stack, and render the complete interface so it appears directly inside the notebook, as described in the list that follows:

```python
def display_interface(self):
    """Display the complete interface"""

    # Control panel
    controls = widgets.VBox([
        self.title,
        self.agent_selector,
        widgets.HTML("<b>Quick Examples:</b>"),
        widgets.HBox(
            self.example_buttons[self.agent_selector.value]),
        self.query_input,
        widgets.HBox([self.submit_button, self.clear_button])
    ])

    # Main interface
    main_interface = widgets.VBox([
        controls,
        widgets.HTML("<b>Output:</b>"),
```

```
        self.output_area
    ])

    display(main_interface)
```

- `widgets.VBox([...])` stacks controls vertically; the inner `HBox` groups example buttons and the action buttons
- `display(main_interface)` renders the composite UI in the current notebook cell

Now that the UI is visible, we'll add behavior for agent switching, loading examples, clearing output, and handling queries.

3. When the chosen agent is switched, the interface updates its example buttons and automatically loads a matching sample query into the input field. This ensures that the interface stays in sync with the selected agent, giving the user relevant example prompts immediately:

```
def on_agent_change(self, change):
    """Handle agent selection change"""
    new_agent = change['new']

    # Update example buttons
    for widget in self.example_buttons[new_agent]:
        widget.layout.display = 'block'

    # Update example text based on agent
    examples = self.examples[new_agent]
    if examples:
        self.query_input.value = examples[0]
```

4. Clicking an example button places its predefined prompt directly into the input field, making it easy to test queries without typing them manually. This is a small convenience that speeds up trying different agent scenarios without manual typing:

```
def load_example(self, button):
    """Load example query when button is clicked"""
    self.query_input.value = button.example_text
```

5. This method then clears the output display, giving a clean slate for the next interaction, and keeping the interface easy to follow. Using `clear_output()` keeps the display tidy between runs, especially during demos:

```python
def clear_output(self, button):
    """Clear the output area"""
    with self.output_area:
        clear_output()
```

Handling query submission

This method takes the active agent and current query, sends the request to the appropriate back-end, and then displays the response in a structured, readable format:

1. We begin with the method signature to establish the entry point for handling a submitted query from the interface:

```python
def handle_query(self, button):
    """Handle query submission"""
```

This method is bound to the `submit_button`. When clicked, it orchestrates clearing the display, validating input, routing by agent type, and printing results or errors.

2. Now, we scope output to the widget, clear previous content, and prepare inputs for processing:

```python
with self.output_area:
    clear_output()

    agent_type = self.agent_selector.value
    query = self.query_input.value.strip()

    if not query:
        print("✖ Please enter a query")
        return

    print(f"🤖 Processing with {self.agent_selector.label}
agent...")
    print(f" Query: {query}")
    print("=" * 60)
```

The with context sends all prints into the output widget, clear_output() wipes old results, inputs are read and validated, and a short header shows which agent will handle the query.

3.   Next comes the try/except skeleton that separates the normal execution path from error handling:

```
try:
    # route by agent type and print structured results
    ...
except Exception as e:
    # print a helpful error and guidance
    ...
```

The try block contains routing and printing logic; the except block provides a graceful fallback so the UI never crashes and the user sees clear next steps.

4.   Inside the try block, we handle the calculator branch first—invoke the agent and print its output:

```
if agent_type == 'calculator':
    result = self.calculator_agent.invoke({"input": query})
    print(" Calculator Result:")
    print(f" {result.get('output', 'Calculation completed')}")
```

This path sends the query to the calculator agent's invoke method and prints a labeled, concise result for arithmetic or simple computations.

5.   The research branch delegates to research_agent.research(query) and prints either an answer or an explicit error:

```
elif agent_type == 'research':
    result = self.research_agent.research(query)
    if result['success']:
        print(" Research Complete:")
        print(f" {result['answer']}")
    else:
        print(f" Research Error: {result['error']}")
```

Here, the helper method returns a structured dictionary. Success prints the answer; failure surfaces the captured error message without raising an exception.

6. The `customer_service` branch calls the multi-agent system, then shows routing info and the final response:

```
elif agent_type == 'customer_service':
    result = self.cs_system.handle_inquiry(query)
    print("◎ Customer Service Response:")
    print(f"🔹 Routed to: {result['agent_name']}")
    print(f" Response: {result['response']}")
```

This path reveals which specialized agent handled the inquiry and displays its message, providing transparency about internal routing decisions.

7. After any branch completes, a closing marker confirms success and visually separates runs:

```
print("\n" + "=" * 60)
print("   Query processing completed!")
```

These final prints add a spacer line and a completion note, making repeated runs easy to scan during demos and testing.

8. Finally, the exception handler converts unexpected failures into friendly guidance without exposing stack traces:

```
except Exception as e:
    print(f"✖ Unexpected error: {str(e)}")
    print("Please try again or contact support.")
```

Any unanticipated error is caught, summarized, and followed by clear next steps, keeping the interface resilient and user-oriented.

This method takes the currently selected agent and user query, first ensuring that the input is valid. It then routes execution to the correct backend (calculator, research, or customer service) and prints structured, labeled outputs. Errors are caught gracefully, making demonstrations smooth, readable, and resilient during interactive exploration.

9. A final message confirms that the class is defined and ready to instantiate:

```
print("  Interactive demo interface class created successfully!")
```

This wraps the setup nicely, so the next step can focus on launching the demo.

Step 10: Launching interactive demo

With the interface defined, we can now launch a live demo in the notebook. This step prints simple usage instructions and creates the interface, which renders automatically through its `display_interface()` method.

Usage instructions

A brief checklist is presented to orient newcomers, giving clear guidance on how to start interacting with the demo effectively:

```
# Display usage instructions
print(" 🚀 Launching Interactive Multi-Agent Demo Interface!")
print("\ni  How to use:")
print("1. Select an agent from the dropdown")
print("2. Click an example button or type your own query")
print("3. Click 'Submit Query' to see the agent in action")
print("4. Try different agents with various types of questions")
print("\n" + "="*60)
```

These instructions frame the experience and reduce confusion during a live workshop.

Creating and displaying the interface

We create an instance of `AgentDemoInterface`, linking it to our agents and allowing the interface to build and display itself inside the notebook:

```
# Create and display the demo interface
demo_interface = AgentDemoInterface()
```

This single line brings the entire system together in a usable UI. You can select an agent, try examples, and watch the outputs stream into the panel.

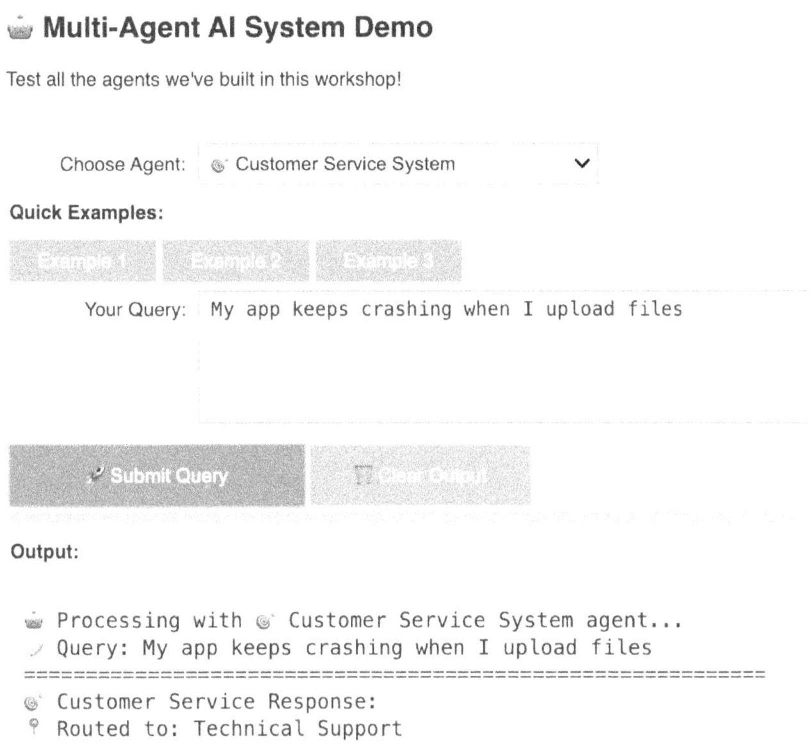

👑 **Multi-Agent AI System Demo**

Test all the agents we've built in this workshop!

Choose Agent: 🎧 Customer Service System ⌄

Quick Examples:

Example 1   Example 2   Example 3

Your Query: My app keeps crashing when I upload files

Submit Query   Clear Output

Output:

```
👑 Processing with 🎧 Customer Service System agent...
✓ Query: My app keeps crashing when I upload files
=================================================================
🎧 Customer Service Response:
📍 Routed to: Technical Support
```

Figure 5.7: UI screen for agent testing

The interface is ready. Don't just read the code—use it. Select an agent, type in a query, and press **Submit Query**. Try the examples or invent your own. Watch how each agent responds differently. This hands-on exploration transforms theory into a tangible, interactive experience.

Step 11: Agent performance testing

Now that the agents and UI are functioning, it's time to measure how they behave under realistic workloads. This step provides a scaffolded performance harness that times responses, counts successes/failures, and summarizes results, making it easy to compare different agents and identify optimization opportunities.

Defining the performance tester class

Testing logic is organized into a dedicated class, and here we outline the test_agent_performance method in scaffold form to highlight its flow without overwhelming detail:

```python
import time
from datetime import datetime


class AgentPerformanceTester:
    """Test and measure agent performance"""

    def __init__(self):
        self.test_results = []

    def test_agent_performance(
        self, agent_name: str, agent_func, test_queries: list
    ):
        """Run multiple queries against an agent and collect timing &
success metrics"""
        # 1) initialize results structure
        # 2) iterate over test queries
        #     - start timer
        #     - attempt the agent call
        #     - on success: compute elapsed, update success counters, build
query_result
        #     - on error: compute elapsed, update failure counters, build
query_result
        #     - append query_result to results
        # 3) compute final averages / success rate
        # 4) persist to self.test_results and print a summary
        # 5) return results

        ...
```

This scaffold outlines the control flow while omitting specific print statements and minor details, keeping attention on the core mechanics you'll measure and report.

Result initialization

The method begins by setting up a results dictionary, establishing counters and storage fields that will track query outcomes, timing, and overall success metrics throughout the performance test:

```
results = {
    'agent_name': agent_name,
    'total_queries': len(test_queries),
    'successful_queries': 0,
    'failed_queries': 0,
    'total_time': 0,
    'average_time': 0,
    'query_results': []
}
```

This dictionary accumulates run-wide metrics and per-query records. It tracks counts, total/average time, and a query_results list for granular analysis or later export.

All tests loop

The method proceeds with a loop over all test queries, timing each attempt, handling both success and error cases, and appending a structured record to the results list for consistency:

```
for i, query in enumerate(test_queries, 1):
    #  start time measurement
    start_time = time.time()
    try:
        #  try running the agent call
        #     e.g., result = agent_func(query)
        #  measure elapsed time on success

        ...
    except Exception as e:
        #  measure elapsed time on error

        ...
    #  append per-query record
    results['query_results'].append(query_result)
```

The loop times each attempt, separates success and error paths, and ensures that every query produces a consistent query_result entry added to results['query_results'].

Process time-measured agent call (success path)

In the success path, the agent's output is captured, execution time is measured, and counters are updated. A structured record is stored, including result_length, to help detect unusually short or long responses:

```python
result = agent_func(query)
end_time = time.time()
execution_time = end_time - start_time

results['successful_queries'] += 1
results['total_time'] += execution_time

query_result = {
    'query': query,
    'success': True,
    'execution_time': execution_time,
    'result_length': len(str(result))
}
```

On success, we compute elapsed time, increment success counters, and store a compact per-query record. Tracking result_length is handy to spot extremely short or unexpectedly long outputs.

Handle error (failure path)

In the failure path, execution time is still measured, failure counters are incremented, and the exception message is captured. This ensures that every query produces a consistent record, even when errors occur:

```python
end_time = time.time()
execution_time = end_time - start_time

results['failed_queries'] += 1
results['total_time'] += execution_time

query_result = {
    'query': query,
    'success': False,
    'execution_time': execution_time,
    'error': str(e)
}
```

Errors still yield a valid record: we time them, increment failure counters, and store the exception text for later review without interrupting the batch run.

Final metrics calculation and persistence

At the end, averages and success rates are computed to summarize performance. The results are stored, a summary is printed, and the framework is ready for iterative testing and refinement:

```python
if results['total_queries'] > 0:
    results['average_time'] = \
        results['total_time'] / results['total_queries']
    results['success_rate'] = \
        results['successful_queries'] / results['total_queries']

self.test_results.append(results)
self.print_performance_summary(results)
```

Average latency and success rate summarize the run's reliability and speed. We then persist the `results` object and emit a concise summary for quick inspection.

With the benchmarking scaffold in place, you can refine prompts, tune tools, or add caching. Then rerun tests to confirm measurable improvements.

Method: printing a summary of metrics

This helper prints a concise report after a run completes:

```python
def print_performance_summary(self, results):
    """Print performance summary"""
    print(f"\n📊 Performance Summary for {results['agent_name']}:")
    print(f"   Total Queries: {results['total_queries']}")
    print(f"   Successful: {results['successful_queries']}")
    print(f"   Failed: {results['failed_queries']}")
    print(f"   Success Rate: {results.get('success_rate', 0):.1%}")
    print(f"   Average Time: {results['average_time']:.2f}s")
    print(f"   Total Time: {results['total_time']:.2f}s")
```

This report surfaces the essential KPIs: throughput, reliability, and latency. You can extend it later to export CSV/JSON for dashboards.

Creating the tester and defining agent-specific functions

We instantiate the tester, define representative queries, and wrap each agent call in a small function that conforms to the agent_func(query) signature, as described in the following list:

```python
# Create performance tester
tester = AgentPerformanceTester()


# Test each agent
print(" 🔬 Starting comprehensive agent performance testing...")


# Test Calculator Agent
calc_queries = [
    "What is 15 + 25?",
    "Calculate 12 * 8",
    "What's 100 / 4?"
]


def test_calculator(query):
    return calculator_agent.invoke({"input": query})['output']
```

- `tester = AgentPerformanceTester()`: Initializes the harness and results store
- `calc_queries`: Small arithmetic suite
- `test_calculator(query)`: Adapts the calculator agent to the expected function signature and extracts the 'output' field

With the calculator path ready, we can add research and customer service wrappers.

Research agent wrapper and queries

This wrapper returns the answer on success and raises when the research agent reports an error:

```python
# Test Research Agent
research_queries = [
    "What is artificial intelligence?",
    "Benefits of renewable energy"
]


def test_research(query):
    result = research_agent.research(query)
```

```
if result['success']:
    return result['answer']
else:
    raise Exception(result['error'])
```

The wrapper enforces a fail-fast policy so errors are logged and counted, producing realistic reliability metrics.

Customer service system wrapper and queries

We route queries through the customer service system and return the human-readable response:

```
# Test Customer Service System
cs_queries = [
    "App crashes on startup",
    "Need refund help"
]

def test_customer_service(query):
    result = cs_system.handle_inquiry(query)
    return result['response']
```

This small adapter isolates how results are extracted without changing the tester's core logic.

Executing the performance runs

We pass each wrapper and its query set to the tester, which prints live progress and a summary per agent, as described in the following list:

```
tester.test_agent_performance("Calculator Agent", test_calculator,
        calc_queries)
tester.test_agent_performance("Research Agent", test_research,
        research_queries)
tester.test_agent_performance("Customer Service", test_customer_service,
        cs_queries)
```

- Each call triggers timing, logging, and a final KPI summary
- Results are appended to tester.test_results for later inspection

At this stage, our agents have been designed, orchestrated, and equipped with an interactive interface. The final step is performance testing, where metrics such as success rate and average response time reveal both individual effectiveness and system-wide behavior. These benchmarks highlight strengths, expose weaknesses, and provide a foundation for iterative improvement. Through refinement of prompts, new tools, or caching strategies, the system can steadily become more reliable and responsive, with each cycle validated against these baselines.

Over the course of the workshop, we progressed from foundational components to a dynamic multi-agent framework. Along the way, we integrated tools, created specialized agents, and built an interactive demo, ensuring that theory was reinforced by hands-on practice. By the conclusion, participants could experiment directly with agents, compare their outputs, and measure performance across tasks. This combination of design, execution, and evaluation showed how simple prototypes grow into scalable, production-ready systems, while also pointing toward creative extensions and real-world applications.

Workshop 2: Visual AI agents with n8n

Sometimes, coding a solution from scratch is not an option—too slow, too complex, or simply not worth the overhead. That's where n8n comes in, giving us the power to rapidly prototype workflows that are both fast and effective. In this workshop, we'll connect financial data, news feeds, and Mistral AI into one automated pipeline, ending with personalized trading insights delivered straight to Telegram. By the end, you'll see how quickly complex ideas can turn into working solutions.

It's time to set the stage. We'll begin by installing and preparing n8n, then connect it with a few free data sources that will power our workflow. These foundations will give us the inputs we need (symbols, price history, and news) that later steps will enrich and analyze.

Step 1: Setting up n8n and free data sources

In this opening step, we lay a stable foundation for our workflow: a consistent n8n environment and freely accessible data streams. You'll launch n8n with Docker, register your instance, tour the interface, and prepare the first Manual Trigger node. With this, the canvas becomes our playground for later AI-powered enrichment. Let's begin:

1. We'll start n8n locally to establish a clean, reproducible baseline across machines:

    ```
    # Launch n8n with Docker
    docker run -it --rm --name n8n -p 5678:5678 -v ~/.n8n:/home/node/.
    n8n docker.n8n.io/n8nio/n8n
    ```

After running this, a local workspace spins up, ready for your first workflow connections. This step unlocks the editor and ensures that you can save, execute, and manage workflows confidently.

2. For first-time users, the n8n registration screen shows the welcome page with a **Get started** button. Once you click on it, you will see the following form for owner account creation:

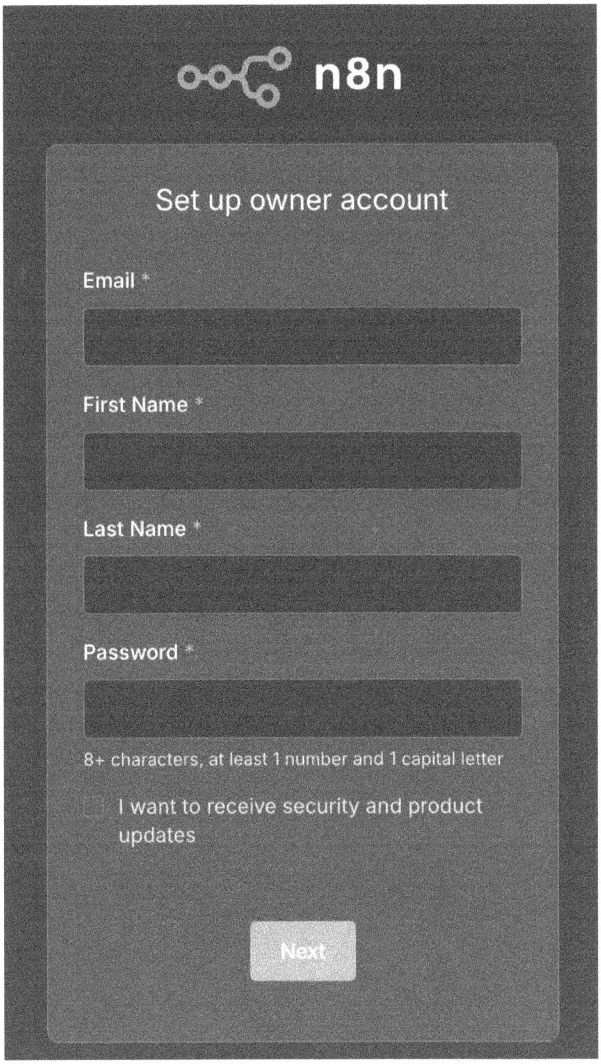

Figure 5.8: The n8n registration screen

Once registered, you'll immediately be able to access the main workspace with a clean canvas:

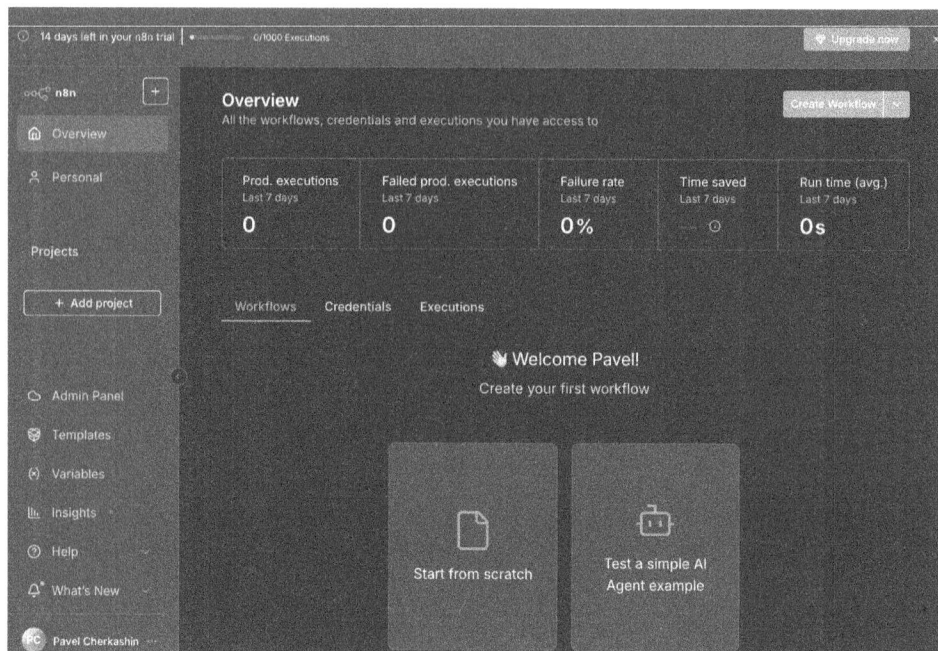

Figure 5.9: Main n8n workspace

3. We now locate and add the **Manual Trigger** node, the essential starting point for our workflow testing. Remember, any node can be searched in the right-hand palette and then simply dragged and dropped onto the canvas, making it quick to assemble even complex flows:

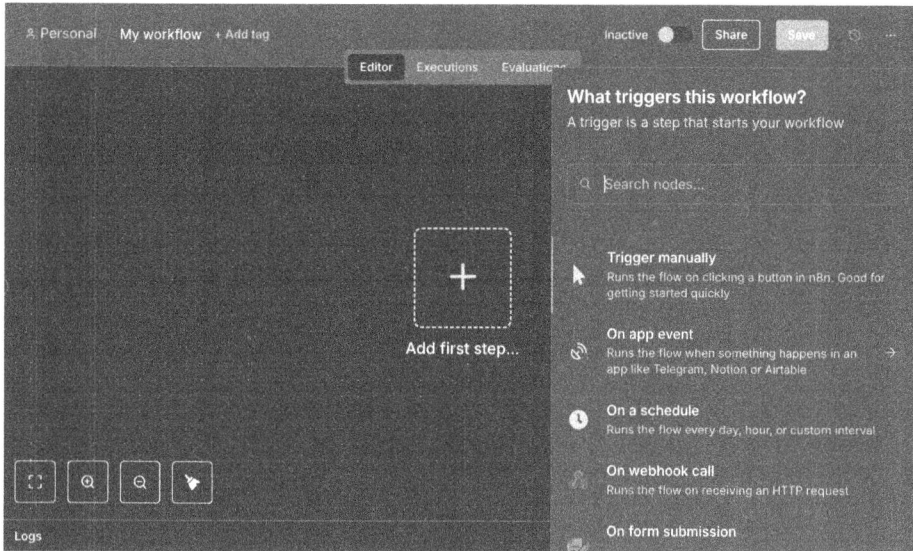

Figure 5.10: Node selection search box

You now have a running n8n, a registered workspace, and know how to add your first trigger node. The interface should feel familiar, the canvas ready. This foundation lets us safely iterate—no mystery, just clarity. Great start! The n8n tool has a heartbeat and a place to grow.

Next, we'll prepare Telegram for friendly notifications, creating a bot and group chat where insights will land.

Step 2: Configuring the Telegram bot and chat for notifications

In this step, we connect automation with people. You'll create a Telegram bot, secure its access token, set up a group chat, and capture the chat ID. This prepares the channel where your workflow will eventually post its insights, making the automation visible and collaborative. We start with Telegram communication with @BotFather.

> Telegram is available on iPhone, Android, Windows, and macOS, so you can use it on whatever device you prefer. If you don't already have an account, signing up is quick and free. Just download the app from `telegram.org/apps` and follow the on-screen steps. You'll be ready to chat with @BotFather in minutes.

The process begins with @BotFather, Telegram's official bot-creation tool. Open Telegram, search for @BotFather, and start a chat with it. Then, follow these steps:

1. To create a new bot by typing /newbot, when prompted, provide a **name** for your bot (this is what users will see). Choose a **username** ending with "bot" (e.g., MistralFinancialInsightBot). @BotFather will reply with a **unique API token**. Copy and store it securely. This token is required to authenticate and connect your bot from code:

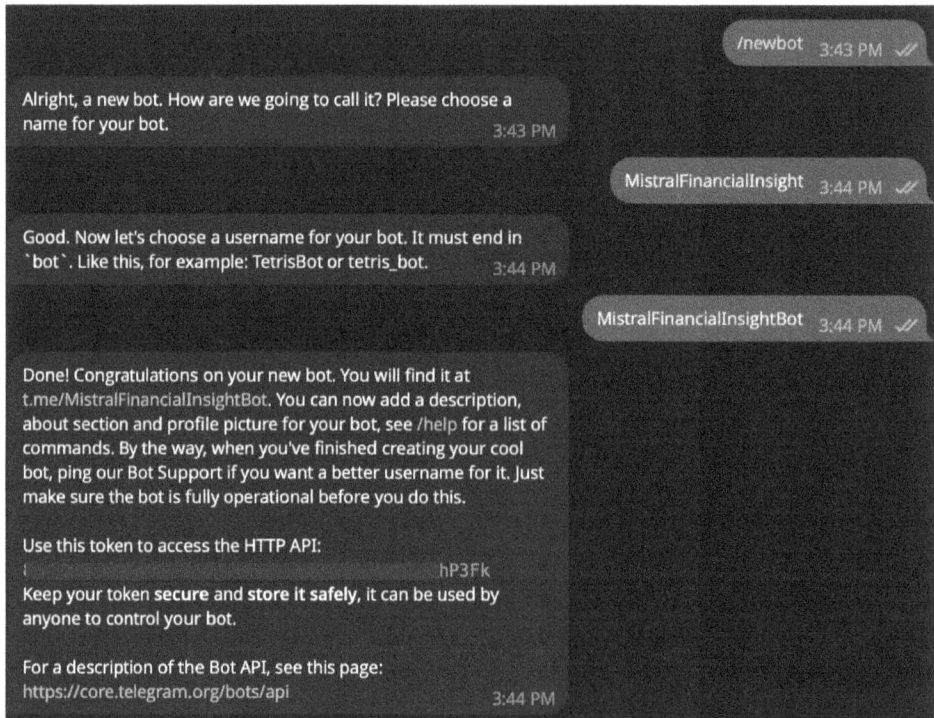

Figure 5.11: Creating a bot

As we can see in *Figure 5.11*, @BotFather returns the essential access token, which you'll need later to authorize n8n.

At this point, be sure to store the bot token securely. It's the key that allows your workflow to post messages reliably.

2. Next, you'll invite our new bot into a chat where results will be delivered. This could be a group of collaborators or your own test space. *Figure 5.12* illustrates the moment your bot is successfully added to a group, confirming it's ready to relay messages:

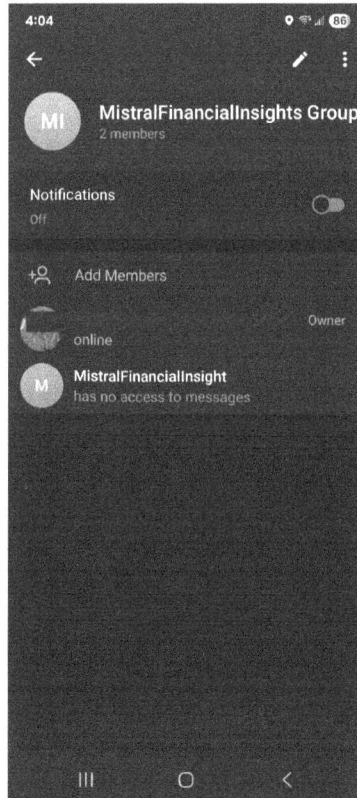

Figure 5.12: Bot added to group

3. To deliver messages, n8n must know exactly where to post them. We'll query Telegram's API to extract the numeric chat identifier. The URL template goes below `https://api.telegram.org/bot<BOT_TOKEN>/getUpdates`. You will need to replace the part of the URL with your own access token you received from `@BotFather`. Then, simply paste it in the browser address bar.

Figure 5.13 depicts the JSON response, where the chat ID is embedded. This value links your workflow to the right conversation:

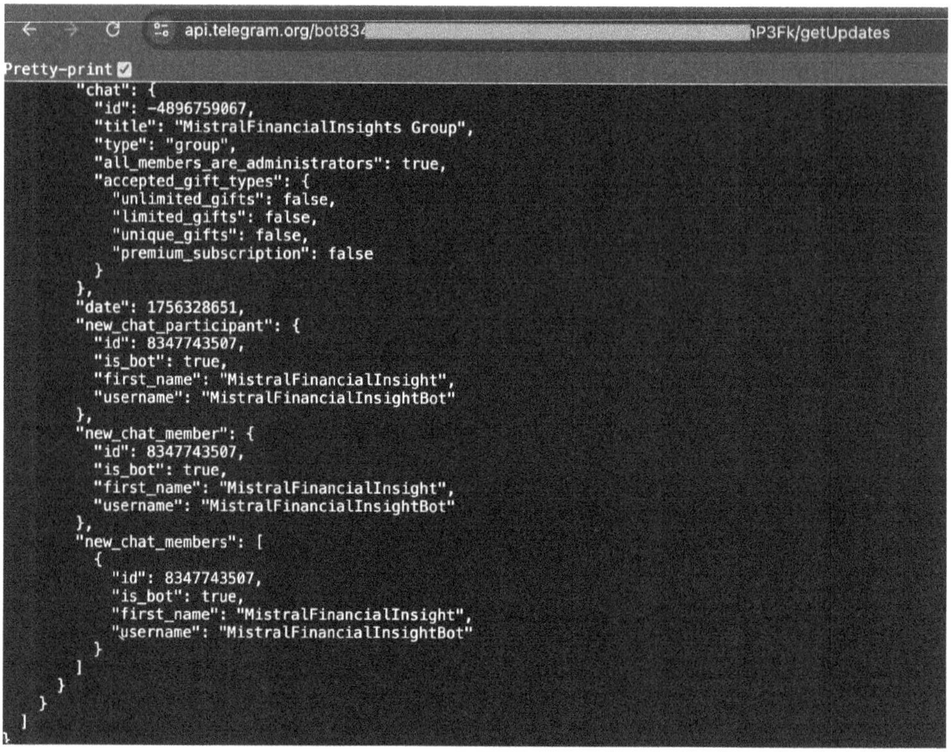

Figure 5.13: Chat ID via API

4. Next, scroll through the JSON until you find the `"chat"` object and note the value of its `"id"` field. In *Figure 5.14*, you'll notice the chat ID clearly highlighted in the payload, making it easy to copy into n8n later.

> Open the JSON in a proper editor such as VS Code or Sublime Text. Formatting and syntax highlighting will make it much easier to spot.

```
"chat": {
  "accepted_gift_types": {
    "limited_gifts": false,
    "premium_subscription": false,
    "unique_gifts": false,
    "unlimited_gifts": false
  },
  "all_members_are_administrators": true,
  "id": -4896759067,
  "title": "MistralFinancialInsights Group",
  "type": "group"
},
```

Figure 5.14: Chat ID highlighted

After completing this step, you now have a Telegram bot created, credentials saved, and the chat ID identified. Notifications now have a defined home. The automation will feel more alive when you open the line between data and dialogue.

Following this, we'll connect a manual trigger to an HTTP request and fetch live finance data from Yahoo to enrich our workflow.

Step 3: Adding a manual trigger and configuring HTTP requests

In this step, we bring dynamic data into play. You'll add a manual trigger to start the workflow on demand, then configure HTTP request nodes that pull market information from Yahoo Finance. These include the most active stocks, top gainers, and top losers, which are perfect seeds for later analysis.

Adding the manual trigger

The manual trigger lets you launch the workflow whenever you want, making it easy to test and refine as we go.

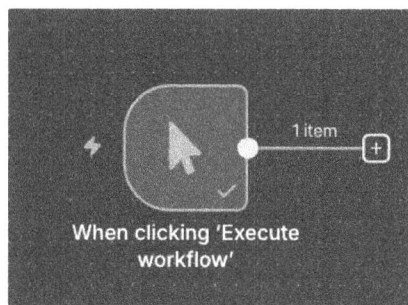

Figure 5.15: Manual trigger node

As shown in *Figure 5.15*, the trigger node sits at the very start of the canvas, ensuring that every execution begins consistently.

Adding the first HTTP request node

Next, connect an **HTTP request** node after the trigger. We'll query the Yahoo endpoint for the most active stocks.

Here is the endpoint URL we'll use for most active stocks: `https://query1.finance.yahoo.com/v1/finance/screener/predefined/saved?count=100&scrIds=most_actives`. This URL instructs Yahoo Finance to return a list of the 100 most active stocks, complete with volumes and price details:

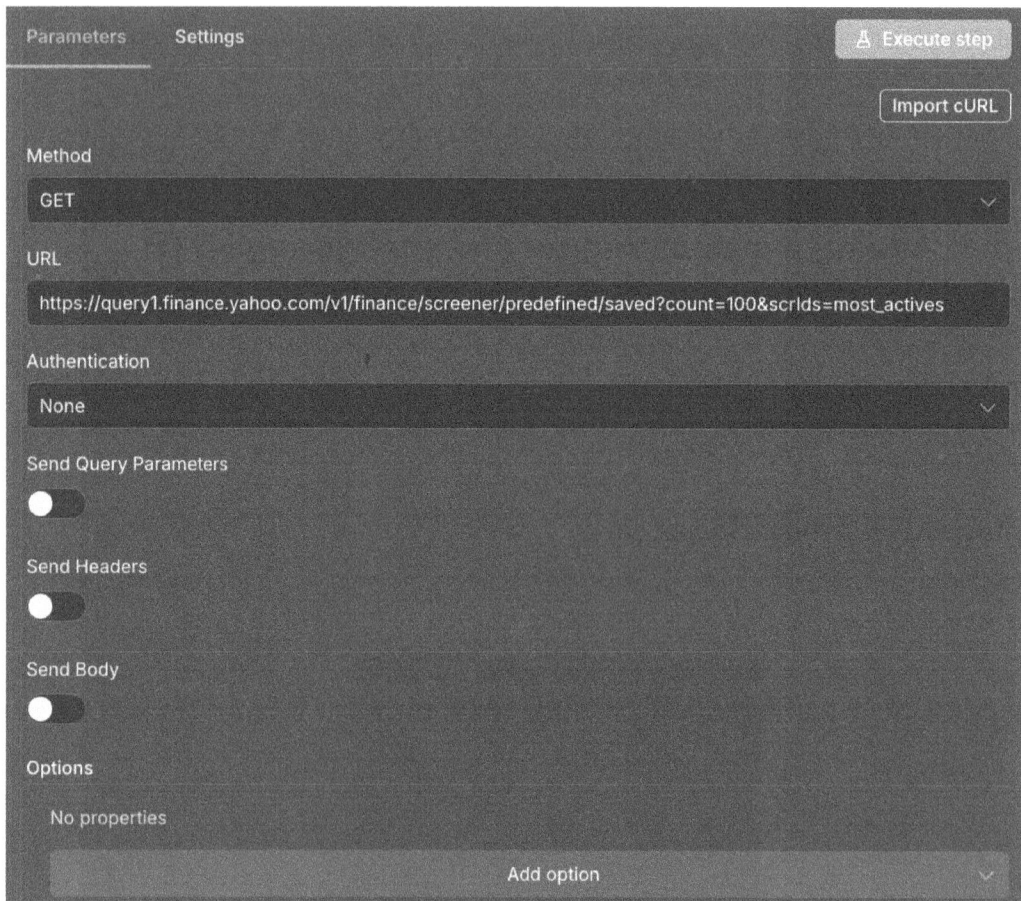

Figure 5.16: HTTP request connected

Figure 5.16 highlights how the HTTP request node connects seamlessly to the trigger, forming the pipeline's first live data connection.

Configuring the HTTP request node

Run the node manually by clicking the **Play** button on it once to confirm the response. The output should display JSON with stock data, ready for further transformation:

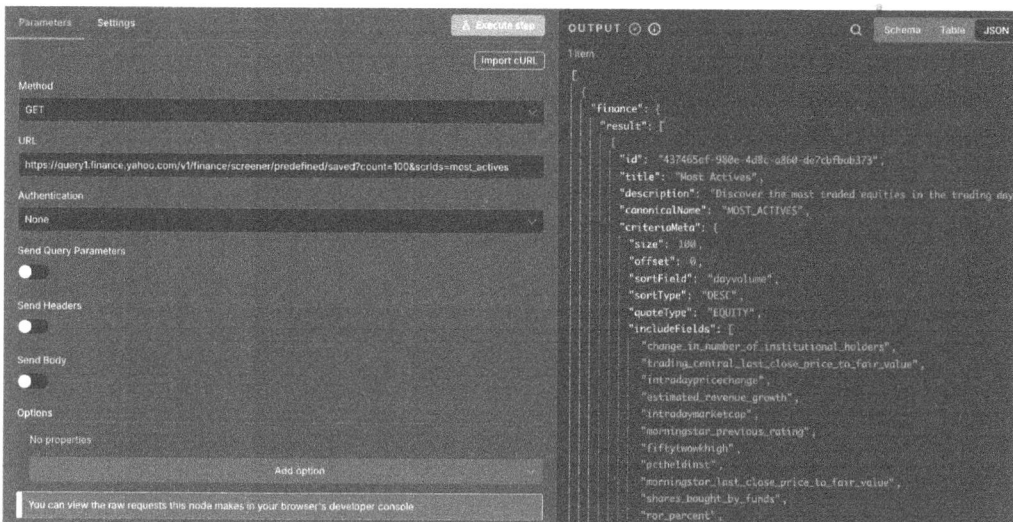

Figure 5.17: Request configuration

In *Figure 5.17*, you'll notice the request parameters and a JSON preview confirming that the node is fetching real-time market data. You can clearly observe how the HTTP request was set up and validated, displaying its parameters alongside the returned JSON data. There is an opportunity to review the raw payload to verify that symbols, prices, and metadata are present.

> Your list of tickers will likely differ, since market activity shifts constantly and new symbols rise to the top among active players.

Duplicating the HTTP requests for gainers and losers

To broaden our market picture, duplicate the node twice. Rename one for day gainers and the other for day losers. Adjust each URL accordingly:

- **Day gainers**: Use this endpoint to capture the day's top risers: `https://query1.finance.yahoo.com/v1/finance/screener/predefined/saved?count=100&scrIds=day_gainers`. This will output JSON with stocks climbing sharply during the session.

- **Day losers**: Use this endpoint to capture the day's steepest decliners: `https://query1.finance.yahoo.com/v1/finance/screener/predefined/saved?count=100&scrIds=day_losers`. This will return JSON with stocks currently trending downward.

After completing this step, your workflow now responds to a manual start, pulls live stock data, and prepares three distinct data streams. The pipeline is no longer static. It's breathing real information. That's a big leap forward.

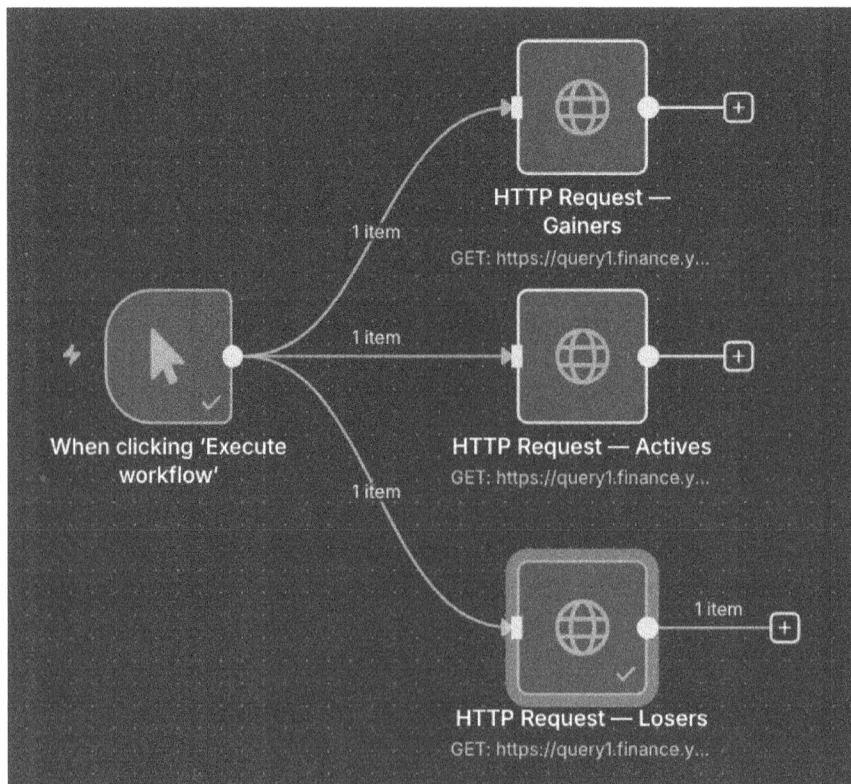

Figure 5.18: Three data gathering HTTP requests run in parallel

Following this, we'll merge the three outputs, remove duplicates, and sort by a useful metric, producing a clean, prioritized list for downstream steps.

Step 4: Merging, deduplicating, and sorting market data

At this point, we've pulled in three separate feeds: most active, top gainers, and top losers. Now, it's time to bring them together. In this step, you'll merge the outputs, eliminate duplicates, and sort the consolidated dataset to create a clean and prioritized list ready for deeper analysis.

Merging the three data streams

Start by adding a Merge node and wiring it to the outputs of your three HTTP requests. This node will unify all results into a single flow for processing.

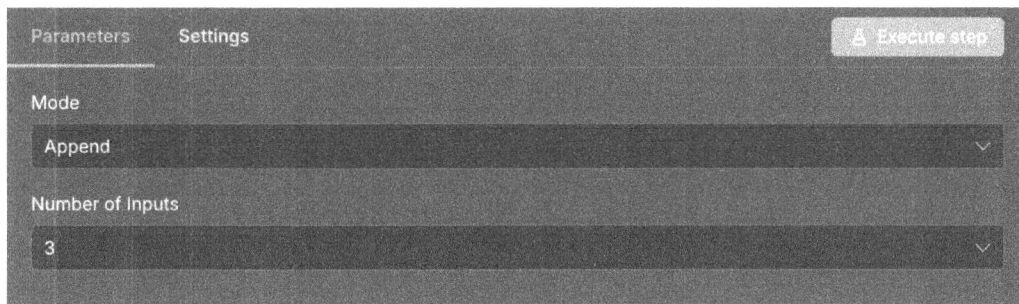

Figure 5.19: Merge node

As shown in *Figure 5.19*, the Merge node visually ties together the three separate outputs, combining them into a single downstream path.

Use the following configuration for the Merge node:

- **Mode: Append** (to stack all results)
- **Number of Inputs: 3**

This ensures that all data items flow into one stream without losing any results.

Removing duplicates

Now, insert a Remove Duplicates node to clean up overlapping stock symbols. This ensures that each ticker appears once, keeping the dataset tidy and accurate.

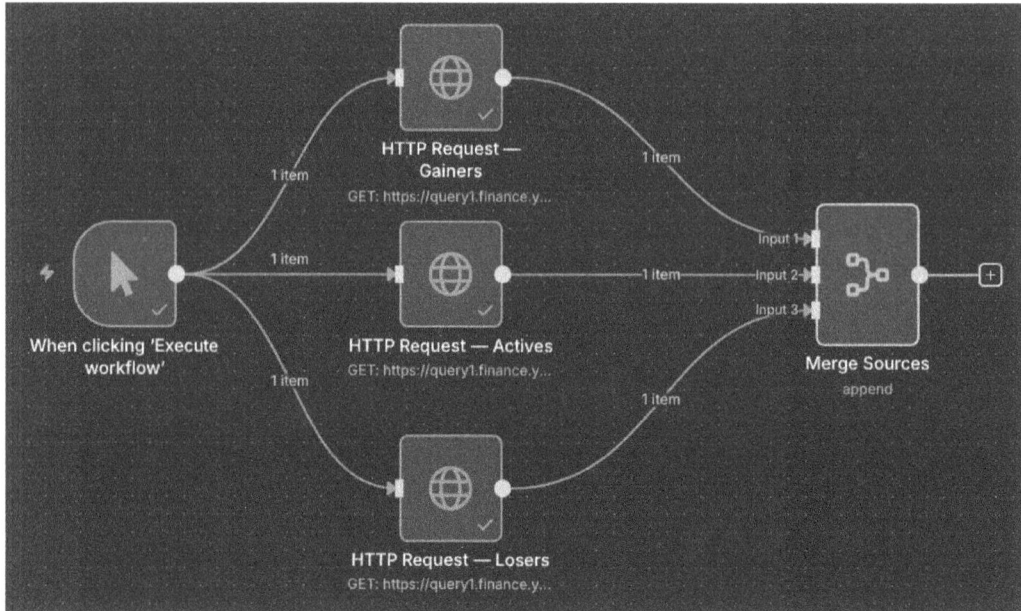

Figure 5.20: Pipeline with Merge Sources connected

As shown in *Figure 5.20*, the pipeline now unites three sources (top gainers, top losers, and most active tickers) into a single flow, ready for downstream processing.

Deduplicating and sorting the data

Finally, add a **Code** node to deduplicate and arrange the data in a meaningful order, such as by percentage change or trading volume.

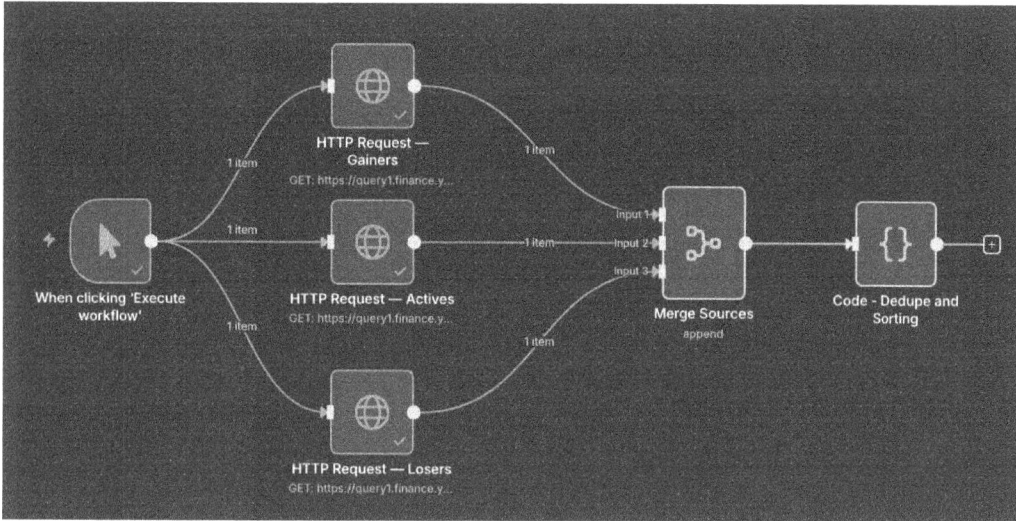

Figure 5.21: The Dedupe and Sorting node added after Merge

This illustration shows the workflow immediately after merging three ticker streams. A **Dedupe and Sorting** node is added to ensure unique symbols and consistent ordering before further processing.

The processing script

The JavaScript for this node is stored in `Code01_Dedupe_and_Sorting.js`. For readability, let's break it down into parts and walk through them.

To start, we define a simple configuration constant:

```
// ---- config
const LIMIT = 5;
```

This sets a cap on how many tickers will be returned after sorting. In our case, the list is limited to five.

> The limit of five is chosen for quick results. Later steps will call external services for each ticker, so keeping this small avoids unnecessary requests.

Now, we introduce helper functions that will handle normalization and filtering:

```
function normNum(v) {
  if (typeof v === 'number' && isFinite(v)) return v;
  if (v == null) return 0;
  const n = parseFloat(String(v).replace('%','').trim());
  return isFinite(n) ? n : 0;
}

function cleanSymbol(s) {
  return (s || '').toString().trim().toUpperCase();
}

function isLikelyEquity(sym, quoteType) {
  if (!sym) return false;
  if (sym.startsWith('^')) return false;
  if (sym.includes('=')) return false;
  if (quoteType && quoteType !== 'EQUITY') return false;
  return true;
}
```

- `normNum(v)` standardizes percentages and numbers
- `cleanSymbol(s)` ensures symbols are uppercase and trimmed
- `isLikelyEquity()` removes non-equity instruments such as indexes and FX pairs

> Don't worry if the math or financial logic seems dense. You don't need full mastery to follow the workshop. Reviewing the code for reference is enough. The important takeaway is understanding where these helper functions fit, while the heavy lifting has already been done for you.

The next piece deals with extracting rows from each input:

```
function extractRowsFromItem(it) {
  const row = it?.json ?? it ?? {};
  const quotes = row.finance?.result?.[0]?.quotes;
  if (Array.isArray(quotes) && quotes.length) {
    return quotes.map(q => ({
      symbol: q.symbol,
```

```
      changePct: normNum(q.regularMarketChangePercent),
      quoteType: q.quoteType
    }));
  }
  return [{
    symbol: row.symbol || row.ticker,
    changePct: normNum(
      row.changePct ??
      row.regularMarketChangePercent ??
      row.changesPercentage ??
      row.percentchange
    ),
    quoteType: row.quoteType
  }];
}
```

This ensures that we handle both structured screener responses and single-row inputs consistently. With that in place, we can collect all rows into one bucket:

```
const bucket = [];
for (const it of items) {
  const rows = extractRowsFromItem(it);
  for (const r of rows) bucket.push(r);
}
```

Next, we deduplicate symbols and filter out anything invalid:

```
const seen = new Set();
const flat = [];
for (const r of bucket) {
  const sym = cleanSymbol(r.symbol);
  if (!isLikelyEquity(sym, r.quoteType)) continue;
  if (seen.has(sym)) continue;
  seen.add(sym);
  flat.push({ symbol: sym, changePct: normNum(r.changePct) });
}
```

Finally, we sort by absolute percentage move and take only the top five. This produces a clean list of equities ranked by their strongest move:

```
flat.sort((a, b) => Math.abs(b.changePct) - Math.abs(a.changePct));
const top = flat.slice(0, LIMIT);

return top.map(x => ({ json: { symbol: x.symbol, changePct: x.changePct }
}));
```

Each row is output as JSON, ready for the next steps. When executed, the **Code** node's output will show five items, each containing a ticker symbol and its percent change.

Rerunning the workflow

Now, rerun the workflow from the manual trigger. All three HTTP requests will execute, the Merge node will append them, and the **Code** node will return a list of five items.

Open the **Code** node to view the output. You should see a structure similar to this:

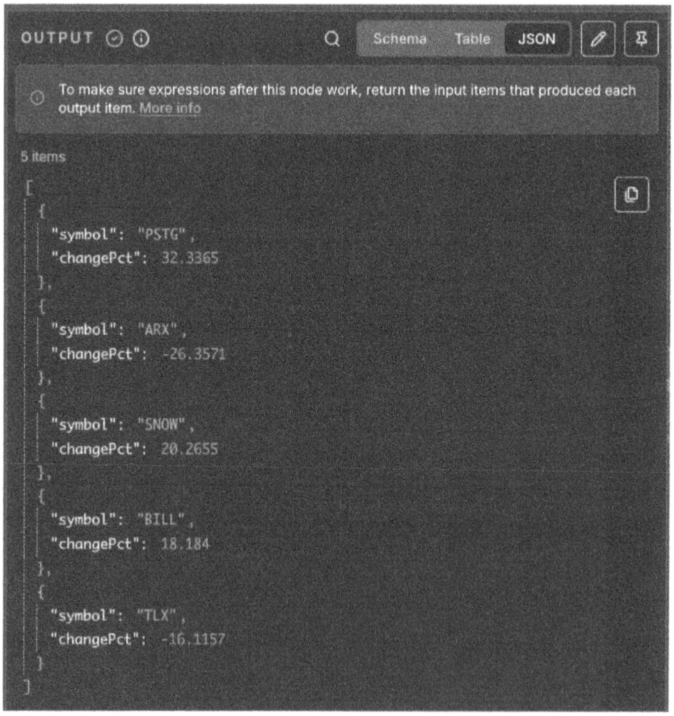

Figure 5.22: Code node output

Figure 5.22 illustrates the resulting list of five tickers, each with its percent change, confirming that the deduplication and sorting logic works. Nice and clean, isn't it?

```
[
  { "symbol": "PSTG", "changePct": 32.3365 },
  { "symbol": "ARX",  "changePct": -26.3571 },
  { "symbol": "SNOW", "changePct": 20.2655 },
  { "symbol": "BILL", "changePct": 18.184 },
  { "symbol": "TLX",  "changePct": -16.1157 }
]
```

> The JSON output is an array where each item contains a symbol attribute. This field acts as the key for all further processing steps, as we will attach additional data to each symbol as the workflow expands.

After completing this step, you now have a deduplicated, sorted list of the top five movers across all three categories. The workflow is no longer just fetching raw feeds, it's already providing structured, ranked insights.

Following this, we'll prepare to attach external intelligence, enhancing each ticker with richer data in the next stage.

Step 5: Configuring Yahoo Finance

To ground decisions in a live market context, we'll fetch intraday series from Yahoo Finance and condense each symbol's history into a single, comparable record. We'll request five days of five-minute **OHLCV** (**open, high, low, close, volume**) bars, then compute quick signals—**z-scores** (standardized moves) and **ATR** (**average true range**, a volatility gauge)—plus a simple volatility flag to guide routing.

> Don't be intimidated by abbreviations such as OHLCV, ATR, or z-score. You don't need deep market math to follow along—the code is provided and can be copy-pasted. This chapter highlights only the most interesting parts for reference, so focus on the flow rather than formulas.

Start by creating an HTTP request node that retrieves the chart data for the current symbol. This call returns arrays suitable for computing context:

- **Method: GET**
- **URL:** `https://query1.finance.yahoo.com/v8/finance/chart/{{ $json.symbol }}`
- **Query Parameters:** `interval=5m`, `range=5d`

This configuration pulls a compact intraday window where trends, shocks, and participation are easy to assess without excessive payload.

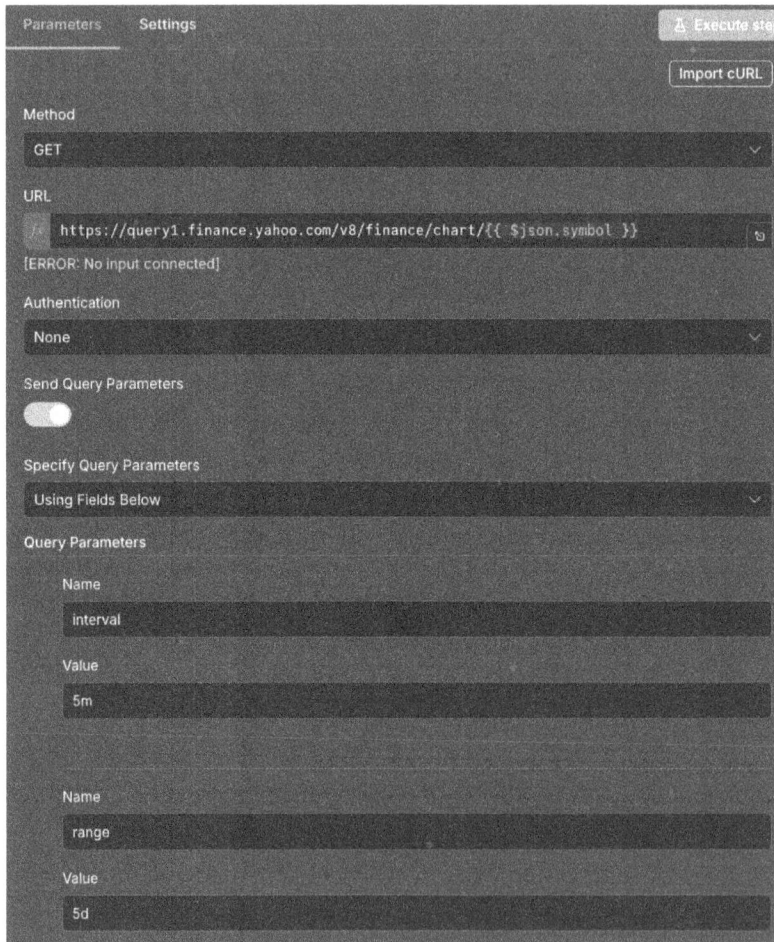

Figure 5.23: Yahoo chart request configured

In *Figure 5.23*, the request shows the `interval` and `range` parameters that shape the returned OHLCV arrays for each ticker.

Attach a **Code** node after the request. Its role is to normalize inputs and return one compact object per ticker: latest price, percent change, short-horizon drift (**zH**), last-bar shock (**z1**), ATR-scaled move, a **volume-spike** flag, and a combined volatilityFlag:

```
// minimal return shape from the parser
return [{
  json: { symbol, price, change, changePercent, z1, zH, moveVsATR,
  volSpike, volatilityFlag, timestamp }
}];
```

This **one in, one out** contract keeps downstream nodes predictable—no list explosions or missing fields when a symbol has sparse data.

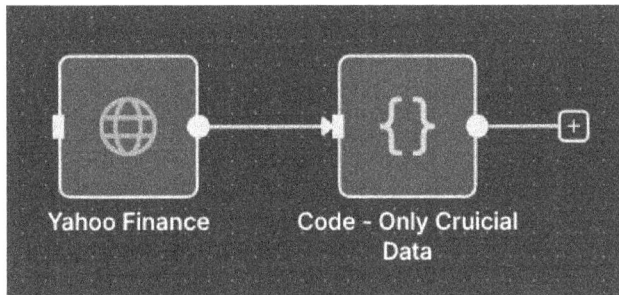

Figure 5.24: Parser after Yahoo request

Figure 5.24 depicts the placement: the **Code** node immediately follows the Yahoo request, converting raw arrays into a single, telemetry-rich item.

Connect to the last node and execute from the very beginning, and confirm that the parser outputs exactly one item per input symbol. When the series is too short, the node should still return a safe stub, avoiding errors while signaling insufficient data.

Next, we'll bring in recent headlines via Google News and keep a few clean snippets per ticker for balanced, human-readable context.

Step 6: Fetching and parsing news (Google News RSS, last two days)

In this step, you'll add a Google News HTTP request per ticker, then run two **Code** nodes in sequence: one to attach each RSS payload to its ticker symbol, and another to parse the RSS XML into a compact list of titles.

Adding the Google News HTTP request

Search for HTTP Request, drag it onto the canvas, and connect it after your Yahoo 5d/5m metrics node (or after the Split in Batches node, if you're batching). Configure the following:

- **Method: GET**

- **URL**: `https://news.google.com/rss/search?q={{$json.symbol}}%20stock%20 when:2d&hl=en-US&gl=US&ceid=US:en`

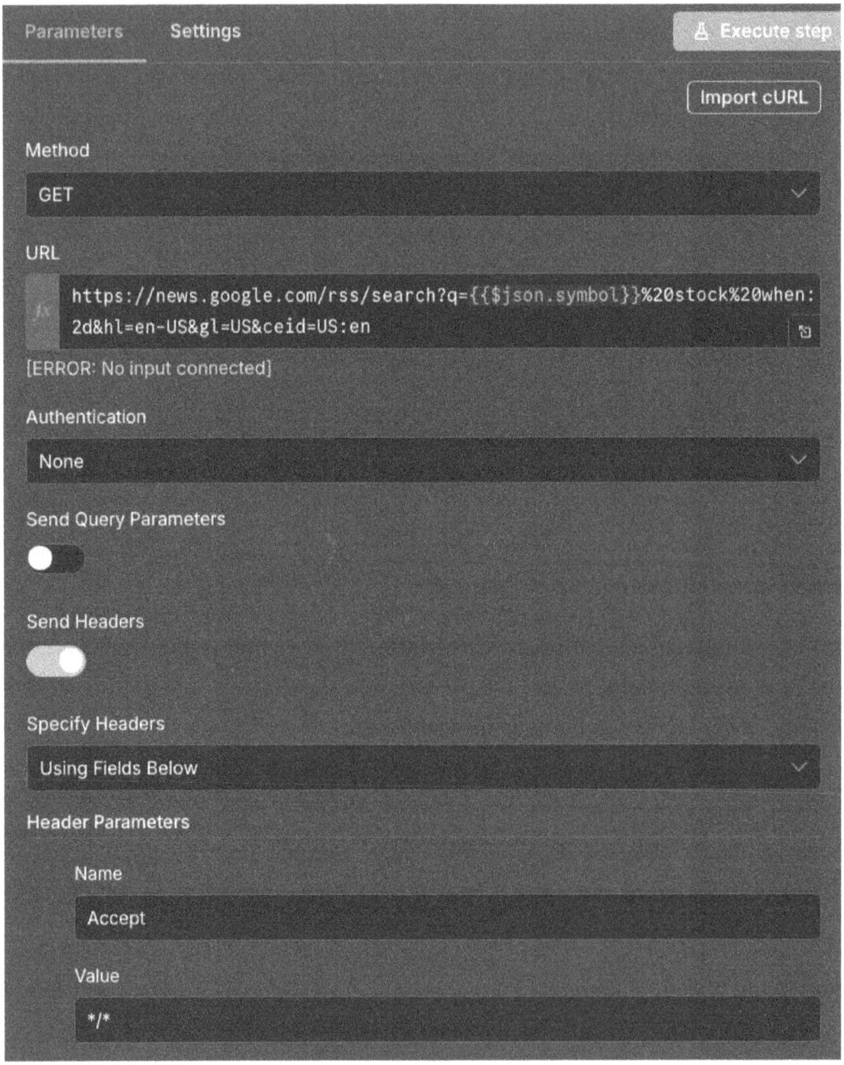

Figure 5.25: HTTP request to Google News configured for per-ticker RSS (last two days)

Wiring two Code nodes after Google News

Drag two **Code** nodes to the canvas and connect them in series after the **Google News** node:

- **Attach Symbol** pairs each RSS payload with the correct ticker
- **Parse RSS** extracts titles (and short snippets) from the RSS XML into a news[] array

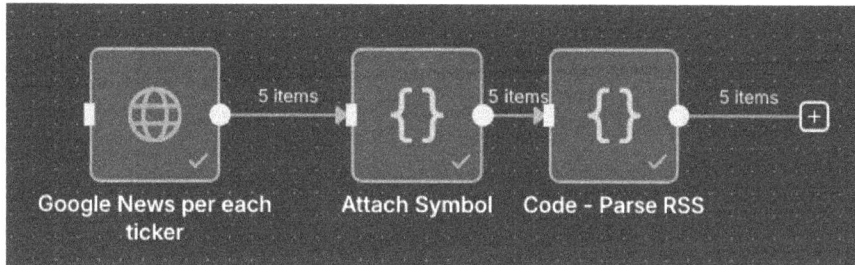

Figure 5.26: Google News HTTP node connected to two Code nodes: Attach Symbol → Parse RSS

Code node 1: Attach Symbol

You can copy and paste the full script from Code03_Attach_Symbol.js. The essential idea is that you take the RSS XML returned for each item and attach the corresponding symbol taken from your earlier dedupe node. Two lines matter most, as explained in the list that follows:

```
const SYMBOLS_NODE = 'Code - Dedupe and Sorting'; // <-- must match the
node's label exactly
const symItems = $items(SYMBOLS_NODE, 0) || [];
```

- SYMBOLS_NODE must match the exact canvas label of the node that outputs { symbol: ... } (your dedupe/sort step)
- symItems pulls all items emitted by that node, giving you the symbol list to align with the current RSS items

The rest of the file walks the input items, pairs each with its symbol, and outputs { symbol, data }, where data carries the raw RSS XML.

> **Important dependency**
>
> This news-fetching subflow will not work in isolation. Until you connect it to the main workflow where ticker symbols are produced (from **Code – Dedupe and Sorting**), the symbol list will be empty. That means there is nothing to request news about and nothing to parse from the RSS feed.

💡 If you renamed your dedupe node, update SYMBOLS_NODE to the new name.

Code node 2: Parse RSS

You can copy and paste the full script from Code04_Parse_RSS.js. The key routine is parseRss(xml, symbol), which turns raw RSS XML into a compact list of strings such as "Title — short description":

```javascript
function parseRss(xml, symbol) {
  const reItem = /<item\b[\s\S]*?<\/item>/gi;
  const blocks = Array.from(xml.matchAll(reItem)).map(m => m[0]);
  if (!blocks.length) return [];

  const reTitle = /<title>([\s\S]*?)<\/title>/i;
  const reDesc  = /<description>([\s\S]*?)<\/description>/i;

  const seen = new Set();
  const out = [];

  for (const block of blocks) {
    const t = stripHtml((block.match(reTitle)?.[1]) || '');
    const d = stripHtml((block.match(reDesc)?.[1]) || '');
    if (!t) continue;

    const key = t.toLowerCase();
    if (seen.has(key)) continue;
    seen.add(key);

    out.push(d ? `${t} — ${d.slice(0, 240)}` : t);
    if (out.length >= 5) break;
  }
  return out;
}
```

This is what it does, step by step:

1. Locates each <item> ... </item> block in the XML

2. Pulls out <title> and <description> per item

3. Cleans HTML/CDATA so you keep readable text

4. Deduplicates by title, truncates the snippet, and limits to a handful of items to keep prompts small

The node outputs one item per ticker as { symbol, news: ["...", "..."] }, ready for your LLM step.

Important dependency

This news-fetching subflow will not work in isolation. Until you connect it to the main workflow where ticker symbols are produced (from **Code – Dedupe and Sorting**), the symbol list will be empty. That means there is nothing to request news about and nothing to parse from the RSS feed.

Making the connections and verifying the run

From **Code – Dedupe and Sorting**, draw two connections:

- To **Yahoo Finance** (5d/5m HTTP request).
- To **Google News** (RSS HTTP request). This is the only change needed in this sub-step.

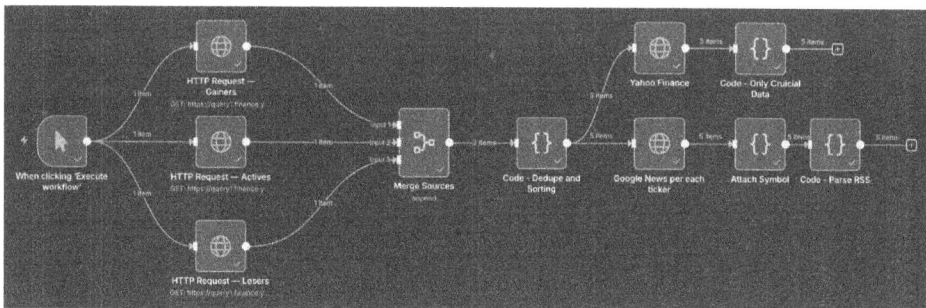

Figure 5.27: Overall workflow: Code – Dedupe and Sorting connected to both Yahoo Finance and Google News branches

We have now reached the spot where we can run the pipeline from the beginning to make sure there are no errors so far.

Rerunning the workflow

Execute the **entire workflow** from the manual trigger. Confirm the following:

- Every node turns green
- Both branches receive items
- There are no errors in any node's execution panel

At this stage, both the market metrics and news feeds are ready, and the next task is to bring them together. By aligning financial signals with their related headlines under each ticker, we create a unified context for Mistral. This sets the ground for *Step 7*, where everything is consolidated into a structured input for deeper analysis.

Step 7: Merging metrics with news and preparing the Mistral prompt

Now that the Yahoo Finance metrics and Google News titles are flowing, we're ready to **merge** them per ticker and pass a tidy, per-symbol bundle into Mistral for a concise BUY/SELL/HOLD note.

Setting up the Merge block

Place a **Merge** node and configure it to combine by field:

- **Mode: Combine**
- **Combine by: Matching fields**
- **Fields to Match:** `symbol`

- **Inputs:**

    - Input 1: The processed **Yahoo Finance** metrics (your 5d/5m **Code** output)

    - Input 2: The parsed **Google News** titles (your Parse RSS **Code** output)

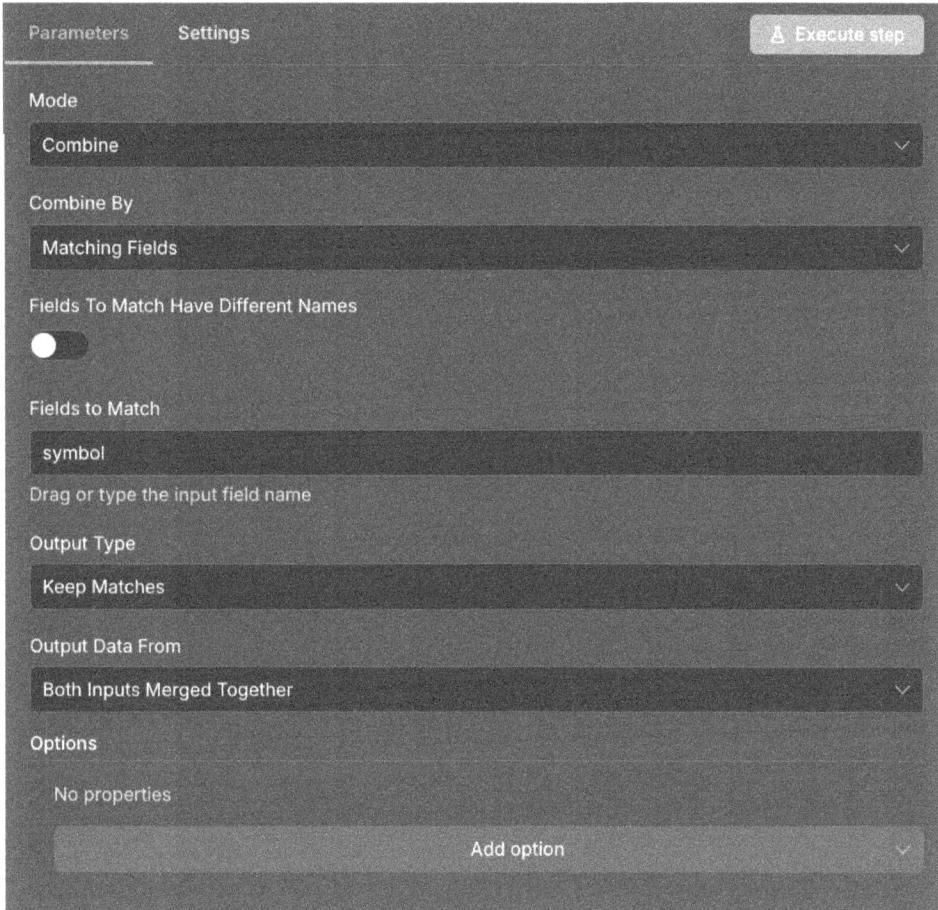

Figure 5.28: Merge node configuration combining two inputs by symbol

Run the node. You should now see one item per ticker that includes both the **financial metrics** and the **news array**. Each item will carry { `symbol`, `...financial fields...`, `news: [ ... ] }`.

```
OUTPUT ⊙ ⓘ                                          Q    Schema    Table    JSON

5 items

[
  {
    "symbol": "PSTG",
    "price": 80.54,
    "change": -0.04,
    "changePercent": -0.05,
    "z1": -0.3,
    "zH": 1.78,
    "moveVsATR": 0.12,
    "volSpike": false,
    "volatilityFlag": false,
    "timestamp": "2025-08-28T20:00:00.000Z",
    "news": [
      "Why Pure Storage Stock Is Soaring After Its Results While Data Storage Rival NetApp Wavers -
      Investor's Business Daily - &lt;a
      href=\"https://news.google.com/rss/articles/CBMinwFBVV95cUxNS3VLTjlhTXVPdjhLZ3dHVGplY05TZzJJR2xVL
      bUpaV1UyWnk4alJuVWVUc2Y5bVI5LUlPNW1scExqSzllaTNnMjd5Y0pPejk5XzhUYWc1blazZDJOb0V1bWZZOEVyY2p1VGhOY
      TllUNEJwem1YSVFRWEJsbC1BdHZ",
      "How to interpret RSI for PSTG stock - 2025 Biggest Moves &amp; Real-Time Sentiment Analysis - N
      &lt;a
      href=\"https://news.google.com/rss/articles/CBMieEFVX3lxTE1rR1FmNG9EdEFTWlN1czRlWmhUWGtKbEU2TTloN
      Q3BUc1ppcDJDRDdzdE1FN2k3b2psNHhXZmZIcnJyVVJUazBtSzdkbXM1RlZZMZVyLWJFVUVNSDAxcVpsMDJGRnpPR1RpVHVSM
      NQ?oc=5\" target=\"_blank\"&gt",
      "$PSTG stock is up 28% today. Here's what we see in our data. - Quiver Quantitative - &lt;a
      href=\"https://news.google.com/rss/articles/CBMioAFBVV95cUxPalZrSW52eDZwbzg3UjY5Y3pIU2l1eHhtczNXW
      eDdvSEVYT2VFS05laZFpaURJRktfUWdGd3A3c1F2N2swbTJDb1Q1ZXpXWkppQ0JIeVE0dTNPZVYwdkhVSzZlZXpDeDdfWXRHL
      TZNuZzhhMWNTMFg1Yldiem9VV0E",
      "Pure Storage Stock (PSTG) Rises 30% on News of Meta Platforms Deal - TipRanks - &lt;a
      href=\"https://news.google.com/rss/articles/CBMimAFBVV95cUx0dDFjYVk5alJuYTJYSHo4YkVJRWY0YlFzUS1DS
      WlBGT3JNdWStZUhsVVdTejlpX052YkFoeVJ6R1NCSjlORHFKbC1EcnV3eUlYT2thTk1HVk82aUJRbS1HTWhRZmctd0hQRlhL
      V281V0FXZ29LX3RNM1lBaHNuTGJ",
      "Pure Storage (PSTG) Raises Revenue Guidance and Completes US$390 Million Share Buyback - Yahoo
      - &lt;a
      href=\"https://news.google.com/rss/articles/CBMihAFBVV95cUxPRHZvSzNzbDZDDdkNmbkdqbzlXeEhwNDBRMXBvM
      NHpRU09lWXNOTkFsOFBOb2Fpc09vNmNwNF83aGZ0VTFKWnZ2NnIwc2VmWTFVMXctR3JaX1Z4UnhmLV9udzZGNjF0cWdQcWMwS
      Z1lHVnhhdjk3ZUtUbkY?oc=5\" t"
    ]
  },
```

Figure 5.29: Output preview showing each merged item with symbol, financial parameters, and news (titles/snippets)

At this stage, we've successfully merged and refined the outputs from both financial metrics and news feeds, creating a single enriched dataset per symbol. The next move is to prepare this information for Mistral. To do that, we'll construct a structured prompt that combines financial indicators with news context, giving the model a clear view for generating actionable recommendations.

Building the Mistral prompt

You can copy and paste the full builder from `Code05_Build_Mistral_Prompt.js`, but let's walk through the most important parts so you know exactly how it works:

1. We define small helpers and limits. We trim long headlines and keep only a handful to control tokens; `fmt` formats numbers safely:

```
const MAX_NEWS = 5;      // keep only a few headlines
const MAX_LINE = 300;    // trim any overly long line
function fmt(n, d = 2) { /* returns 'n/a' or fixed decimals */ }
```

> **Why?**
>
> It keeps prompts short, predictable, and cheap while still informative.

2. We then iterate over merged items. We build **one Mistral request per ticker**, so each symbol gets its own recommendation:

```
for (const itWrap of items) {
  const it = itWrap.json || {};
  // …
}
```

> **Why?**
>
> Per-item calls make routing, retries, and downstream posting (Telegram) straightforward.

3. Next, we assemble the news block. We take your news array (titles/snippets) and render each as a bullet; empty lists get a polite stub:

```
const newsLines = Array.isArray(it.news) ? it.news : [];
const newsBlock = newsLines
  .filter(Boolean)
  .slice(0, MAX_NEWS)
  .map(s => String(s).slice(0, MAX_LINE))
  .map(s => `- ${s}`)
  .join('\n') || '– no notable news –';
```

Why?

Mistral sees a compact, scannable set of recent headlines relevant to the ticker.

4. Following that, we compose the user prompt (triple-quoted, task-first). The user content starts with Task, then Details, and News last. It's formatted to produce a **Telegram-ready MarkdownV2** message (no JSON):

```
const userContent = `"""
Task:
Provide a concise stock recommendation for Telegram.
Output must be a single MarkdownV2 message, no JSON, no code blocks.

Format:
*${it.symbol || 'SYM'}*
Score: *X/10*
Recommendation: *BUY/SELL/HOLD*
Projection (1w): *N.NN%*
Rationale: <one sentence>
Uncertainty: <one sentence>

Details:
Symbol: ${it.symbol || 'n/a'}
Timestamp: ${it.timestamp || 'n/a'}
Last price: ${fmt(it.price)}
Day change: ${fmt(it.change)} (${fmt(it.changePercent)}%)
Risk: z1=${fmt(it.z1)}, zH=${fmt(it.zH)}, moveVsATR=${fmt(it.
moveVsATR)}, volSpike=${Boolean(it.volSpike)},
volatilityFlag=${Boolean(it.volatilityFlag)}

News (last 2 days):
${newsBlock}
"""`;
```

*   The **system prompt** sets strict formatting expectations
*   The **user prompt** carries the **task**, your **metrics**, and **news** context

> **Why this order?**
>
> Putting Task first tends to improve compliance; News goes last as supporting evidence.

Declare the system prompt and request body

We ask for **one concise MarkdownV2 message**, explicitly disallowing JSON or code blocks. Then, we package system and user into messages;

```
{
  model: "mistral-small-latest",
  temperature: 0.3,
  messages: [
    {
      role: "system",
      content: "You are a financial analytics assistant. Return one
concise Telegram-ready MarkdownV2 message only. Do not return JSON. Do not
use code blocks. Properly escape MarkdownV2 special characters."
    },
    { role: "user", content: userContent }
  ]
}
```

- **System prompt**: Sets formatting rules (Telegram-ready, no JSON, no code blocks, escape special characters)
- **Model and temperature**: Small, steady model with low-variance output for consistent formatting

The expected result is that Mistral will return a **single MarkdownV2 message** in choices[0]. message.content, ready to send straight to Telegram. It will look like this:

- *SYM*
- Score: *X/10*
- Recommendation: *BUY/HOLD/SELL*
- Projection (1w): *N.NN%*
- Short **rationale** and an **uncertainty** line

Now that the JSON body is in place, the next move is to pass it into an **HTTP Request** node. This will transmit our merged financial and news data to the Mistral API for analysis.

Step 8: Sending prompts to Mistral and delivering to Telegram

At this stage, we are ready to call the Mistral API and then later forward each MarkdownV2 response to Telegram:

1. We'll begin by creating the Mistral HTTP request. Add an **HTTP Request** node after your **Code – Build Mistral Prompt** node. Set **Method** to **POST**, **Body Content Type** to **JSON**, and **Body** to the output of the builder (e.g., {{$json}}).

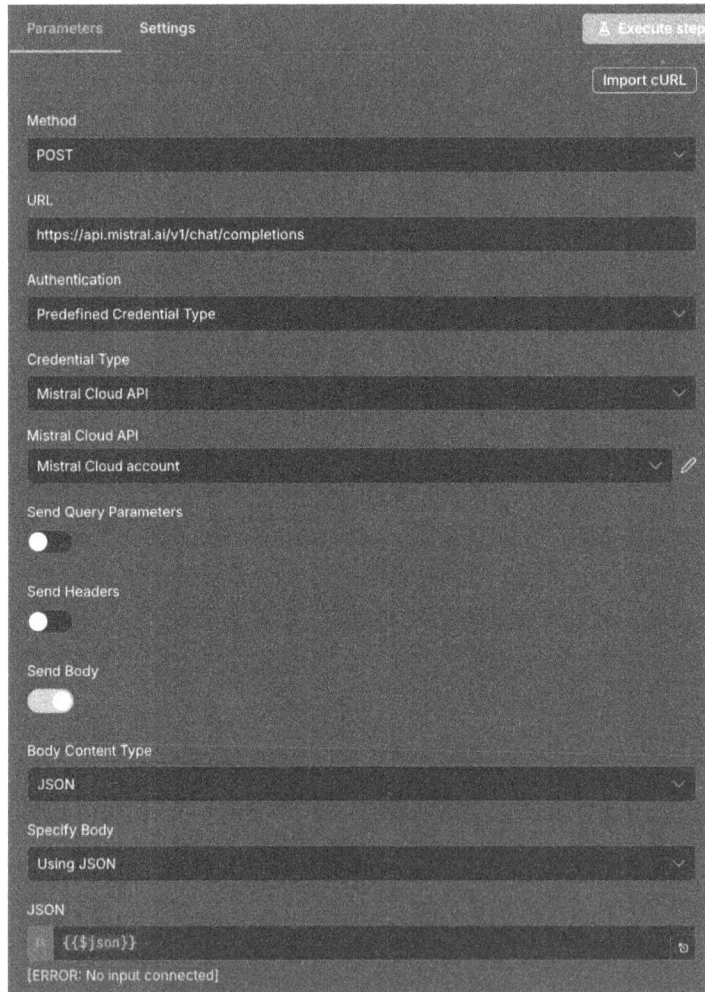

Figure 5.30: HTTP Request node set up for Mistral inference

2. Then, configure Mistral authentication. Open the node's **Authentication** dropdown, choose **Mistral Cloud API** (built-in), and paste your Mistral API access key. Save this as a reusable credential (e.g., Mistral - Workshop).

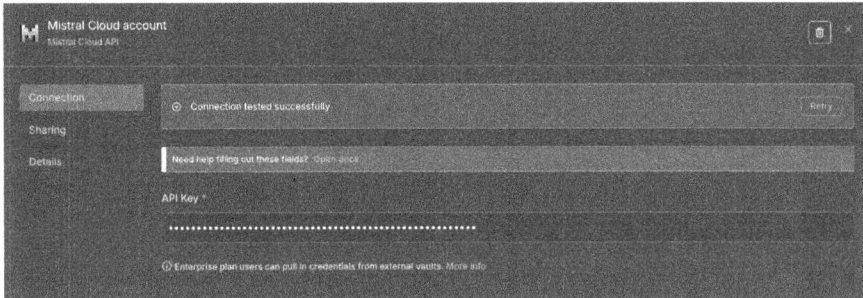

Figure 5.31: Mistral Cloud API credential with the access key stored as a named credential

3. Click **Execute Node**. The response should include a single message per item, accessible at choices[0].message.content and already formatted as MarkdownV2 (per *Step 7*).

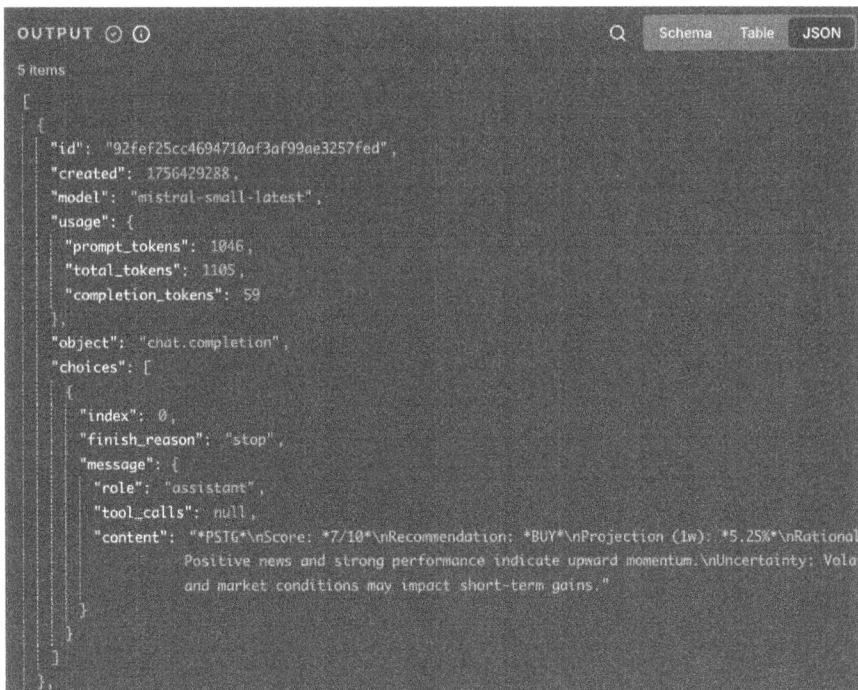

Figure 5.32: Successful Mistral response

4. With the response safely returned from Mistral, we now shift focus to extracting the actual recommendation text. The key content is nested in the JSON reply, under the `{{$json["choices"][0]["message"]["content"]}}` path. This value holds the insights we'll forward downstream, making it the bridge between model output and our final delivery channel.

5. We connect Mistral to Telegram by adding a **Telegram → Send Message** node and connecting it after the Mistral node. In **Text**, use the assistant content directly, as in this example:

    - **Text** (expression): `{{$json["choices"][0]["message"]["content"]}}`
    - **Parse Mode: MarkdownV2**

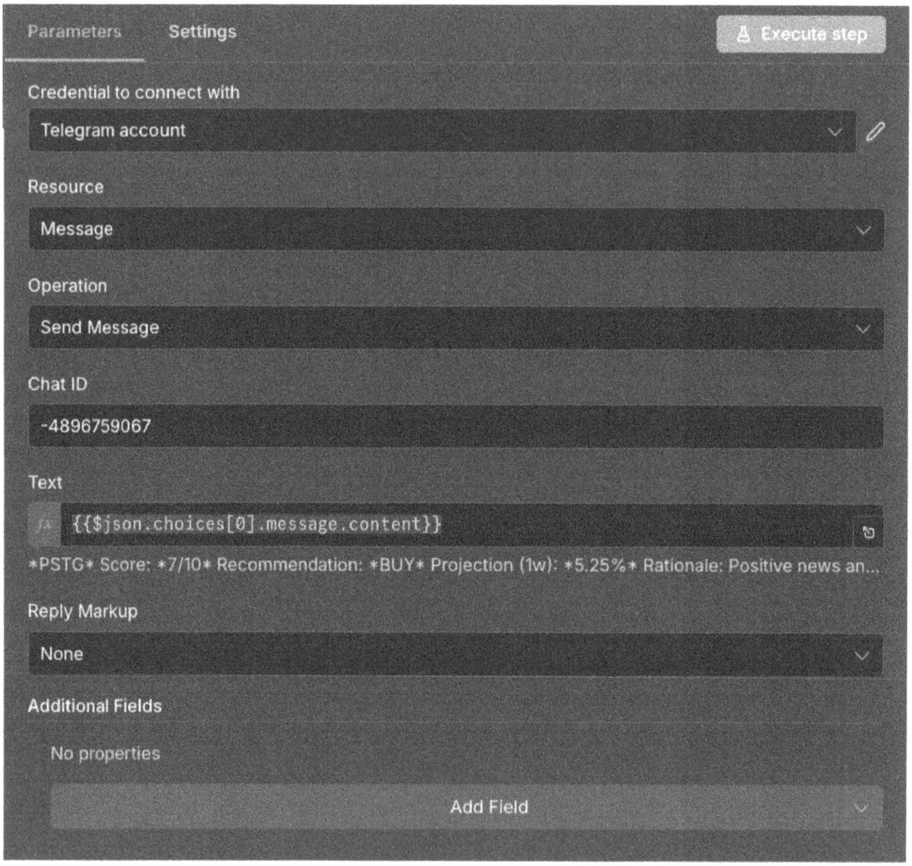

Figure 5.33: Telegram Send Message with Chat ID and credential

6. If the Telegram credential is not configured yet, you must set it up in n8n. Please use the access token you received from @BotFather. Enter this token into the workflow as a Telegram credential.

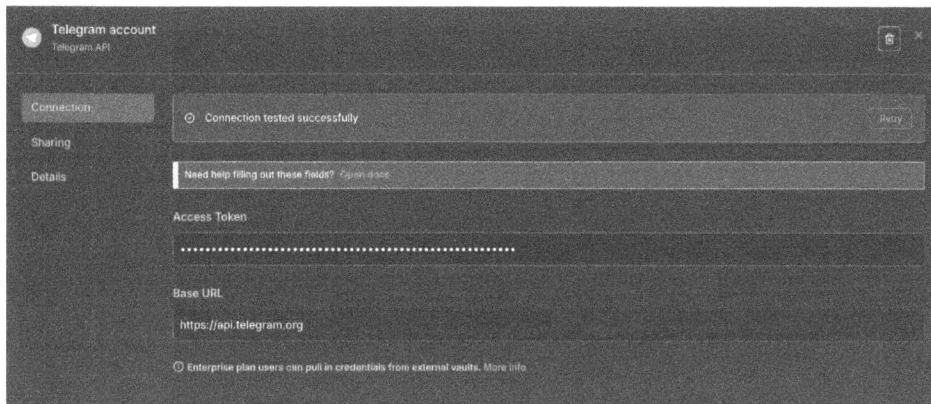

Figure 5.34: Telegram account credential setup with access token

At this point, we are approaching the successful completion of our solution. With Telegram fully connected, the stage is set to run the pipeline as one seamless workflow, ensuring that every node processes correctly and delivers insights to the chat without errors.

🔍**Quick tip**: Need to see a high-resolution version of this image? Open this book in the next-gen Packt Reader or view it in the PDF/ePub copy.

🔓**The next-gen Packt Reader** is included for free with the purchase of this book. Scan the QR code OR go to https://packtpub.com/unlock, then use the search bar to find this book by name. Double-check the edition shown to make sure you get the right one.

Step 9: Run the entire workflow

Run the entire workflow starting from the manual trigger. Make sure all nodes execute successfully without errors and that every item flows through to the end, delivering Telegram messages.

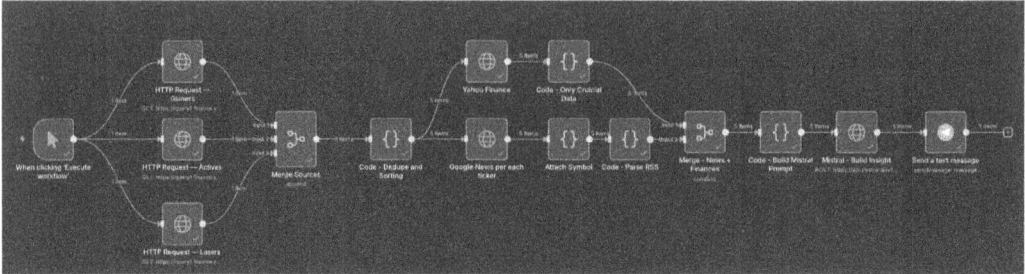

Figure 5.35: Final successful workflow

Open your Telegram chat on your phone—you should see five messages delivered, each containing financial insights with symbol, score, recommendation, one-week projection, and rationale, just like on the screen.

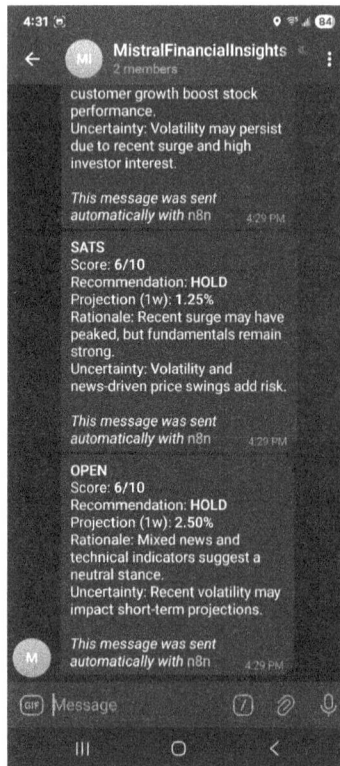

Figure 5.36: Mobile screenshot showing the Telegram message received in the target chat

By completing this step, we achieved a full end-to-end workflow, from market data and news collection, through Mistral analysis, all the way to clear Telegram delivery. It's a cool demonstration of how n8n can orchestrate complex flows with minimal code while producing tangible, actionable insights right in your pocket.

Summary

The workshop brought the theory of agents to life step by step. We began by setting up dependencies and verifying our connection to the Mistral API, ensuring that the foundation was ready. With this in place, we built our first tool—a simple calculator—and then wrapped it into a basic agent. From there, we expanded capabilities by adding a web search tool and assembling a research agent that could combine reasoning with external information. The journey continued with specialized customer service agents, each tuned for a specific role, and culminated in a multi-agent system that collaborated to solve tasks together. Finally, the interactive demo allowed us to test these systems in real scenarios, watching them reason, retry, and adapt. The practical lesson is clear: agents are already usable, adaptable, and valuable in real workflows today.

With agents explored in depth, we're ready to take on the next major leap: **retrieval-augmented generation (RAG)**. If agents gave us adaptability, RAG gives us memory on steroids—the ability to ground reasoning in vast knowledge bases. In the coming chapter, you'll see how retrieval and generation fuse into one powerful workflow.

Extracurricular

Having built a solid foundation in working with embeddings, you're now ready to explore more advanced and creative applications. Let these exercises spark new ideas for your own projects:

- **Build a custom n8n pipeline**: Start from scratch and design your own automated workflow inside n8n. Combine new data feeds, AI analysis, and delivery channels, practicing rapid prototyping skills while tailoring the workflow to your unique trading objectives.
- **Connect n8n with Discord**: Extend your workflow beyond Telegram by integrating n8n with Discord webhooks or bots. This lets trading insights automatically flow into dedicated channels, making it easier to collaborate with communities in real time.
- **Embed charts in n8n messages**: Enhance your n8n workflow by attaching candlestick charts or technical studies as images in outbound messages. This creates visually rich financial updates, helping traders grasp key insights quickly instead of reading only raw text.

- **Replace Code nodes with n8n built-ins:** Rebuild sections of the workflow using only n8n's native nodes, such as **Set**, **IF**, **Merge**, or **Math**. This reduces code complexity, lowers maintenance effort, and highlights n8n's true no-code automation potential.

- **Re-implement the n8n pipeline in code:** Take the automated workflow you've built in n8n and replicate it entirely in Python or Node.js. This exercise strengthens coding skills and reinforces understanding of the automation logic behind each pipeline step.

- **Experiment with Make (Integromat):** Design a multi-step scenario that pulls from APIs, branches on conditions, and reacts dynamically. Notice how adding reasoning (an LLM) would elevate it beyond pure automation.

- **Hybrid agent challenge:** Pick a real task (e.g., summarizing meeting notes, then auto-updating Trello). Build half with a no-code tool such as Zapier and half with an LLM agent framework. Reflect on where each shines, and where agents add the missing spark.

Join our Discord and Reddit space

You're not the only one navigating fragmented tools, constant updates, and unclear best practices. Join a growing community of professionals exchanging insights that don't make it into documentation.

Stay informed with updates, discussions, and behind-the-scenes insights from our authors. Join our Discord at `https://packt.link/z8ivB` or scan the QR code below:	Connect with peers, share ideas, and discuss real-world GenAI challenges. Follow us on Reddit at `https://packt.link/0rExL` or scan the QR code below:

6

Unpacking RAG Workflows

The journey of discovery lies not in seeking new landscapes, but in having new eyes.

— Marcel Proust

Language models are typically trained on large volumes of publicly available data. While this gives them a broad understanding of the world, it also means their knowledge is frozen at the moment training ends. But what if you have your own knowledge—internal documentation, private datasets, or domain-specific facts—and you want the model to generate answers based on that? What if you need every user query to be grounded in facts, checked against your sources, and shaped by up-to-date information? This is exactly where **Retrieval-Augmented Generation (RAG)** comes in.

This chapter is your guide to navigating RAG as if on an ocean voyage, where each stop reveals key parts of the RAG process: indexing, retrieval, and generation. Through practical workshops, we'll go through each of these stops of the RAG journey, from basic implementations to advanced techniques such as multi-query routing and refined indexing. By the end, you'll have the skills to navigate RAG with confidence, building robust systems that handle complex questions seamlessly.

In a nutshell, this chapter will cover the following topics:

- Problem statement
- RAG architecture
- Workshop 1: Bootstrap RAG implementation
- Workshop 2: Multi-query approach
- Workshop 3: Zoom into atomic sub-queries
- Workshop 4: Generification approach

Technical requirements

To implement RAG effectively, certain tools and API keys are essential. Here is a quick list of technical requirements needed:

- **Google Colab**: Easy cloud-based coding and experiments
- **Pinecone API key**: Access to vector database for indexing
- **Mistral AI API key**: Language model integration for generation
- **LangSmith API key**: Advanced language processing and analysis tools

Problem statement

In today's data-rich world, finding precise and contextually relevant information within vast databases can be daunting. RAG offers a solution by combining data retrieval with generative AI to deliver comprehensive, accurate responses.

This chapter addresses the problem of navigating and leveraging diverse data sources, such as vector stores, graph DBs, and SQL databases, to answer complex queries. We'll explore techniques to optimize indexing, retrieval, and generation processes, helping you implement RAG to handle high volumes of data seamlessly. By the end, you'll have the tools to build systems that transform raw data into insightful, context-rich answers.

RAG architecture

The RAG process is a powerful way to combine stored knowledge with the generative abilities of modern AI. The core of RAG lies in three sequential phases: indexing, retrieval, and generation. Each phase builds upon the previous one, transforming vast amounts of raw data into clear, context-aware answers.

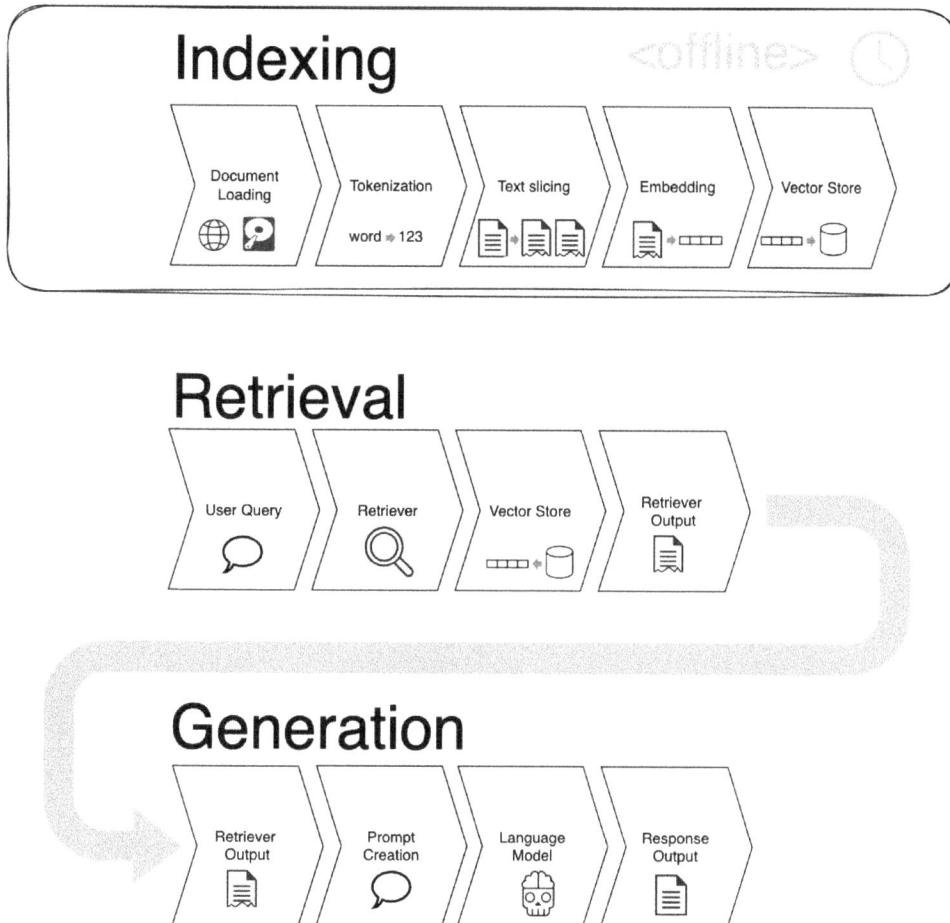

Figure 6.1: RAG phases

You can think of the process illustrated in *Figure 6.1* as a voyage. At Indexing Harbor, information is carefully sorted and stored—like goods being placed in different warehouses, each suited to its cargo. Vector stores capture the essence of language, graph DBs map relationships, and SQL databases organize structured records. Here, the data is also cut into smaller, manageable pieces, making it easier to locate and retrieve later.

From the harbor, we set sail toward the Retrieval Islands, where we search for exactly what is needed. Each island represents a different retrieval strategy: one focuses on simple reference lookups, another on metadata-driven searches, while others bring in whole documents or broader context. Together, they ensure we gather the most relevant knowledge for the task at hand.

Finally, we arrive at Generation Island, where all the collected material is brought together. Here, snippets, context, and metadata are woven into a clear, coherent answer—turning raw information into something ready to use.

Now that we've sketched the journey, let's look more closely at each phase (indexing, retrieval, and generation) to understand how they work in practice.

Indexing

Indexing is the foundational step in RAG that transforms raw information into organized, searchable formats to make retrieval quick and efficient. This phase typically happens upfront, long before a user interacts with the system. During indexing, documents or other sources are structured into formats suitable for rapid lookup. Here's a closer look at each key element in the indexing phase:

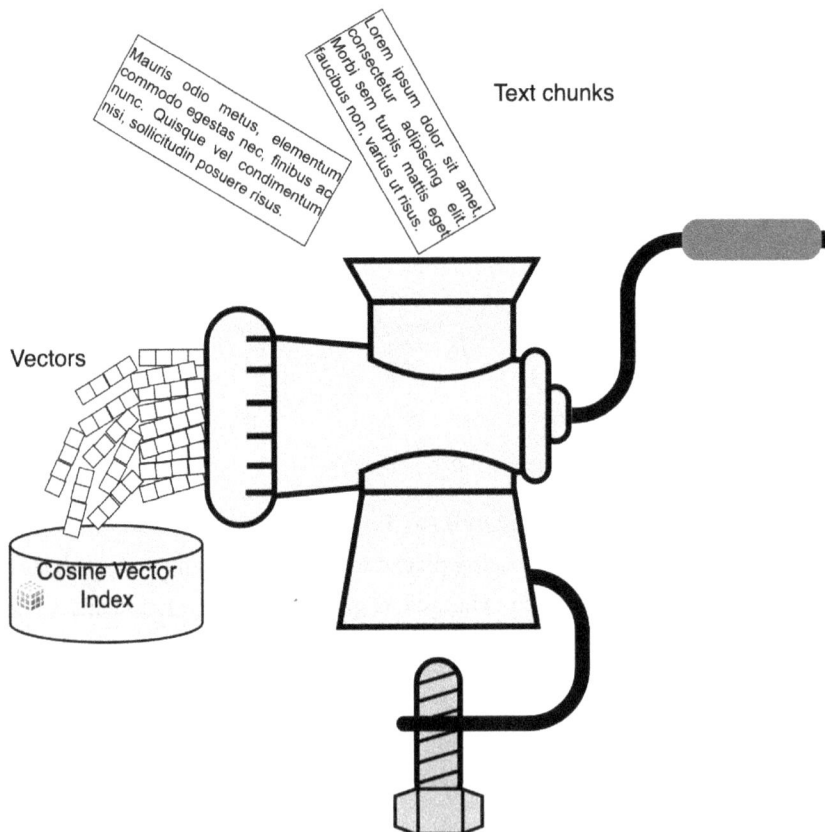

Figure 6.2: Indexing analogy

The illustration depicts text chunks entering a grinder or mincer, symbolizing the process of embedding generation. As the text is processed, it is transformed into high-dimensional vectors—compact numerical representations capturing the semantic meaning of the text—ready for storage in a vector database.

Indexing occurs far before the user submits any queries. By indexing in advance, we create a searchable *map* of information. This pre-processing enables the system to respond quickly by avoiding delays that would occur if we attempted to structure data on demand.

Types of indexed data

In RAG, different types of databases serve specific purposes during the indexing phase, and each offers unique methods for organizing and retrieving information. Here's a deeper look into the roles of graph DBs, vector stores, and Lucene indexes in this process.

Graph DBs

Graph DBs (graph databases) are designed to capture relationships between data points, using nodes (entities) and edges (connections) to represent data and their associations. In a RAG system, graph DBs are particularly useful for storing keywords and tracking their connections based on their likelihood of appearing together in relevant documents—such as resumes or profiles. For instance, keywords such as "machine learning," "data analysis," and "Python" may appear together in resumes, linked with higher likelihoods if commonly associated with similar job roles.

Graph DBs perform searches using Cypher queries. Cypher is a specialized language that efficiently traverses these relationships to identify patterns. This method makes graph DBs such as Neo4j an excellent choice for scenarios where relationships and keyword clustering are critical. With Neo4j, Cypher queries can quickly identify resumes that have certain combinations of skills, such as a focus on data science and programming languages, allowing RAG to return contextually rich results.

Vector stores

Vector stores excel at handling semantic relationships by encoding information as high-dimensional vectors, capturing subtle meanings and contexts. This format enables RAG systems to perform similarity-based searches, which are particularly effective for natural language processing. In *Chapter 3*, we covered Pinecone a popular vector store that scales effectively for production, as well as Chroma, an in-memory vector store option well-suited for local or smaller applications.

Vector stores are ideal when search requirements go beyond simple keywords, such as when a query involves finding documents with similar meaning. By representing each text chunk as a vector, these stores allow RAG to compare the semantic similarity of various documents, ensuring that responses reflect nuanced, context-aware understanding.

Lucene indexes

Lucene indexes provide a more traditional approach to indexing, focusing on keyword-based searches. They're useful in scenarios where a precise match with specific terms is needed, making them ideal for highly structured data or where specific terms define the information being sought. Lucene breaks down documents into tokens and creates an inverted index, mapping each keyword to its location within documents. This enables fast, efficient keyword lookups, making Lucene a strong choice for cases where precise, term-based queries are required.

Relational databases

Relational databases (RDBs) store data in structured tables with defined relationships, making them ideal for highly organized information such as customer records or transaction data. In RAG, RDBs efficiently support queries involving specific relationships and conditions, where precise and structured filtering is needed. SQL-based queries ensure quick, reliable access to this organized data.

Persistent binary trees and distributed caches

Persistent binary trees store data in a hierarchical, binary structure, allowing efficient searching, insertion, and deletion. These trees are especially useful for ordered data, enabling quick retrieval by traversing sorted nodes. Tools such as LevelDB and RocksDB offer persistent binary tree structures optimized for fast reads and writes, often used in scenarios requiring low-latency access to structured data.

Distributed caches, on the other hand, provide temporary, in-memory storage across multiple nodes, ideal for high-speed access to frequently requested data. Popular tools such as Redis and Hazelcast offer distributed caching solutions that reduce database load and speed up retrievals, making them suitable for real-time, low-latency applications in RAG systems.

In a RAG context, combining these different indexing methods allows for a highly flexible retrieval system. Graph DBs help identify relational patterns in keywords; vector stores provide context-aware similarity matching; and Lucene supports quick, exact keyword lookups. Together, they create a robust foundation for handling diverse and complex queries in RAG.

Initial document loading

To kick off indexing, we first load documents, either from a file system or directly from the web. For instance, using LangChain's **WebBaseLoader** allows you to load content directly from a URL.

```
from langchain_community.document_loaders import WebBaseLoader

# load from a web source
loader = WebBaseLoader(
    "https://www.gutenberg.org/cache/epub/2701/pg2701.txt")
books = loader.load()
```

In this code, WebBaseLoader loads a plain text document from a provided URL, capturing the content to begin indexing.

Slicing the text

To prepare data for indexing, it's often broken into smaller segments, or "chunks." Text slicing allows us to divide a document into parts, improving retrieval efficiency by isolating only the relevant parts of information.

- **Chunk size**: This defines the maximum length of each segment. In RAG, a smaller chunk size increases retrieval precision but can raise the number of chunks.

- **Chunk overlap**: Overlap between chunks ensures no context is lost when text is divided. By overlapping, each chunk contains some part of its neighbor, preserving continuity of information.

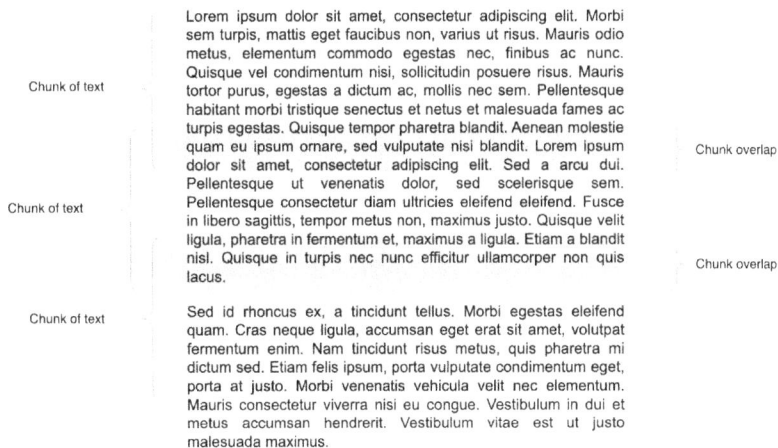

Figure 6.3: Text slicing to chunks with overlaps

The illustration demonstrates text slicing with overlap, where a larger text is divided into smaller chunks, each containing overlapping segments from neighboring chunks. This overlap ensures that contextual continuity is preserved, enabling more accurate retrieval and generation in downstream processes. Here's a basic example of text slicing:

```
from langchain.text_splitter import RecursiveCharacterTextSplitter

text_splitter = RecursiveCharacterTextSplitter.from_tiktoken_encoder(
    chunk_size=300,
    chunk_overlap=50)

splits = text_splitter.split_documents(books)
# assume Books is a collection of longs texts
```

In this example, `chunk_size` is set to 300, meaning each chunk will be a maximum of 300 tokens, while `chunk_overlap` is set to 50, meaning each chunk overlaps its neighbor by 50 tokens. This overlap keeps the segments contextually connected, aiding retrieval accuracy.

Embeddings

Once text is processed, embeddings are generated and stored in a vector store for similarity searches. Embeddings transform text into numerical vectors that capture semantic meaning, a concept explored in detail in *Chapter 3*.

```
from langchain_mistralai import MistralAIEmbeddings
embd = MistralAIEmbeddings()
query_result = embd.embed_query(question)
document_result = embd.embed_query(document)
```

The following takes place in this example:

- `MistralAIEmbeddings` generates embeddings for both the query and the document
- `embed_query` turns the text into a vector for storage or comparison

In summary, the indexing phase begins with loading documents from sources such as files or the web, followed by tokenization and text slicing into manageable chunks. Each chunk is then transformed into vector embeddings (or graph ciphers or SQL statements), capturing semantic meaning, and saved in index storage such as VectorDB, ensuring efficient retrieval for RAG applications.

Retrieval

Retrieval activates when a user query is received. The query, in its original form or after being split into simpler sub-queries, is directed to the retriever. The retriever's role is to consult the indexes created during the indexing phase, scanning them for the most relevant information. This might involve searching across different types of storage—such as data lakes, SQL or NoSQL databases, or even cloud-based repositories—depending on where the needed data resides. Retrieval's aim is to identify and load the information most relevant to the question, often in the form of text passages, metadata, or summarized insights that directly relate to the query's context.

To achieve optimal relevance, the retriever may employ advanced search methods, including similarity searches within vector databases, graph traversal within graph DBs, or structured queries within SQL databases. Additionally, LLMs can assist in this phase by transforming or rephrasing the user's query to make it more precise or even breaking down complex questions into smaller, targeted queries. These techniques can further improve the match between the query and retrieved information. Retrieval is thus about bridging the gap between the indexed knowledge base and the user's question, ensuring only the most pertinent data is sent to the generator.

In the following retrieval example, we'll be using Pinecone as our vector database for retrieving relevant documents. Pinecone's efficient, similarity-based vector search allows us to locate the most contextually relevant passages quickly, making it a powerful choice for retrieval in RAG.

Preparing the retriever

The first step in retrieval is to create a `retriever` object that will search the vector store (Pinecone) for the most relevant document embeddings. This code snippet sets up the retriever:

```python
from langchain_mistralai import MistralAIEmbeddings
from langchain_community.vectorstores import Pinecone

# Initialize the vector store with Mistral embeddings
# and indexed documents

vectorstore = Pinecone.from_documents(
    index_name='book-passages',
    documents=splits,
```

```
        embedding=MistralAIEmbeddings()
)


# Create the retriever with specified search parameters
# (k=1 for the top result)


retriever = vectorstore.as_retriever(search_kwargs={"k": 1})
```

- `Pinecone.from_documents(...)`: This initializes the vector store using the `book-passages` index, where documents represent the pre-processed, split text chunks
- `MistralAIEmbeddings()`: This function generates embeddings for each document, capturing semantic meaning for accurate retrieval
- `retriever = vectorstore.as_retriever(...)`: This creates a retriever with k=1, which limits results to the single most relevant document for each query

> In this chapter, we use LangChain wrappers around the embedding and retrieval processes. This approach simplifies integration by stacking components like Lego bricks, allowing us to work with embeddings and Pinecone retrieval seamlessly without directly interacting with the Pinecone SDK.

Retrieving documents from the vector store

Once the retriever is prepared, we can query it with a specific question to retrieve the relevant document:

```
# Retrieve relevant documents based on the user query
docs = retriever.get_relevant_documents(
    "What is the name of the ship in Moby Dick?")
```

`retriever.get_relevant_documents(...)` executes the search query. Here, it locates the top matching document for `What is the name of the ship in Moby Dick?`.

The result of this retrieval will be a set (or in our case, just one item, because k=1) of passages relevant to the question. This is not the answer yet; it is just the chunk of text that likely contains the answer.

In the retrieval phase, we initialize a vector retriever using Pinecone, which enables efficient, similarity-based searches of pre-indexed document embeddings. This retriever setup helps locate the most relevant document passages for each user query.

Now that the retrieval part has been covered, we can use the fetched information as a context for preparing the smart, summarized answer—the generation phase.

Generation

Generation is where the answer takes shape, transforming retrieved data into a cohesive, human-readable response. Powered by an LLM, the generator synthesizes the retrieved information along with the user's original question, any existing context (such as prior chat history), and metadata from the knowledge base. The LLM processes this entire input set to craft a response that reads naturally, addresses the query accurately, and maintains contextual continuity.

The generation phase may be called on the LLM multiple times. For example, the LLM might answer the question from different perspectives or explore additional angles before synthesizing these responses into one coherent answer. This multi-step approach is especially useful for complex queries that require a nuanced response, as it enables the system to consider various facets of the question before arriving at a final answer. Additionally, the LLM might employ summarization techniques to refine its output, filtering out redundant information and ensuring clarity.

In the RAG workflow, the LLM's primary role is to enhance generation, but it can also support other phases by reformulating questions or summarizing retrieved data. By leveraging the LLM at multiple stages, the RAG system creates answers that are both insightful and easy to understand. Generation is thus the final step in transforming raw data into actionable insights, ensuring that users receive clear, comprehensive responses.

The generation section in RAG is where retrieved information is transformed into a coherent, human-readable answer. We accomplish this by preparing a prompt, initializing the language model (LLM), and creating a chain to combine these components. Here's a step-by-step explanation of the code involved.

Preparing the prompt

The prompt we prepare will contain the original question and additional context. This is the way we inject dynamic data from our knowledge base:

```python
from langchain_mistralai import ChatMistralAI
from langchain.prompts import ChatPromptTemplate


# Prompt template for LLM input
template = """Answer the user question with given the context
Question: {question}

Context: {context}
"""

prompt = ChatPromptTemplate.from_template(template)
```

- `template`: This is a string that sets the structure of the prompt. It instructs the model to answer based exclusively on the provided context, ensuring relevant, focused responses.
- `{context}`: This is a placeholder for the retrieved documents or information snippets from the retriever, inserted dynamically during the chain's execution.
- `{question}`: This is a placeholder for the user's query, allowing the prompt to stay general while being applied to different questions.

Preparing the LLM

This one-liner prepares the LLM SDK object pointed to Mistral AI:

```python
llm = ChatMistralAI(
    model_name="mistral-large-latest",
    temperature=0)
```

- `model_name="mistral-large-latest"`: Specifies the model variant of Mistral AI to use for generating responses
- `temperature=0`: Controls response randomness; a lower temperature (0) makes responses more deterministic and focused, ideal for factual answers

Creating and invoking the chain

The following code snippet demonstrates the construction of a trivial chain, `Prompt -> LLM`, and invocation of this chain with given parameter values, the question and the context:

```
chain = prompt | llm
chain.invoke({
    "context": docs,
    "question":"What is the name of the ship in Moby Dick?"})
```

- `chain = prompt | llm`: Combines the prompt and LLM into a chain, allowing data flow from prompt generation directly into the LLM, making it modular and easy to stack components.
- `chain.invoke(...)`: Executes the chain, passing in the specific context (the retrieved document snippets) and question. The model generates an answer based on this input.

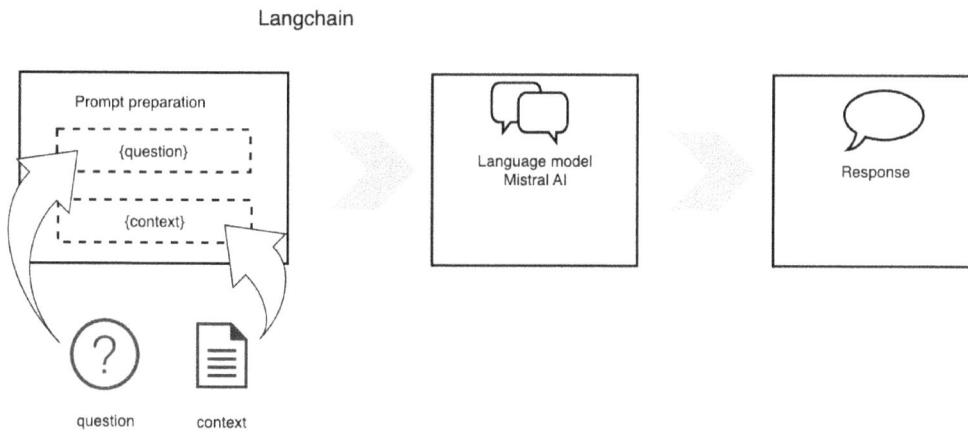

Figure 6.4: Parameterized prompt and chain illustration

Figure 6.4 showcases a parameterized prompt, where placeholders like {context} and {question} are dynamically filled with relevant information during runtime. Connected to the chain, it visually represents the seamless flow of data from input (retrieved context and user question) through the prompt to the language model, generating precise and context-aware responses.

Interaction between retrieval and generation models

RAG operates through a two-part architecture: the retriever and the generator. The retriever searches a document database or external source to gather the most relevant information. This data is then passed to the generator, which crafts a response in natural language based on the retrieved knowledge. The seamless interaction between these components ensures the model remains both coherent in conversation and factually accurate, balancing generative fluency with knowledge retrieval.

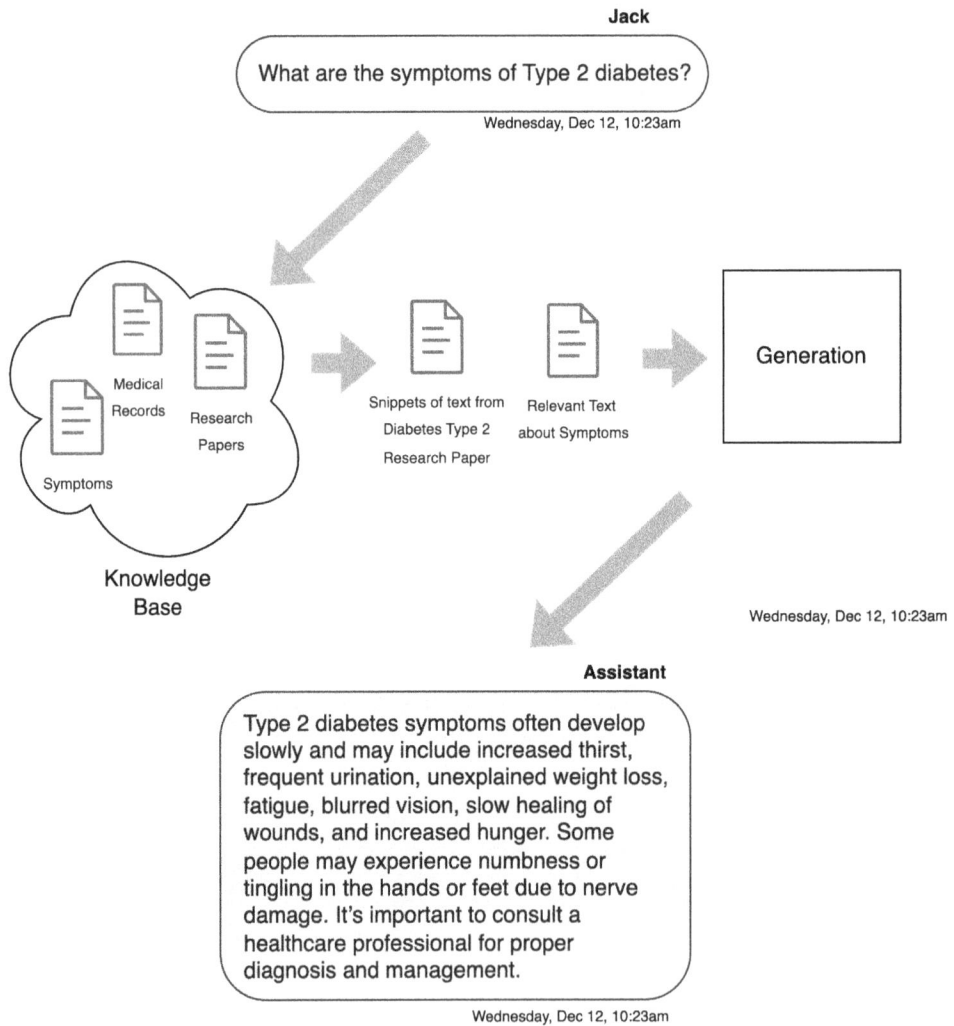

Figure 6.5: The two-level architecture of the retriever and generator

Figure 6.5 illustrates the two-level architecture of the retriever and generator in a RAG pipeline. At the first level, the retriever searches the vector database to identify and extract relevant context based on the user's query. At the second level, the generator combines this context with the query to produce a coherent, human-readable response using a language model. This architecture ensures that the system retrieves only the most pertinent information and delivers precise, contextually enriched answers.

Challenges and trade-offs in RAG systems

While RAG offers several benefits, there are challenges, particularly around performance, latency, and scalability. The retrieval process can introduce delays, especially when searching through large datasets, affecting response time. Scalability is another challenge, as larger databases require more computational resources. Additionally, balancing the accuracy of retrieval with the coherence of generative responses can be tricky, as over-reliance on retrieval might lead to less fluid conversations, while insufficient retrieval may reduce factual accuracy.

Figure 6.6 illustrates the dependency between retrieval depth and response time in a RAG pipeline. As retrieval depth increases (i.e., the number of documents retrieved for context), response time also grows due to the additional processing required. While deeper retrieval can improve response accuracy by providing more context to the generator, it comes at the cost of higher latency. This figure highlights the importance of balancing retrieval depth to optimize both response quality and system efficiency, ensuring a seamless user experience.

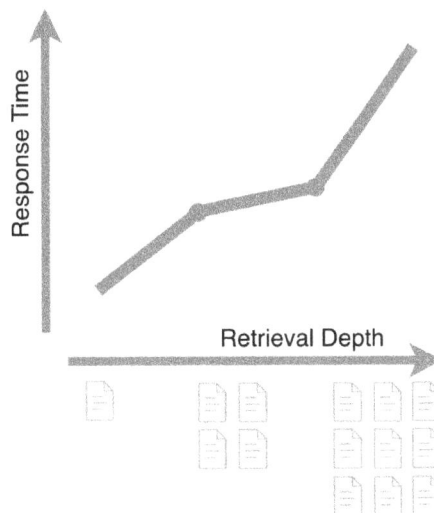

Figure 6.6: Dependency between retrieval depth and response time

And with that, this section highlighted how blending knowledge retrieval with generative AI creates more accurate, contextually rich responses. Now let's get our hands dirty with *Workshop 1: Bootstrap RAG Implementation*, where we'll build a foundational RAG pipeline from scratch. This workshop will guide you through indexing, retrieval, and generation, setting the stage for more advanced techniques. Let's get started by creating a functional RAG workflow!

Workshop 1: Bootstrap RAG implementation

In this workshop, we'll apply the principles of RAG to build a complete pipeline, integrating indexing, retrieval, and generation. We'll start by preparing our data, creating embeddings, and storing them in a vector database. Next, we'll configure the retrieval process to pull relevant context based on specific questions. Finally, we'll combine the retrieved context with a language model to generate informative responses. This hands-on exercise will reinforce the techniques discussed in the chapter, equipping you to build RAG systems that transform data into actionable insights.

Step 1: Prepare the environment

To begin the RAG workshop, make sure you have the following resources and API keys set up:

- **GitHub Colab notebooks**: Access the Colab notebook on GitHub for the exercises: `https://github.com/PacktPublishing/Learn-Mistral`

    - For Pinecone: `/Chapter-6/Ch06_WS1_RAG_Base_PINECONE.ipynb`
    - For in-memory Chroma DB: `Chapter-6/Ch06_WS1_RAG_Base_CHROMADB.ipynb`

- **LangSmith API key**: Obtain and set up your LangSmith API key for advanced language processing integration.

- **HuggingFace token**: Obtain your Hugging Face token and store it securely using the key icon in Google Colab's left panel. Instead of hardcoding, retrieve the token with `userdata.get` and assign it to `os.environ['HF_TOKEN']` in your script. This ensures secure, clean integration with Hugging Face APIs.

- **Pinecone API key and index setup**: Prepare a PineconeDB API key for vector storage and retrieval. Set up a Pinecone index:

    ```
    Index name: book-passages
    Dimension: 1024 (to match embedding output size)
    Metric: Cosine similarity (to measure similarity between embeddings)
    ```

- **Mistral AI API key**: Make sure you have a Mistral AI key to enable access to the language model for generation tasks.

After configuring these resources, open the notebook, enter your API keys in the notebook, and ensure the Pinecone index is ready for storing and retrieving embeddings. This setup will allow you to complete the workshop exercises smoothly.

Why do we need LangSmith?

LangSmith is a toolkit for optimizing language model workflows, especially in applications such as RAG. It integrates with LangChain to streamline model setup, monitoring, and debugging, enabling robust, scalable applications. With features for experimentation and performance tracking, LangSmith ensures that language model systems deliver accurate, reliable responses, making it an essential tool for high-quality, production-grade LLM applications.

Refer to the LangSmith documentation at `https://docs.smith.langchain.com/` (Get Started Guide) for more tutorials on observability, evaluation, prompt engineering, SDK usage, and more.

You could also refer to LangSmith Reference at `https://docs.smith.langchain.com/reference` for technical details such as API endpoints, Python and JS/TS SDKs, architecture, data schemas, and more.

Why do we need the Mistral AI API key?

In contrast to *Chapter 3*, where embeddings were computed locally, this chapter leverages the cloud version of Mistral AI to calculate embeddings directly in the cloud. By using Mistral AI's cloud service through LangChain, we can benefit from scalable, high-performance embedding generation without relying on local resources. This setup requires a Mistral AI API key, enabling seamless access to cloud-based embeddings, which are ideal for large-scale, real-time applications.

Preparing required libraries

Traditionally, we start our workshop Colab by installing the necessary dependencies. This ensures that each component required for the exercises, such as language models, vector stores, tokenizers, and support libraries, is readily available. Here, we install key libraries using `pip`:

```
! pip install langchain_community langchain_mistralai langchainhub
langchain tiktoken langchain-pinecone
```

This command loads the required libraries in a single step, making setup straightforward for immediate use in Colab. Alternatively, you could manage dependencies by listing them in a `requirements.txt` file, which includes each package and version number if needed. This file can be uploaded or linked to Colab with the following:

```
!pip install -r requirements.txt
```

Using `requirements.txt` provides version control and reusability, particularly useful for sharing and maintaining projects across environments. This approach is recommended when working collaboratively or when you need to maintain consistency across multiple sessions.

Initializing environment variables

To ensure a seamless setup for our workshop, we first initialize environment variables to authenticate and connect to necessary services.

```
import os
os.environ['LANGCHAIN_TRACING_V2'] = 'true'
os.environ['LANGCHAIN_ENDPOINT'] = 'https://api.smith.langchain.com'
os.environ['LANGCHAIN_API_KEY'] = '<LangChain API Key goes here>'
os.environ['MISTRAL_API_KEY'] = '<Mistral API Key goes here>'
os.environ['HF_TOKEN'] = '<HuggingFace token goes here>'
os.environ['PINECONE_API_KEY'] = '<Pinecode API Key goes here>'
```

> Instead of hardcoding API keys in your code, you can securely manage them using the key icon on the left panel in Google Colab. Store your keys there as user secrets and access them in your code using `userdata.get('KEY_NAME')` to keep your credentials safe and your notebook cleaner.

Each variable secures access to its respective service, enabling us to trace, connect, and perform vector searches.

Preparing user prompts

In this step, we prepare a list of user prompts, or questions, for querying the RAG system about Moby Dick. Each question is a prompt designed to retrieve specific information from the text:

```
questions = [
    "Who is the main character in Moby Dick?",
    "Who is Ishmael, and why is he important?",
    "What role does Queequeg play in Moby Dick?"]
```

Notice that each question is tailored to elicit meaningful responses on characters and plot elements, setting up focused RAG retrieval and generation. Now that we've set up our environment
and prepared a list of questions to explore, it's time to move into the first major phase of our RAG
workflow: indexing.

Step 2: Indexing

In this section, we'll process the text of Moby Dick, split it into manageable chunks, and generate
embeddings. These embeddings will be stored in our vector database, creating a foundation for
efficient and accurate retrieval when answering our questions.

Loading text from a URL

In this step, we load the full text of Moby Dick directly from a URL. This prepares the document
for indexing and further processing.

```python
from langchain_community.document_loaders import WebBaseLoader
# there can be multiple urls
loader = WebBaseLoader(
    "https://www.gutenberg.org/cache/epub/2701/pg2701.txt")
books = loader.load()
```

This code allows us to fetch multiple documents by adding additional URLs if needed. The books
variable now contains the full text, ready for splitting and embedding.

WebBaseLoader in LangChain is a versatile tool designed for loading content from web pages.
It simplifies the process of retrieving documents by fetching the text from specified URLs and
preparing it for downstream processing.

The parameters of WebBaseLoader are as follows:

- url: (Required) A single URL or a list of URLs to fetch content from
- headers: (Optional) Allows custom HTTP headers to be added to the request, which can
  be useful for handling specific content types or passing API tokens
- timeout: (Optional) Sets a timeout for the request in seconds, ensuring the loader does
  not hang if a web page is slow to respond

Here's an example of WebBaseLoader:

```
loader = WebBaseLoader(
    url=[
        "https://example.com/text1",
        "https://example.com/text2"],
    headers={"User-Agent": "Mozilla/5.0"})
```

> If we need to load an HTML page, WebBaseLoader can handle it, but we might need
> to apply additional processing to clean or parse the HTML into readable text. In such
> cases, you could pair WebBaseLoader with HTML parsers, such as BeautifulSoup,
> to extract only the main content sections before passing it through the RAG pipeline.

Splitting text into chunks

In this step, we split the loaded text into smaller chunks, preparing it for efficient indexing and retrieval. Each chunk maintains context while fitting within token limits.

```
from langchain.text_splitter import RecursiveCharacterTextSplitter

text_splitter = RecursiveCharacterTextSplitter.from_tiktoken_encoder(
    chunk_size=300,
    chunk_overlap=50)

# Make splits
splits = text_splitter.split_documents(books)
len(splits)
```

Here's the output:

```
1412
```

This output shows that the text was split into 1,412 chunks, each sized and overlapped for optimal retrieval quality.

Grinding text to vectors and sending to the vector store

In this step, we convert text chunks into vector embeddings and store them in a vector database for efficient retrieval. Each vector represents the semantic meaning of a text chunk.

```python
from pinecone import Pinecone
from langchain_mistralai import MistralAIEmbeddings
# Not langchain_community.vectorstores
from langchain_pinecone import PineconeVectorStore

# Initialize Pinecone client
pc = Pinecone(api_key=os.environ["PINECONE_API_KEY"])
index = pc.Index("book-passages")

# Create LangChain vectorstore
vectorstore = PineconeVectorStore(
    index=index,
    embedding=MistralAIEmbeddings(),
    text_key="text"
)
```

Here, each text **chunk** in splits is converted to a vector using Mistral AI embeddings, and these vectors are then stored in Pinecone under the book-passages index, enabling rapid similarity-based retrieval.

At this point, make sure the Pinecode book-passages index is prepared. To set up the book-passages index in Pinecone with the correct configuration, follow these steps in the Pinecone UI:

1. Log in to your Pinecone account and navigate to the **Indexes** section.
2. Create a new index by selecting the **Create Index** button.
3. Configure the index:

    ```
    Index Name: Enter book-passages to match the name used in our code.
    Dimensions: Set to 1024 to match the Mistral embedding output size.
    Metric: Choose Cosine Similarity for efficient similarity-based
    searches.
    ```

4. Save the Index by confirming your settings.

book-passages ⊛

METRIC	DIMENSIONS	HOST
cosine	1024	https://book-passages-6k0twet.svc.aped-4627-b74a.pinecone.io ⧉

CLOUD	REGION	TYPE
aws AWS	us-east-1 ⧉	Serverless

Figure 6.7: Example Pinecone index configuration

After creating the index, you'll see it listed on your Pinecone dashboard. To confirm, take a screen-shot of *Figure 6.7* showing the book-passages index with 1024 dimensions and cosine similarity. This screenshot will serve as a reference to ensure the configuration matches the requirements for our RAG workshop.

With our text chunks now converted into vector embeddings and securely stored in Pinecone, we're ready to move on to the next major phase of our RAG workflow: retrieval.

Step 3: Retrieval

In this section, we'll set up a retriever to query our vector store and pull the most relevant text passages based on specific user questions. This retrieval step forms the foundation for generating contextually accurate answers.

Let's retrieve the most relevant vector from the Pinecone vector store based on the first question in our list, using a retriever object to locate the top match:

```
retriever = vectorstore.as_retriever(search_kwargs={"k": 1})
docs = retriever.invoke(questions[0])
docs[0]
```

- search_kwargs={"k": 1}: Specifies that we want only the top-ranked document (k=1) returned for each query
- questions[0]: Uses the first question in our list as the search query
- docs[0]: Outputs the most relevant document based on the query, allowing us to inspect the retrieved content

The output shows the retrieved document based on the input question, providing the relevant text from Moby Dick along with metadata about its source:

```
Document(id='f5c42f4c-015d-4b4e-89ee-8aaab8dd7441',
metadata={'source': 'https://www.gutenberg.org/cache/epub/2701/
pg2701.txt'}, page_content='him—him—" faltering hard for a word, and
screwing his hand round and\r\nround as though uncorking a bottle—
"like him—him—"\r\n\r\n\r\n"Corkscrew!" cried Ahab...')
```

- `metadata` contains the source URL (`https://www.gutenberg.org/cache/epub/2701/pg2701.txt`), identifying the origin of the retrieved content.

- `page_content` displays the relevant text snippet where Captain Ahab and Starbuck discuss Moby Dick. This passage highlights Ahab's obsession and the fateful encounter with the whale, offering rich context for answering the question.

With our relevant passages successfully retrieved from the vector store, we're now ready to move into the generation phase.

Step 4: Generation

In this step, we'll bring together the retrieved data and transform it into readable answers using a language model. The following steps will guide us through setting up a prompt template, initializing the language model, and creating a simple chain to generate responses. Finally, we'll test our setup by running the chain for each of our prepared questions.

Initializing a prompt template for the generator

We define a prompt template to instruct the language model on how to answer based on the provided context. This template helps ensure that responses are focused and relevant to the given question.

```
from langchain_mistralai import ChatMistralAI
from langchain.prompts import ChatPromptTemplate

# Prompt
template = """Answer the question based only on the following context:
    {context}

    Question: {question}
```

```
"""
```

```
prompt = ChatPromptTemplate.from_template(template)
prompt
```

- template: A multi-line string instructing the model to answer the question solely based on the context provided. {context} and {question} are placeholders that will be dynamically filled with relevant data.

- ChatPromptTemplate.from_template(template): Initializes the prompt structure, preparing it to receive input for context and question placeholders.

  The output shows the initialized prompt template in detail:

```
ChatPromptTemplate(input_variables=['context',
'question'], input_types={}, partial_variables={},
messages=[HumanMessagePromptTemplate(prompt=PromptTemplate(input_
variables=['context', 'question'], input_types={}, partial_
variables={}, template='Answer the question based only on the
following context:\n{context}\n\nQuestion: {question}\n'),
additional_kwargs={})])
```

- ChatPromptTemplate indicates the template structure, displaying the input variables— context and question.

- messages contains a structured representation of the prompt for the language model, ensuring it's ready to dynamically insert specific context and question values for generating responses. This structure enables flexibility and reusability across various questions.

Using prompt templates from LangChain Hub

LangChain's Hub provides a centralized collection of community-shared prompt templates, which you can use to accelerate your development process. These templates are designed to support various applications, from RAG to summarization and question-answering.

You can pull a prompt template directly from LangChain Hub using the hub.pull() method:

```
from langchain import hub
# Pull a predefined RAG prompt template from the LangChain Hub
prompt_template = hub.pull("rlm/rag-prompt")
```

In this example, `hub.pull("rlm/rag-prompt")` downloads a prompt template named "rlm/rag-prompt" from LangChain Hub, which can be used directly in your RAG setup.

> LangSmith's Hub is like a shared toolbox built by the community. It's packed with ready-to-use prompt templates that you can explore, adapt, and drop straight into your own RAG workflows. Instead of starting from scratch, you can learn from what others have already built and tested.
>
> You can search the hub by keyword or tag, which makes discovery simple. For example, try looking up terms such as *rag-prompt* or *retrieval-qa-chat*, or browse by tags such as **SQL**, **Summarization**, **Writing**, or **RAG** to find templates that fit your use case.
>
> One prompt worth checking out right away is `rlm/rag-prompt-mistral`. You can experiment with it directly in the playground here: `https://smith.langchain.com/hub/rlm/rag-prompt-mistral`. To see the full catalog, head to LangChain Hub at `https://smith.langchain.com/hub`. Using these community-tested templates can save you time, improve consistency, and help you build more effective RAG systems.

Initializing the LLM

Now, we'll initialize the LLM that will generate responses based on retrieved data and the prompt template. Here, we're using Mistral AI's chat model to create consistent, fact-based answers.

```
llm = ChatMistralAI(model_name="mistral-large-latest", temperature=0)
```

- `model_name="mistral-large-latest"` specifies the version of the Mistral model we want to use, ensuring up-to-date performance.
- `temperature=0` controls response randomness. A temperature of 0 makes responses highly deterministic, ideal for generating accurate, focused answers to factual questions.

This setup prepares the LLM to generate structured responses based on our context and questions.

Initializing a simple chain

Next, we create a simple chain that combines the prompt template with the language model, streamlining the process from input to output.

This chain will take our context and question, pass them through the prompt, and generate a response with the LLM.

```
chain = prompt | llm
```

- `prompt`: The prompt template prepared in *Step 4.1*, containing placeholders for context and question, structured to guide the LLM's response
- `|`: A pipeline operator that links the prompt and language model, passing the output of the prompt directly into the LLM
- `llm`: The initialized language model (`ChatMistralAI`), which generates responses based on the formatted prompt

This chain simplifies the RAG process, enabling a single, reusable structure for querying and generating responses.

Invoking the chain for a given user question

In this step, we use the chain to answer a specific question. The chain combines the prompt, context, and question, and then the LLM generates a concise response.

```
chain.invoke({"context":docs,"question":questions[0]})
```

- `chain.invoke(...)`: Runs the chain, sending input values directly to the model for processing.
- `"context":docs`: Supplies the retrieved document context, helping the LLM focus on relevant information for the answer.
- `"question":questions[0]`: Passes the first question in the list, asking the LLM to respond specifically to this query. The output will be as follows:

```
AIMessage(content='The main character in Moby Dick is Captain
Ahab.', additional_kwargs={}, response_metadata={'token_usage':
{'prompt_tokens': 397, 'total_tokens': 409, 'completion_
tokens': 12}, 'model': 'mistral-large-latest', 'finish_reason':
'stop'}, id='run-e051f82a-afdb-49d3-8f68-372006715325-0', usage_
metadata={'input_tokens': 397, 'output_tokens': 12, 'total_tokens':
409})
```

- `AIMessage(content=...)`: Displays the LLM's answer, identifying Captain Ahab as the main character in Moby Dick

- response_metadata: Provides details such as token usage (prompt_tokens, completion_ tokens), the model used (mistral-large-latest), and the reason for completion (finish_ reason).

- usage_metadata: Shows the token count breakdown, indicating the input and output token usage for this request.

This response confirms that the chain works as expected, delivering accurate and efficient answers based on context.

Testing all questions

In this final step, we test the chain on multiple questions. The chain retrieves relevant context, formats the prompt, invokes the LLM, and processes output for each question, delivering accurate, structured answers.

```python
from langchain_core.output_parsers import StrOutputParser
from langchain_core.runnables import RunnablePassthrough


rag_chain = (
    {"context": retriever, "question": RunnablePassthrough()}
    | prompt
    | llm
    | StrOutputParser()
)


for question in questions:
    print("--------------")
    print(question)
    print(rag_chain.invoke(question))
```

- {"context": retriever, "question": RunnablePassthrough()}: Initializes the chain with two main inputs:

- context: The retriever object, which searches the vector database to pull relevant context based on the question, ensuring the LLM has the most contextually relevant data.

- question: A RunnablePassthrough() object that passes each question through the chain without modification, holding the user's query for the LLM to address.

- RunnablePassthrough(): Allows questions to flow directly to the chain without modification, acting as a placeholder.

- `| prompt | llm | StrOutputParser()`: Chains the prompt, LLM, and output parser to form a complete RAG process.

- `| prompt`: The pipeline operator (`|`) links the context and question inputs to the prompt template. This template structures the information by placing the retrieved context and question into a formatted prompt, guiding the LLM's response to stay relevant to the provided context.

- `| llm`: Connects the prompt to the LLM—in this case, ChatMistralAI, which generates responses based on the structured prompt.

- `| StrOutputParser()`: Parses the raw output from the LLM into a clean string format, ensuring the response is readable and suitable for display.

- `rag_chain.invoke(question)`: Executes the chain for each question, using the RAG pipeline to produce accurate, context-driven answers by combining retrieval, prompt formatting, model generation, and output parsing.

The output will be as follows:

```
------------
Who is the main character in Moby Dick?
The main character in Moby Dick is Captain Ahab.
------------
Who is Ishmael, and why is he important?
Ishmael is the narrator of the story. He is important because the
story is told from his perspective, and he is interacting with other
characters, such as Captain Peleg, to potentially join a ship's
crew.
------------
What role does Queequeg play in Moby Dick?
Queequeg is a harpooneer in Moby Dick.
```

Each response is accurate and contextually relevant, confirming that the RAG chain works effectively across multiple queries. This process enables consistent, structured answers for complex questions.

Let's step into LangSmith to inspect how our application behaves by tracing call sequences, reviewing outputs, and analyzing metrics in a unified console.

RunnableSequence TRACE

Before diving into individual steps, it is useful to view the RAG pipeline as a whole. LangSmith provides a **TRACE** view that captures the execution of the entire workflow in sequence, making it easier to assess overall performance and resource usage.

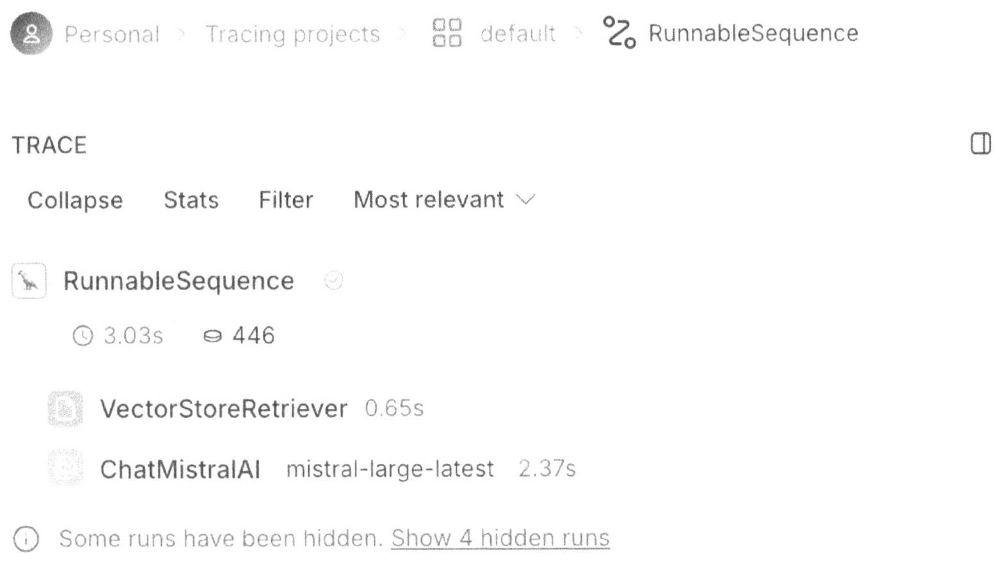

Personal > Tracing projects > default > RunnableSequence

TRACE

Collapse   Stats   Filter   Most relevant ∨

RunnableSequence ⊘

  ⏱ 3.03s   ⊜ 446

  VectorStoreRetriever 0.65s

  ChatMistralAI mistral-large-latest 2.37s

ⓘ Some runs have been hidden. Show 4 hidden runs

Figure 6.8: RunnableSequense TRACE – LangSmith screen

Figure 6.8 illustrates this **RunnableSequence** trace, which summarizes the process through the following key details:

- **VectorStoreRetriever**: Took 0.65 seconds to complete and retrieve the relevant context.
- **ChatMistralAI**: Took 2.37 seconds to generate a response, using the mistral-large-latest model. The total number of tokens used (446) is displayed alongside latency.
- **Total Workflow Duration**: 3.03 seconds, showing the total time taken from the beginning of retrieval to the final answer generation.

VectorStoreRetriever

Retrieval is the first active phase of the pipeline, where the system locates relevant context to ground the model's response.

VectorStoreRetriever	Add to ∨ ⬆ ✎

Run Feedback Metadata	⧉ Run ID ⧉ Trace ID ⬚

Input ∨

```
1    query: Who is Ishmael, and why is he important?
```

YAML ↕

Rendered Output ∨

DOCUMENTS 1

📄 I made no doubt, was all eagerness to vanish from before the awak...   +1

START TIME
11/01/2024, 10:48:56 PM

END TIME
11/01/2024, 10:48:57 PM

TIME TO FIRST TOKEN
N/A

STATUS
⊘ Success

TOTAL TOKENS
0 tokens

LATENCY
◷ 0.65s

TYPE
Retriever

Figure 6.9: VectorStoreRetriever – LangSmith screen

As shown, the LangSmith interface organizes this step into three clear views:

- **Input**: This screen shows the initial input query, "Who is Ishmael, and why is he important?"

- **Rendered Output**: The retriever searches the vector store (likely powered by Pinecone or a similar service) and finds a relevant document snippet to answer the question. The retrieved text includes part of a passage from Moby Dick, providing context related to Ishmael.

- **Metadata**: The right sidebar provides execution details, such as the start and end time, latency (0.65 seconds), and status (success). This indicates that the retrieval phase was completed quickly and successfully.

ChatMistralAI

Once the retriever has supplied the relevant context, the generation phase takes over, where the LLM synthesizes the retrieved information into a coherent response. The following screen captures the completion of the generation phase in the RAG workflow:

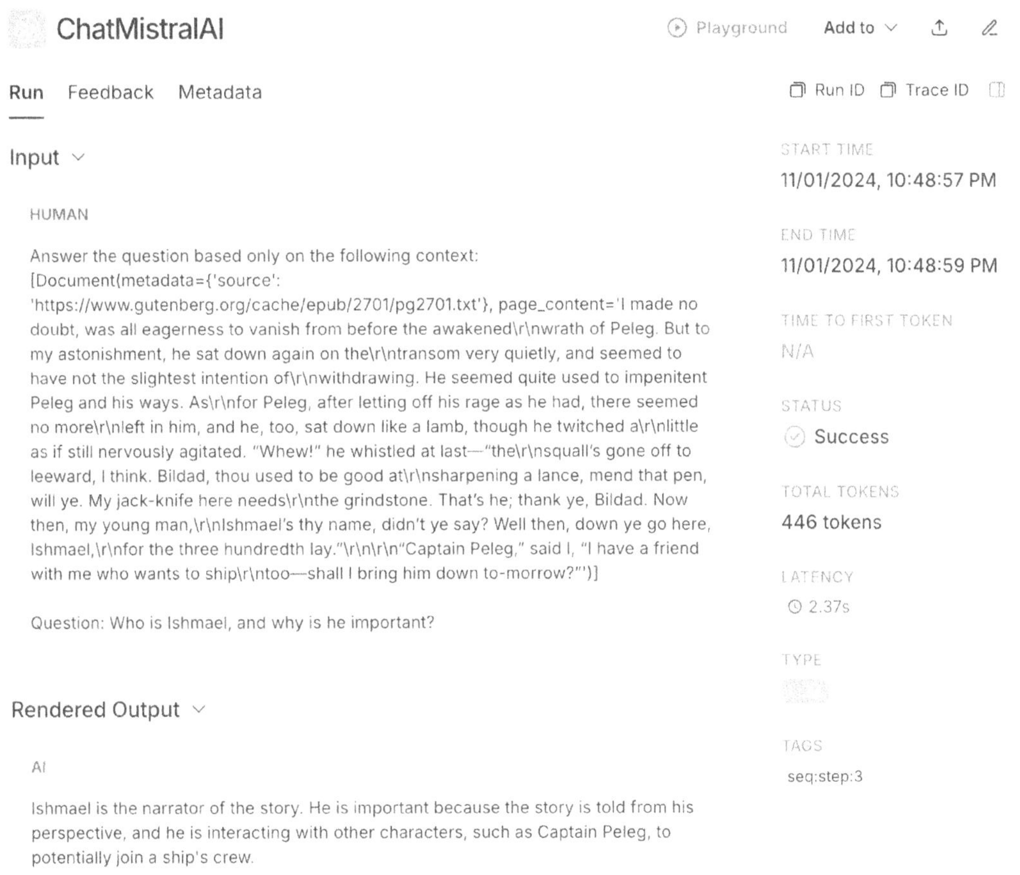

ChatMistralAI   ▶ Playground   Add to ∨   ↥   ✎

Run   Feedback   Metadata   ⧉ Run ID   ⧉ Trace ID   ⬚

Input ∨   START TIME
                                                 11/01/2024, 10:48:57 PM
HUMAN
                                                 END TIME
Answer the question based only on the following context: 11/01/2024, 10:48:59 PM
[Document(metadata={'source':
'https://www.gutenberg.org/cache/epub/2701/pg2701.txt'}, page_content='I made no   TIME TO FIRST TOKEN
doubt, was all eagerness to vanish from before the awakened\r\nwrath of Peleg. But to   N/A
my astonishment, he sat down again on the\r\ntransom very quietly, and seemed to
have not the slightest intention of\r\nwithdrawing. He seemed quite used to impenitent   STATUS
Peleg and his ways. As\r\nfor Peleg, after letting off his rage as he had, there seemed   ⊘ Success
no more\r\nleft in him, and he, too, sat down like a lamb, though he twitched a\r\nlittle
as if still nervously agitated. "Whew!" he whistled at last—"the\r\nsquall's gone off to   TOTAL TOKENS
leeward, I think. Bildad, thou used to be good at\r\nsharpening a lance, mend that pen,   446 tokens
will ye. My jack-knife here needs\r\nthe grindstone. That's he; thank ye, Bildad. Now
then, my young man,\r\nIshmael's thy name, didn't ye say? Well then, down ye go here,   LATENCY
Ishmael,\r\nfor the three hundredth lay."\r\n\r\n"Captain Peleg," said I, "I have a friend   ⏱ 2.37s
with me who wants to ship\r\ntoo—shall I bring him down to-morrow?"')]
                                                 TYPE
Question: Who is Ishmael, and why is he important?

                                                 TAGS
Rendered Output ∨   seq:step:3

AI

Ishmael is the narrator of the story. He is important because the story is told from his
perspective, and he is interacting with other characters, such as Captain Peleg, to
potentially join a ship's crew.

Figure 6.10: ChatMistralAI – LangSmith screen

The LangSmith interface in *Figure 6.10* breaks down this phase into the following components:

- **Input:** This section shows the prompt created for the LLM. It includes the following:

    The directive, "Answer the question based only on the following context."

    The retrieved context (the document snippet retrieved in the previous step).

    The question, "Who is Ishmael, and why is he important?"

- **Rendered Output**: The LLM's response is displayed in the **AI** section:

  ```
  Ishmael is the narrator of the story. He is important because the
  story is told from his perspective, and he is interacting with other
  characters, such as Captain Peleg, to potentially join a ship's
  crew.
  ```

  This is a direct, contextually accurate answer to the question based on the retrieved information.

- **Metadata**: The sidebar on the right provides further execution details:

  ```
  Total tokens: 446 tokens were used in this generation (prompt +
  response).
  Latency: 2.37 seconds, showing the time taken by the LLM to process
  the input and generate an output.
  Status: Success, indicating that the LLM completed the task without
  issues.
  ```

The same traces are available for each of those user questions we ran through the RAG chain. You can browse them on your own once you complete the workshop.

In this workshop, we didn't just build a RAG pipeline. We set out on a journey to unlock the full potential of AI-driven knowledge retrieval. RAG is a pursuit of understanding, a relentless quest to bring clarity from the depths of data. With the techniques you've learned, you're now equipped to navigate your own course, uncovering and shaping insights hidden in the vast oceans of information. Sail onward and let your RAG systems guide you on this exciting voyage of discovery!

Understanding the next workshops

In the next three workshops, we'll dive deeper into our multi-step retrieval and generation approach, each building upon the concepts we've introduced.

In *Workshop 2*, we'll explore **multi-query generation**. Here, we create varied rephrasing of the same question to uncover multiple perspectives, enriching our retrieval process by viewing the topic from different angles.

Workshop 3 will focus on **detailed sub-queries**, where we narrow down on specific aspects of a question to gather precise and nuanced information. This approach allows us to capture finer details and add depth to our responses.

Finally, *Workshop 4* introduces **step-back generification**. We'll rephrase questions to broaden their scope, providing contextual understanding by situating topics within a larger framework, and giving us a comprehensive view.

Multi-query Prompt `Workshop 2`

Multi-query prompts are like photographing a subject from different angles, capturing unique perspectives. Each rephrased question is a "new angle," revealing different aspects of the topic. Together, they provide a richer, more complete understanding by covering more ground than a single view.

Detalized Sub-queries `Workshop 3`

Detailed subqueries are like zooming in on a subject to capture finer details. Each subquery focuses on specific aspects, revealing nuances and in-depth information that a broad question might overlook. This approach enhances the answer by adding intricate details.

Step-Back Generification `Workshop 4`

Step-back generification is like zooming out to capture the surrounding landscape. By rephrasing the question in broader terms, it helps situate the topic within a wider context, offering a comprehensive view that includes the big picture

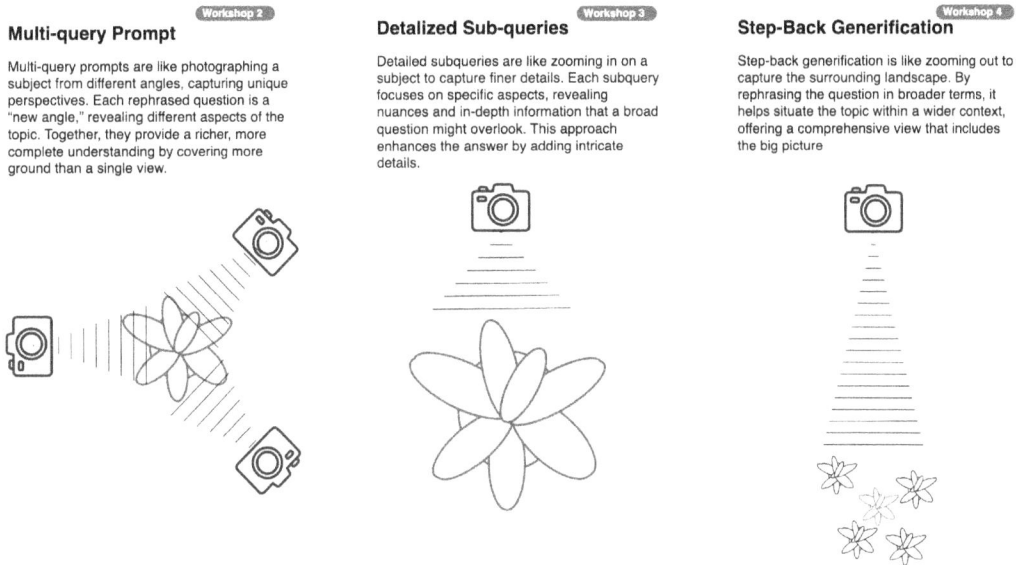

Figure 6.11: Approaches and their analogies

Together, these workshops and their illustrated approaches will guide us toward creating responses that are both detailed and contextually rich. Having those grounds covered, let us move on to *Workshop 2: Multi-query approach*, where we'll enhance retrieval by rephrasing a single question into multiple variations.

Workshop 2: Multi-query approach

In this workshop, we explore a multi-step approach to improve the relevance and objectivity of answers generated from vector-based search systems. Often, a single query may limit the range of information retrieved, as it relies on exact phrasing to yield relevant matches. Here, we tackle this by first rephrasing the user's question in several ways to cover multiple perspectives. Each variation is designed to uncover different facets of information that may otherwise be missed in a traditional similarity search.

Once the rephrased queries are prepared, we execute a vector search for each version, retrieving a broader set of documents that contain unique insights. This variety helps counteract potential biases and limitations of a single search phrase. In the final generation phase, we aggregate and analyze the diverse answers collected, synthesizing them into a well-rounded, summarized response. By answering the question from different angles, we create a more objective and comprehensive answer, giving users the benefit of multiple perspectives in one cohesive result. This method enhances the depth and accuracy of responses, making it ideal for complex questions.

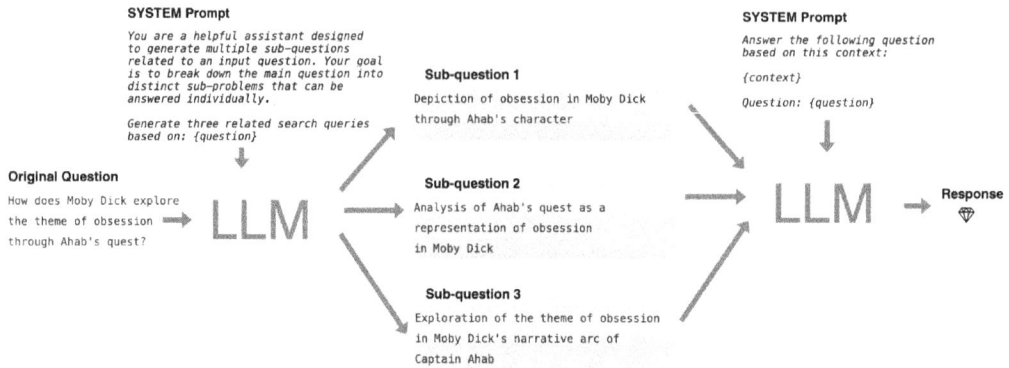

Figure 6.12: Multi-query approach

Figure 6.12 illustrates the multi-query approach, where a single question is rephrased into multiple variations to improve retrieval accuracy. Each variation explores different perspectives, enhancing the relevance of retrieved documents. The final step combines the retrieved context to generate a comprehensive and high-quality response using the language model.

Step 1: Prepare the environment

The environment preparation for this workshop is identical to previous setups. The only differences are as follows:

- The Colab notebook file to use is `Chapter-6/Ch06_WS2_RAG_multi_query_*.ipynb`
- The set of questions has been updated specifically for this workshop
- The retrieval and generation parts of RAG have been reworked and use a *multi-query* and *drill-down* approach

Access the Colab notebook on GitHub for the exercises:

- For Pinecone DB: `Chapter-6/Ch06_WS2_RAG_multi_query_PINECONE.ipynb`
- For Chroma DB: `Chapter-6/Ch06_WS2_RAG_multi_query_CHROMADB.ipynb`

The steps to prepare the required libraries remain the same as for the previous workshop. You'll install and import the same set of libraries to ensure consistency and compatibility with our environment, allowing us to focus on the unique aspects of this workshop without reconfiguring the setup:

```
! pip install langchain_community langchain_mistralai langchainhub
langchain tiktoken langchain-pinecone
```

Similarly, we'll reuse the same set of environment variables from *Workshop 1* to connect with LangSmith, Mistral, and Pinecone:

```
import os

os.environ['LANGCHAIN_TRACING_V2'] = 'true'
os.environ['LANGCHAIN_ENDPOINT'] = 'https://api.smith.langchain.com'
os.environ['LANGCHAIN_API_KEY'] = '<Lagchain API Key goes here>'
os.environ['MISTRAL_API_KEY'] = '<Mistral API Key goes here>'
os.environ['PINECONE_API_KEY'] = '<Pinecone API Key goes here>'
```

Preparing user prompts

We provide a variety of user prompts to simulate different query perspectives. For efficiency and faster processing, many of these prompts are commented out initially. This allows you to run the RAG setup smoothly without processing all queries at once. Once you confirm that the RAG pipeline is working as expected, we recommend uncommenting additional prompts to explore the full range of questions.

```
questions = [ "What does Moby Dick say about humanity's struggle against nature?",
"How does Moby Dick explore the theme of obsession through Ahab's quest?",
"How is Captain Ahab portrayed as both a hero and a villain in Moby Dick?",
#   "What motivates Ishmael to join the Pequod, and how does he change throughout the novel?",
#   "What does the white whale symbolize in Moby Dick, and how does it relate to Ahab's obsession?",
#   "How does the novel Moby Dick use the ocean as a symbol of the unknown?",
#   "How does Melville's narrative style in Moby Dick contribute to the sense of adventure and mystery?",
#   "How does Ishmael's perspective shape the reader's understanding of the story in Moby Dick?",
#   "How does Moby Dick reflect 19th-century views on fate and destiny?",
#   "What philosophical questions does Melville raise about human existence and purpose in Moby Dick?",
#   "How does Melville use imagery to depict the sea as both beautiful and terrifying in Moby Dick?",
#   "How does Moby Dick describe the vastness and danger of the open
```

```
sea?",
#    "What moral dilemmas do the crew members face in Moby Dick?",
#    "How does Moby Dick present Ahab's pursuit of revenge as both
justified and self-destructive?"
]
question = questions[0]
```

To streamline the preparation steps, we initialize the question variable with the first item in the questions list. This setup allows you to test and refine each stage without loading multiple queries, keeping the focus on optimizing the process before expanding to the full set of prompts.

Step 2: Indexing

Indexing in this workshop follows the exact same steps as in *Workshop 1*. We begin by setting up the vector index, ensuring it's optimized for storing and retrieving embeddings based on our document corpus. Next, we process each document, converting it into embeddings that capture semantic meaning. These embeddings are then stored in the index, allowing for quick, similarity-based retrieval in later stages.

The code is the same and fully implemented in Ch06_WS2_RAG_multi_query_*.ipynb. We will skip the explanation and move on to the next step.

Step 3: Retrieval

In this workshop's retrieval step, we'll take an enhanced, exploratory approach to uncovering valuable information from our documents. Here's the plan:

1. **Initialize and explore**: We'll start by setting up a "drill-down" prompt to generate diverse rephrased questions based on the original query. Let's pause here to examine these rephrased prompts closely, observing how each one reveals different angles of the question.

2. **Vector search and merge**: With these variations in hand, we'll perform a vector search to find all relevant documents for each rephrased query, then merge the unique content pieces. This step enriches the answer by pooling diverse insights.

3. **Generate a comprehensive answer**: Finally, we'll pass the original question and the merged content to our RAG model. This approach brings together multiple perspectives, enabling the model to provide a well-rounded, comprehensive response.

This enhanced retrieval method allows us to uncover layers of meaning and depth, giving richer, more nuanced answers than a single query approach.

Initialize the retriever

In this step, we define our retriever to locate the most relevant documents based on similarity to our query. By setting k to 1 in `search_kwargs`, we are instructing the retriever to return only the top result for each query. This approach helps us focus on the single most relevant document for each prompt, ensuring that we capture the closest match without additional noise from less relevant documents:

```
retriever = vectorstore.as_retriever(search_kwargs={"k": 1})
```

Initializing a drill-down prompt template

In this step, we're setting up a prompt to generate diverse rephrasing of our original question. This multi-query approach allows us to create several variations of the same question, each capturing a unique perspective. These rephrased questions help in retrieving a richer variety of documents by uncovering information that might be missed in a single, straightforward search. By broadening the query scope, we improve the quality of information gathered to generate a comprehensive answer.

The following starting snippet imports `ChatPromptTemplate`, which we use to structure the prompt. This template helps us specify the details of how we want our rephrased questions to be generated:

```
from langchain.prompts import ChatPromptTemplate
```

We then define our prompt template. The template instructs the LLM to produce five different variations of the input question, each designed to approach the topic from a new angle. This helps us overcome limitations of distance-based similarity search by covering a broader conceptual range:

```
# Multi Query: Different Perspectives
template = """Generate five unique variations of the given user question
to improve document retrieval from a vector database.
The goal is to create diverse perspectives on the question, helping to
mitigate limitations of distance-based similarity search.
Separate each alternative question with a new line. Original question:
{question}"""
```

This prompt setup generates rephrased versions of the question that reveal different angles and facets of the topic. By retrieving content based on multiple perspectives, we can gather a more comprehensive set of documents that cover the subject in greater depth and detail.

Then we create an instance of `ChatPromptTemplate` called `prompt_perspectives`, allowing us to reuse this prompt template with different questions as input.

```
prompt_perspectives = ChatPromptTemplate.from_template(template)
```

Next, we import `StrOutputParser` to format output as strings and `ChatMistralAI`, which we use as the language model to process the prompt:

```
from langchain_core.output_parsers import StrOutputParser
from langchain_mistralai import ChatMistralAI
```

Finally, we perform multi-query generation:

```
generate_queries = (
    prompt_perspectives
    | ChatMistralAI(temperature=0)
    | StrOutputParser()
    | (lambda x: x.split("\n"))
)
```

- `prompt_perspectives`: The prompt template we defined is fed as the input.
- `ChatMistralAI(temperature=0)`: We use `ChatMistralAI` to generate text, setting temperature to 0 for deterministic responses. This ensures the LLM generates consistent, rephrased questions.
- `StrOutputParser()`: Parses the output into a plain string format.
- `(lambda x: x.split("\n"))`: Splits the output by newline to obtain a list of individual rephrased questions.

With our multi-query setup ready, we're now prepared to examine the rephrased questions. In the next step, we'll observe each variation and see how it broadens the scope of our search. This will allow us to ensure that each question captures a unique angle, enhancing the quality and diversity of the information retrieved.

Generating rephrased questions

In this step, we loop through each question in our list, generating multiple rephrased versions of each question. By viewing these rephrased prompts, we gain insight into how different angles of the question might reveal varied content, broadening the scope of our retrieval process. Each rephrased question helps us capture different facets of the original inquiry, creating a richer basis for document retrieval.

The following loop iterates over each question, generates five rephrased versions using generate_queries, and prints both the original question and each rephrased version:

```
for question in questions:
    print("--------------")
    print(question)
rephrased_questions = generate_queries.invoke({"question":question})
for rephrased_question in rephrased_questions:
    print("\t"+rephrased_question)
```

Here's the output snippet:

```
--------------
What does Moby Dick say about humanity's struggle against nature?
1. In what ways does Herman Melville's "Moby Dick" explore the theme of
human conflict with nature?
2. How does the novel "Moby Dick" portray the struggle between mankind and
natural forces?
3. Examine the depiction of humanity's battle against nature as presented
in "Moby Dick".
4. In the context of "Moby Dick", how can we understand the literary
treatment of human's fight against nature?
5. How does Melville use the story of "Moby Dick" to illustrate and
critique humanity's attempt to dominate nature?
--------------
```

For the original question, What does Moby Dick say about humanity's struggle against nature?, the generated rephrased questions reveal different perspectives on the theme. For example, How does Melville use the story of Moby Dick to illustrate and critique humanity's attempt to dominate nature? resents a critical lens, focusing on humanity's intent to control nature, while Examine the depiction of humanity's battle against nature as presented in Moby Dick offers a more analytical approach. This variation allows us to retrieve a broader range of relevant content.

Now that we have generated diverse rephrasing for each question, we're ready to initialize the retrieval chain. In the next section, we'll collect a unique list of documents based on each rephrased query and then invoke the chain to gather the most relevant information for our final response.

Initializing and calling the retrieval chain

We will now set up a function to consolidate and deduplicate documents retrieved for each rephrased question. By taking a "unique union" of the documents, we ensure that only one copy of each relevant piece of content is included in our final collection, improving efficiency and reducing redundancy. This setup will help us create a more streamlined and comprehensive response by minimizing repetitive information.

Let us run through the code. As a starter, we import `dumps` and `loads` to handle the serialization and deserialization of document objects. This allows us to convert documents to strings for deduplication, then revert them back to their original format:

```
from langchain.load import dumps, loads
```

We then define the `get_unique_union` function, which takes a list of lists (each representing documents retrieved per query) and returns a unique set of documents:

```
def get_unique_union(documents: list[list]):
    """ Unique union of retrieved docs """
```

Next, we flatten the nested list of documents into a single list and serialize each document to a string format using `dumps`. This makes it easier to deduplicate:

```
# Flatten list of lists, and convert each Document to string
flattened_docs = [dumps(doc) for sublist in documents for doc in sublist]
```

We use a set to remove duplicate documents based on their string representation, then convert it back to a list for consistency:

```
# Get unique documents
unique_docs = list(set(flattened_docs))
```

The unique document strings are deserialized back into their original format with `loads`, preparing them for further use:

```
# Return
return [loads(doc) for doc in unique_docs]
```

Next, we set up `retrieval_chain`, which generates query rephrasings, retrieves relevant documents for each query, and then deduplicates them through `get_unique_union`:

```
# Retrieve
retrieval_chain = generate_queries | retriever.map() | get_unique_union
```

The chain is invoked with the original question, producing a unique list of relevant documents:

```
docs = retrieval_chain.invoke({"question":question})
```

We check the length of the unique documents list to understand how many distinct documents have been retrieved:

```
len(docs)
```

With our unique list of documents ready, we're prepared to assemble and invoke the final RAG chain.

Step 4: Generating a summarized response

In this final step, we combine the unique documents retrieved earlier with the original question to generate a cohesive and well-rounded response. This approach allows the model to answer complex questions based on a thorough review of relevant content. By drawing on multiple sources and perspectives, we produce a detailed answer that offers nuanced insights into each question.

We begin by importing essential libraries: `itemgetter` for extracting specific elements from a dictionary, `ChatMistralAI` to power our language model, and `RunnablePassthrough` for handling data through pipelines.

```
from operator import itemgetter
from langchain_mistralai import ChatMistralAI
from langchain_core.runnables import RunnablePassthrough
```

The following template instructs the model to answer the question based on the context provided. It allows the model to access necessary background information when formulating its response.

```
# RAG
template = """Answer the following question based on this context:

{context}

Question: {question}
"""
```

The prompt instructs the language model to focus on the provided context when answering the question, ensuring that the response is grounded in specific information retrieved from the documents. This prompt guides the model to synthesize information from various sources, resulting in a coherent and comprehensive answer.

We then create a prompt using the preceding defined template, which will be used to format the context and question for the model.

```
prompt = ChatPromptTemplate.from_template(template)
```

Further, we initialize the language model with a temperature of 0, ensuring deterministic responses that focus on accuracy over creativity:

```
llm = ChatMistralAI(temperature=0)
```

We then set up the RAG chain:

```
final_rag_chain = (
    {"context": retrieval_chain, "question": itemgetter("question")}
    | prompt
    | llm
    | StrOutputParser()
)
```

1. We provide a dictionary with context from `retrieval_chain` and the question from `itemgetter("question")`.
2. This dictionary is passed through the prompt, formatted for the model.
3. `llm` generates a response based on the formatted input.
4. `StrOutputParser()` converts the output to a readable string format.

For each question, we print the original question, followed by its rephrased versions generated by `generate_queries`. Additionally, `final_rag_chain` is invoked to produce a detailed answer based on the retrieved context and rephrased prompts, and the result is displayed.

```
for question in questions:
    print("-------------")
    print(question)
    rephrased_questions = generate_queries.invoke({
        "question": question})
```

```
for rephrased_question in rephrased_questions:
    print("\t" + rephrased_question)
print("\nAnswer: ")
print(final_rag_chain.invoke({"question": question}))
```

The fragment of the output is displayed here:

```
-------------
How does Moby Dick explore the theme of obsession through Ahab's quest?
1. In what ways does Herman Melville's "Moby Dick" depict the theme of
relentless pursuit, as exemplified by Captain Ahab's fixation on the white
whale?
2. How does Melville use the character of Ahab in "Moby Dick" to delve
into the psychological implications of obsession throughout the narrative?
3. Explore how the theme of obsession is portrayed in "Moby Dick", with
particular focus on Ahab's unyielding hunt for Moby Dick and its impact on
the crew.
4. In the context of "Moby Dick", how can the exploration of Ahab's
fixation on the white whale be seen as a metaphorical representation of
obsession?
5. How does Melville's portrayal of Ahab's obsessive quest for revenge
against Moby Dick in "Moby Dick" contribute to the overall thematic
development of obsession?

Answer:
Moby Dick explores the theme of obsession through Ahab's quest for the
white whale, Moby Dick. Ahab's fixation on revenge against the whale is
so strong that it consumes him entirely, causing him to abandon all other
considerations and focus solely on his vendetta. This monomania is evident
in his determination to hunt down and kill Moby Dick, even at the cost of
his own life and the lives of his crew.

The document highlights how Ahab's obsession extends beyond just the White
Whale, as he may have developed a general hatred towards all sperm whales.
This suggests that his obsession has become all-consuming, affecting his
judgment and behavior towards other aspects of the voyage.
```

```
Furthermore, Ahab recognizes the need to keep his crew's focus on more
immediate concerns rather than the distant and abstract goal of killing
Moby Dick. He understands that prolonged meditation on the terror of
the voyage could undermine their courage and reliability. Therefore, he
ensures that there are temporary interests and employments to keep them
occupied and "healthily suspended" for the final dash towards the whale.

In summary, Moby Dick uses Ahab's relentless pursuit of the white whale
to explore the theme of obsession, demonstrating how it can consume a
person's thoughts, judgments, and actions, affecting not only their own
life but also the lives of those around them.
```

For the question, How does Moby Dick explore the theme of obsession through Ahab's quest?, the output includes five rephrased questions that each examine different facets of Ahab's obsession with Moby Dick. The answer that follows synthesizes this information to provide a multi-dimensional view of Ahab's fixation. It describes Ahab's overwhelming obsession, his impact on the crew, and how Melville uses this narrative to explore the consequences of single-minded revenge.

LangSmith metrics overview

Now, we haven't looked into LangSmith metrics for a while, have we? This overview provides a quick snapshot of our RAG pipeline's performance, showing how each step from rephrasing questions to retrieving and deduplicating documents contributes to building comprehensive answers. By tracking metrics such as latency and output, we ensure each stage works efficiently for accurate, well-rounded responses.

Runs overview

The screen in *Figure 6.13* provides an overview of the different components in the LangSmith **Runs** sequence. Each row shows a specific operation, such as **ChatMistralAI**, **ChatPromptTemplate**, **get_unique_union**, and **VectorStoreRetriever**, along with their respective input and output snippets. The **Name** column lists each component, and the **Input** and **Output** columns display data processed in each stage.

Runs   Threads   Monitor   Setup

≡ Filters   ⟋ Last 7 days   Root Runs   LLM Calls   All Runs   ▥ Columns

	Name	Input	Output	Error
⊘	🔲 ChatMistralAI	human: Answer the fo...	ai: In Moby Dick, Captain Ahab is portrayed as both a hero and a villain in se...	
⊘	🔲 ChatPromptTemplate	How is Captain Ahab ...	{"messages":[{"content":"Answer the following question based on this cont...	
⊘	🔲 get_unique_union	[[{"metadata":{"sourc...	[{"metadata":{"source":"https://www.gutenberg.org/cache/epub/2701/pg27...	
⊘	🔲 VectorStoreRetriever	5. How can the portra...	[{"metadata":{"source":"https://www.gutenberg.org/cache/epub/2701/pg27...	
⊘	🔲 VectorStoreRetriever	4. How does Melville ...	[{"metadata":{"source":"https://www.gutenberg.org/cache/epub/2701/pg27...	
⊘	🔲 VectorStoreRetriever	3. Could we analyze C...	[{"metadata":{"source":"https://www.gutenberg.org/cache/epub/2701/pg27...	
⊘	🔲 VectorStoreRetriever	2. How does the char...	[{"metadata":{"source":"https://www.gutenberg.org/cache/epub/2701/pg27...	
⊘	🔲 VectorStoreRetriever	1. In what ways does ...	[{"metadata":{"source":"https://www.gutenberg.org/cache/epub/2701/pg27...	
⊘	🔲 RunnableEach<VectorStoreRetriever:	["1. In what ways does...	[[{"metadata":{"source":"https://www.gutenberg.org/cache/epub/2701/pg2...	

Figure 6.13: All Runs for this workshop

This high-level summary allows tracking the flow of data across the pipeline and identifying the output generated at each step.

VectorStoreRetriever

The screenshot in *Figure 6.14* zooms in on the **VectorStoreRetriever** component within the LangSmith pipeline:

TRACE   🔲   🔲 **VectorStoreRetriever**   Add to ⌄   ⬆   ✎

Collapse   Stats   Filter
                                                      Run   Feedback   Metadata   🗗 Run ID 🗗 Trace ID 🔳
Most relevant ⌄

⌕ RunnableSequence ⊘   Input ⌄   START TIME
    ⏱ 8.23s   ⊝ 1,594   11/13/2024, 05:37:47 PM
                                                        1   query: 1. In what ways does Herman
   🔲 map:key:context 2.38s   ⌄   Melville's Moby Dick present Captain   END TIME
                                                            Ahab as a heroic figure and as an   11/13/2024, 05:37:47 PM
      🔲 ChatMistr... mistral-s... 1.85s   antagonist?
                                                                                                         TIME TO FIRST TOKEN
      🔲 VectorStoreRetriever 0.49s   YAML ⌄   N/A
      🔲 VectorStoreRetriever 0.42s
      🔲 VectorStoreRetriever 0.47s   STATUS
      🔲 VectorStoreRetriever 0.47s   Rendered Output ⌄   ⊘ Success
      🔲 VectorStoreRetriever 0.51s
      🔲 get_unique_union 0.00s   DOCUMENTS 1   TOTAL TOKENS
   🔲 ChatMistral... mistral-sm... 5.84s   0 tokens
                                                        🗋 of his manner. "Captain Ahab." "What! the cap... +1
ⓘ Some runs have been hidden. Show 8   LATENCY
   hidden runs   ⏱ 0.49s

Figure 6.14: VectorStoreRetriever run details

As you can see, this view displays details about the input query (in this case, a rephrased version of the original question) and the resulting output, which includes a document retrieved from the vector store. This document is based on semantic similarity with the query and provides content relevant to the question about Captain Ahab in Moby Dick. The screen also shows the retrieval latency, confirming that the process succeeded within a specific timeframe.

ChatMistralAI

This view provides a detailed view of the **ChatMistralAI** component, which is responsible for generating rephrased versions of the user's question.

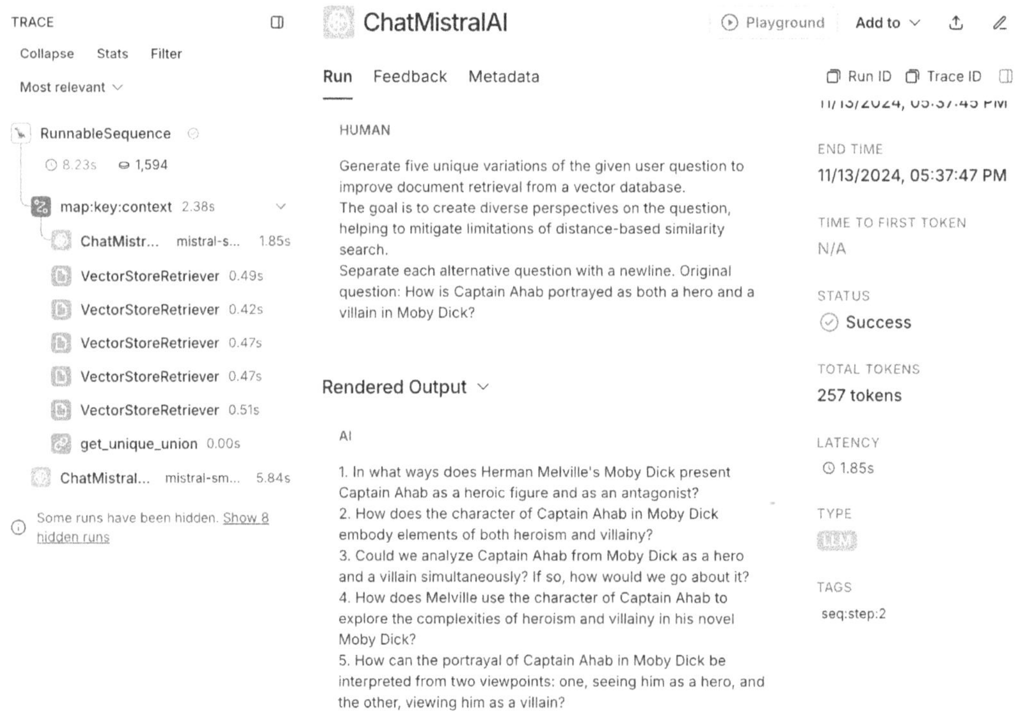

TRACE   ⊡   ⚙ **ChatMistralAI**   ▶ Playground   Add to ∨   ⬆   ✎

Collapse   Stats   Filter   Run   Feedback   Metadata   ⬚ Run ID   ⬚ Trace ID   ⬚

Most relevant ∨   ──   11/13/2024, 05:37:45 PM

⚙ **RunnableSequence** ⓘ   HUMAN   END TIME
   ⊙ 8.23s   ⊘ 1,594   Generate five unique variations of the given user question to   11/13/2024, 05:37:47 PM
                                                                   improve document retrieval from a vector database.
   ⬚ map:key:context 2.38s   ∨   The goal is to create diverse perspectives on the question,   TIME TO FIRST TOKEN
                                                                   helping to mitigate limitations of distance-based similarity   N/A
      ⚙ ChatMistr... mistral-s... 1.85s   search.
                                                                   Separate each alternative question with a newline. Original   STATUS
      ▣ VectorStoreRetriever 0.49s   question: How is Captain Ahab portrayed as both a hero and a   ⊘ Success
                                                                   villain in Moby Dick?
      ▣ VectorStoreRetriever 0.42s
                                                                                                                                        TOTAL TOKENS
      ▣ VectorStoreRetriever 0.47s   257 tokens

      ▣ VectorStoreRetriever 0.47s   Rendered Output ∨   LATENCY
                                                                                                                                        ⊙ 1.85s
      ▣ VectorStoreRetriever 0.51s   AI
                                                                                                                                        TYPE
      ⚙ get_unique_union 0.00s   1. In what ways does Herman Melville's Moby Dick present   ⬚ TEXT
                                                                   Captain Ahab as a heroic figure and as an antagonist?
   ⚙ ChatMistral... mistral-sm... 5.84s   2. How does the character of Captain Ahab in Moby Dick   TAGS
                                                                   embody elements of both heroism and villainy?   seq:step:2
ⓘ Some runs have been hidden. Show 8   3. Could we analyze Captain Ahab from Moby Dick as a hero
   hidden runs   and a villain simultaneously? If so, how would we go about it?
                                                                   4. How does Melville use the character of Captain Ahab to
                                                                   explore the complexities of heroism and villainy in his novel
                                                                   Moby Dick?
                                                                   5. How can the portrayal of Captain Ahab in Moby Dick be
                                                                   interpreted from two viewpoints: one, seeing him as a hero, and
                                                                   the other, viewing him as a villain?

Figure 6.15: ChatMistralAI run details

This view includes both the input prompt, instructing the AI to produce question variations, and the generated output, a list of rephrased questions that each offer a unique angle on the original query. The latency and token count are also displayed, helping to evaluate the performance and efficiency of this step. This component plays a key role in diversifying queries for improved document retrieval.

Next, we'll explore *Workshop 3: Zoom into atomic sub-queries*, where we'll break down complex questions into smaller, focused sub-queries. This approach ensures precise retrieval and allows for detailed responses by addressing each sub-problem individually. Let's learn how this technique refines our RAG process!

Workshop 3: Atomic sub-queries

In *Workshop 3*, we'll continue refining our retrieval approach, building on the techniques from *Workshop 2*. However, instead of generating rephrased variations of the original question, we'll take a different path by breaking down the main question into a series of smaller, **atomic sub-queries**. This approach allows us to target specific elements within a complex question, capturing detailed information piece by piece.

Each atomic question focuses on a distinct aspect of the original question, helping us retrieve precise, nuanced content that might otherwise be missed. By combining these smaller pieces, we'll create a comprehensive, well-rounded answer. We'll zoom in as a photographer would with their camera to look closer at the finer points of the topic, enhancing the depth of our response.

In the following steps, we'll set up the sub-queries and explore how this focused retrieval approach enriches our answers, allowing us to gather detailed insights from each facet of the question.

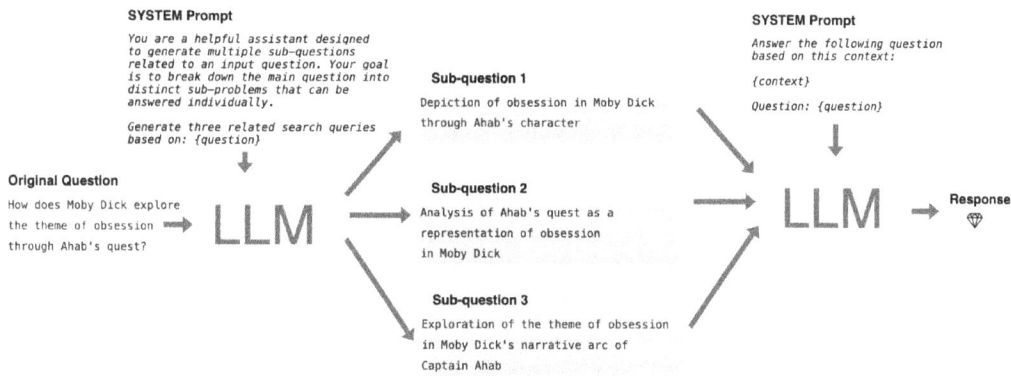

Figure 6.16: Approach overview

Figure 6.16 illustrates a structured approach where an original question is broken into sub-questions via a system prompt. These sub-questions guide the targeted retrievals, and their combined context is used by the LLM to generate a detailed and comprehensive response. This method enhances precision and depth in complex queries.

Step 1: Prepare the environment

The environment preparation for this workshop is identical to previous setups. The only differences are as follows:

- The Colab notebook file to use is `Chapter-6/Ch06_WS3_RAG_chain_of_thought_and_decomposition_*.ipynb`.

- The set of questions has been updated specifically for this workshop.

- The retrieval and generation parts of RAG have been reworked and use a *chain-of-thought* and *decomposition* approach.

Access the Colab notebook on GitHub for the exercises:

- For Pinecone DB: `Chapter-6/Ch06_WS3_RAG_chain_of_thought_and_decomposition_PINECONE.ipynb`

- For Chroma DB: `Chapter-6/Ch06_WS3_RAG_chain_of_thought_and_decomposition_CHROMADB.ipynb`

The remainder of the setup remains unchanged. To avoid repetition, the explanation is omitted as it is identical to the setup in *Workshop 1*.

Step 2: Indexing

The entire *Step 2: Indexing* section is the same as *Workshop 1*. To avoid redundancy, the explanation is omitted. Let's fast-forward to the most interesting part—**retrieval** and **generation**—where we'll see our refined approach in action!

Step 3: Retrieval

In this step, we follow a similar structure to the one we used in previous setups. We start by initializing the retriever and setting up a detailed drill-down prompt. Next, we break down the original question into smaller, focused sub-questions and retrieve relevant information for each from the vector store.

Once we have gathered responses to these detailed queries, we wrap everything up into a final generation prompt. This prompt combines the rich, context-specific answers from the vector store along with the original user question, allowing the LLM to generate a comprehensive, nuanced response based on all the relevant content we've collected.

This approach ensures that the answer reflects both the breadth and depth, synthesizing multiple aspects of the topic into a well-rounded result.

Init retriever

In this step, we set up a retriever that will pull relevant documents from our vector store based on similarity to each of our detailed sub-questions.

```
retriever = vectorstore.as_retriever(search_kwargs={"k": 1})
```

By specifying `"k"=1` in `search_kwargs`, we're instructing the retriever to return only the single most relevant document for each query. This ensures that we focus on the most pertinent information without including extra data that may dilute the specificity of our answers.

With the retriever now configured, we're ready to initialize the drill-down prompt. This prompt will guide the LLM in crafting responses based on the focused, detailed context retrieved for each sub-question, creating a rich foundation for our final answer.

Initializing a drill-down prompt template

In this step, we're preparing a prompt to generate detailed sub-questions from the original query. By breaking the question down into smaller, manageable parts, we can focus on distinct aspects, each requiring specific context. This approach allows us to retrieve more targeted and relevant information, enhancing the depth and accuracy of the final response.

Let us run through this code, starting with the following block. We import `ChatPromptTemplate`, which we'll use to structure the prompt for generating sub-questions:

```
from langchain.prompts import ChatPromptTemplate
```

Next, we define the prompt template. It instructs the LLM to create three specific sub-questions related to the original query, each designed to focus on different facets of the main question. This template is crucial for generating varied yet relevant sub-questions:

```
# Multi Query: Different Perspectives
template = """You are a helpful assistant designed to generate multiple
sub-questions related to an input question.
Your goal is to break down the main question into distinct sub-problems
that can be answered individually.
Generate three related search queries based on: {question} and output each
query on a new line."""
```

> The prompt directs the LLM to break the main question into three distinct sub-questions, providing unique angles for more precise retrieval. Each sub-question focuses on a different aspect of the original query, helping us retrieve a broader range of information to construct a thorough answer.

We then create an instance of `ChatPromptTemplate` named `prompt_perspectives`, which allows us to input different questions while using the same template format:

```
prompt_perspectives = ChatPromptTemplate.from_template(template)
```

The following lines then import `StrOutputParser` for parsing the model's output into string format, and `ChatMistralAI`, the language model we'll use for generating responses:

```
from langchain_core.output_parsers import StrOutputParser
from langchain_mistralai import ChatMistralAI
```

We then define the generate_queries pipeline:

```
generate_queries = (
    prompt_perspectives
    | ChatMistralAI(temperature=0)
    | StrOutputParser()
    | (lambda x: x.split("\n"))
)
```

- prompt_perspectives is the input template with the question to be rephrased
- ChatMistralAI(temperature=0) generates responses with a deterministic approach due to the temperature being set to 0
- StrOutputParser() formats the output as a string
- (lambda x: x.split("\n")) splits the output into a list of sub-questions, each on a new line

Generating detailed questions

In this step, we're using our generated sub-question prompt to create multiple sub-problems for each main question. By decomposing the original question into focused, detailed sub-questions, we can retrieve information on specific aspects of the query, making our answer more comprehensive. This structured approach allows us to tackle complex topics in a way that captures different nuances and perspectives.

```
for question in questions:
    print("--------------")
    print(question)
sub_problems = generate_queries.invoke({"question":question})
for sub_problem in sub_problems:
    print("\t"+sub_problem)
```

This code iterates over each main question, generating a set of focused sub-questions for each one. For each question, it first prints a separator and the question itself. Then, it calls generate_queries to create sub-questions that break down the original question into smaller, targeted components. Finally, it prints each generated sub-question, making it easy to identify distinct aspects of the main topic for more precise information retrieval.

We get the following output fragment:

```
--------------
What does Moby Dick say about humanity's struggle against nature?
1. "Themes of Moby Dick related to human struggle with nature"
2. "Analysis of Moby Dick's portrayal of man versus nature"
3. "Interpretations of the novel Moby Dick on the conflict between
humanity and nature"
```

The output consists of the original question followed by three generated sub-questions, each focusing on a distinct element of the query. For example, for the main question, What does Moby Dick say about humanity's struggle against nature?, the sub-questions are as follows:

- "Themes of Moby Dick related to human struggle with nature" – focuses on over-arching themes
- "Analysis of Moby Dick's portrayal of man versus nature" – examines how this struggle is depicted
- "Interpretations of the novel Moby Dick on the conflict between humanity and nature" – seeks various viewpoints on the conflict

Preparing a unique union

In this step, we're setting up a process to retrieve and deduplicate documents related to our sub-questions, ensuring that only unique content is retained. This approach is similar to what we implemented in *Workshop 2*, where we explained each part in detail.

```python
from langchain.load import dumps, loads


def get_unique_union(documents: list[list]):
    """ Unique union of retrieved docs """
    # Flatten list of lists, and convert each Document to string
    flattened_docs = [dumps(doc) for sublist in documents
                                 for doc in sublist]


    # Get unique documents
    unique_docs = list(set(flattened_docs))


    # Return
```

```
        return [loads(doc) for doc in unique_docs]

    # Retrieve
    retrieval_chain = generate_queries | retriever.map() | get_unique_union
    docs = retrieval_chain.invoke({"question":question})
```

This code flattens the retrieved documents, converts each to a string for easy deduplication, and then returns only the unique documents. This setup helps us avoid redundant content, streamlining our information for a more focused final answer.

Generating a summarized response

In this final generation step, we combine the context collected from our sub-queries to generate a comprehensive answer to the original question. This process is similar to *Workshop 2*, where we created a prompt for generating answers based on retrieved context. Here, we use a similar approach to integrate detailed, deduplicated information for a nuanced response.

```
from operator import itemgetter
from langchain_mistralai import ChatMistralAI
from langchain_core.runnables import RunnablePassthrough
from langchain.prompts import ChatPromptTemplate
from langchain_core.output_parsers import StrOutputParser

# RAG
template = """Answer the following question based on this context:

{context}

Question: {question}
"""

prompt = ChatPromptTemplate.from_template(template)

llm = ChatMistralAI(temperature=0)

final_rag_chain = (
    {
        "context": retrieval_chain,
        "question": itemgetter("question"),
```

```
    }
    | prompt
    | llm
    | StrOutputParser()
)


for question in questions:
    print("-------------")
    print(question)

    rephrased_questions = generate_queries.invoke({"question": question})

    for rephrased_question in rephrased_questions:
        print("\t" + rephrased_question)
        print("\nAnswer: ")

    print(final_rag_chain.invoke({"question": question}))
```

This should give us the following output:

```
How does Moby Dick explore the theme of obsession through Ahab's quest?
1. "Depiction of obsession in Moby Dick through Ahab's character"
2. "Analysis of Ahab's quest as a representation of obsession in Moby
Dick"
3. "Exploration of the theme of obsession in Moby Dick's narrative arc of
Captain Ahab"

Answer:
Moby Dick explores the theme of obsession through the character of Ahab
...

The passage describes how ...
The passage also notes that ...
Furthermore, the passage highlights ...

Overall, Moby Dick uses Ahab's obsession with the white whale to explore
themes of revenge, power, and the all-consuming nature of fixation...
```

The actual response text was shortened, but the structure of the response persists.

For the question, `How does Moby Dick explore the theme of obsession through Ahab's quest?`, the output includes the following:

- Several variations of the main question, each focusing on specific aspects of obsession in Moby Dick.
- A comprehensive response that analyzes Ahab's obsession in multiple dimensions. It details how Ahab's fixation on Moby Dick evolves into an all-consuming monomania, impacting his judgment and actions.

With our final answer generated, we've completed the process of refining a complex query into detailed sub-questions, retrieving relevant information, and synthesizing it into a comprehensive response. This workshop has demonstrated how to achieve depth and clarity in answers by structuring queries and combining detailed insights.

Grab a cup of coffee before we start *Workshop 4: Generification approach*, where we'll explore how to transform specific questions into broader, step-back queries. This technique provides a wider perspective, enabling the system to generate more comprehensive and insightful responses to complex topics. Let's see how generification enhances our RAG workflow!

Workshop 4: Generification approach

In *Workshop 4*, we take a new approach to refining our retrieval and generation process by creating *step-back questions*. These are broader, more generalized versions of the original user question. Instead of narrowing down the focus, as we did with drill-down sub-questions, step-back questions allow us to explore the topic within a wider context.

For example, if the original question is *"What are the economic impacts of tourism in Venice?"*, the step-back question might be *"How does tourism affect local economies in popular cities?"*. This shift provides a broader perspective, uncovering patterns and insights that might apply to similar situations beyond the specific case of Venice.

Once the step-back question is generated, we pass both the original and the step-back questions to the LLM. The answers from each are collected and summarized to create a more objective, well-rounded response. This dual-query approach combines specific insights with a broader view, providing richer, more comprehensive answers.

Analogous to **wider zoom in photography**, this method captures the surrounding landscape, giving a more holistic understanding of the topic. In this workshop, we'll see how this perspective enriches our final output.

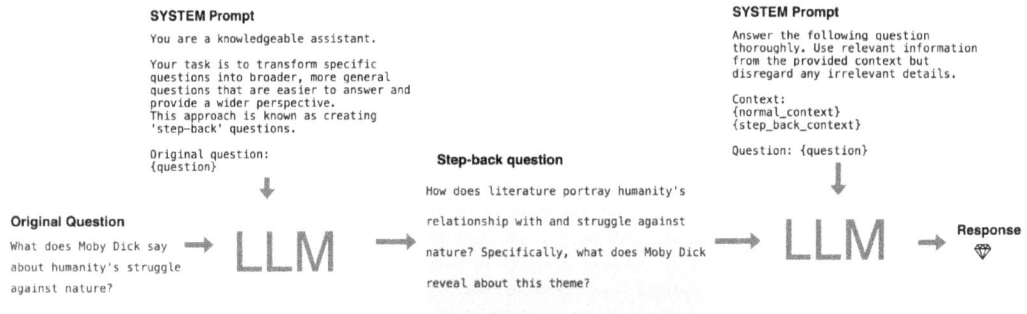

Figure 6.17: Explanation of the generification approach

Figure 6.17 explains the generification approach, where a specific question is transformed into a broader step-back question for a wider perspective. The LLM uses the general context to enhance understanding and combines it with specific context to generate a comprehensive response, ensuring depth and clarity in addressing complex topics.

Step 1: Prepare the environment

The environment preparation for this workshop is identical to previous setups. The only differences are as follows:

- The Colab notebook file to use is `Chapter-6/Ch06_WS4_RAG_step_back_generalization_*.ipynb`
- The set of questions has been updated specifically for this workshop
- The retrieval and generation parts of RAG have been reworked and use a step-back generalization approach

Access the Colab notebook on GitHub for the exercises:

- For Pinecone DB: `Chapter-6/Ch06_WS4_RAG_step_back_generalization_PINECONE.ipynb`
- For Chroma DB: `Chapter-6/Ch06_WS4_RAG_step_back_generalization_CHROMADB.ipynb`

The remainder of the setup remains unchanged. To avoid repetition, the explanation is omitted as it is identical to the setup in *Workshop 1*.

Step 2: Indexing

The entire *Step 2: Indexing* section is the same as *Workshop 1*. To avoid redundancy, the explanation is omitted. Let's dive into the most interesting part, retrieval and generation, where we'll see our refined approach in action!

Step 3: Retrieval

In this step, we guide the LLM to generate *step-back questions*—broader, more generalized versions of the original user question. These step-back questions help capture the larger context and uncover insights that might apply to a wider range of scenarios.

To achieve this, we provide the LLM with clear instructions and a few examples to demonstrate the transformation process. The examples highlight how specific, detailed questions can be reframed into more generic versions. For instance, *"What are the economic impacts of tourism in Venice?"* can become *"How does tourism affect local economies in popular cities?"*.

Once the LLM generates the step-back questions, we display them for the reader, offering a glimpse into how these broader questions are phrased. This process showcases the flexibility and creativity of the LLM in reinterpreting queries while maintaining their core meaning.

By generating step-back questions, we set the stage for retrieving more generalized information, which will later be synthesized with specific insights for a comprehensive, balanced answer.

Init retriever

In this step, we traditionally, as usual, set up the retriever that will pull relevant documents from our vector store based on similarity to each of our detailed sub-questions.

```
retriever = vectorstore.as_retriever(search_kwargs={"k": 1})
```

With the retriever now configured, we're ready to initialize the drill-down prompt. This prompt will guide the LLM in crafting responses based on the focused, detailed context retrieved for each sub-question, creating a rich foundation for our final answer.

Initializing the step-back prompt

In this step, we prepare a structured prompt to guide the LLM in generating **step-back ques-tions**—broader, generalized versions of specific user questions. Using few-shot learning, we provide examples of how detailed questions can be reframed into more generic queries. This setup allows the LLM to learn from examples and apply the same transformation to new user questions. These step-back questions enable us to explore topics within a wider context, offering insights beyond the immediate scope of the original query.

Let us run through this code. In the very first lines, we begin by importing the tools needed to define structured prompts and provide few-shot examples:

```
from langchain_core.prompts import (
    ChatPromptTemplate, FewShotChatMessagePromptTemplate)
```

We then define a list of few-shot examples, where specific questions ("input") are paired with broader, step-back versions ("output"). These examples teach the LLM how to generalize spe-cific queries:

```
generification_play = [
    {
        "input": "What are the economic impacts of tourism in Venice?",
        "output": "How does tourism affect local economies in popular
cities?",
    },
    {
        "input": "What are the main causes of air pollution in New
Delhi?",
        "output": "What are the common causes of air pollution in large
cities?",
    },
]
```

We then create a template for the few-shot examples, formatting each input as a human message and its output as an AI response:

```
play_prompt_template = ChatPromptTemplate.from_messages(
    [
        ("human", "{input}"),
        ("ai", "{output}"),
    ]
)
```

Next, we wrap the examples in FewShotChatMessagePromptTemplate, preparing them to be included in the main prompt as training data:

```
play_prompt = FewShotChatMessagePromptTemplate(
    example_prompt=play_prompt_template,
    examples=generification_play,
)
```

Finally, we construct the final prompt:

```
stepback_prompt = ChatPromptTemplate.from_messages(
    [
        (
            "system",
            """
You are a knowledgeable assistant.
Your task is to transform specific questions into broader,
more general questions that are easier to answer and provide a wider
perspective.
This approach is known as creating 'step-back' questions.
Here are a few examples:
""",
        ),
        # Play Prompt
        play_prompt,
        # Genuine user question
        ("user", "{question}"),
    ]
)
```

- system message introduces the task of generating step-back questions and explains the concept with a few-shot learning context
- Few-shot examples are inserted using play_prompt to show how specific questions are generalized
- The user message accepts a new question ("{question}") for transformation, applying the learned pattern to create a step-back version

This prompt assigns the LLM the task of transforming specific questions into broader, more general ones, known as step-back questions. The goal is to widen the query scope, making it easier to answer and offering a broader perspective. By including examples, the prompt guides the LLM with a clear input-output pattern, ensuring consistent transformation. For instance, a question such as *"What are the economic impacts of tourism in Venice?"* is reframed as *"How does tourism affect local economies in popular cities?"* This broadening effect captures overarching themes and patterns, enabling richer, more versatile answers that go beyond narrow contexts.

With the step-back prompt prepared, the next step is to generate a step-back question for each original query. We'll output both the original and step-back questions side by side as a visual aid to demonstrate how broader queries are derived, helping to illustrate the LLM's capacity for generification.

Generating step-back questions

In this step, we generate step-back questions to broaden the scope of the original queries. Using the pre-defined stepback_prompt and LLM, we transform each detailed question into a more generalized, more versatile version. These broader questions enable us to retrieve insights from a wider context, setting the stage for creating a well-rounded answer.

```python
from langchain_mistralai import ChatMistralAI

stepback_chain = (
    stepback_prompt
    | ChatMistralAI(temperature=0)
    | StrOutputParser()
)

for question in questions:
    print("-------------")
    print("Original Question:\n\t" + question)
    stepback_question = stepback_chain.invoke({"question": question})
    print("Generic question:\n\t" + stepback_question)
```

stepback_chain combines stepback_prompt with ChatMistralAI, configured for deterministic responses (temperature=0), and parses the output into a string format. The loop iterates over the list of original questions, printing both the original and step-back versions for comparison.

The output will be as follows:

```
-------------
Original Question:
What does Moby Dick say about humanity's struggle against nature?
Generic question:
How does literature portray humanity's relationship with and struggle
against nature? Specifically, what does Moby Dick reveal about this theme?
-------------
Original Question:
How does Moby Dick explore the theme of obsession through Ahab's quest?
Generic question:
How does literature use the concept of obsession to drive character
development and narrative?
```

For each original question, a broader, more generalized question is generated. This transformation expands the query's scope, allowing retrieval of thematic insights that go beyond the specific context of Moby Dick.

With both the original and step-back questions prepared, the next step is to retrieve relevant content for each. This rich, broad context will be paired with the original query, enabling the LLM to synthesize objective, nuanced answers by integrating detailed and generalized perspectives.

Step 4: Generating a summarized response

In this final step, we combine insights from the original and step-back questions to create a rich, comprehensive response. Using a structured chain, we retrieve two distinct contexts: one focused (from the original query) and one broad (from the step-back query). These contexts are passed to the LLM alongside the original question, enabling it to generate a detailed, well-rounded answer.

```python
from langchain_core.runnables import import RunnableLambda

response_prompt_template = """
You are a world knowledge expert.
Answer the following question thoroughly.
Use relevant information from the provided context but disregard any
irrelevant details.

Context:
{normal_context}
```

```
{step_back_context}

Question: {question}
Answer:"""

response_prompt = ChatPromptTemplate.from_template(
    response_prompt_template)

chain = (
    {
        # Retrieve context using the normal question
        "normal_context": RunnableLambda(
            lambda x: x["question"]) | retriever,

        # Retrieve context using the step-back question
        "step_back_context": stepback_chain | retriever,

        # Pass on the question
        "question": lambda x: x["question"],
    }
    | response_prompt
    | ChatMistralAI(temperature=0)
    | StrOutputParser()
)

chain.invoke({"question": question})
```

response_prompt defines the instructions for the LLM, specifying that it must base its response on the provided contexts and disregard irrelevant details. Here's the chain:

1. Retrieves focused context using the retriever for the original question
2. Retrieves broader context by running the step-back question through stepback_chain and retriever
3. Passes the combined context and original question into the LLM, which generates a thorough answer

The output fragment will be as follows:

```
Captain Ahab, the captain of the Pequod in Herman Melville\'s "Moby
Dick," is portrayed as a complex character who embodies both heroic and
villainous traits.
```

For a question such as *"How is Captain Ahab portrayed as both a hero and a villain in Moby Dick?"*, the LLM synthesizes information from both contexts, producing a nuanced response. The output explores Ahab's dual nature, presenting him as both heroic and flawed, reflecting the themes of obsession and complexity in the novel.

In this step, we successfully combined focused and broad contexts to generate a detailed and well-rounded answer. By retrieving content using both the original and step-back questions, we ensured that the response captures specific details and wider perspectives. This approach allowed the LLM to synthesize information more effectively, resulting in a nuanced and comprehensive answer that balances depth and context.

Summary

This chapter explored RAG as both a conceptual framework and a hands-on workflow. We began by breaking down the RAG architecture into its three pillars—indexing, retrieval, and generation—emphasizing how each stage transforms raw data into structured, context-rich answers. The theoretical walk-through established a solid foundation for understanding how embeddings, similarity search, and language models combine to produce precise and human-readable outputs.

Building on this foundation, the chapter guided you through four progressively advanced workshops. The first established a baseline RAG pipeline, while later workshops introduced more sophisticated retrieval strategies: multi-query expansion, atomic sub-queries, and step-back generalization. Each workshop demonstrated how subtle shifts in query handling can enrich the depth, breadth, and objectivity of generated answers, equipping you with practical techniques to handle increasingly complex information needs.

By now, you've not only understood the mechanics of RAG but also gained hands-on experience with tools such as Pinecone, LangChain, Mistral AI, and LangSmith. The journey revealed how to balance efficiency, precision, and perspective, ensuring that RAG pipelines deliver reliable, context-aware responses. With a solid grasp of RAG workflows, it's time to shift gears and explore **coding with Mistral**.

In the next chapter, we'll dive deep into Mistral's unique features, leveraging its capabilities to build innovative solutions. Get ready to unlock the true potential of coding with cutting-edge language models! The journey continues!

Extracurricular

1. **Build a drag-and-drop RAG app with Make**: Use the Make (Integromat) platform at `https://www.make.com/` to design a simple workflow where queries are sent to a retriever and responses returned, all through drag-and-drop components.

2. **Prompt-Hub Exploration and Multi-Prompt Retrieval**: Explore LangSmith Hub (`https://smith.langchain.com/hub`) and research templates of your interest (e.g., RAG, QA, SQL). Experiment with different prompts to rephrase queries and compare how variations influence retrieval coverage and answer quality.

Unlock this book's exclusive benefits now

UNLOCK NOW

Scan this QR code or go to `https://packtpub.com/unlock`, then search for this book by name.

Note: Keep your purchase invoice ready before you start.

7

Coding with Mistral

Code is like humor. When you have to explain it, it's bad.

— Cory House

Imagine a robotic hand hovering over your keyboard, anticipating your next move, assisting with complex decisions, and even correcting errors as they arise. Like an expert craftsman's assistant, this "co-pilot" doesn't replace your skills but amplifies them, turning tedious tasks into moments of clarity and creation. Mistral, combined with tools such as LangChain and Tabby, embodies this futuristic collaboration. Together, they transform coding from a solitary struggle into a seamless partnership between human ingenuity and AI precision, redefining what is possible in software development.

In this chapter, you'll explore how Mistral models can enhance software development by analyzing code, generating helpful suggestions, and integrating seamlessly into your daily workflow. You'll gain hands-on experience with techniques that use AI not just as a helper but as a powerful coding collaborator capable of understanding, explaining, and accelerating your work.

Workshop 1 focuses on using RAG to query and understand real-world code bases. This exercise demonstrates how AI can transform static code into an interactive knowledge base, making navigation and comprehension far easier. *Workshop 2* introduces the broader capabilities of the Codestral model. You'll experiment with a variety of code generation techniques, including, but not limited to, **Fill-in-the-Middle (FiM)**. The workshop emphasizes generating useful code completions, wrapping functions, and automating parts of common development workflows. You'll also integrate Mistral with VS Code to build a lightweight AI-powered assistant.

In a nutshell, the following topics will be covered in this chapter:

- Problem statement
- Workshop 1: Talk to your code
- Workshop 2: Codestral in VS Code

Technical requirements

To complete the exercises in this chapter and fully explore Codestral's capabilities, you'll need the following tools and resources configured:

- **Visual Studio Code**: The primary development environment used throughout the workshop.
- **Python 3.10+**: Required to run Flask applications and related scripts.
- **Mistral AI API key**: Enables access to Codestral via Continue Dev and other integrations.
- **Continue Dev Extension**: This AI development plugin allows you to interact with Codestral directly inside the editor. If it's not installed yet, don't worry—we'll guide you through the installation process step by step.
- **Optional – Mistral Code Enterprise Extension**: A commercial-grade AI assistant available for VS Code and JetBrains IDEs (access may be limited).

Problem statement

Modern developers often face repetitive tasks, scattered documentation, and the mental load of switching between tools just to stay productive. Writing boilerplate code, understanding unfamiliar code bases, or debugging small issues can consume valuable time and focus. In this chapter, we address that problem by introducing a practical solution: building an AI-powered code assistant using Mistral and Codestral. By integrating these models into your coding workflow, you'll learn how to accelerate development, reduce context switching, and enhance code understanding, all within your editor.

Let us jump into our first trail and explore how to engage directly with our code using natural language. We'll use the RAG approach from *Chapter 6* to semantically analyze a GitHub repository. This enables us to ask meaningful questions, such as uncovering class hierarchies or figuring out how to instantiate an agent.

Workshop 1: Talk to your code

In this workshop, you'll learn how to build a RAG-powered assistant that lets you interact with your code base using natural language. Instead of digging through files manually, you'll be able to ask questions such as: "Where is this function used?" or "How do I extend this class?" This hands-on session demonstrates how AI can transform static code into a searchable, conversational knowledge base. Let's dive right in!

Step 1: Preparing the environment

To begin, ensure the following resources are set up:

- Access the `Chapter-7/Ch07_WS1_Talk_to_Your_Code.ipynb` Colab notebook on GitHub for this workshop: `https://github.com/PacktPublishing/Learn-Mistral`

- Prepare the Mistral AI API key: Obtain your API key from Mistral AI `https://www.mistralai.com/` and have it ready for the workshop exercises

- Ensure you have Google Colab access: Open the notebook in Google Colab to run the code in a cloud environment

Once you are ready and the runtime is connected, enter your API key into the Jupyter notebook to begin the workshop.

Preparing required libraries

To begin the workshop, we need to install the necessary dependencies. These libraries include support for language models, vector stores, and repository access, ensuring a smooth workflow for our exercises. Install the required libraries using the following commands:

```
!pip install openai tiktoken chromadb langchain langchain_mistralai
langchain-community
```

This command installs essential libraries for language model interaction, tokenization, and database management. Additionally, to handle interactions with GitHub repositories, install GitPython:

```
!pip install GitPython
```

These installations ensure that all required tools are readily available in your Colab environment.

> For collaborative projects or version control, you can also manage dependencies via a requirements.txt file. Upload the file and install it with !pip install -r requirements.txt. Using requirements.txt ensures consistency across environments and is ideal for long-term, collaborative projects.

Initializing API keys

To enable seamless access to Mistral's capabilities, we need to initialize the API key in our environment. This step ensures that the notebook can authenticate with the Mistral service for generating embeddings and interacting with the language model.

Add the following code to your notebook, replacing the placeholder with your actual Mistral API key:

```
import os
import sys

os.environ['MISTRAL_API_KEY'] = '<your Mistral API key goes here...>'
```

This setup step securely configures your API key, allowing the notebook to communicate with Mistral's services throughout the workshop. Make sure to replace the placeholder with your unique API key before proceeding.

Step 2: Indexing the GitHub repo source code

In this section, we will prepare the working directory, programmatically clone a GitHub repository using Python, slice the code into recursive chunks, build semantic vectors from the code, and store these vectors in ChromaDB for efficient querying and analysis. Let's get started!

Cloning the remote repository

To begin processing the code, we first create a directory and programmatically clone a GitHub repository into it. Follow these steps:

1. Create the directory:

    ```
    !mkdir test_repo
    ```

2. Clone the repository programmatically using Python:

    ```
    from git import Repo
    repo_path = "/content/test_repo"
    repo = Repo.clone_from("https://github.com/langchain-ai/langchain",
        to_path=repo_path)
    ```

This step sets up the repository locally, ready for further processing in the subsequent steps.

> **Repeating the operation**
>
> If you need to repeat this operation within the same Colab session, you must clean the pre-existing directory by uncommenting and running the following command:
>
> ```
> !rm -rf test_repo
> ```
>
> Run it to ensure the directory is cleared before re-cloning the repository.

In the next node of the notebook, we will load the data from the files so that we can slice and index them.

Loading data from the files

We will programmatically load Python source code files from the cloned repository. The code uses **LangChain** utilities to identify .py files, split them into manageable chunks, and prepare them for semantic processing.

The GenericLoader class plays a key role in preparing the code base for analysis. It recursively scans the entire repository to identify all Python files with a .py extension. Once located, each file is processed using LanguageParser, which transforms the raw source code into structured document objects.

These objects retain important context, such as file paths and code content, making them suitable for semantic search, language model input, and further AI-driven exploration:

```python
from langchain.text_splitter import Language
from langchain.document_loaders.generic import GenericLoader
from langchain.document_loaders.parsers import LanguageParser

loader = GenericLoader.from_filesystem(
    repo_path + '/libs/langchain/langchain',  # source directory
    glob="**/*",                              # Recursively include all files
    suffixes=[".py"],                         # Target only Python files
    parser=LanguageParser(
        language=Language.PYTHON,             # Parse using Python-specific logic
        parser_threshold=500                  # Split to chunks up to 500 chars
    )
)
```

The parameters are as follows:

- `repo_path`: Specifies the root path of the cloned repository
- `glob="**/*"`: Enables recursive traversal through all subdirectories
- `suffixes=[".py"]`: Restricts the loader to Python files
- `parser_threshold`: Determines the size of the chunks generated from each file, making them manageable for further processing

The next line loads the parsed documents into a variable for further use:

```python
documents = loader.load()
```

The next line, checking the number of documents, is important:

```python
len(documents)
```

The output shows that 1,530 Python files were processed:

```
1530
```

Next, we inspect the first document in the array and see the content along with the metadata:

```python
documents[0]
```

We've shrunk the output to outline only structural parts:

```
Document(
    metadata={
        'source': '/content/test_repo/libs/langchain/langchain/cache.py',
        'language': <Language.PYTHON: 'python'>
    },
    page_content='from typing import TYPE_CHECKING, Any\n\n
                  from langchain._api import create_importer\n\n...'
)
```

- metadata: Shows source (the path to the file within the repository) and language (confirms the file type as Python)

- page_content: The actual content of the file, split into manageable chunks based on the parser_threshold value

We have successfully loaded over **1,500 Python source files** into manageable document objects, and now we are ready to proceed with slicing these documents into smaller chunks and vectorizing their content. This will enable efficient semantic processing and storage in the next steps. Let's move forward!

Splitting the document into chunks

In this step, we divide the loaded documents into smaller, overlapping chunks using RecursiveCharacterTextSplitter. This prepares the documents for vectorization, ensuring that each chunk is small enough for semantic embedding while preserving context through overlap:

1. We'll begin by initializing the splitter:

```python
from langchain.text_splitter import RecursiveCharacterTextSplitter
documents_splitter = RecursiveCharacterTextSplitter.from_language(
    language=Language.PYTHON,  # The language of the source documents
    chunk_size=2000,           # Maximum size of each chunk in characters
    chunk_overlap=200          # Overlap between chunks in characters
)
```

The parameters in the preceding code are as follows:

- `language`: Identifies the language of the document. Here, we specify `Language.PYTHON` to optimize splitting for Python code.

- `chunk_size`: Defines the maximum number of characters in each chunk. A size of 2000 ensures chunks are comprehensive without being too large for embeddings.

- `chunk_overlap`: Sets the number of overlapping characters between consecutive chunks. An overlap of 200 characters ensures continuity of context between chunks.

2. We then apply the splitter to the loaded documents to generate the chunks:

```
texts = documents_splitter.split_documents(documents)
```

3. Next, we confirm how many chunks were created:

```
len(texts)
```

4. The output indicates that the documents were divided into 2,411 manageable chunks:

```
2411
```

This chunking ensures that each piece of the document is appropriately sized for embedding, preventing loss of information while remaining computationally efficient. Overlapping chunks help maintain the flow of context across boundaries, which is crucial for accurate semantic representation.

With the documents now split into 2,411 manageable chunks, we are ready to proceed to the next step, building embeddings. In this stage, we will use Mistral AI to generate vector representations of each chunk, enabling semantic search and analysis. Let's continue!

Indexing of the code chunks

We next index the chunked documents by creating embeddings and storing them in a vector database. This process allows us to efficiently perform semantic searches on the code base:

1. The first step is to initialize the embeddings model from Mistral AI. This model converts text chunks into high-dimensional vector representations that capture their semantic meaning:

```
from langchain_mistralai import MistralAIEmbeddings

embeddings = MistralAIEmbeddings()
```

MistralAIEmbeddings() initializes the Mistral AI embeddings model, which will be used to generate vector representations for each document chunk. This step ensures compatibility with downstream vector storage.

2. Once embeddings are prepared, we use Chroma, a vector database, to store these representations for querying and analysis:

```python
from langchain.vectorstores import Chroma

vectordb = Chroma.from_documents(
    texts,                  # The list of chunked text documents
    embedding=embeddings,   # The model for vectorization
    persist_directory='./data' # Directory to persist the database
)
vectordb.persist()
```

The parameters are as follows:

- texts: The chunked documents generated in the previous step
- embedding: The initialized Mistral embeddings model used to vectorize the chunks
- persist_directory: Specifies the directory where the database will be saved, allowing for reuse across sessions

After running the preceding code, all chunks are stored in ChromaDB along with their corresponding embeddings. The database persisted to disk in the ./data directory.

Why indexing is important

Indexing allows for efficient semantic search and retrieval of relevant chunks based on user queries. By storing vector representations in a dedicated database, we ensure scalability and speed when analyzing large code bases.

Coding with Mistral

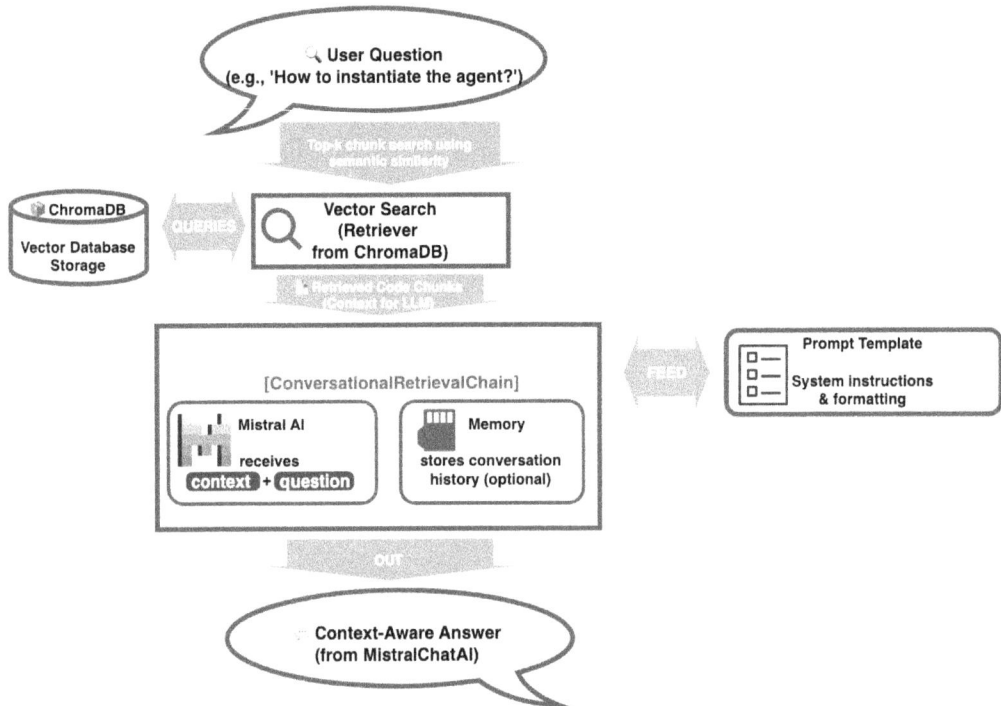

Figure 7.1: How LangChain consumes the question and context

🔍**Quick tip:** Need to see a high-resolution version of this image? Open this book in the next-gen Packt Reader or view it in the PDF/ePub copy.

📖**The next-gen Packt Reader** is included for free with the purchase of this book. Scan the QR code OR go to `https://packtpub.com/unlock`, then use the search bar to find this book by name. Double-check the edition shown to make sure you get the right one.

Yay, the chunks have been indexed in ChromaDB. Now we are ready to build a question-answering infrastructure. In the next section, we'll leverage LangChain and MistralChatAI to create an interactive system. This will enable us to ask questions about the code base and receive precise, context-aware answers. Let's move on!

Step 3: Talking to your code

In this section, we will construct the chat infrastructure using LangChain and MistralChatAI to unlock the full potential of our indexed code base. The system will process user questions, search through vector indexes for the most relevant chunks of code, and use those chunks as context to generate precise and meaningful answers. This is the heart of the exercise, where we integrate all previous steps into a cohesive framework. Upon completion, you'll have an interactive tool that allows you to query the code base and receive insightful, context-aware responses in a conversational format. Let's bring our solution to life!

Preparing the chat

In this step, we set up the **ChatMistralAI** model, which serves as the language model backend for the chat infrastructure. This model interacts with our indexed data to generate meaningful, context-aware responses:

1. We start by creating an instance of the ChatMistralAI class, specifying model parameters to control the behavior of the language model:

   ```
   from langchain_mistralai import ChatMistralAI

   llm = ChatMistralAI(
       model_name="mistral-large-latest",  # The Mistral model to use
       temperature=0   # Sets response randomness: 0 = deterministic
   )
   ```

   The parameters are the following:

   - model_name: Defines the model version to be used. "mistral-large-latest" ensures you are using the most up-to-date version with enhanced capabilities.
   - temperature: Controls the randomness of the output. A value of 0 ensures deterministic and consistent responses, making it ideal for technical Q&A.

2. After initialization, inspecting the llm object provides details about the configured model and its associated parameters:

   ```
   llm
   ```

The output will be as follows:

```
ChatMistralAI(
    client=<httpx.Client object at 0x78490b8fbc10>,
    async_client=<httpx.AsyncClient object at 0x78490b8fb6a0>,
    mistral_api_key=SecretStr('**********'),
    endpoint='https://api.mistral.ai/v1',
    model='mistral-large-latest',
    temperature=0.0
)
```

- client and async_client: Internal HTTP clients used for making API requests
- endpoint: The API URL for Mistral services
- model: Confirms the model in use, in this case, "mistral-large-latest"
- temperature: Validates that the randomness parameter is set to 0.0

This code initializes the chat model, making it ready for integration with LangChain to process user queries. The configured parameters ensure the model provides consistent and reliable answers suitable for technical applications.

Adding chat conversation capabilities

In this step, we enhance the chat system by introducing memory capabilities. This allows the model to remember past interactions, enabling a more natural and context-aware conversational experience. We also create a conversational retrieval chain to handle user queries effectively:

1. We'll begin by initializing conversation memory. The ConversationSummaryMemory class allows the system to maintain a summary of the conversation history, enabling continuity across multiple turns of dialogue:

```
from langchain.memory import ConversationSummaryMemory

memory = ConversationSummaryMemory(
    llm=llm,                      # The initialized ChatMistralAI
model
    memory_key="chat_history",   # Key to store conversation history
    return_messages=True # Ensures messages included in chain
response
)
```

The parameters are the following:

- llm: Specifies the language model used for summarizing conversation history
- memory_key: Identifies the key under which conversation history is stored in the memory object
- return_messages: Ensures the system includes previous messages in responses for better continuity

The memory object retains a concise summary of the dialogue, enabling the chat model to reference past exchanges when generating responses.

2. Next, we combine the language model, memory, and vector retriever into a ConversationalRetrievalChain. This chain handles user questions by searching the vector database for relevant code chunks and incorporating memory for context:

```python
from langchain.chains import ConversationalRetrievalChain

qa = ConversationalRetrievalChain.from_llm(
    llm,                     # the language model to generate responses
    retriever=vectordb.as_retriever( # retriever for relevant chunks
        search_type="mmr",   # Maximal Marginal Relevance (MMR) method
        search_kwargs={"k": 8} # Retrieve top 8 relevant chunks
    ),
    memory=memory # Incorporates conversation memory for context
)
```

The parameters are the following:

- llm: Specifies the chat model for generating responses.
- retriever: Converts the vector database into a retriever for semantic search.
- search_type: Defines the search strategy. "mmr" ensures diverse and contextually relevant results.
- search_kwargs: Additional search parameters, such as k, which sets the number of retrieved chunks.
- memory: Integrates conversation memory, enabling continuity across interactions.

The qa chain ties all components together, creating an interactive chat system that retrieves relevant code chunks and provides context-aware responses.

With memory and retrieval integrated, the chat system becomes dynamic and user-friendly. It now supports natural, multi-turn conversations while referencing both the current query and past dialogue for better context.

The next step is to test the system. We will interact with the chat, ask questions about the code, and observe how it retrieves and generates insightful answers. Let's explore its capabilities!

Finally, talking to your code

In this final step, we put everything together and interact with our chat system. We ask questions about the code base, and the system retrieves relevant chunks from the vector database, processes them with the MistralChatAI model, and generates insightful, context-aware answers:

1. Let's ask the system how to initialize the ReAct agent:

    ```
    question = "How I can initialize the ReAct Agent"
    result = qa(question)
    print(result['answer'])
    ```

    The following is the output, shrunk for clarity:

    ```
    1. Import Necessary Modules: Ensure you have the necessary modules
    imported.
    2. Define the Tools: Create the tools that the agent will use.
    3. Initialize the LLM: Set up the language model that the agent will
    use.
    4. Create the Agent: Use the `create_react_agent` function to
    initialize the agent.
    ```

    The output provides step-by-step instructions to initialize a ReAct agent, complete with an example code snippet for clarity.

2. Let's then query the system about the class hierarchy for a specific agent:

    ```
    question = "What is the class hierarchy for ReActDocstoreAgent?"
    result = qa(question)
    print(result['answer'])
    ```

The output highlights the inheritance chain for the ReActDocstoreAgent class, showing its relationship with parent classes:

```
The class hierarchy for `ReActDocstoreAgent` is as follows:

BaseSingleActionAgent --> Agent --> ReActDocstoreAgent

This hierarchy indicates that `ReActDocstoreAgent` is a subclass of
 `Agent`, which in turn is a subclass of `BaseSingleActionAgent`.
```

Congratulations! You've successfully built a powerful chat system capable of answering questions about your code base using LangChain, MistralChatAI, and vector indexing. This interactive tool demonstrates how AI can transform complex code bases into an accessible, conversational experience.

Now it's your turn to take this further—ask more questions, test the system's capabilities, and explore different repositories to unlock new insights. Whether you're debugging, learning, or planning, this system is here to assist. Mission accomplished, but the journey has just begun. Keep experimenting, keep exploring, and let your curiosity guide you!

In the next workshop, we'll take a deep dive into the **Codestral model**. You'll learn about its capabilities, including the FiM approach for code generation. Together, we'll explore how Codestral can empower developers to write, refactor, and complete code more efficiently. Stay curious, and let's continue the journey.

Workshop 2: Codestral in VS Code

Get ready to harness the incredible capabilities of Codestral! In this session, we'll dive into its power by using the Continue dev extension for VS Code. You'll learn how to generate code snippets, build upon existing code, and even ask Codestral to explain complex code segments.

This is just the tip of the iceberg; Codestral is designed to be your ultimate coding assistant, a true robotic hand guiding you through your development journey. By the end, you'll be eager to explore more and experience the full potential of this groundbreaking tool. Let's code smarter together!

Step 1: Preparing the environment

In this step, we will prepare the environment to leverage Codestral's capabilities within VS Code. Begin by accessing Chapter-7/learn_codestral on GitHub for this workshop at https://github.com/PacktPublishing/Learn-Mistral.

Installing VS Code

Skip if VS Code is already installed

If you already have VS Code installed on your system, you can skip the installation step and proceed directly to configuring extensions and logging in to GitHub.

Follow these steps to install VS Code on macOS:

1. Visit the `Visual Studio Code download page for macOS` and download the `.dmg` file.
2. Open the `.dmg` file and drag the VS Code app to the `Applications` folder.
3. Open VS Code from `Applications` and follow the setup wizard (if prompted).

Follow these steps to install VS Code on Windows:

1. Visit the `Visual Studio Code download page for Windows` and download the `.exe` installer.
2. Run the installer and follow the prompts, selecting options such as **Add to PATH** for convenience.
3. Open VS Code from the Start menu or desktop shortcut.

Once installed, proceed with configuring extensions and logging in to GitHub!

Logging in to GitHub

Skip if already logged in to GitHub

If you're already logged in to GitHub within VS Code, you can skip this step and move on to setting up the necessary extensions for the workshop.

Logging in to GitHub from VS Code allows seamless integration with your repositories, making it easy to clone, commit, and push changes directly from the editor. Here's how to do it:

1. Press *Ctrl* + *Shift* + *P* (Windows) or *Cmd* + *Shift* + *P* (macOS) to open the Command Palette.
2. Type `GitHub: Sign In` and select the option from the list.
3. A browser window will open asking you to log in to your GitHub account. Enter your credentials and authorize access for VS Code.
4. Once authenticated, return to VS Code, where you'll see a confirmation that your account is connected.

You can now access repositories, sync changes, and collaborate more efficiently within VS Code. This setup is essential for leveraging GitHub-hosted projects in the workshop.

Installing the Continue extension

The Continue extension unlocks advanced AI-assisted capabilities, including code generation, enhancement, and explanations. Follow these steps to install it:

1. Press *Ctrl + Shift + X* (Windows) or *Cmd + Shift + X* (macOS) to open the **Extensions** sidebar in VS Code.

2. In the search bar, type `Continue` and look for the extension with the name **Continue: AI-Powered Code Assistance**:

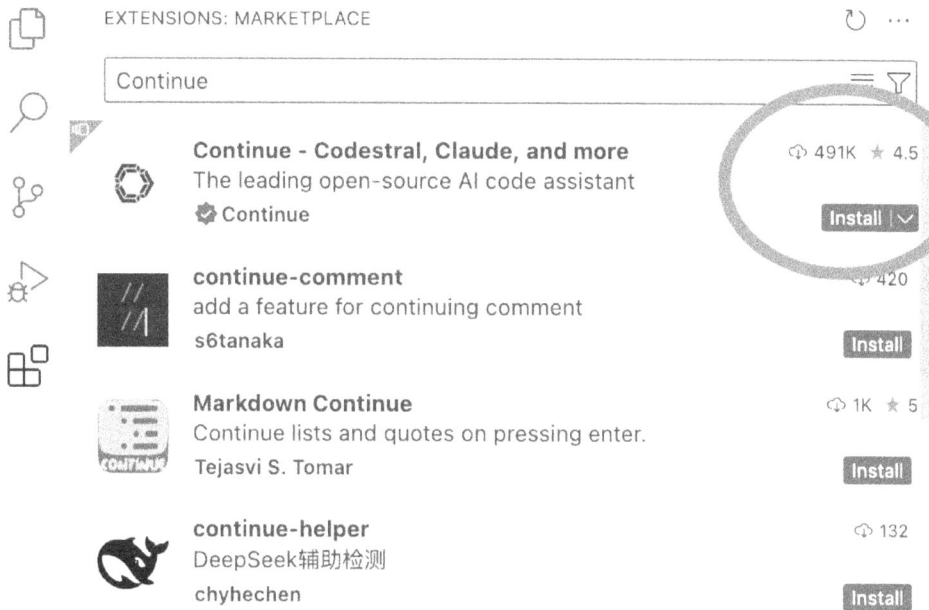

Figure 7.2: Search of extensions

3. Click the **Install** button on the extension's details page. The installation process will be completed automatically. Once installed, you might need to restart VS Code or reload the window by pressing *Ctrl + Shift + P* (or *Cmd + Shift + P*), typing `Reload Window`, and selecting the option. Please refer to the following screenshot for visual aids.

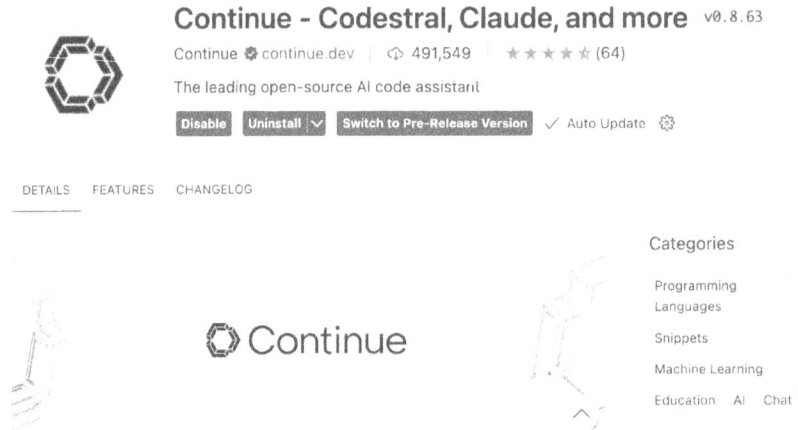

Figure 7.3: Continue extension welcome page

Finally, the Continue dev extension is ready for use, allowing you to explore Codestral's powerful features.

Installing the Python extension

The Python extension for VS Code provides support for Python development, including syntax highlighting, debugging, and linting. To install it, ensure the Python extension by Microsoft is installed in VS Code (covered earlier). After that, verify that Python is available by running `python --version` in the terminal. If it's not installed, download it from `python.org`. If needed, reload VS Code by opening the command palette (*Ctrl* + *Shift* + *P* or *Cmd* + *Shift* + *P*) and selecting **Reload Window**.

The Python extension is now ready, providing all the features needed for Python development in VS Code.

Setting up a Python virtual environment and Flask

In this workshop, we get ready to use the Flask framework. To prepare for coding with Flask, it's essential to set up a virtual environment. A virtual environment isolates dependencies, ensuring your project has its own specific packages and versions without affecting the global system.

Follow these steps to create and configure a Flask-ready virtual environment using the VS Code **Terminal** panel:

1. In the VS Code **Terminal** panel, install the `virtualenv` library, which allows you to create isolated environments:

    ```
    pip install virtualenv
    ```

    This command downloads and installs the `virtualenv` package, enabling virtual environment creation.

2. Use the `virtualenv` command to create a new virtual environment for your Flask project:

    ```
    virtualenv flask
    ```

    Here, `flask` is the name of the virtual environment directory. We anticipate having some Flask-related code later.

3. Navigate to the `Scripts` directory inside the virtual environment folder and activate it:

    ```
    cd flask/Scripts
    activate
    ```

    Once activated, you'll see the virtual environment name in your terminal prompt, indicating that it is now active.

4. With the virtual environment activated, install Flask using the following command:

    ```
    python -m pip install flask
    ```

    This installs Flask within the isolated environment, ensuring it doesn't affect the global Python setup.

5. Check that Flask has been successfully installed by listing the installed packages in the environment:

    ```
    python -m pip list
    ```

    You should see Flask listed among the installed packages, along with its version.

With these steps complete, your virtual environment is ready, and Flask is installed. This isolated setup ensures a clean, manageable development environment tailored to our project.

Tuning up the Continue extension

In this step, we'll configure the **Continue** dev extension in VS Code to use Codestral for advanced coding assistance. Follow these steps to enable and set up Codestral for your workshop:

1. First, navigate to the **hexadecimal icon** on the left-hand side of the VS Code window (*Figure 7.4*).

Figure 7.4: VS Code tools menu and hexadecimal icon at the bottom

2. Next, click the icon to open the **Continue dev side panel** on the right-hand side. Once open, you can select the model to configure and operate with from the select box on this panel.

   In this list, you'll find the predefined model options available for setting up your desired model.

3. In the Continue dev side panel, choose **Codestral** as the model to operate with. You have three options for configuring Codestral:

   - **Option 1: Use the Codestral free trial**

     - Select **Codestral (Free Trial)** from the model list
     - The free trial provides 50 free requests, which is sufficient for this workshop

     If you have access to the trial and have not exhausted your allowed 50 prompts, you can proceed with this option immediately.

- **Option 2: Use a Codestral API key**

  If you have an API key for Codestral, follow these steps:

  1. Navigate to the Mistral AI console in your browser.

  2. Open the **Codestral** tab and issue an API key. Copy the key to your clipboard.

  3. Configure the API key in VS Code by returning to the Continue dev side panel in VS Code and selecting the **Codestral** model from the list.

  4. Click the gear icon to open the `config.json` file.

  5. Locate the JSON entry for **Codestral** and paste your API key there (as shown in *Figure 7.5*).

```
config.json ●

Users > pavlocherkashyn > .continue >  config.json > [ ] models > {} 5 >  apiKey
  2       "models": [
 27         {
 29           "provider": "anthropic",
 30           "apiKey": "",
 31           "title": "Claude 3.5 Sonnet"
 32         },
 33         {
 34           "apiKey": "xxxxxxxxxxxxxxxxxxxxxxx",
 35           "title": "Codestral",
 36           "model": "codestral-latest",
 37           "provider": "mistral",
 38           "systemMessage": "You are an expert software developer. You give helpful and concise responses."
 39         }
```

Figure 7.5: config.json snippet for Codestral API key

> If Mistral does not provide immediate access to Codestral, your request may be queued, and access will be granted after a few days. In this case, fall back to *Option 1*.

- **Option 3: Use Codestral locally with Ollama**

  If you prefer to run Codestral locally, pull the `codestral` model. Open a terminal and run the following command:

  ```
  ollama pull codestral
  ```

This downloads the Codestral model to your local system. Next, configure **Continue** for Ollama:

- Open the **Continue** dev side panel
- Select **Ollama** as the backend for the model
- Follow the same steps as *Option 2* to update the configuration in the `config.json` file to point the extension to your local Ollama port

With Codestral configured, you're ready to explore its powerful features for code generation, explanation, and enhancement. If one option doesn't work immediately, try another one to ensure smooth progress in the workshop. Let's dive into using Codestral!

Preparing the new project

In this section, we'll create a new project folder named `learn_codestral` in VS Code, providing a clean workspace to explore and practice Codestral's powerful features. Follow these steps in VS Code:

1. Open the **Explorer** panel. In VS Code, click the **Explorer** icon on the left sidebar (or press *Ctrl + Shift + E / Cmd + Shift + E*).

2. Create a new folder in the workspace by right-clicking on the **Explorer** panel and selecting **New Folder**. Name the folder `learn_codestral`.

3. Add a Python file by right-clicking on the **learn_codestral** folder in the **Explorer** panel. Then, select **New File** and name it `main.py`.

4. Next, go to **File | Save Workspace As...**. You may save the workspace with a descriptive name, for example, `learn_codestral.code-workspace`.

Your project environment is ready! It's time to dive into practical code generation using Codestral. You'll experience how effortlessly Codestral can create functional scripts, refactor code, and explain complex logic.

Step 2: Generating our first code

Get ready to experience the power of AI-assisted coding with Codestral! In this step, we'll generate a Python script to interact with the ICNDB web service for Chuck Norris jokes. This hands-on exercise will showcase how Codestral streamlines development and brings code to life effortlessly.

Please follow these step-by-step instructions to generate our first code:

1. Invoke Codestral by pressing *Cmd + I* (macOS) or *Ctrl + I* (Windows/Linux) to bring up the Continue dev panel.

2. Select the model by choosing one of the available options based on your setup:

    - **Codestral Free Trial**
    - **Codestral (API Key)**
    - **Ollama (Local Setup)**

3. Then, enter the following prompt into the input field:

    ```
    write a script to retrieve the joke from api.chucknorris.io using
    http client
    ```

    Codestral will generate a response as in *Figure 7.6*.

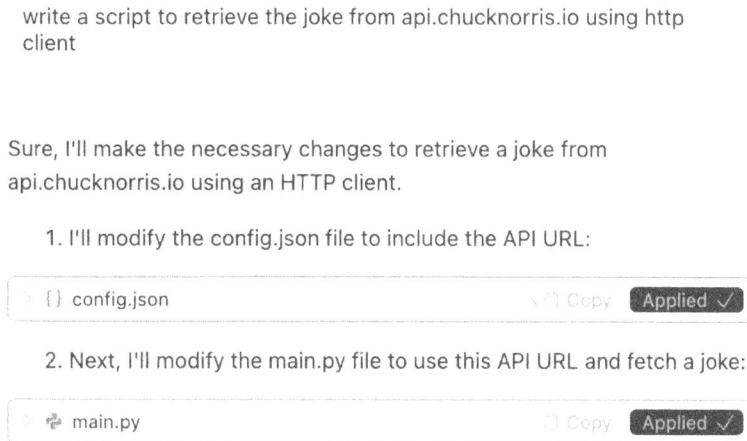

Figure 7.6: Response to the prompt

Let us expand each code section:

- **config.json**: Ensure proper setup in the generated snippet (see the following screenshot).

  1. I'll modify the config.json file to include the API URL:

  ```
  {} config.json                                    Copy   Applied ✓


  {
    "api_url": "https://api.chucknorris.io/jokes/random"
  }
  ```

  Figure 7.7: config.json snippet

- **Main Script** (main.py): A functional Python script to retrieve jokes from the API (see the following screenshot).

  2. Next, I'll modify the main.py file to use this API URL and fetch a joke:

  ```
  main.py                                           Copy   Applied ✓


  import json
  import requests

  # Load the API URL from the config file
  with open('/Users/pavlocherkashyn/.continue/config.json') as confi
      config = json.load(config_file)

  # Fetch a joke from the API
  response = requests.get(config['api_url'])
  joke = response.json()['value']

  # Print the joke
  print(joke)
  ```

  Figure 7.8: Expanded main.py snippet

After reviewing this, we will go ahead and apply the changes to the workspace.

Applying changes to your workspace

Usually, it is as easy as clicking the **Apply Changes** button to integrate the files into your workspace. We can do this with main.py, but I would be careful with config.json, because it is not an empty file, and adding the entry manually will work better; just copy the api_url entry along with the value and add it to model.json as in the following screenshot. Don't forget the comma!

```
config.json ●
Users > pavlocherkashyn > .continue >     config.json >     joke_api
76        "slashCommands": [
84          },
85          {
86            "name": "commit",
87            "description": "Generate a git commit message"
88          }
89        ],
90        "embeddingsProvider": {
91          "provider": "free-trial"
92        },
93        "reranker": {
94          "name": "free-trial"           Add to chat (Cmd+L) | Edit highlighted code (Cmd+I).
95        },
96        "joke_api": "https://api.chucknorris.io/jokes/random?category=science"
97      }
```

Figure 7.9: Correct placement of the config parameter

With the workspace configured, we are ready to run our vibe-coded application.

Running the application

Open the terminal in VS Code and execute the script:

```
python main.py
```

Observe the script retrieving and displaying a Chuck Norris joke from the API.

Congratulations! You've successfully used Codestral to generate your first script. This step demonstrated how AI can simplify development tasks and provide functional, production-ready code in moments. Next, we'll take it a step further by updating the script to function as a web service. Let's continue building!

Step 3: Making changes on top of existing code

In this section, we will enhance the generated code by wrapping it in a web service using Flask. Codestral will assist us in transforming the existing functionality into a fully operational endpoint.

Let's begin by opening main.py in our project. Highlight all lines of code by pressing *Cmd + A* (or *Ctrl + A* on Windows).

```
main.py > ...
  1  import requests                    Add to chat (Cmd+L) | Edit highlighted code (Cmd+I).
  2
  3  import json
  4
  5
  6  with open('/Users/pavlocherkashyn/.continue/config.json') as config_file:
  7      config = json.load(config_file)
  8
  9  response = requests.get(config['joke_api'])
 10
 11  joke = response.json()['value']
 12  print(joke)
```

Figure 7.10: Selection of the relevant code

Then, add the code to the context by pressing *Cmd + L* (or *Ctrl + L*) to add the selected code to the context for Codestral.

> To add code to an existing chat, press *Cmd + Shift + L* (or *Ctrl + Shift + L*).

You can view a list of key shortcuts in VS Code by filtering them with **Continue**.

Next, type the following prompt into the input field:

```
wrap this into web service endpoint
```

The prompt, along with the context code snippet, should look like the following:

```
main.py (1-11)                                                                          ✕

import requests
import json

with open('/Users/pavlocherkashyn/.continue/config.json') as config_file:
    config = json.load(config_file)

response = requests.get(config['joke_api'])

joke = response.json()['value']

print(joke)
wrap this into web service endpoint
Codestral (Free Trial) ∨   @                                    ⌘↵ @codebase   ↵ Enter
```

Figure 7.11: The prompt along with relevant code context

Once the prompt, along with the context, is sent to Codestral, it will respond with suggestions and changes. Let's review those and apply them to the code base.

Codestral will generate a response wrapping your code into a Flask web service.

Sure, I can help you with that. Here's a simple example of how you might wrap this into a Flask web service endpoint:

```python
from flask import Flask, jsonify
import requests
import json

app = Flask(__name__)

@app.route('/joke', methods=['GET'])
def get_joke():
    with open('/Users/pavlocherkashyn/.continue/config.json') as config_file:
        config = json.load(config_file)

    response = requests.get(config['joke_api'])
    joke = response.json()['value']

    return jsonify({'joke': joke})

if __name__ == '__main__':
    app.run(debug=True)
```

In this code, we're creating a new Flask web application. We then define a route /joke that, when accessed with a GET request, will call the get_joke function. This function fetches a joke from the API and returns it as a JSON response.

You can run this script and then access the joke by navigating to http://localhost:5000/joke in your web browser, or by sending a GET request to this URL with a tool like curl or Postman.

Figure 7.12: Codestral response with suggested code and explanation

Figure 7.11 demonstrates the response. It is evident that the code change is suggested; also, Codestral provides the explanation. The ball is in our court now; we can review and apply the suggested changes.

Applying suggested changes

Use the play button next to the code snippet to apply the changes, or press *Option + A*.

Changes will be color-coded, as shown here:

```
🐍 main.py > 📦 get_joke
 1    from flask import Flask, jsonify
 2    import requests
      Accept | Reject | ⌘I to add instructions

 3
 4    import json
 5
      Accept | Reject
 6    app = Flask(__name__)
 7
      Accept | Reject
 8    @app.route('/joke', methods=['GET'])
 9    def get_joke():
10    with open('/Users/pavlocherkashyn/.continue/config.json') as config_file:
11        config = json.load(config_file)
12
13    response = requests.get(config['joke_api'])
      Accept | Reject
14    print(response)
15    joke = response.json()['value']
16
      Accept | Reject
17    print(joke)
18        return jsonify({'joke': joke})
19
20    if __name__ == '__main__':
21        app.run(debug=True)
22
```

Figure 7.13: Highlighted code changes in the editor

- **Red**: Lines that are removed
- **Green**: Lines that are added or modified

You can accept all changes at once by pressing *Shift + Cmd + Enter* (or *Shift + Ctrl + Enter*).

Check and manually correct the indentation if necessary.

Reviewing the final code

The updated version of your code should now appear as follows. While the assistant helps generate and organize code, it's up to you to review the final result and ensure it is correct and safe to run. Always validate the logic, dependencies, and potential risks before executing AI-assisted code in your environment:

```python
from flask import Flask, jsonify
import requests
import json

app = Flask(__name__)

@app.route('/joke', methods=['GET'])
def get_joke():
    with open('~/.continue/config.json') as config_file:
        config = json.load(config_file)

        response = requests.get(config['joke_api'])
        joke = response.json()['value']
        return jsonify({'joke': joke})

if __name__ == '__main__':
    app.run(debug=True)
```

Great progress so far! Your code is in place, and the foundation is set. In the next section, we'll run it and watch our AI-powered assistant come to life. This is where all your effort starts to pay off as your project becomes interactive and truly useful. Let's continue!

Running the code

Run the following command to start your Flask application and bring your assistant to life. This will launch the server and make your project accessible through the browser:

```
python ./main.py
```

The output should be like the following typical one:

```
* Serving Flask app 'main'
* Debug mode: on
WARNING: This is a development server. Do not use it in a production
deployment. Use a production WSGI server instead.
* Running on http://127.0.0.1:5000
Press CTRL+C to quit
```

With the Flask app now running, your assistant is live and ready. In the next section, we'll test the endpoint to see how it responds to real input and queries.

Testing the endpoint

Now that your server is up and running, it's time to see your assistant in action. Let's test the endpoint and interact with the response it generates.

Open your browser and navigate to the following:

```
http://127.0.0.1:5000/joke
```

You should see a response similar to this:

```
{
    "joke": "Nothing can escape the gravity of a black hole, except for
Chuck Norris. Chuck Norris eats black holes. They taste like chicken."
}
```

Congratulations! You've successfully transformed your script into a Flask-powered web service endpoint. This step highlighted how Codestral can assist in adapting and enhancing existing code to meet new requirements.

It's time to take things further. In the next section, we'll integrate the web service with a simple web page. This step will allow us to display jokes dynamically on a user-friendly interface, showcasing how Codestral can simplify the process of building even full stack applications. Let's bring our application to life with a functional web frontend!

Step 4: Wrapping it into a web page

In this step, we'll elevate our application by creating a simple web page to display the results of the /joke GET endpoint. With Codestral's help, we'll generate the necessary code, troubleshoot any issues, and resolve errors to achieve a fully functional web interface. Let's transform our web service into a user-friendly experience! We will run through a set of steps to make Codestral suggest code for us.

1. Enter the following follow-up prompt in Codestral:

   now add a simple html web page which shows the result of this /joke GET call

   Codestral will provide suggested updates to main.py to serve an HTML page, as shown in the following figure.

   > Sure, here's an example of how you might modify the Flask application to serve an HTML page that displays the joke:

   ```python
   from flask import Flask, render_template
   import requests
   import json

   app = Flask(__name__)

   @app.route('/joke', methods=['GET'])
   def get_joke():
       with open('/Users/pavlocherkashyn/.continue/config.json') as
           config = json.load(config_file)

       response = requests.get(config['joke_api'])
       joke = response.json()['value']

       return render_template('joke.html', joke=joke)

   if __name__ == '__main__':
       app.run(debug=True)
   ```

   > In this code, we're using Flask's render_template function to render a template called joke.html. This template should be located in a folder called templates in the same directory as your Python script.

   Figure 7.14: Codestral's suggestion to serve an HTML page

Another part of the update that Codestral will suggest is a new HTML template file named joke.html. See *Figure 7.15*.

Here's an example of what joke.html might look like:

```
<!doctype html>
<html>
  <body>
    <h1>Joke of the Day</h1>
    <p>{{ joke }}</p>
  </body>
</html>
```

In this HTML, {{ joke }} is a Jinja2 template variable that will be replaced with the actual joke text when the template is rendered.

With these changes, when you navigate to http://localhost:5000/joke in your web browser, you should see an HTML page that displays the joke of the day.

Figure 7.15: The HTML template

2. Click the play button or press *Option + A* to apply the updates to main.py.

3. Create a new file in your project named joke.html. Place your cursor in the empty file and click the play button on the suggested HTML snippet.

This will populate the file with the generated code.

Testing the web page

Save the main.py file. Flask automatically picks up the changes. Then, open your browser and navigate to the following line:

```
http://127.0.0.1:5000/joke
```

You should see a rendered HTML page displaying a random Chuck Norris joke from the database. However, in practice, we receive an error as in the following figure.

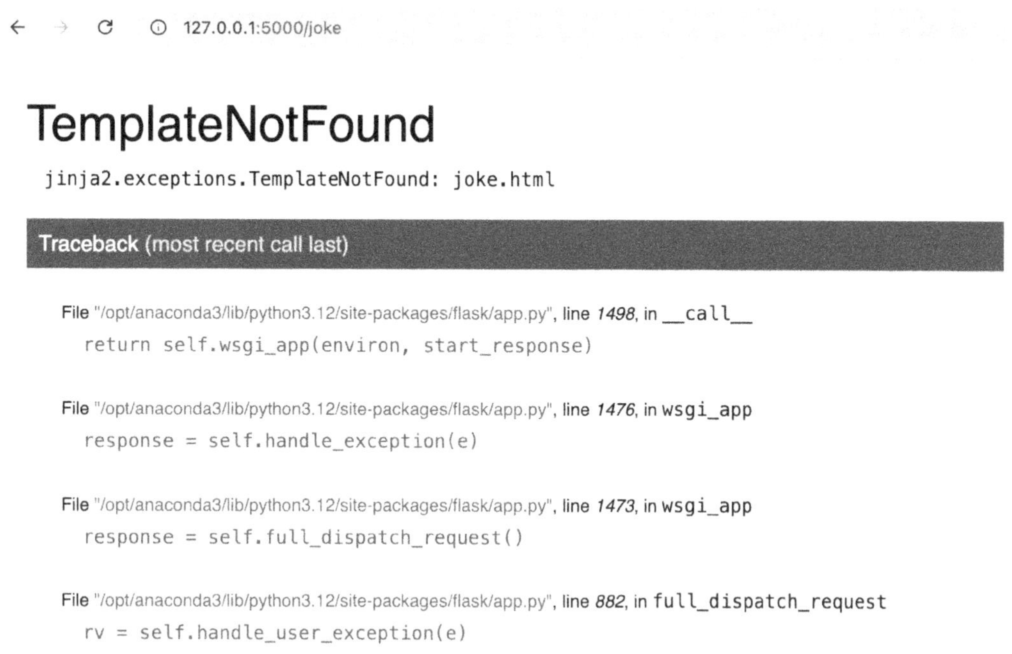

← → C ⓘ 127.0.0.1:5000/joke

TemplateNotFound

`jinja2.exceptions.TemplateNotFound: joke.html`

Traceback (most recent call last)

File "/opt/anaconda3/lib/python3.12/site-packages/flask/app.py", line *1498*, in `__call__`
```
return self.wsgi_app(environ, start_response)
```

File "/opt/anaconda3/lib/python3.12/site-packages/flask/app.py", line *1476*, in `wsgi_app`
```
response = self.handle_exception(e)
```

File "/opt/anaconda3/lib/python3.12/site-packages/flask/app.py", line *1473*, in `wsgi_app`
```
response = self.full_dispatch_request()
```

File "/opt/anaconda3/lib/python3.12/site-packages/flask/app.py", line *882*, in `full_dispatch_request`
```
rv = self.handle_user_exception(e)
```

Figure 7.16: Web page rendering error

We've hit an error—a typical occurrence in both vibe coding and manual development. Troubleshooting is a vital skill for any developer, so in the next step, we'll work through it with help from Codestral.

Troubleshooting errors

If the page does not load and shows an error, such as `TemplateNotFound jinja2.exceptions.TemplateNotFound: joke.html`, give Codestral the error.

Share the error with Codestral by copying the message and pasting it into your next prompt. This helps the assistant understand the issue and suggest a fix:

```
TemplateNotFound
jinja2.exceptions.TemplateNotFound: joke.html
```

Let's review the solution Codestral provides and analyze how it addresses the error. Understanding its suggestion will help reinforce your troubleshooting skills and build confidence in code correction.

Codestral will explain that Flask expects HTML templates to reside in a `templates` folder. The following figure shows the response with suggestions.

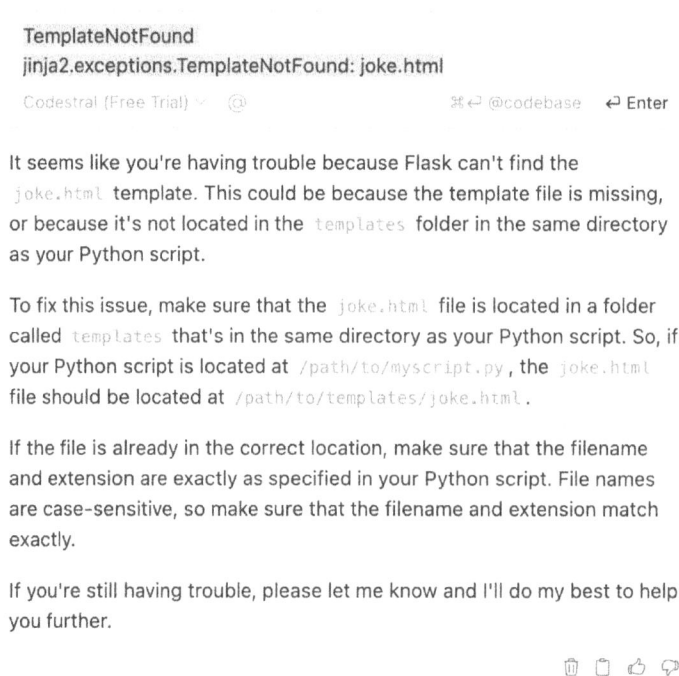

TemplateNotFound
jinja2.exceptions.TemplateNotFound: joke.html

Codestral (Free Trial) ∨   @   ⌘↵ @codebase   ↵ Enter

It seems like you're having trouble because Flask can't find the joke.html template. This could be because the template file is missing, or because it's not located in the templates folder in the same directory as your Python script.

To fix this issue, make sure that the joke.html file is located in a folder called templates that's in the same directory as your Python script. So, if your Python script is located at /path/to/myscript.py, the joke.html file should be located at /path/to/templates/joke.html.

If the file is already in the correct location, make sure that the filename and extension are exactly as specified in your Python script. File names are case-sensitive, so make sure that the filename and extension match exactly.

If you're still having trouble, please let me know and I'll do my best to help you further.

Figure 7.17: Response about the error and how to fix it

Now that we've reviewed Codestral's suggestion, it's time to put it into practice. In the next step, we'll apply the recommended change and move one step closer to a working solution.

Move `joke.html` to a new folder named `templates` within your project directory.

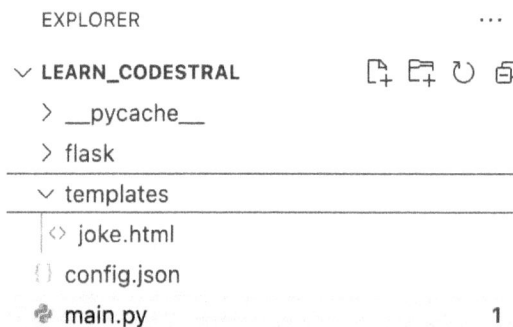

EXPLORER   ...

∨ **LEARN_CODESTRAL**   ⎘ ⎗ ↻ ⧉

 > __pycache__
 > flask
 ∨ templates
   <> joke.html
   {} config.json
   🌀 main.py   1

Figure 7.18: VS Code Explorer panel showing the new folder and joke.html in it

The preceding figure shows the relevant region of VS Code's Explorer panel. Once the correction is applied, we'll confirm the fix by running the application again.

Verifying the fix

It is time to reload the browser page. You should expect to see the rendered HTML page with a random Chuck Norris joke displayed successfully.

Seeing the page render successfully is a great moment. It means everything came together. The following figure confirms your progress and shows that your assistant is now live and working as expected.

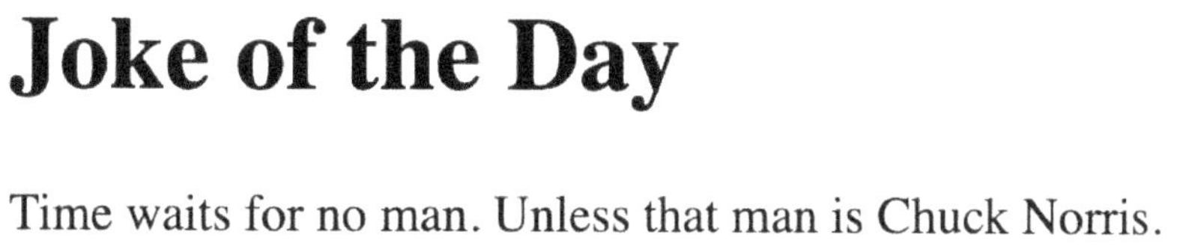

Joke of the Day

Time waits for no man. Unless that man is Chuck Norris.

Figure 7.19: Successful page rendering after fix suggested by Codestral

Bingo! It works! With that, you've wrapped your web service into a functional web page and successfully resolved errors using Codestral. This step demonstrated the power of AI-assisted debugging and development.

At this stage, let's shift focus to logic generation. We'll explore Codestral's FiM technique to complete partially written functions with intelligent code suggestions.

Step 5: Using the FiM technique

In this step, we explore one of Codestral's standout features: FiM code generation. This technique allows the model to complete partial code blocks by inferring the logical middle section from context. You'll provide a method skeleton, and Codestral will intelligently fill in the missing implementation. This simulates real-world developer workflows and showcases how Codestral can act as a productive coding partner.

To explore Codestral's FiM capabilities, we'll create a file with a partially implemented function and let the AI fill in the missing logic:

1. Start by creating a new file named `fim.py`. You can do this by duplicating the existing `fim_bare.py` file. This ensures we have a clean and consistent starting point. The `fim_bare.py` file content looks as follows:

```
def fibonacci(n):
    # TODO: compute the nth Fibonacci number
    pass
```

2. Open `fim.py` in VS Code and select the entire function body, including the `def` line and the `pass` placeholder. Add to context.

3. With the code selected, press *Cmd + L* (or *Ctrl + L* on Windows/Linux) to bring the code into the Continue dev chat panel.

4. In the prompt field, type the following:

```
fill in the logic for this function
```

You'll notice that Codestral carefully considers the function name and structure and responds with a complete implementation that fits the context.

This smooth and intentional flow demonstrates the power of FiM in real development work. It doesn't just guess, but rather infers meaning from structure and intent, giving you exactly what you need without overcomplicating the process.

After applying the suggested code, your `fim.py` file should now look like this:

```
def fibonacci(n):
    if n <= 0:
        return 0
    elif n == 1:
        return 1
    else:
        return fibonacci(n - 1) + fibonacci(n - 2)
```

The FiM technique demonstrates how Codestral can bridge the gap between high-level design and implementation, making it a smart assistant for completing code logically. Whether you're sketching ideas, prototyping functions, or filling in missing code in legacy projects, FiM speeds up the process with intelligent suggestions. Let's now move on to our final step, learning from the code, where we'll ask Codestral to explain and teach us what it just helped create.

Step 6: Learning from code

In this step, we'll harness the mentoring capabilities of Codestral to deepen our understanding of the code. By treating Codestral as an expert mentor, we'll receive thorough, line-by-line explanations of a key function in our application. This will not only clarify the code's functionality but also enhance your programming knowledge:

1. Open your `main.py` file and select the following lines of code:

    ```python
    @app.route('/joke', methods=['GET'])
    def get_joke():
    with open('~/.continue/config.json') as config_file:
    config = json.load(config_file)

    response = requests.get(config['joke_api'])
    joke = response.json()['value']

    return render_template('joke.html', joke=joke)
    ```

2. Press *Cmd* + *L* (or *Ctrl* + *L* on Windows/Linux) to start a new chat with Codestral and add the selected snippet to the context.

3. To interact with your assistant, type the following prompt into the chat:

    ```
    please explain the code
    ```

4. Once entered, press *Enter* to send it to Codestral. This will trigger the model to analyze the code and return an explanation, helping you better understand its structure and behavior.

Codestral will generate a detailed, line-by-line explanation of the selected code snippet. Each line will be broken down to explain its purpose and how it fits into the overall function. The following figure demonstrates how it looks.

This is a Python script that uses the Flask web framework to create a simple web application. The script defines a route for the URL '/joke' that accepts GET requests. When a GET request is made to this URL, the function `get_joke()` is executed.

Here's a breakdown of the code:

1. `@app.route('/joke', methods=['GET'])` : This is a decorator that Flask provides to assign URLs in our app to functions easily. In this case, the function `get_joke()` is assigned to the '/joke' URL and can only be accessed via GET requests.

2. `with open('/Users/pavlocherkashyn/.continue/config.json') as config_file:` : This line opens the 'config.json' file located at the specified path and assigns the file object to 'config_file'. The 'with' statement is used for resource management and ensures that the file is properly closed after it is no longer needed.

3. `config = json.load(config_file)` : This line uses the 'json' module to parse the JSON data from the 'config.json' file and assigns the resulting Python object to 'config'.

4. `response = requests.get(config['joke_api'])` : This line uses the 'requests' library to send a GET request to the URL specified in 'config['joke_api']'. The response from the server is assigned to 'response'.

5. `joke = response.json()['value']` : This line parses the JSON data from the response and assigns the value of the 'value' key to 'joke'.

6. `return render_template('joke.html', joke=joke)` : Finally, the function returns a rendered HTML template called 'joke.html'. The 'joke' variable is passed to the template as a parameter, which means that it can be accessed and used in the template to display the joke to the user.

Figure 7.20: Thorough code explanation provided as a response

Great news! Codestral responded with a detailed explanation, breaking down the code with clarity and nuance. It didn't just describe what each part does, but offered insights into structure, logic, and intent. This kind of thoughtful response turns code into something readable, learnable, and less intimidating. A true milestone in building your AI-powered coding assistant!

By leveraging Codestral as a mentor, you've gained an in-depth understanding of your code's functionality and design. This exercise demonstrated how Codestral's expert knowledge can serve as a valuable learning tool, enriching your coding experience.

Summary

Across multiple hands-on workshops, we explored how Codestral can support developers as a powerful coding assistant. From setting up the environment in VS Code to generating Flask web services, building simple web interfaces, and integrating with external APIs, we saw how Codestral simplifies common development tasks.

We also tackled troubleshooting scenarios, such as resolving template errors, where Codestral's guidance helped clarify project structure and improve debugging skills. Beyond just code generation, Codestral acted as a mentor, offering clear, line-by-line explanations that deepened our understanding of how the code works.

Overall, these workshops highlighted Codestral's value in streamlining development, accelerating learning, and bridging backend and frontend components with ease.

With Codestral as your partner, the possibilities for innovation and learning are endless. Let's continue to build, explore, and grow!

In the next chapter, we explore how Mistral models support practical security tasks, including analyzing PCAP files, inspecting logs for anomalies, and detecting vulnerabilities such as SQL injection and cross-site scripting in source code. Through real-world examples, you'll see how these models assist security teams by accelerating detection, guiding remediation, and helping make informed decisions during log analysis and code reviews.

Extracurricular

This optional activity introduces **Mistral Code Enterprise**, a powerful AI assistant integrated into your code editor. It's designed to support inline completion, refactoring, explanations, and more. Here's how to set it up quickly in VS Code:

> **On licensing**
>
> Mistral Code Enterprise operates under a commercial license, which typically requires a paid subscription. However, certain categories of users, such as researchers, educators, students, open source maintainers, and selected enterprise evaluators, may be eligible to request free access.

You can apply for access or check eligibility directly via the Mistral Code welcome screen or Mistral's official website.

- Ensure VS Code is installed. This was already covered in *Workshop 2*. If you've followed that, you're good to go.
- Install the Mistral Code extension. Open the **Extensions** panel in VS Code. Search for Mistral Code Enterprise or go directly to `https://marketplace.visualstudio.com/items?itemName=mistralai.mistral-code`. Click **Install**, and allow your browser to open it in VS Code:

Mistral Code Enterprise

Mistral AI | ⬇ 1,589 installs | ★ ★ ★ ★ ★ (3) | Free

Your AI coding copilot powered by state-of-the-art Mistral coding models

[**Install**]   Trouble Installing? ↗

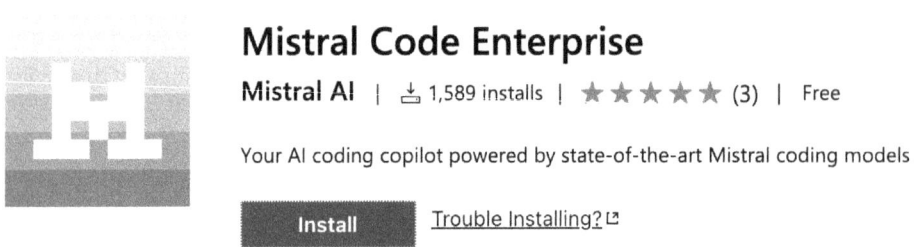

Figure 7.21: Mistral Code Enterprise

- Log in to your Mistral account. Click the **M** icon in the left sidebar of VS Code. A welcome screen will appear, prompting you to log in. Follow the authentication flow to activate your assistant:

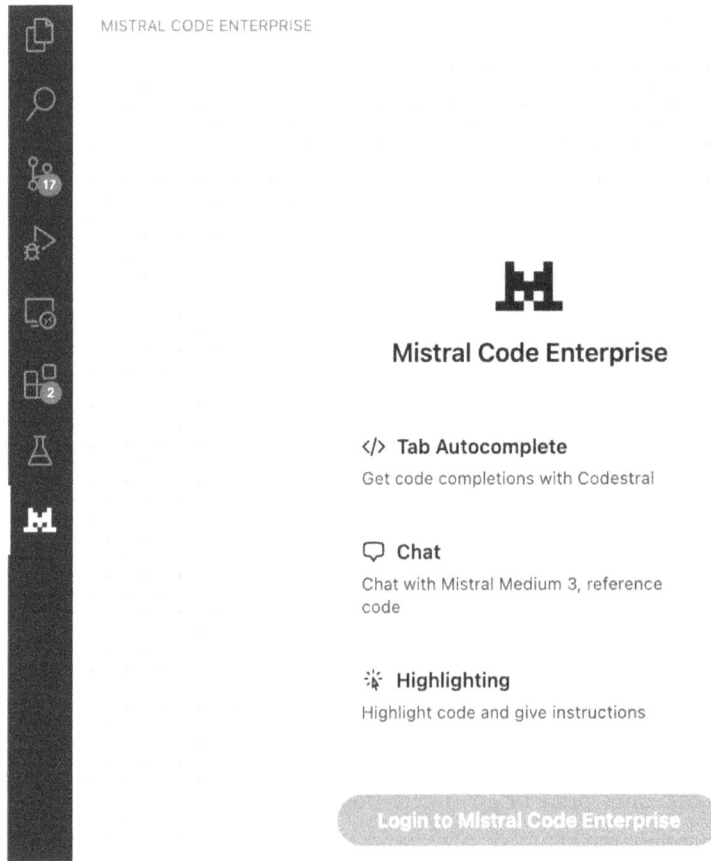

MISTRAL CODE ENTERPRISE

M

Mistral Code Enterprise

</> Tab Autocomplete
Get code completions with Codestral

💬 Chat
Chat with Mistral Medium 3, reference code

☀ Highlighting
Highlight code and give instructions

(**Login to Mistral Code Enterprise**)

Figure 7.22: Mistral Code Enterprise home screen

- **JetBrains alternative**: If you're using IntelliJ, PyCharm, or other JetBrains IDEs, you can install the same plugin from the JetBrains Marketplace at `https://plugins.jetbrains.com/plugin/27493-mistral-code-enterprise`.

- For more details about features and use cases, see the official launch announcement at `https://mistral.ai/news/mistral-code`.

- Once installed and logged in, you can use Mistral Code to complete code, explain snippets, or build directly in your editor, using natural prompts. Happy coding and experimenting!

Join our Discord and Reddit space

You're not the only one navigating fragmented tools, constant updates, and unclear best practices. Join a growing community of professionals exchanging insights that don't make it into documentation.

Stay informed with updates, discussions, and behind-the-scenes insights from our authors. Join our Discord at `https://packt.link/z8ivB` or scan the QR code below:	Connect with peers, share ideas, and discuss real-world GenAI challenges. Follow us on Reddit at `https://packt.link/0rExL` or scan the QR code below:

8

Building Smarter Defenses with Mistral

An ounce of prevention is worth a pound of cure.

—Benjamin Franklin

Security is the backbone of any modern digital infrastructure, where every log entry tells a story, and every anomaly could signal a potential threat. This chapter explores the power of AI-driven log analysis in protecting systems, applications, and data. We'll examine techniques from firewall logs to SQL injection detection to identify, mitigate, and prevent attacks. We'll also cover endpoint security and cloud security, emphasizing actionable insights and automation using LLMs. By the end, you'll have a comprehensive understanding of how advanced tools and strategies can transform security challenges into manageable tasks.

This chapter covers the following main topics:

- Problem statement
- Security applications
- Workshop: Code and cloud security with Mistral

Technical requirements

To complete this chapter successfully, make sure you have the following tools and setup ready.

- **GitHub access**: You'll need access to the following GitHub repository to download reference code and workshop files: `https://github.com/PacktPublishing/Learn-Mistral`. Make sure to specifically navigate to the `Chapter-8` folder.

- **Visual Studio Code**: If not yet installed, set up VSCode from `https://code.visualstudio.com/`. This will be your primary IDE throughout the workshop.

- **Continue dev extension**: Install the Continue AI extension from the VSCode Marketplace. This is the interface we'll use to communicate with the Mistral-based Codestral model.

- **Codestral LLM access**: You'll need one of the following options: set up a free Codestral trial or paid API access with an API key.

With all the tools and environment ready, you're well-equipped to dive in!

Problem statement

Modern security challenges often lie hidden within the complexities of application code, where vulnerabilities such as SQL injection or insecure dependencies can jeopardize systems. Identifying and mitigating these risks requires practical strategies. That's where tools such as the Mistral LLM step in, helping you catch problems early with smart features such as input sanitization, parameterized queries, and automated vulnerability detection—all without the heavy lifting.

Security applications

In an ever-evolving digital landscape, security applications are no longer optional. According to Verizon's 2025 Data Breach Investigations Report, exploiting vulnerabilities is now the initial access vector in 20% of breaches, a 34% year-over-year increase (*Reference:* `https://www.indusface.com/blog/key-cybersecurity-statistics/`).

Threats range from subtle vulnerabilities in application code to large-scale data breaches, and the stakes have never been higher. This section introduces cutting-edge approaches to fortifying systems against cyber risks, leveraging the power of Mistral LLM to automate and enhance security measures.

In this section, we'll journey through critical areas of security, including analyzing firewall logs to detect anomalous traffic and compliance violations, identifying SQL injection vulnerabilities in application code, and safeguarding endpoints against malware and data exfiltration.

Cloud security, authentication protocols, and advanced AI-driven user behavior analytics also take center stage, ensuring a robust understanding of how to shield digital assets effectively.

Rule compliance auditing

Firewall rules define which traffic is permitted or denied, and misconfigurations can significantly weaken your network's security. For instance, overly permissive rules, such as allowing unrestricted access on sensitive ports, expose your system to unauthorized access and potential attacks. Conducting regular audits helps identify these vulnerabilities and ensures your firewall rules align with the principle of least privilege.

Consider the following Terraform snippet defining an AWS security group. This configuration includes ingress rules for SSH, HTTP, and HTTPS.

> **Challenge: Can you spot the overtrust?**
>
> This security group is like leaving all your doors wide open with a welcome sign.
>
> **Hint:** When you see 0.0.0.0/0, think "open to the world." Does every server really need SSH, HTTP, and HTTPS access from anywhere? And what about letting all outbound traffic through without limits? That's not tight security; that's a red carpet for attackers.

```
resource "aws_security_group" "example" {
  name        = "example-security-group"
  description = "Security group for example application"
  vpc_id      = aws_vpc.main.id

  # Allow SSH access
  ingress {
    from_port   = 22
    to_port     = 22
    protocol    = "tcp"
    cidr_blocks = ["0.0.0.0/0"]
  }

  # Allow HTTP access
  ingress {
    from_port   = 80
```

```
    to_port     = 80
    protocol    = "tcp"
    cidr_blocks = ["0.0.0.0/0"]
  }

  # Allow HTTPS access
  ingress {
    from_port   = 443
    to_port     = 443
    protocol    = "tcp"
    cidr_blocks = ["0.0.0.0/0"]
  }

  # Egress rule
  egress {
    from_port   = 0
    to_port     = 0
    protocol    = "-1"
    cidr_blocks = ["0.0.0.0/0"]
  }

  tags = {
    Name = "example-security-group"
  }
}
```

Okay, as we can see, protocols HTTP and HTTPS are all open to the entire internet, as well as an unrestricted egress rule.

Manually reviewing such configurations for potential risks is tedious and error-prone, especially in complex environments. Instead, you can leverage the Mistral LLM to automate the process. A refined prompt tailored for this task could be the following:

```
Analyze the following Terraform script and identify any configurations
that violate the least privilege principle or are overly permissive.
Provide specific recommendations for improvement.
```

When processed by Mistral, the model identifies potential misconfigurations and offers action-able suggestions:

```
Potential misconfigurations:
- SSH ingress rule (port 22) allows unrestricted access. Recommend
limiting to trusted IPs.
- HTTP ingress rule (port 80) is open to the entire internet. Suggest
restricting access based on application requirements.
- Open egress rule permits all outbound traffic. Recommend narrowing the
scope to specific destinations and protocols.

Suggested action: Update ingress rules to use restricted CIDR ranges and
refine the egress rule to align with application needs.
```

By automating this analysis, Mistral streamlines compliance auditing, reducing the risk of over-sight. It provides clear guidance for securing configurations, allowing your team to focus on im-plementing the necessary changes. This approach ensures your firewall rules are both effective and aligned with security best practices.

> In our workshop in the second half of this chapter, we will dive deeper into analyz-ing Terraform scripts to ensure they adhere to the principle of least privilege. Using Codestral, we'll identify overly permissive configurations, such as unrestricted in-gress or egress rules, and learn how to secure them effectively, aligning with best practices for cloud security.

Firewall logs analysis

Firewall logs are like a treasure trove of data – if you know what to look for. They record every interaction between your network and the outside world, but making sense of all that noise can feel overwhelming. That's where the Mistral LLM steps in, helping you quickly spot patterns and focus on what really matters.

In this section, we'll dive into practical ways to make firewall logs work for you, learn how to spot weird traffic that might signal a DDoS attack or unauthorized access attempts, use geolocation analysis to flag traffic from shady regions or known bad actors, check whether your firewall rules are playing by the book, and keep your setup secure.

We'll also show you how to sort alerts into categories, so you can tackle the big problems first, and use AI to uncover new threats you might not even know to look for. By the end, you'll know how to turn raw log data into useful insights and take action fast.

Anomalous traffic detection

Every network tells a story through its traffic, but hidden within the steady flow of data are unusual patterns that can signal a looming threat. Detecting these anomalies, such as sudden spikes in traffic during a DDoS attack or repeated access attempts from suspicious IPs, can mean the difference between staying secure and falling victim to an attack. With the help of the Mistral LLM and Codestral, this process can become more streamlined, turning logs into actionable insights in a matter of moments.

Spotting DDoS traffic

DDoS attacks often result in a flood of requests from multiple IPs targeting the same endpoint. These attacks can overwhelm your network, making it crucial to identify the source quickly. For instance, consider the following sample log entries:

```
2023-12-28T10:15:12Z SRC_IP=192.168.1.5 DEST_IP=10.0.0.8 DEST_PORT=443
PROTOCOL=TCP BYTES_SENT=0 BYTES_RECEIVED=124
2023-12-28T10:15:12Z SRC_IP=192.168.1.6 DEST_IP=10.0.0.8 DEST_PORT=443
PROTOCOL=TCP BYTES_SENT=0 BYTES_RECEIVED=124
2023-12-28T10:15:13Z SRC_IP=192.168.1.7 DEST_IP=10.0.0.8 DEST_PORT=443
PROTOCOL=TCP BYTES_SENT=0 BYTES_RECEIVED=124
```

Manually analyzing these logs to detect patterns can be tedious and error-prone. This is where the Mistral LLM excels. Let's feed logs into Mistral with a prompt such as the following:

```
Analyze the logs and identify source IPs with high traffic targeting a
single destination.
```

Mistral processes the data and provides a summary:

```
Potential DDoS detected:
  - SRC_IP: 192.168.1.5, Requests: 100
  - SRC_IP: 192.168.1.6, Requests: 98
  - SRC_IP: 192.168.1.7, Requests: 95
Suggested action: Block these IPs temporarily.
```

This output not only identifies the problematic IPs but also offers actionable advice, such as temporarily blocking the offenders. By automating the detection and recommendation process, Mistral allows you to focus on mitigation instead of manual analysis.

Identifying port scanning attempts

Port scans are another common threat, where attackers probe multiple ports on a single machine to find vulnerabilities. Detecting these scans requires tracking connections over time to identify patterns. For example, here's a sample log:

```
2023-12-28T11:00:15Z SRC_IP=203.0.113.5 DEST_IP=10.0.0.8 DEST_PORT=22
PROTOCOL=TCP
2023-12-28T11:00:16Z SRC_IP=203.0.113.5 DEST_IP=10.0.0.8 DEST_PORT=80
PROTOCOL=TCP
2023-12-28T11:00:17Z SRC_IP=203.0.113.5 DEST_IP=10.0.0.8 DEST_PORT=443
PROTOCOL=TCP
```

Manually analyzing logs for patterns indicative of port scanning can be time-consuming and error-prone, especially when dealing with large datasets. By leveraging a language model, such as Mistral 8B, you can automate this process. The model can quickly identify suspicious activities by processing the log entries and providing actionable insights with a well-crafted prompt like the following one:

```
Analyze the following network packets and detect potential port scanning
activities. If detected, provide the source IP, list the targeted ports,
and suggest an appropriate action.
```

The model processes the data and provides a concise and actionable response, highlighting suspicious activity, targeted ports, and recommended next steps:

```
Port scanning detected from
SRC_IP: 203.0.113.5
Ports targeted: 22, 80, 443
Suggested action: Add to dynamic block list.
```

This analysis pinpoints the source of the port scanning activity and the specific ports targeted, allowing for an effective response. By blocking the offending IP or enhancing monitoring on the affected machine, you can mitigate the threat swiftly and strengthen your network's overall security posture.

Addressing unauthorized access attempts

Brute force attacks are a persistent issue, often involving repeated failed login attempts targeting specific systems or accounts. Identifying these attempts manually from logs can be labor-intensive and error-prone, particularly in environments with high traffic. Automated analysis using the Mistral LLM offers a faster and more reliable approach, helping to detect patterns and suggest countermeasures.

For example, consider the following log entries:

```
2023-12-28T12:30:10Z SRC_IP=198.51.100.7 DEST_PORT=22 STATUS=FAILED
2023-12-28T12:30:11Z SRC_IP=198.51.100.7 DEST_PORT=22 STATUS=FAILED
2023-12-28T12:30:12Z SRC_IP=198.51.100.7 DEST_PORT=22 STATUS=FAILED
```

Instead of manually analyzing these logs for repeated attempts, you can utilize a language model such as Mistral. By providing the logs and a well-crafted prompt, the model can efficiently process the data and provide actionable insights. A suitable prompt could be the following:

```
Analyze the logs for repeated failed login attempts. Identify the source
IP, the number of attempts, and recommend appropriate mitigations.
```

The model processes the logs and provides a clear and concise output:

```
Repeated failed login attempts detected from SRC_IP: 198.51.100.7
Attempts: 50 within 5 minutes
Suggested action: Enforce IP blocking and review SSH access policies.
```

This output not only identifies the offending source IP but also suggests specific mitigations, such as enforcing IP blocks and reviewing access policies. By automating the detection and response process, Mistral streamlines threat management, allowing security teams to act swiftly and reduce the risk of unauthorized access.

We've flagged suspicious behavior in the logs—DDoS bursts, port scans, and brute force attempts. The next step is to add geographic context so we can separate routine noise from riskier traffic. Geolocation-based analysis uses region and threat-intel signals to enrich each event, making triage faster. Let's look at that next.

Geolocation-based analysis

Understanding where traffic originates is a critical component of identifying potential threats to your network. Geolocation analysis allows you to detect traffic originating from high-risk regions or known malicious IPs, which often serve as early indicators of malicious activity.

However, manually analyzing logs for such patterns is not only labor-intensive but prone to human error. Leveraging Mistral LLM automates this process, enabling quick and accurate analysis of geolocation metadata.

For example, consider the following log entries, which include geolocation information:

```
2023-12-28T14:05:22Z SRC_IP=45.67.89.101 DEST_IP=10.0.0.8
GEOLOCATION=Unknown REGION="Eastern Europe"
2023-12-28T14:05:23Z SRC_IP=203.0.113.88 DEST_IP=10.0.0.8
GEOLOCATION=Known Malicious REGION="Asia"
```

> To enhance geolocation analysis, you can integrate IP geolocation databases such as MaxMind's GeoLite2 into tools such as Wireshark. This allows for real-time mapping of IP addresses to their geographic locations, providing valuable context for traffic patterns and aiding in the identification of high-risk regions or malicious IPs.

Manually identifying and categorizing traffic from suspicious regions can be daunting, especially when logs are voluminous. To streamline this, you can provide these logs to the Mistral LLM using a prompt that directs the model to highlight any high-risk traffic sources. A rephrased and focused prompt could look like this:

```
Review the logs and identify traffic from suspicious regions or known
malicious IPs. Provide the source IP, the region or geolocation, and
recommend appropriate actions.
```

When processed, Mistral generates insights like the following:

```
Suspicious traffic detected:
- SRC_IP: 45.67.89.101 (Region: Eastern Europe, Geo: Unknown)
- SRC_IP: 203.0.113.88 (Region: Asia, Geo: Known Malicious)
Suggested action: Monitor or block these IPs.
```

This output not only pinpoints the source IPs and their associated regions but also suggests actionable steps, such as blocking or monitoring the identified traffic. By automating geolocation analysis, Mistral not only saves valuable time but also enhances accuracy, enabling security teams to focus on proactive measures. This approach ensures a more robust and efficient defense against evolving threats.

Now that we can detect anomalies and understand where they originate, the challenge is alert volume.

Alert prioritization

One of the greatest challenges in managing network security is sifting through the sheer volume of alerts generated by modern systems. Not all alerts are of equal importance; some may indicate critical threats requiring immediate action, while others are simply routine notifications. Without proper prioritization, security teams risk wasting time on low-priority issues, potentially leaving serious threats unaddressed. Automating the categorization of these alerts helps streamline response efforts, allowing teams to focus on what matters most.

Consider the following log entries, representing different types of network events:

```
2023-12-28T15:10:12Z SRC_IP=198.51.100.1 EVENT="Unauthorized access
attempt"
2023-12-28T15:10:15Z SRC_IP=192.0.2.5 EVENT="Login failure"
2023-12-28T15:10:17Z SRC_IP=192.0.2.5 EVENT="Login failure"
2023-12-28T15:10:18Z SRC_IP=192.0.2.5 EVENT="Login failure"
2023-12-28T15:10:20Z SRC_IP=192.0.2.5 EVENT="Login failure"
2023-12-28T15:10:25Z SRC_IP=203.0.113.50 EVENT="Routine connection
established"
```

Manually analyzing these logs to determine their urgency can be inefficient and error-prone, particularly in high-traffic environments. To automate this process, the Mistral LLM can analyze the logs and assign appropriate severity levels, prioritizing them for immediate action when necessary. A suitable prompt might be the following:

```
Analyze the following logs and categorize them as critical, warning, or
informational. Provide recommendations for appropriate actions based on
the severity of each event.
```

Mistral processes these logs and delivers actionable insights:

```
Critical: Unauthorized access attempt (SRC_IP: 198.51.100.1) — Block
immediately and investigate.
Warning: Repeated login failures (SRC_IP: 192.0.2.5) — Monitor and enforce
rate-limiting.
Informational: Routine connection established (SRC_IP: 203.0.113.50) — No
action needed.
```

By automating this analysis, Mistral enables security teams to quickly identify and respond to critical events, such as unauthorized access attempts, while monitoring lower-priority warnings, such as repeated login failures. This prioritization not only reduces response time but also ensures that security resources are allocated efficiently, addressing threats before they escalate.

Even with tighter rules and sharper context, some threats still sneak through. So, what's next? We turn to spotting the unusual—the patterns that break the mold. In the next section, we'll explore how anomaly detection helps catch zero-day threats before they make headlines.

Zero-day threat detection

Zero-day threats are among the most challenging security risks, exploiting unknown vulnerabilities that leave systems exposed to sophisticated attacks. Unlike traditional threats, which can often be mitigated with predefined rules, zero-day exploits require advanced anomaly detection techniques. The Mistral LLM excels in identifying these patterns, offering insights that enable rapid response and mitigation. Let's explore two examples of anomalous traffic patterns that could indicate a potential zero-day threat.

Example 1: Rapidly fluctuating traffic volume

One potential indicator of a zero-day threat is abnormal fluctuations in traffic volume. Such patterns may suggest data exfiltration, traffic shaping, or other unauthorized activity. Consider the following log entries:

```
2023-12-28T14:00:01Z SRC_IP=192.168.1.20 DEST_IP=10.0.0.8 BYTES_SENT=500KB
PROTOCOL=TCP
2023-12-28T14:00:05Z SRC_IP=192.168.1.20 DEST_IP=10.0.0.8 BYTES_SENT=5MB
PROTOCOL=TCP
2023-12-28T14:00:06Z SRC_IP=192.168.1.20 DEST_IP=10.0.0.8 BYTES_SENT=20KB
PROTOCOL=TCP
2023-12-28T14:00:07Z SRC_IP=192.168.1.20 DEST_IP=10.0.0.8 BYTES_SENT=100MB
PROTOCOL=TCP
2023-12-28T14:00:08Z SRC_IP=192.168.1.20 DEST_IP=10.0.0.8 BYTES_SENT=1KB
PROTOCOL=TCP
```

Manually identifying these irregularities is time-consuming and error-prone, especially when monitoring large datasets. By leveraging the Mistral LLM, you can automate this process using a targeted prompt such as the following:

```
Analyze the following logs for unusual traffic patterns that may indicate
emerging threats. Highlight anomalies and recommend appropriate actions to
mitigate potential risks.
```

When processed, Mistral provides the following actionable insights:

```
Emerging threat detected:
- Traffic volume fluctuates abnormally from SRC_IP: 192.168.1.20.
- Potential indicator of data exfiltration or traffic shaping attempts.
Suggested action: Monitor the system closely and review logs for signs of
unauthorized data transfers.
```

These insights highlight the irregular behavior, allowing security teams to take immediate action, such as isolating the source or strengthening data monitoring.

Example 2: Irregular session establishment and termination

Another suspicious pattern involves unusual session behavior, where a source IP frequently establishes and terminates sessions within a short time. This could indicate connection probing or attempts to exploit session vulnerabilities. Review the following log entries:

```
2023-12-28T14:05:10Z SRC_IP=203.0.113.25 DEST_IP=10.0.0.8 EVENT="Session
start" PROTOCOL=TCP
2023-12-28T14:05:11Z SRC_IP=203.0.113.25 DEST_IP=10.0.0.8 EVENT="Session
end" PROTOCOL=TCP
2023-12-28T14:05:12Z SRC_IP=203.0.113.25 DEST_IP=10.0.0.8 EVENT="Session
start" PROTOCOL=TCP
2023-12-28T14:05:13Z SRC_IP=203.0.113.25 DEST_IP=10.0.0.8 EVENT="Session
end" PROTOCOL=TCP
2023-12-28T14:05:14Z SRC_IP=203.0.113.25 DEST_IP=10.0.0.8 EVENT="Session
start" PROTOCOL=TCP
```

Such frequent session changes can easily be missed during manual review, but Mistral's anomaly detection capabilities make it simple to identify and prioritize. Let's consider the same as in the previous example:

```
Analyze the following logs for unusual traffic patterns that may indicate
emerging threats. Highlight anomalies and recommend appropriate actions to
mitigate potential risks.
```

Mistral's response draws attention to the anomaly and provides clear next steps to address the potential threat, such as tracking sessions or further isolating the source for deeper analysis:

```
Emerging threat detected:
- Irregular session establishment and termination from SRC_IP:
203.0.113.25.
```

```
- Behavior consistent with potential connection probing or session
hijacking attempts.
Suggested action: Investigate the source IP and implement session tracking
mechanisms for further monitoring.
```

By automating the detection of anomalous traffic patterns, the Mistral LLM allows security teams to quickly identify and respond to zero-day threats. Whether it's fluctuating traffic volumes or erratic session behavior, these insights enable proactive threat mitigation, reducing the risk of exploitation. With tools such as Mistral and Codestral, you gain a significant advantage in safeguarding critical systems against unknown vulnerabilities.

From geolocation-based filtering to zero-day anomaly detection, Mistral LLM revolutionizes how we handle firewall logs and security workflows. Its ability to automate geolocation analysis, audit firewall rules, prioritize alerts, and detect emerging threats simplifies complex tasks and enhances decision-making. This seamless integration of AI into security operations ensures that organizations stay ahead of attackers, responding faster and smarter to potential risks. By combining practical tools with AI-driven insights, these approaches turn raw data into actionable intelligence, enabling a more robust and efficient defense strategy.

The next layer of defense lies in understanding the stateful nature of connections. Stateful firewall logs provide deeper insights into session behaviors, revealing patterns such as incomplete handshakes, persistent attempts, and protocol misuse. Let's explore how analyzing these logs strengthens network security further.

Stateful firewall logs

Imagine your network as a busy highway, with countless vehicles (connections) passing through every second. Stateful firewalls are like the vigilant traffic controllers of this highway, not just tracking who comes and goes, but also monitoring how each vehicle behaves at every stage of its journey. By analyzing stateful firewall logs, we can uncover potential threats hidden in incomplete sessions, unusual timings, or strange protocol behaviors. With the help of Mistral LLM, this process becomes even more intuitive, turning cryptic logs into clear, actionable insights.

Session tracking

Connections in a network typically follow a predictable handshake pattern: SYN, SYN-ACK, ACK. This sequence ensures that both ends of the connection are ready to communicate. However, when the sequence breaks (like a car stalling mid-journey), it can disrupt operations and signal malicious activity. Such disruptions often indicate attempts to overwhelm or exploit the system.

Let's look at a specific example of suspicious traffic:

```
2023-12-28T17:10:45Z SRC_IP=203.0.113.5 DEST_IP=10.0.0.8 DEST_PORT=80
PROTOCOL=TCP STATE=SYN_SENT
2023-12-28T17:10:46Z SRC_IP=203.0.113.5 DEST_IP=10.0.0.8 DEST_PORT=80
PROTOCOL=TCP STATE=SYN_SENT
2023-12-28T17:10:47Z SRC_IP=203.0.113.5 DEST_IP=10.0.0.8 DEST_PORT=80
PROTOCOL=TCP STATE=SYN_SENT
```

In this case, the source IP repeatedly sends SYN requests but never completes the handshake. This behavior is a classic sign of a SYN flood attack, a technique used to overwhelm the target system by exhausting its resources. Identifying such patterns manually can be a time-consuming and error-prone process, especially in high-traffic environments.

To simplify the analysis, we can use the Mistral LLM to automatically detect potential SYN floods by analyzing the logs. Here's an updated prompt to ensure the response includes the required format:

```
Analyze the following logs for incomplete sessions and potential SYN
flood attacks. Provide the source IP, the count of SYN_SENT states, and
recommend appropriate actions.
```

Mistral processes the data and provides a clear and actionable response:

```
Potential SYN flood detected:
- SRC_IP: 203.0.113.5
- SYN_SENT count: 100 within 10 seconds
Suggested action: Apply rate limiting and monitor for continued behavior.
```

This output highlights the problem and offers immediate steps to mitigate the risk. Rate limiting can reduce the impact of the attack by limiting the number of connections from the offending IP, while continued monitoring ensures the system remains secure.

Protocol misuse

Protocols are like designated lanes on a highway, each carefully designed to handle specific types of traffic. HTTP traffic flows through one lane, while SMTP occupies another. But what happens when a protocol strays into the wrong lane? For instance, running SMTP on a port typically used for HTTP signals suspicious activity that could indicate a misconfiguration or a potential exploit. Identifying and addressing these anomalies is key to maintaining a secure and efficient network.

Consider this log entry, which demonstrates a case of protocol misuse:

```
2023-12-28T14:00:10Z SRC_IP=192.0.2.5 DEST_PORT=8080 PROTOCOL=SMTP
```

Here, SMTP is operating on port 8080, a port commonly reserved for HTTP traffic. Such discrepancies might result from errors, or they could indicate an attacker attempting to bypass security measures. Detecting and addressing these issues manually can be time-consuming and prone to oversight, particularly in networks with high traffic volumes.

To simplify this process, we can use the Mistral LLM to analyze the logs and identify protocol misuses. Here's an updated prompt that ensures the response includes all necessary details:

```
Analyze the following logs for unexpected protocol usage on non-standard
ports. Provide the source IP, protocol used, port number, and recommend
actions to address the issue.
```

When processed, Mistral provides a clear and actionable response:

```
Protocol misuse detected:
- SRC_IP: 192.0.2.5
- Protocol: SMTP on port 8080
- Suggested action: Investigate the source IP and enforce protocol-port
mapping rules to prevent unauthorized usage.
```

This response highlights the misuse and provides a recommended course of action. Investigating the source IP can reveal whether the behavior results from a misconfiguration or a more serious threat. Enforcing strict protocol-port mappings helps prevent unauthorized activities and ensures the network operates within its intended boundaries.

By automating the detection of protocol misuses, Mistral enables security teams to quickly identify and address anomalies. This not only enhances the efficiency of network management but also reduces the risk of potential exploits, keeping your infrastructure secure and reliable.

Stateful firewall logs are a goldmine of insights into network behavior, allowing you to uncover threats ranging from incomplete handshakes to protocol misuse. With the Mistral LLM, analyzing these logs becomes straightforward and actionable. By identifying issues, suggesting responses, and automating tasks such as dynamic block list updates, Mistral turns complex data into simple solutions, ensuring your network remains secure and resilient.

On real-time log processing

Real-time log processing isn't always feasible due to the high volume and complexity of network logs, often requiring significant computational resources. However, with the availability of local deployment options such as Mistral 8B and Mistral Nemo, close-to-real-time analysis becomes achievable even on limited infrastructure. Running Mistral locally allows for efficient, low-latency processing, enabling organizations to monitor and respond to threats without relying on costly cloud solutions or external dependencies. This approach balances performance with resource availability, making it a practical choice for businesses aiming to enhance their security posture without overextending their operational budget.

Other security applications

Let's now explore how Mistral LLMs can enhance cybersecurity across multiple domains. From detecting endpoint threats and abnormal user behavior to monitoring file integrity and cloud misconfigurations, Mistral can support real-time analysis and automation. Let's look at its role in strengthening authentication, authorization, and identifying potential data exfiltration risks:

- **Endpoint security, malware behavior prediction**: Predicting malware behavior is like identifying a hidden predator in the wild: seemingly harmless until it strikes. By analyzing code snippets with Mistral, you can uncover malicious patterns early, even identifying zero-day threats. A real-life example includes Stuxnet, a highly sophisticated malware that targeted industrial systems by hiding in legitimate-looking code (referenced material: `https://www.codeproject.com/articles/246545/stuxnet-malware-analysis-paper`).

- **File integrity monitoring**: Critical system files, once tampered with, can compromise the entire system. In the 2017 NotPetya attack, unauthorized file changes led to widespread damage. Mistral can monitor file integrity in real time, alerting you to any unauthorized modifications (referenced material: `https://css.csail.mit.edu/6.566/2018/readings/stuxnet.pdf`).

- **Data exfiltration detection (unusual data transfers)**: Massive or repeated data exports often signal exfiltration attempts. In 2014, the Sony Pictures breach involved gigabytes of sensitive data stolen over weeks. Using Mistral, you can identify such anomalies by analyzing network logs and flagging transfers to unknown destinations (referenced material: `https://www.itgovernance.co.uk/blog/global-data-breaches-and-cyber-attacks-in-december-2023-2241916765-records-breached`).

- **Authentication and authorization (credential abuse detection)**: Credential stuffing and brute-force attacks continue to pose significant cybersecurity threats. In 2024, 35% of organizations reported identity-related breaches due to brute-force attacks, including credential stuffing and password spraying (referenced material: `https://www.beyondtrust.com/blog/entry/the-state-of-identity-security-identity-based-threats-breaches-security-best-practices?utm_source=chatgpt.com`). Additionally, in 2023, credential stuffing accounted for approximately 10% of data breaches (referenced material: `https://jumpcloud.com/blog/password-statistics-trends?utm_source=chatgpt.com`). Mistral can analyze login attempts in real time, detecting and blocking abusive patterns to mitigate these threats.

- **Application code vulnerability identification**: The OWASP Top 10 lists critical web vulnerabilities such as XSS and CSRF. Mistral identifies these flaws in your application code by scanning for insecure patterns, offering fixes to strengthen your code base (referenced material: `https://github.com/x86byte/Stuxnet-Rootkit`).

- **User behavior analytics (UBA) (command and control patterns)**: C2 servers are often used in advanced attacks, such as the 2020 SolarWinds breach. Mistral can identify known C2 communication patterns from logs, enabling early detection and disruption of these malicious channels (referenced material: `https://css.csail.mit.edu/6.566/2018/readings/stuxnet.pdf`).

- **Cloud misconfiguration monitoring**: Misconfigurations are responsible for 73% of cloud security issues, as seen in the 2018 Tesla cloud breach. Mistral analyzes configuration files such as Terraform and CloudFormation to detect open ports, overly permissive roles, and insecure defaults (referenced article: `https://www.cloudcomputing-news.net/news/misconfiguration-was-the-number-one-cause-of-cloud-security-incidents-in-2021/`).

- **Cloud storage security**: Publicly exposed storage buckets have led to numerous breaches, such as the 2017 Verizon data leak. Mistral can analyze bucket policies, ensuring that sensitive data is properly secured (referenced material: `https://www.osibeyond.com/blog/cloud-services-misconfiguration-problem/`).

We've taken a stroll through some of the most critical areas of modern cybersecurity, from spotting sneaky malware to flagging odd data transfers and locking down misconfigured cloud setups. It's not rocket science, but it's definitely a bit more than "just click here to secure." Thankfully, Mistral makes heavy lifting easier by catching anomalies and serving up actionable insights.

Ready to roll up your sleeves? In the upcoming workshop, we'll get hands-on with SQL injection analysis and tackle cloud configuration scripts. You'll see how Mistral can uncover vulnerabilities faster than your boss can say, "What's a SQL injection?" The focus is on turning raw logs and scripts into clear insights that support more secure systems.

By the end of this section, you will see how AI-assisted analysis can streamline complex security tasks and prepare you to apply the same techniques to other high-risk scenarios.

Practical workshop: Code and cloud security with Mistral

In this workshop, we'll uncover vulnerabilities hiding in plain sight, such as overly permissive cloud configurations, sneaky SQL injections, and XSS risks. With tools such as Visual Studio Code, the Continue extension, and Mistral's powerful analysis, we'll not only detect these threats but learn how to fix them like pros. By the end, you'll be armed with skills to outsmart potential attackers!

Step 1: Environment setup

In the first step of our preparation, we'll cover essential set-up tasks to ensure a smooth start to the workshop. We'll begin by installing Visual Studio Code, a powerful code editor ideal for this project. Next, we'll access the reference material in the GitHub repository, which contains all necessary files and scripts. We'll then install the Continue dev extension, which enhances our coding experience with AI-driven assistance. Following that, we'll set up Codestral using a free trial or through an API-compatible local deployment, enabling advanced security analysis features such as code review and vulnerability detection. Finally, we'll prepare a new project workspace to organize and manage our work effectively. These foundational steps will set the stage for our hands-on exploration of security applications:

1. To set up the environment for the workshop, you'll need a code editor such as Visual Studio Code. It's a lightweight yet powerful tool widely used for development. While installation steps may vary slightly depending on your operating system, the process is straightforward: download, install, and launch the editor. For detailed step-by-step instructions, refer to *Chapter 7, Workshop 2*, where we've outlined the entire setup process in a clear and comprehensive way. No need to reinvent the wheel here. Just follow along in *Chapter 7*, and you'll be ready to roll!

Skip if VS Code is already installed

If you already have Visual Studio Code installed on your system, you can skip the installation step and proceed directly to configuring extensions and logging into GitHub.

2. For the workshop setup, you'll need access to the project files hosted on GitHub. Visit the main project repository at `https://github.com/PacktPublishing/Learn-Mistral` and navigate to `/Chapter-8`. These files contain the scripts and data needed for hands-on exercises. Be sure to download or clone the repository before starting!

3. To enhance your Visual Studio Code experience, you'll need to set up the Continue extension for AI-powered code assistance. It streamlines coding with features such as auto-completion and contextual suggestions. For detailed installation and configuration steps, refer to *Chapter 7*, *Workshop 2*, *Step 1.3*. Follow those instructions, and you'll have the extension ready in no time!

4. To set up the Codestral model for the Continue extension in Visual Studio Code, you have several options. You can use the free trial, which is sufficient for this workshop, or opt for the paid version with a configured API key. Alternatively, if you prefer local processing, integrate it with Ollama on your computer. For detailed setup instructions, refer to *Chapter 7*, *Workshop 2*. Follow the steps there to ensure smooth integration and get started with Codestral.

5. Finally, to kick off the workshop, we'll initiate a new project called `security_usecases`. You can either copy the entire folder with all the necessary files from the `Chapter-8` folder in the repository (`https://github.com/PacktPublishing/Learn-Mistral`) or create your own files as you progress through the exercises. Simply copy the provided code snippets into your files and work with them to explore the workshop steps one by one.

Step 2: Cloud security analysis

In this step, we'll analyze a too-permissive Terraform script to uncover security risks stemming from excessive permissions and open ports. Such configurations violate the principle of least privilege, potentially exposing your infrastructure to unnecessary vulnerabilities. Using Codestral, we'll identify and address these issues to strengthen your cloud security posture.

Please follow these steps:

1. Open the provided Terraform script (`too-permissive.terraform`). Focus on security group configurations that define ingress and egress rules.

2. Then identify the vulnerable code by reviewing the following lines:

```
resource "aws_security_group" "example" {
  name        = "example-security-group"
  description = "Security group"
  vpc_id      = aws_vpc.main.id

  ingress {
    from_port   = 22
    to_port     = 22
    protocol    = "tcp"
    cidr_blocks = ["0.0.0.0/0"] # Open SSH access
  }

  ingress {
    from_port   = 80
    to_port     = 80
    protocol    = "tcp"
    cidr_blocks = ["0.0.0.0/0"] # Open HTTP access
  }

  egress {
    from_port   = 0
    to_port     = 0
    protocol    = "-1"
    cidr_blocks = ["0.0.0.0/0"] # Open all traffic
  }
}
```

These configurations allow unrestricted access to SSH and HTTP and open all egress traffic, exposing the application to unnecessary risks. Additionally, identify the next lines:

```
# Inline policy with wide permissions
inline_policy {
  name    = "example-inline-policy"
```

```
policy = jsonencode({
  Version = "2012-10-17"
  Statement = [
    {
      Effect   = "Allow"
      Action   = "*"
      Resource = "*" # Overly permissive role
    }
  ]
})
}
```

As seen in the preceding Terraform configuration, the inline IAM policy grants overly broad permissions without restriction. Using Codestral, we analyze this code and flag it as a security risk. Unrestricted access like this can lead to privilege escalation or lateral movement, emphasizing the need to apply the principle of least privilege in policy definitions.

3. Next, we highlight all lines (*CMD + A*) and press *CMD + L* to add the entire file snippet to a new Codestral chat context. The reason we do this is because the first part of the file has an inline IAM policy that grants universal "Action": "*" and "Resource": "*" access, a dangerously permissive setup that violates least privilege and poses a major security risk.

4. Then, use the following prompt:

```
You are a security-focused AI expert. Your task is to review the
following Terraform script for potential security misconfigurations.
Analyze the script step-by-step and identify any issues related to
overly permissive rules, unnecessary open ports, and violations of
the principle of least privilege.

Analysis Tasks:

  1. Identify and describe misconfigurations, focusing on overly
permissive ingress and egress rules.
  2. Suggest specific improvements to enforce the principle of
least privilege.
  3. Provide general best practices for securing cloud
infrastructure.

Please structure your analysis as follows:
```

```
    1. Identified Misconfigurations: - [Short description of the
issue] - [Line numbers or location in the code] - [Impact or
potential exploit]
    2. Mitigation Recommendations: - [Suggested configuration
changes] - [Best practices]
    3. Secure Configuration Recommendations: - [General advice on
secure cloud configurations]


    Focus on actionable recommendations and specific examples of how
to improve the security posture.
```

With the prompt submitted, the model produces a structured response that highlights misconfigurations, suggests mitigations, and outlines secure configuration practices. To make sense of these results, we'll walk through each part of the analysis in turn. First, we'll review the part of the response identifying the found vulnerable misconfigurations:

1. Identified Misconfigurations:

- Overly Permissive Ingress Rules: The security group allows SSH (port 22), HTTP (port 80), and HTTPS (port 443) access from any IP address (0.0.0.0/0). This can pose a security risk as it exposes these services to the internet, potentially allowing unauthorized access or attacks.
    - Line numbers: 16-18, 22-24
    - Impact: Unauthorized access or denial-of-service attacks.
- Overly Permissive Egress Rules: The security group has an open egress rule that allows all outbound traffic (protocol -1) to any IP address (0.0.0.0/0). This is a security risk as it allows the instance to communicate with any external resource, which may not be necessary or desirable.
    - Line number: 30-33
    - Impact: Unintended data leakage or communication with malicious resources.
- Overly Permissive IAM Role: The IAM role has an inline policy that grants full permissions ("*") to all resources (""). This violates the principle of least privilege and exposes the instance to potential unauthorized actions.
    - Line numbers: 40-50
    - Impact: Unauthorized actions on AWS resources.

Figure 8.1: Terraform script – identified misconfigurations

Let us take a closer look at the identified misconfigurations and analyze them:

- **Overly permissive ingress rules**: As we can see from the response, allowing SSH, HTTP, and HTTPS access from any IP address (**0.0.0.0/0**) exposes the application to the internet without restriction. This creates a significant attack surface for unauthorized access or denial-of-service attacks. Limiting access to trusted IP ranges is critical to reducing this risk.

- **Overly permissive egress rules**: As highlighted, the open egress rule permits all outbound traffic to any IP address, which poses a risk of unintended data leakage or communication with malicious resources. By restricting egress to only necessary IPs and ports, you can better control and monitor outbound connections.

- **Overly permissive IAM role**: The response points out that granting full permissions to all resources violates the principle of least privilege. This opens the door to unauthorized actions on AWS resources, which could lead to severe consequences such as accidental deletions or privilege escalations. Limiting permissions to only what is necessary helps mitigate these risks.

Now, let us investigate mitigation recommendations:

2. Mitigation Recommendations:

    ◦ Limit Ingress Rules: Restrict the ingress rules to only allow necessary traffic from trusted sources. Use specific IP addresses or security group IDs instead of using the broad 0.0.0.0/0 CIDR block.
        ▪ Example: Replace "0.0.0.0/0" with the specific IP addresses or CIDR blocks of trusted sources.
    ◦ Limit Egress Rules: Restrict the egress rules to only allow necessary outbound traffic. Consider using security group rules or network ACLs to control outbound traffic.
        ▪ Example: Remove the open egress rule and add specific rules for required outbound traffic.
    ◦ Limit IAM Role Permissions: Follow the principle of least privilege and grant the IAM role only the necessary permissions. Avoid using the "*" action or resource.
        ▪ Example: Specify the specific actions and resources required by the instance.

Figure 8.2: Terraform script mitigation recommendations

Let us take a closer look at these mitigation recommendations and analyze them:

- What **limiting ingress rules** involves is narrowing access to only the traffic that's absolutely necessary and from trusted sources. Replacing the **0.0.0.0/0** CIDR block with specific IP addresses or ranges ensures your system isn't left exposed to potential intruders while still maintaining essential connectivity.

- The essence of **limiting egress rules** lies in controlling outbound traffic with precision. By eliminating the open egress rule and introducing targeted rules, you prevent unintended communications and data leakage, ensuring only authorized and necessary connections are allowed.

- The principle behind **limiting IAM role permissions** is to provide just enough access for the role to perform its job. Moving away from overly broad * permissions and specifying exact actions and resources creates a tighter security posture, reducing the risk of unauthorized actions and privilege escalation.

Next, let us review the secure configuration recommendations. The following recommendations outline key strategies for enhancing your cloud security by addressing overly permissive configurations. These steps leverage AWS best practices to control access, reduce exposure, and monitor network activity effectively.

3. Secure Configuration Recommendations:

- Use Security Groups for Instance-Level Access Control: Use security groups to control inbound and outbound traffic at the instance level.
- Implement Network ACLs for Subnet-Level Access Control: Use network ACLs to add an additional layer of security at the subnet level.
- Use IAM Roles and Policies for Access Control: Use IAM roles and policies to manage access to AWS resources. Follow the principle of least privilege and grant only the necessary permissions.
- Enable VPC Flow Logs: Enable VPC flow logs to capture information about traffic flowing in and out of your instances. This can help identify unauthorized or suspicious traffic.
- Regularly Review and Update Security Configurations: Regularly review and update security configurations to ensure they are still aligned with the organization's security policies and best practices.

Figure 8.3: Secure configuration recommendations

Let us take a closer look at the secure configuration recommendations and analyze them:

- The essence of using security groups for instance-level access control is to filter traffic and allow only authorized connections, reducing exposure to threats.
- Implementing network ACLs for subnet-level access control means adding another security layer to filter traffic before it reaches instances.
- The principle behind using IAM roles and policies for access control is to grant only the permissions necessary, minimizing unauthorized access risks.
- The goal of enabling VPC flow logs is to track traffic and identify suspicious activity for better threat monitoring.

This exercise step highlights the risks of overly permissive cloud configurations, such as unrestricted SSH access and open egress rules. By using Codestral to pinpoint these vulnerabilities, you can implement tighter security measures, reinforcing the principle of least privilege and minimizing your attack surface. With secure configurations in place, your cloud environment will be far better protected against potential threats.

With this solid understanding of how to secure cloud environments through proper access controls and traffic monitoring, it's time to shift our focus to application-level vulnerabilities. In the next step, we'll dive into SQL injection detection, exploring how improperly handled user inputs can compromise your database. Let's uncover these risks and learn how to safeguard your data!

Step 3: SQL injection detection

Security vulnerabilities, like hidden cracks in a foundation, can compromise an entire system. Detecting and addressing them proactively ensures a solid defense. In this step, we'll analyze Java Servlet code to uncover common issues such as SQL injection and learn how to strengthen our applications using actionable insights from Codestral. Overall, this exercise will demonstrate how to detect and mitigate security risks in real-world code.

1. We'll start by opening the `JdbcServlet.java` file. Focus on lines 14–66, which contain the logic for handling user inputs and database queries.

2. Copy lines 14–66 into your clipboard. Pay special attention to line 39, where user input is directly concatenated into the SQL query.

    ```
    String sql = "SELECT * FROM users WHERE username = '" + param + "'";
    ```

    This exposes the application to SQL injection, a common and dangerous vulnerability. For example, a malicious user could inject SQL commands to drop tables or extract sensitive data, bypassing the intended functionality.

3. Press *CMD + L* to add the selected code snippet to a new chat context in the Continue extension. This will allow Codestral to analyze the code.

Prompt structuring tip

- Start by telling the LLM who it is (e.g., "You are a security expert").
- List the tasks you want (e.g., find vulnerabilities, suggest fixes).
- Finally, define the format of the response you expect.
- Clear roles, clear goals, and clear structure lead to better results.

Paste the following prompt into the Codestral chat:

```
You are a security-focused AI expert. Your task is to review the
following Java Servlet code for potential vulnerabilities. Analyze
the code step-by-step and identify any issues related to security,
code quality, or best practices.

    Analysis Tasks:

    1. Identify and describe security vulnerabilities, focusing on
risks like SQL injection, hardcoded credentials, and improper error
```

handling.

2. Suggest improvements to mitigate each identified vulnerability.

3. Recommend secure coding practices for handling user input, database queries, and sensitive information.

4. If applicable, highlight any code smells or violations of coding best practices.

Please provide your analysis in the following structure:

1. Identified Vulnerabilities: - [Short description of the issue] - [Line numbers or location in the code] - [Impact or potential exploit]

2. Mitigation Recommendations: - [Suggested code improvements] - [Best practices]

3. Secure Coding Recommendations: - [General advice on secure coding]

Focus on actionable recommendations and specific examples of how to improve the code.

Codestral will analyze the code and highlight vulnerabilities. Here's an example of what you might see:

1. Identified Vulnerabilities:

- SQL Injection: Line 37 - The SQL query is crafted by concatenating the user input directly into the query string. This allows an attacker to manipulate the query and potentially execute unintended SQL commands, leading to data leakage or modification.
- Hardcoded Credentials: Lines 24-26 - The database credentials are hardcoded into the servlet, which poses a significant security risk. If the source code is compromised, the attacker can easily access the database.
- Improper Error Handling: Line 41 - The exception message is directly sent to the client in the case of an error. This could potentially leak sensitive information about the application or the database to the attacker.

Figure 8.4: Identified vulnerabilities in Java code

Figure 8.4 illustrates the Codestral response flagging key security concerns in a vulnerable JDBC code snippet, such as SQL injection, hardcoded credentials, and error exposure. SQL injection reflects a broader neglect of trust boundaries. By directly embedding user input into a query, the code grants attackers a chance to *redefine logic*, access data, or escalate privileges. It's a classic sign of missing validation and poor separation between data and commands.

Meanwhile, hardcoded credentials and error exposure suggest a lack of secret management hygiene. Storing database credentials in plain sight is a shortcut that could have a devastating impact if the repo is leaked. Similarly, returning raw error messages to the client makes internal logic visible to outsiders, offering attackers breadcrumbs toward exploitation. Both indicate an absence of layered security thinking.

Next, let us investigate mitigation recommendations:

2. Mitigation Recommendations:

    ○ SQL Injection:
        ▪ Use Prepared Statements: Instead of concatenating the user input into the query string, use a PreparedStatement. This separates the SQL code from the data, preventing SQL injection.
        ▪ Example:

```
String sql = "SELECT * FROM users WHERE username = ?";
PreparedStatement pstmt = conn.prepareStatement(sql);
pstmt.setString(1, param);
ResultSet rs = pstmt.executeQuery();
```

    ○ Hardcoded Credentials:
        ▪ Store credentials securely: Store the credentials in a secure location, such as environment variables or a secure vault. Do not hardcode them in the source code.
    ○ Improper Error Handling:
        ▪ Implement a custom error page: Instead of sending the exception message directly to the client, implement a custom error page. This page should display a generic error message to the user without leaking sensitive information.

Figure 8.5: Mitigation recommendations for vulnerable Java code

Figure 8.5 illustrates a safer approach to SQL query construction using prepared statements. This method helps eliminate SQL injection risks by cleanly separating SQL logic from user input, ensuring malicious values cannot alter the intended query behavior.

In addition, the figure emphasizes that hardcoded credentials should be avoided. Instead, developers are encouraged to store sensitive credentials in environment variables or secure vaults, reducing exposure in case of source code compromise.

Lastly, for improper error handling, a recommended best practice is to serve generic error messages through a custom error page. This prevents leakage of technical details that could aid attackers in probing system weaknesses.

Now, let us investigate coding recommendations:

3. Secure Coding Recommendations:

    ◦ Use parameterized queries or prepared statements to protect against SQL injection.
    ◦ Never store sensitive information in the source code. Use secure methods to store and retrieve credentials.
    ◦ Implement proper error handling to prevent the leakage of sensitive information to the client.
    ◦ Validate and sanitize user input to ensure it is in the expected format and does not contain malicious content.
    ◦ Use secure communication protocols, such as HTTPS, to encrypt data in transit.
    ◦ Implement access control mechanisms to restrict access to sensitive resources and data.
    ◦ Regularly update and patch the application to protect against known vulnerabilities.

Figure 8.6: Secure coding recommendations for vulnerable Java code

Figure 8.6 presents a broader set of secure configuration practices that go beyond single vulnerabilities and address holistic application hygiene. The guidance includes using parameterized queries to defend against injection, avoiding hardcoded secrets, and sanitizing input to stop malicious payloads. It also stresses proper error handling, using HTTPS for encrypted transport, and keeping software up to date, together forming a layered, proactive security posture.

Codestral provides a comprehensive analysis, detailing vulnerabilities, potential exploits, and actionable solutions. This feedback not only helps fix immediate issues but also establishes a foundation for secure coding practices, ensuring the application's resilience against future attacks.

Through this process, we've learned how to identify and fix security risks, an important skill for building safe software. We've gained a clear understanding of SQL injection vulnerabilities and how to address them. With Codestral's help, we've tackled risks and adopted secure coding practices, making our applications more secure.

Next, we'll dive into **Cross-Site Scripting (XSS)**, another common and dangerous vulnerability. You'll learn how attackers exploit unsanitized user inputs to inject malicious scripts and how to defend your applications with effective validation and sanitization techniques. Let's continue fortifying our defenses!

Step 4: Cross-site scripting detection

In this step, we'll explore **Cross-Site Scripting (XSS)** vulnerabilities in a PHP script that takes a URL parameter and includes it unescaped in the response. XSS allows attackers to inject malicious scripts into web applications, potentially compromising user data or control.

Let's begin:

1. Open or create the PHP file and save the following code as `vulnerable.php`:

    ```php
    <?php

    if (isset($_GET['input'])) {
        $input = $_GET['error'];
        echo "<div>Error: $input</div>";
    } else {
        echo "<div>No input provided.</div>";
    }
    ?>
    ```

2. Then, identify the vulnerable code. Focus on **lines 3–4**:

    ```
    3          $input = $_GET['input'];
    4          echo "<div>Error: $input</div>";
    5      } else {
    ```

    Figure 8.7: Vulnerable PHP code passage

    *   Line *3* captures user input from the error URL parameter without any validation or sanitization.

    *   Line *4* echoes the input directly into the HTML, which could allow an attacker to inject a malicious script, such as `<script>alert('XSS');</script>`.

3. Use the Continue extension to analyze the code. Press *CMD + L* to add the snippet to a new chat context for Codestral to process. Paste this prompt into Codestral:

    ```
    You are a security-focused AI expert. Your task is to review the
    following PHP script for potential vulnerabilities. Analyze the
    code step-by-step and identify any issues related to security, code
    quality, or best practices.

    Analysis Tasks:

    1. Identify and describe security vulnerabilities, focusing on
    risks like XSS, improper input handling, and output sanitization.
    ```

2. Suggest improvements to mitigate each identified
vulnerability.

3. Recommend secure coding practices for handling user input and
preventing XSS attacks.

Please provide your analysis in the following structure:

1. Identified Vulnerabilities: - [Short description of the
issue] - [Line numbers or location in the code] - [Impact or
potential exploit]

2. Mitigation Recommendations: - [Suggested code improvements] -
[Best practices]

3. Secure Coding Recommendations: - [General advice on secure
coding]

Focus on actionable recommendations and specific examples of how
to improve the code.

The response from Codestral should be similar to this:

1. Identified Vulnerabilities:

  ◦ Cross-Site Scripting (XSS) Vulnerability: The script directly outputs user-provided data without proper sanitization or encoding.
    ▪ Line numbers: 4
    ▪ Impact: An attacker could inject malicious JavaScript code into the 'input' parameter, which would then be executed in the browser of any
      user who views the page. This could lead to various attacks, such as session hijacking, defacement of the website, or the theft of sensitive
      data.

2. Mitigation Recommendations:

  ◦ Use the `htmlspecialchars()` function to encode special characters in the user-provided data, preventing them from being interpreted as HTML
    or JavaScript.
    ▪ Suggested code improvements:

      ```
      $input = htmlspecialchars($_GET['input'], ENT_QUOTES, 'UTF-8');
      ```

  ◦ Consider using a more secure method of input handling, such as prepared statements or parameterized queries, when dealing with databases. In
    this case, since the script does not interact with a database, this is not applicable.

3. Secure Coding Recommendations:

  ◦ Always sanitize and validate user input before using it in your application.
  ◦ Use output encoding functions to prevent XSS attacks.
  ◦ Use least privilege principle, i.e., only grant necessary permissions to the application.
  ◦ Keep your software up-to-date with the latest security patches.
  ◦ Follow the principle of defense in depth, i.e., use multiple layers of security.
  ◦ Limit the amount of sensitive data that is stored or processed by the application.
  ◦ Implement a secure error handling mechanism that does not leak sensitive information to the user.
  ◦ Use a secure communication protocol (HTTPS) to protect data in transit.

Figure 8.8: Codestral response on vulnerable PHP snippet

As we can see, the LLM response in *Figure 8.8* thoroughly identifies the XSS vulnerability, its impact, and actionable mitigation steps, such as using `htmlspecialchars()` to sanitize output. It emphasizes secure coding practices, including input validation, output encoding, and defense-in-depth strategies. This clear and actionable feedback equips developers to address vulnerabilities effectively and build more secure applications.

This overall exercise demonstrates how easily XSS vulnerabilities can arise from unsanitized user input. By using Codestral, we can quickly identify these risks and implement proper mitigations, such as escaping user input and validating URL parameters. These practices are critical for protecting users and ensuring the security of web applications.

Summary

In this chapter, we explored the multifaceted world of modern cybersecurity, diving deep into key security applications and practical vulnerability analysis. We began by examining firewall logs to detect anomalies and prioritize threats, followed by a focus on stateful firewall logs to uncover incomplete sessions and protocol misuse. SQL injection detection highlighted the risks of insecure database interactions and the importance of parameterized queries. Endpoint security emphasized predicting malware, ensuring configuration compliance, and monitoring critical files, while data exfiltration detection revealed the dangers of unusual transfers, encryption misuse, and insider threats.

We also covered authentication and authorization, identifying overly permissive access controls and detecting credential abuse. Application code security brought attention to OWASP vulnerabilities, dependency risks, and custom threat patterns. User behavior analytics helped us recognize session anomalies, command and control patterns, and phishing attempts. Cloud security underlined the importance of misconfiguration monitoring and storage security, while automation with Mistral showcased the power of LLMs for generating playbooks and analyzing logs. The hands-on workshop solidified these concepts through practical exercises: securing a Terraform script, identifying SQL injection in JDBC code, and mitigating XSS vulnerabilities in a PHP script. Together, these skills provide a solid foundation for tackling real-world security challenges.

In the next chapter, we move into more open-ended territory with advanced take-home RAG challenges. You'll brainstorm, build, and evaluate your own retrieval-augmented generation solutions, applying what you've learned to real-world scenarios. Don't worry. *Chapter 10* and *Chapter 11* return to a more guided format, but with fun, optional extracurricular activities to stretch your skills further.

Extracurricular

1. **Analyze suspicious packets with Wireshark**: Dive into real-world packet captures and investigate anomalies using Wireshark. Then, paste selected packet summaries or logs into your Mistral LLM setup and ask it to flag abnormal patterns, detect suspicious IPs, or explain the significance of certain protocols, like a virtual SOC analyst helping you sharpen your instincts. Links:

    *   `https://www.malware-traffic-analysis.net/`
    *   `https://digitalcorpora.org/?s=pcap`

2. **Explore real-world vulnerabilities in CVE/CWE databases**: Use the CVE and CWE databases to study past cases of security misconfigurations. Feed a CVE summary or CWE description to Mistral and ask for an explanation, risk summary, or even Terraform-specific analogies. It's a great way to blend reading with hands-on AI guidance that tailors learning to your style. Links:

    *   `https://www.cve.org/`
    *   `https://cwe.mitre.org/`
    *   `https://nvd.nist.gov/`

9

Take-Home RAG Challenges

The best way to predict the future is to invent it.

—Alan Kay

RAG has unlocked new possibilities for AI by seamlessly combining retrieval and generation. Yet, the most exciting potential lies in what remains unexplored. Adapting RAG for specialized domains such as law, medicine, and finance demands precision, creativity, and technical depth. Challenges such as optimizing embeddings, fine-tuning for specific applications, and integrating real-time data streams push the limits of existing implementations. The complexity intensifies in multi-modal scenarios, where text meets images, code, or even live environments.

This chapter presents a high-level challenge: take these advanced ideas and transform them into actionable projects. Experiment with new retrieval mechanisms, redefine performance benchmarks, and innovate across modalities. Imagine novel applications and engineer systems that adapt dynamically to ever-changing information landscapes.

Your mission is clear: break down these challenges into tangible steps, experiment boldly, and contribute to shaping the next frontier of RAG. The future of intelligent systems isn't just in understanding information. It's in discovering new ways to retrieve, generate, and create.

This chapter will cover the following main topics:

- Helful code examples
- Problem statement
- Challenge 1: Revolutionize software QA with RAG testing
- Challenge 2: Build a real-time news summarizer with RAG

Helpful code examples

To reinforce the concepts covered in this chapter, we've included several Jupyter notebooks packed with hands-on, ready-to-run code. You can find all examples in the `Learn-Mistral` repository at `https://github.com/PacktPublishing/Learn-Mistral`:

- `Ch09_01_various_integrations.ipynb`: Explore real-time data integration with external services. This notebook provides working code for Jira issue tracking, Slack bots, RSS feed parsing, GDELT news retrieval, and News API connectivity. You'll learn how to authenticate, make API calls, fetch and parse data, and use it in downstream applications.

- `Ch09_02_indexing.ipynb`: Dive into vector indexing using Mistral embeddings integrated with vector databases such as Weaviate and Milvus. Follow end-to-end workflows for embedding text, creating indexes, inserting vectors, and executing efficient searches using cosine similarity.

- `Ch09_03_custom_embedding.ipynb`: See how to design your own domain-specific embeddings, such as fashion vectors, and build a full pipeline to generate, index, and query them. Great for cases where pretrained models don't align with your domain needs.

- `Ch09_04_data_parsing_and_organization.ipynb`: This is a comprehensive notebook demonstrating end-to-end text handling: parsing PDFs and HTML, cleaning using Beautiful Soup and pandas, summarizing with Transformers, extracting named entities, and performing hashtag tagging. Ideal for workflows involving unstructured document ingestion, metadata extraction, and semantic enrichment.

These notebooks serve as practical templates for building and extending real-world AI-enhanced data pipelines. Explore the repository to modify, test, and integrate scenarios into your own projects.

Problem statement

The world increasingly values individuals who can think independently, engineer creatively, and solve ambiguous problems with clarity. In real-world AI applications, there are no step-by-step guides; only high-level goals and messy data. This chapter invites you to train the skill that matters most: transforming complex challenges into structured solutions. Through open-ended, hands-on RAG projects, you'll practice breaking problems down, making smart architectural choices, and building systems that adapt and scale. The ability to design without a template, reason across layers, and prototype ideas fast is a competitive edge. Let's exercise that mindset and have fun doing it.

Let's begin with a real-world challenge: using RAG to improve software testing. QA teams often deal with long test cases, bug reports, and repeated tasks. What if you could build a system that quickly finds the right information (test steps, logs, or past fixes) right when it's needed? This challenge is your chance to design a smarter, faster, and more responsive QA workflow.

Challenge 1: Revolutionize software QA with RAG testing

Software QA can be tedious, with scattered documentation and repetitive debugging. A RAG assistant can simplify this by automatically finding test cases, summarizing bug histories, and offering context-aware suggestions, thus shifting QA from a reactive task to a proactive, streamlined process.

For example, a new QA intern joins a mobile app development team. To understand the testing approach, they sift through outdated Excel sheets and read hundreds of lines of test scripts across GitHub and Google Docs. They feel overwhelmed. With the use of RAG's helping hand, the intern can ask the QA Assistant, "What are common bugs in the login module?" It summarizes failed test scenarios, shows recent authentication issues, and even recommends which tests to rerun. The learning curve shrinks from weeks to days.

Let's look at another example. A QA engineer at a fintech company is testing a payment flow. They encounter a bug when simulating failed credit card payments. To investigate, they dig through Jira tickets, search Confluence for test scripts, and scan Slack for hints, wasting 45 minutes without clarity. Now, with the help of RAG, the QA engineer types the error message into a QA assistant. It instantly returns the exact test case used in the last similar bug, links to a matching bug fix from three months ago, and suggests possible misconfigured API headers all within seconds.

These examples reveal a pattern: repetitive searches, scattered documentation, and missed insights slow QA work down. To fix that, this challenge proposes a focused pipeline (ingestion, retrieval, and generation) powered by RAG. The following illustration outlines its key components and how they fit together.

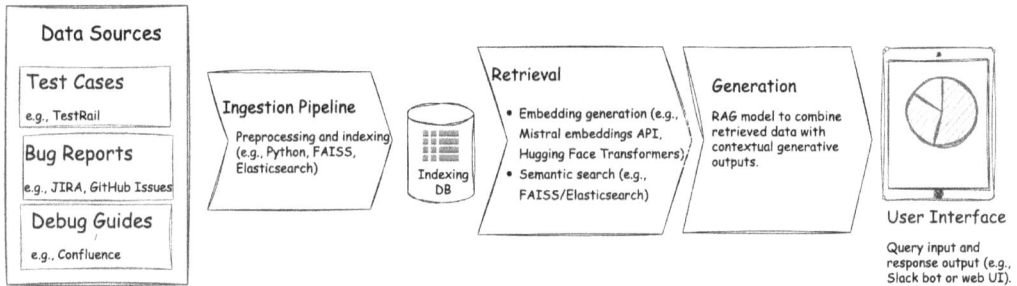

Figure 9.1: High-level architecture of the QA RAG system

🔍 **Quick tip:** Need to see a high-resolution version of this image? Open this book in the next-gen Packt Reader or view it in the PDF/ePub copy.

📖 **The next-gen Packt Reader** is included for free with the purchase of this book. Scan the QR code OR go to `https://packtpub.com/unlock`, then use the search bar to find this book by name. Double-check the edition shown to make sure you get the right one.

In the steps that follow, you'll define the scope of your QA assistant, ingest and structure real test data, design a retrieval pipeline, and fine-tune the system so it performs in real-world scenarios. Think of it as a hackathon-style exercise where creativity matters as much as precision.

Step 1: Define the scope of your QA RAG system

Start by clarifying what your QA RAG system will achieve. Think of its purpose as a virtual assistant for QA engineers, capable of fetching test cases, debugging steps, or summaries of known issues. Identify specific use cases where it can provide the most value, such as retrieving test cases for complex features or generating explanations for common software bugs. To implement this effectively, explore APIs such as Atlassian Jira's REST API to programmatically fetch bug reports and test cases. For additional data, consider integrating with tools such as GitHub Issues or CI/CD systems such as Jenkins.

Before jumping into building your RAG assistant, spend time gathering insights from the people on the ground like your QA engineers. Ask them the following questions directly:

- What are your biggest time sinks?
- Where do you repeatedly search for answers?
- Which issues keep resurfacing?

Their feedback will help you identify real pain points and prioritize features. You might discover that they waste time hunting down test cases, or that triaging bugs involves flipping between Jira, Slack, and outdated Confluence docs. These are golden opportunities where a RAG assistant could help. Build around their needs, not assumptions.

As an exercise, design a scenario where the system retrieves and summarizes test cases for a "Login Page" issue. Visualize how an engineer would query the system and how the ideal response should look.

As a result, you should have a clear vision of your RAG system's purpose and scope: what problems it solves, how it fits into QA workflows, and which tools and APIs it integrates with.

Stretch goal

Go beyond static retrieval by designing a proactive query suggestion feature. Integrate your RAG system with CI/CD pipelines such as Jenkins or GitLab to monitor recent build failures or test results. Use this data to automatically generate and suggest queries to QA engineers, such as "Retrieve test cases related to failed module X" or "Debug steps for memory allocation issues."

This feature will simulate an assistant that responds to queries but also anticipates potential QA needs.

Additionally, experiment with setting up priority levels for test cases based on their historical frequency of failures or criticality. For example, use Jira's REST API to extract issue priorities and labels, then integrate this metadata into your RAG system. Test how prioritizing critical issues changes the relevance of retrieved information.

Step 2: Ingest relevant data sources

A RAG system thrives on high-quality data. Begin by gathering the essential data sources that QA engineers rely on daily. These might include test case repositories extracted from platforms such as TestRail, historical bug reports from Jira or GitHub Issues, and debugging guides stored in Confluence pages. To prepare this data for your system, build an ingestion pipeline using Python and libraries such as **pandas** to clean and preprocess the information.

For quick prototyping, you can collect and merge data from multiple sources using tools such as **n8n**, which allows no-code/low-code workflows for pulling from Jira, GitHub, or Confluence. Once the process is validated, you can rewrite it in Python for greater control and scalability.

Once the data is cleaned, index it using a retrieval engine such as FAISS or Elasticsearch. This indexing process ensures that your system can quickly and accurately retrieve relevant information based on user queries. For example, you might experiment with combining debugging guides and bug reports to test how data diversity influences retrieval quality.

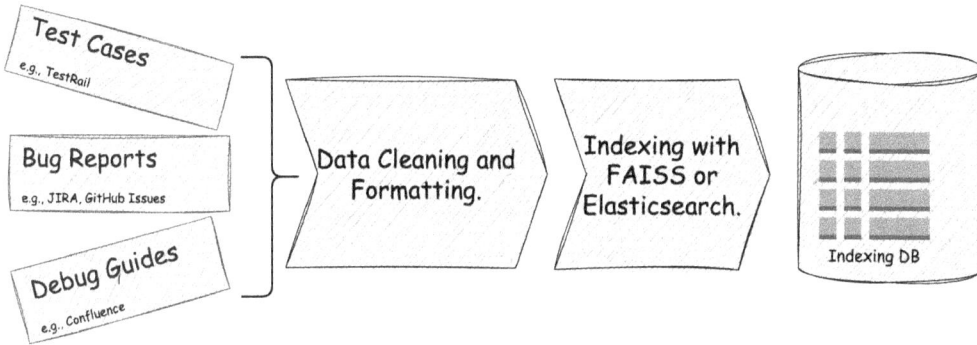

Figure 9.2: Ingestion pipeline workflow

The figure illustrates the ingestion pipeline workflow, detailing data preprocessing, indexing with Elasticsearch or FAISS, and preparation for retrieval.

> **Reference material**: Code examples for all integrations in this chapter, including Jira, Slack, RSS, GDELT, and the News API, are provided in the Jupyter notebook in `Chapter-9/Ch09_01_various_integrations.ipynb`. Use it to explore working pipelines, test credentials, and adapt the patterns to your own applications.

> For early prototyping, consider using a lightweight, local instance of Elasticsearch with a simple `docker-compose.yml` setup. It allows you to quickly test indexing strategies, run semantic or keyword queries, and iterate on document structure. Tools such as Kibana or Postman can help you visualize and experiment with your data through REST APIs; no full backend needed during this phase. Once the indexing pipeline works well locally, scale to managed Elasticsearch services such as Amazon OpenSearch for production.

You should end up with a structured dataset (cleaned, normalized, and indexed) from sources such as test repos, bug reports, and debug docs. It should be query-ready via your vector store (FAISS) or search engine (Elasticsearch), making your retrieval pipeline fast and developer-testable out of the box.

Stretch goal

Try incorporating a dynamic element into your ingestion pipeline by adding real-time data feeds from platforms such as Slack or Microsoft Teams channels used by QA teams. Use their respective APIs to fetch conversations or shared files related to bugs and test cases, preprocess them, and include them in your dataset. This will test your pipeline's ability to handle live, unstructured data and seamlessly integrate it with static sources such as TestRail or Jira.

Additionally, experiment with multi-language data preprocessing. If your QA team operates in a global environment, consider including test cases and bug reports in multiple languages, then implement a translation layer (e.g., Google Translate API) before indexing. Analyze how this affects retrieval performance for diverse user queries.

Step 3: Design the retrieval process

The retrieval process is the heart of your RAG system. Focus on building a robust pipeline that fetches the most relevant data for each query. Use tools such as FAISS or Elasticsearch to implement the retrieval layer and enhance it with embeddings generated from models such as OpenAI's API or **sentence-transformers**.

Imagine a scenario where a user asks, "What's the test case for a user authentication error?". Your retrieval process should identify and return a relevant test script, along with any supporting documentation.

Seamless web UI integration

If you're using the web UI from *Chapter 2* and want to connect it to your custom RAG system without giving up features such as voice input or the familiar chat interface, you don't need to modify the UI or patch the source code. Instead, mimic the API that the UI expects—typically, a POST request to /api/generate with a JSON payload such as the following:

```
{{
    "prompt": "What's the test case for login errors?",
    "system": "You are a helpful QA assistant.",
    "options": {}

}
```

You can write a lightweight wrapper (e.g., using **FastAPI**) that accepts this request and routes the prompt to your own RAG pipeline. Perform retrieval, compose context, and run generation behind the scenes, then return the result in streaming chunks, just as **Ollama** would.

This trick allows you to reuse the UI completely, including voice-to-text, streaming output, and message formatting, while swapping out the backend brain. It's simple, efficient, and keeps your focus on improving the assistant's intelligence instead of on rebuilding what already works well.

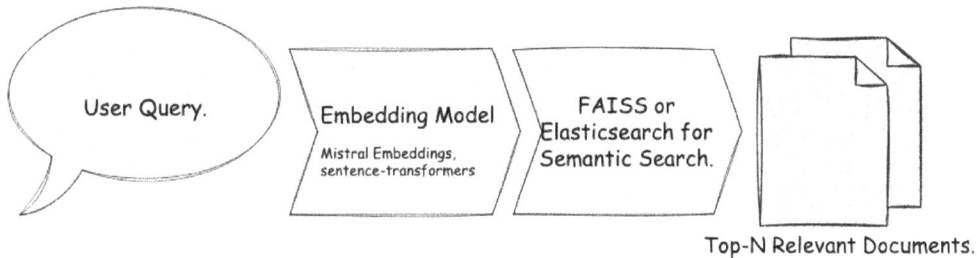

Figure 9.3: Retrieval process workflow

The preceding figure illustrates the retrieval process, showing how user queries are converted into embeddings for efficient semantic search using Elasticsearch or FAISS.

- **Reference material:**
- Vector indexing and semantic search examples using Mistral embeddings with Weaviate and Milvus are covered in `Chapter-9/Ch09_02_indexing.ipynb`
- For custom embedding workflows, such as designing and indexing your own vectors for fashion items, refer to `Chapter-9/Ch09_03_custom_embedding.ipynb`

Together, these notebooks provide end-to-end solutions for vector creation, storage, and retrieval using both pretrained and domain-specific embeddings.

You should end up with a working retrieval pipeline that returns the most relevant documents for a given query. The pipeline should use embeddings to enable semantically accurate results, making it far more effective than basic keyword search.

> **Stretch goal**
>
> Extend your retrieval system by integrating a **hybrid search approach** that combines both semantic search (using embeddings) and traditional keyword-based search. Test how this hybrid approach improves retrieval relevance, especially for edge cases where semantic models might misinterpret specific technical terms or unique identifiers in test cases.
>
> Additionally, implement a **query expansion module**. Use techniques such as synonym expansion or related term generation (e.g., "login failure" expanded to "authentication error" or "credential mismatch"). Test how query expansion influences the diversity and accuracy of retrieved results. You can experiment with libraries such as NLTK or WordNet to build your expansion logic.
>
> For a more advanced challenge, create a feedback loop where QA engineers can mark retrieved results as "relevant" or "not relevant." Use this feedback to fine-tune the retrieval engine, dynamically improving relevance for similar future queries.

Step 4: Fine-tune the RAG system

Fine-tuning your RAG system ensures that it performs well for software testing scenarios. Start by preparing a high-quality dataset that includes labeled examples of queries and corresponding ideal responses. Use this dataset to fine-tune your system using frameworks such as Hugging Face Transformers.

For example, consider a query such as "Steps to debug a memory leak issue." Your fine-tuned RAG system should retrieve a detailed set of steps from debugging guides and enrich them with generated tips. To push your system further, explore how it handles ambiguous queries, such as "performance issues in backend services." Experiment with prompt engineering to clarify ambiguous user inputs and generate more context-aware outputs.

Fine-tuning with efficiency and ease

Fine-tuning a large model may sound heavy, but with the right approach, it can be surprisingly manageable and efficient. A great starting point is the DigitalOcean guide *Fine-Tune Mistral-7B with LoRA: A Quickstart Guide*, which walks through using QLoRA (4-bit quantization + LoRA) on modest hardware such as an A6000 GPU: `https://www.digitalocean.com/community/tutorials/mistral-7b-fine-tuning`.

You'll find a production-ready code base in the Mistral-FineTune GitHub repo (`https://github.com/mistralai/mistral-finetune`), and a fully executable Colab tutorial at `https://colab.research.google.com/github/mistralai/mistral-finetune/blob/main/tutorials/mistral_finetune_7b.ipynb`.

These resources will guide you through environment setup, dataset formatting, and training workflows using transformers, `peft`, and `trl`.

To adapt this to your QA RAG system, use real-world debugging questions and structured answers as training examples. The model will learn to retrieve and generate context-aware, precise outputs tailored to your QA workflow, all while staying lightweight and GPU-friendly. Start with a small dataset, track performance, and iterate.

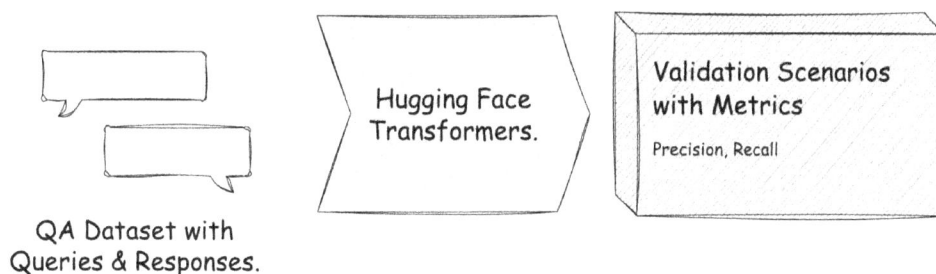

QA Dataset with Queries & Responses.

Hugging Face Transformers.

Validation Scenarios with Metrics

Precision, Recall

Figure 9.4: Fine-tuning workflow

The preceding figure outlines the fine-tuning workflow, demonstrating how labeled datasets are used to train and validate a tailored generative model.

Reference material: The `Chapter-9/Ch09_04_data_parsing_and_organization.` `ipynb` notebook demonstrates how to parse PDF and HTML content, clean and organize text using pandas and Beautiful Soup, apply sentence transformers for summarization, extract entities with NER, and enrich documents with hashtag tagging. It's a complete workflow for transforming raw text into structured, searchable data.

The expected result is a fine-tuned RAG model tailored to software QA tasks, capable of combining retrieved data with context-aware generative outputs that are precise and actionable for testers.

Stretch goal

Take your fine-tuning a step further by introducing **domain-specific embeddings** tailored to software engineering language. Train embeddings on repositories such as Stack Overflow or open source GitHub Issues to create a more context-aware retrieval and generation process. Compare the performance of your RAG system with generic embeddings versus these custom-trained embeddings.

Another interesting challenge is to implement **zero-shot** or **few-shot learning scenarios**. Instead of labeling a large dataset, provide just a few high-quality examples during fine-tuning to see how well the system generalizes to unseen queries. This will help you explore the efficiency and flexibility of fine-tuning for real-world QA scenarios.

For an advanced challenge, experiment with **multi-turn query understanding** by fine-tuning the system to handle follow-up queries. For instance, after querying, "Steps to debug a memory leak," the next query might be, "What tools can I use for heap analysis?". Fine-tune the system to maintain context across queries and provide cohesive responses.

Step 5: Validate outputs

Testing and validating your RAG system is crucial to ensure its effectiveness. Begin with manual validation by querying the system with common software bugs and comparing its responses to known solutions. Measure metrics such as precision, recall, and relevance to assess its performance.

In addition to manual tests, automate the validation process by writing test cases that evaluate the system's output against predefined criteria. For instance, create a CI/CD pipeline that automatically runs these tests whenever new data is ingested or when updates are made to the retrieval or generation components. By integrating tools such as Jenkins or GitLab, you can maintain a high level of system reliability.

Automate feedback loops for confidence at scale

Testing your RAG system isn't just about proving it works. It's about building confidence that it stays reliable as it grows. Start small: use a spreadsheet or JSON file to track known queries and ideal answers. Manually test your system against these to catch obvious gaps in accuracy, tone, or context relevance.

Once you're confident in a baseline, shift into automation. Wrap these cases into Python unit tests using `pytest` or `unittest`. Use **assert** logic to compare model output against expected keywords or semantic similarity scores. For embeddings-based validation, libraries such as `sklearn` or `sentence-transformers` can calculate cosine similarity between reference and generated answers.

Next, plug these tests into a CI/CD pipeline—Jenkins, GitLab, or GitHub Actions work well. Whenever you update your data, retriever, or model weights, the pipeline should rerun validations automatically.

This creates a feedback loop that alerts you to regression in quality early, long before users notice. Over time, this transforms your QA assistant from a promising prototype into a production-ready tool you can trust.

By the end of this step, your RAG system should consistently return accurate and relevant outputs, backed by a robust validation process. Both manual testing and automated test cases, integrated into CI/CD pipelines, should verify its reliability and ensure performance remains stable as data and components evolve.

Stretch goal

Enhance your validation process by introducing **stress testing scenarios**. Simulate high query loads using tools such as Apache JMeter or Locust and measure how the system maintains accuracy and response time under pressure. Evaluate the impact of concurrent queries on both retrieval and generation components and identify bottlenecks for further optimization.

Another micro challenge is to implement a **real-world QA test suite** by extracting a set of queries directly from production logs or team conversations (e.g., Slack or Jira). Compare the system's responses to actual resolutions provided by QA engineers. This will give you a practical benchmark for assessing how well your RAG system performs in real-world scenarios.

For a deeper exploration, develop an **error analysis dashboard** that logs incorrect or incomplete responses. Use these logs to identify common failure points in retrieval or generation and refine the system iteratively. Include metrics such as false positives or failure-to-retrieve cases to guide improvements.

Step 6: Optimize and scale

To prepare your system for real-world deployment, focus on optimization and scalability. Start by tuning the retrieval engine to handle large datasets efficiently. Explore advanced indexing methods or caching mechanisms to reduce latency. For instance, caching high-frequency queries can significantly improve response times.

Scaling your system involves managing larger data volumes and distributed workloads. Use cloud-based storage solutions, such as **Amazon S3** for scalable data storage and consider tools such as **Milvus** or **Weaviate** for distributed indexing. Experiment with scaling strategies to maintain performance as the dataset grows.

For optimization, try pregenerating embeddings and storing them as .npy or .parquet files, rather than computing them on the fly. This allows you to reload them quickly into FAISS or Elasticsearch and benchmark different retrieval setups. You can also test memory footprint and retrieval speed by toggling between dense and sparse vector types.

For scalability trials, simulate distributed behavior by running multiple retrieval nodes locally using tools such as Docker Compose, mimicking how you'd shard indexes across Milvus or Weaviate in production.

If you haven't yet configured cloud resources, no rush. *Chapter 10* will walk you through setting up your AWS account, generating access keys, and creating your first S3 buckets for ingestion and retrieval. For now, you can iterate locally and get familiar with performance baselines.

The expected result is a highly efficient, scalable system optimized for low latency and capable of handling large datasets and distributed indexing without performance degradation.

Stretch goal

Experiment with **dynamic caching strategies** by implementing intelligent caching layers that prioritize high-frequency queries or queries with long retrieval times. Use tools such as Redis or Memcached to cache query results and compare the impact on latency for different query types.

For an advanced challenge, introduce **adaptive indexing** by implementing time-based indexing updates. For example, prioritize indexing of recent data over older datasets to ensure that the system is optimized for real-time use cases while maintaining efficiency for archival queries.

Step 7: Integrate with QA workflows

Once optimized, integrate your RAG system into existing QA workflows for seamless usability. One approach is to create a chatbot interface that QA engineers can query directly from collaboration tools such as Slack or Microsoft Teams. Another idea is to connect your system with Jira, so it can automatically suggest solutions for newly created issues.

Use n8n as a smart playground to prototype your QA assistant's integration. It's perfect for connecting Slack, Jira, or your own FastAPI service, without diving into full-stack code. You can simulate real workflows and test how your RAG responds in context. This approach helps validate ideas quickly and identify user-experience gaps early. It's a low-friction way to get your assistant interacting with real systems before you move to production-level integration. Give it a spin before coding everything by hand.

Next, focus on user experience by designing an intuitive interface. Add features such as autocomplete suggestions for common queries or flow diagrams to visualize complex debugging steps. For a fun challenge, build a Slack bot using the Slack API and test how QA teams interact with it. Gather feedback to refine the user experience further.

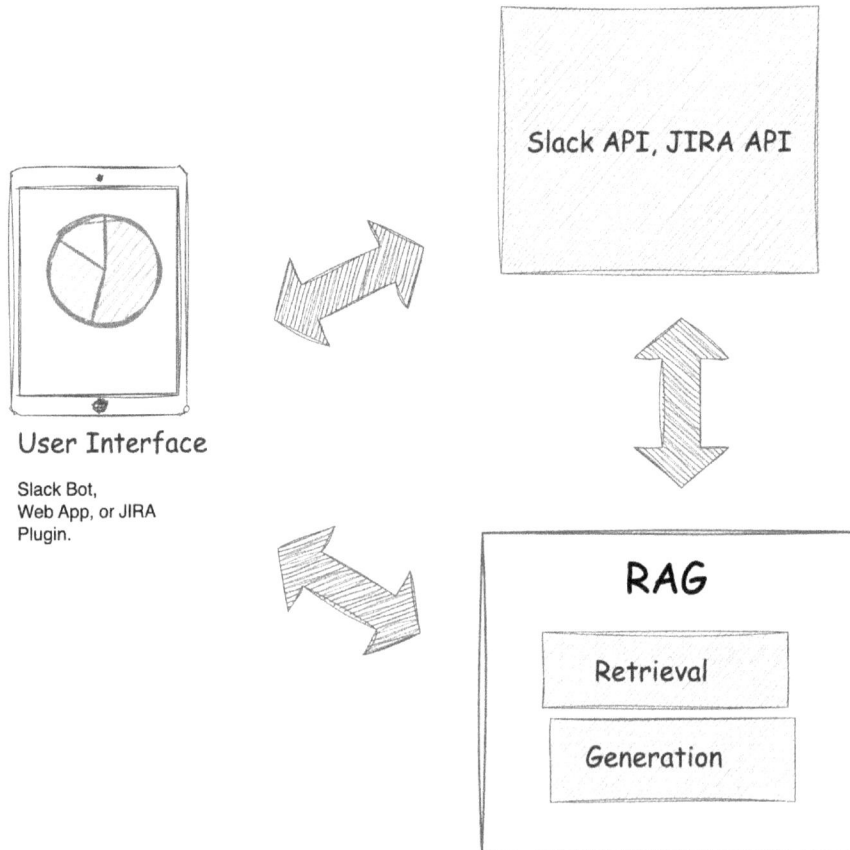

Figure 9.5: Integration with QA workflows

The figure illustrates how the QA RAG system integrates with existing workflows, connecting tools such as Jira, Slack, and CI/CD pipelines.

Reference material: In `Chapter-9/Ch09_01_various_integrations.ipynb`, you'll find hands-on examples for integrating external data sources, including Jira, Slack, RSS feeds, the GDELT project, and the News API. This notebook helps you connect, authenticate, and retrieve real-time data from these platforms for downstream processing or integration into larger AI workflows.

The expected result is to have a fully integrated system that QA engineers can easily access through tools such as Slack or Jira, providing real-time assistance and improving overall testing productivity.

Stretch goal

Take the integration further by implementing proactive notifications. Configure your RAG system to monitor ongoing activities in Jira or Slack and automatically suggest solutions or test cases when specific keywords or patterns appear. For example, if a new issue with "login failure" is created in Jira, the system could recommend related debugging guides and test cases without needing a user query.

The next level-up exercise is to develop a multi-platform integration. Extend your chatbot to work not only on Slack but also on Microsoft Teams, Discord, or Telegram. Test how the RAG system performs across different collaboration platforms and optimize the user experience for each.

For a more advanced challenge, integrate a visual debugging assistant. Allow the RAG system to generate flowcharts or step-by-step visual guides for complex issues. Use libraries such as `diagram-js` or `draw.io` integrations to generate these visualizations dynamically based on the retrieved data.

Once your QA RAG system is complete, it's time to share it with the world. Prepare a polished demonstration that highlights its capabilities, such as retrieving and generating debugging tips or automating common QA queries. Use metrics such as response accuracy and system speed to showcase its effectiveness.

Consider open-sourcing your project on GitHub to invite collaboration and feedback. Write a detailed README file with setup instructions, examples, and use cases. For an engaging presentation, record a two-minute video demo that captures your system in action and share it with the QA or AI community for feedback.

Takeaway

Building a QA RAG system is a chance to rethink how software testing can be supported by advanced AI tools. Each outlined step, from data ingestion to fine-tuning and integration, offers an opportunity to innovate, solve real-world challenges, and create something that directly impacts the productivity and efficiency of QA processes.

Imagine the potential of a system that doesn't just retrieve relevant information but actively enhances how QA engineers work. By applying these concepts, you're not just learning but shaping the future of software testing. This challenge invites you to step into a creative and experimental mindset, using AI as a powerful tool to simplify and improve complex tasks.

To go further and experiment by yourself, take the outlined concepts and make them your own. Experiment with tools, refine ideas, and bring your system to life. The possibilities for transforming QA are immense, and it's your chance to lead the way.

The next challenge takes you into the fast-paced world of real-time news aggregation. You'll explore how to build a dynamic RAG system capable of retrieving and summarizing breaking news from diverse live sources. Get ready to design an innovative, scalable solution that combines real-time data processing with powerful generative capabilities!

Challenge 2: Build a real-time news summarizer with RAG

News moves fast, and so does the need to make sense of it. From breaking headlines to detailed analysis, the constant flow of information can overwhelm even the most dedicated reader. This challenge explores how RAG can cut through the noise by fetching the latest stories and turning them into concise, relevant summaries tailored to a user's query.

Figure 9.6 shows the high-level design of this system. Multiple live sources (RSS feeds, public APIs, and even Telegram channels) feed into an ingestion pipeline that cleans and structures data before indexing it in real time with tools such as Kafka and Elasticsearch. A retrieval layer then processes user queries with embeddings to locate the most relevant articles, while a fine-tuned summarization model condenses them into clear, actionable outputs.

Finally, the results are delivered through user interfaces such as a web app or a chatbot integration, making dynamic news accessible in formats users already rely on.

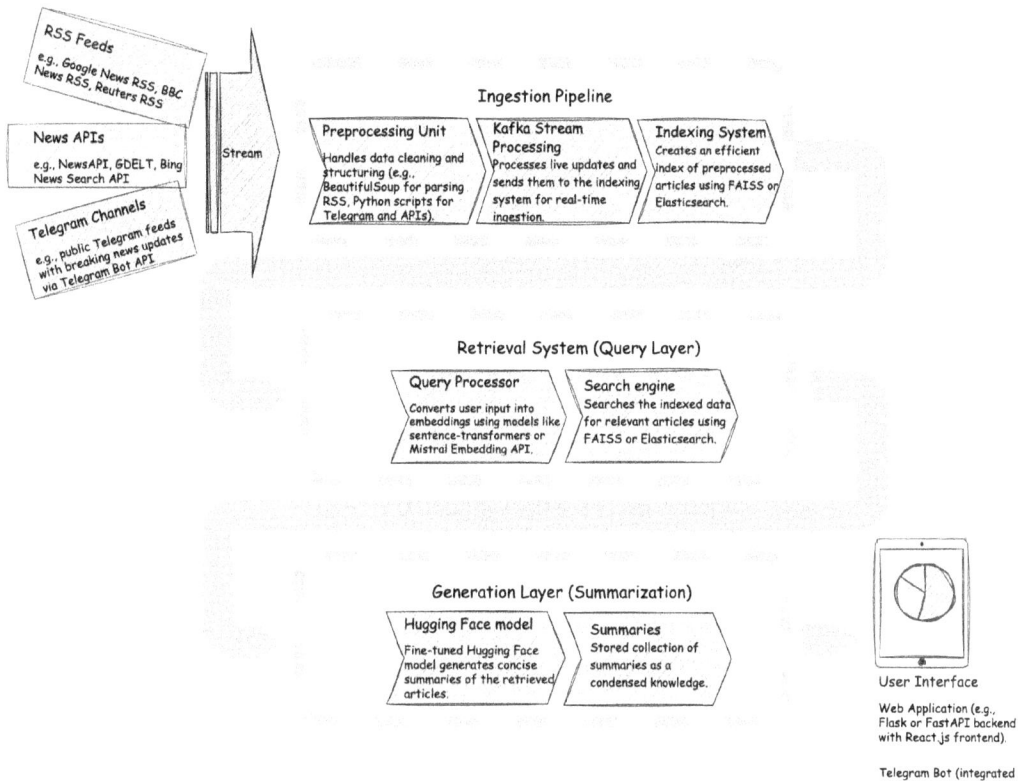

Figure 9.6: News summarizer: design draft

Your mission is to design and build this system as a personal news aggregator, one that blends retrieval speed with summarization accuracy, all while keeping pace with real-time updates.

To support your experimentation, we've included fully functional Jupyter notebooks for each major integration covered in this chapter. Use the following:

- `Chapter-9/Ch09_01_various_integrations.ipynb` explores Jira, Slack, RSS, GDELT, and News API connections

- `Ch09_02_indexing.ipynb` demonstrates vector indexing using Mistral embeddings with Weaviate and Milvus

- `Ch09_03_custom_embedding.ipynb` walks you through creating and searching your own custom embeddings

- Finally, `Ch09_04_data_parsing_and_organization.ipynb` focuses on parsing real-world PDFs and HTML, structuring the data, and enhancing it with sentence transformers, **named entity recognition** (**NER**), and hashtags

Each step challenges you to balance engineering discipline with creativity, resulting in a tool that doesn't just report the news but helps users see the signal in the noise.

Step 1: Integrate live news feeds and public APIs

The first step is to gather data from live news sources and APIs. Use feeds such as Google News RSS, public APIs such as **NewsAPI**, or open datasets such as **GDELT** for large-scale news coverage. Configure your system to fetch and preprocess articles in real time. Build a simple ingestion pipeline to clean and structure incoming data. You can preprocess using tools such as Python's **pandas** and **Beautiful Soup** for cleaning and organizing raw data into a usable format.

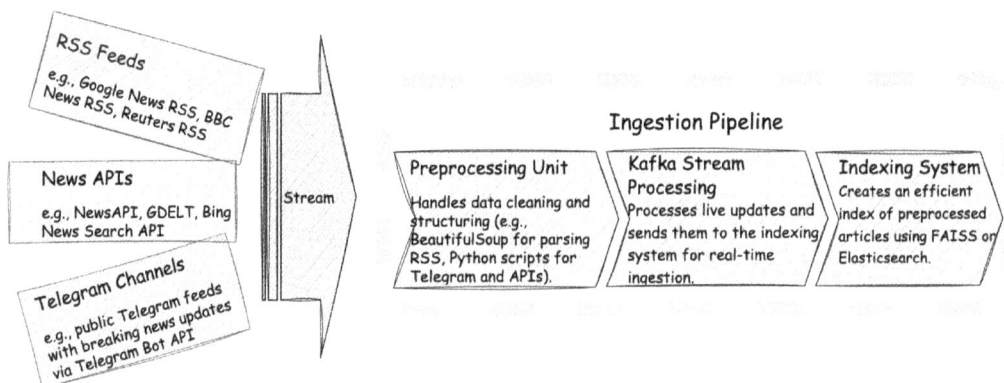

Figure 9.7: Ingestion of the live news

The preceding figure demonstrates live news ingestion using Telegram, RSS feeds, and APIs.

Reference material: All code examples for this chapter are organized into four Jupyter notebooks for easy exploration and reuse:

- **Integrations**: Ch09_01_various_integrations.ipynb includes Jira, Slack, RSS, GDELT, and News API demos

- **Vector indexing**: Ch09_02_indexing.ipynb covers Mistral embeddings with Weaviate and Milvus

- **Custom embeddings**: Ch09_03_custom_embedding.ipynb shows how to create and query your own vector space

- **Data parsing and NLP**: Ch09_04_data_parsing_and_organization.ipynb guides you through parsing, cleaning, summarizing, NER, and hashtag tagging

> To experiment with near real-time ingestion, use n8n or Make.com to build a no-code/low-code automation workflow. Trigger data collection with RSS feeds such as Google News or Reddit headlines, then pipe the articles through a cleanup step using prebuilt Python functions or HTTP nodes calling your FastAPI service. This mirrors best practices from *Chapter 5*, letting you prototype ingestion, transformation, and downstream RAG integration without writing full backend code up front.

By the completion of this stage, you should have a working ingestion pipeline that continuously collects and preprocesses real-time news articles. The output should be clean, structured data, ready for semantic indexing and retrieval within your RAG system.

Stretch goal

> Take your ingestion pipeline to the next level by integrating real-time data streams. Use **Kafka** to continuously process incoming articles and filter them by region, language, or topic before they even hit your vector store. This allows you to keep your dataset fresh, focused, and highly relevant, perfect for building dynamic QA or news-based assistants. Stream processing also opens doors to time-sensitive triggers and alerts, making your RAG system not just reactive but also responsive.

Step 2: Build a retrieval system for relevant articles

Design a retrieval system to fetch articles that match user queries. Start by indexing your pre-processed articles using a scalable search engine such as Elasticsearch or FAISS. Use embeddings generated with tools such as OpenAI's API or **sentence-transformers** to enable semantic searches. This approach ensures that your system can match the meaning of a query rather than relying solely on keyword overlap.

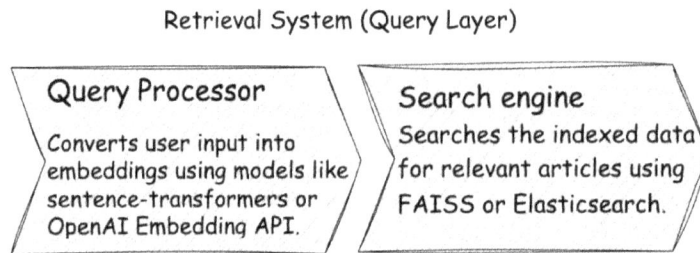

Retrieval System (Query Layer)

Query Processor

Converts user input into embeddings using models like sentence-transformers or OpenAI Embedding API.

Search engine

Searches the indexed data for relevant articles using FAISS or Elasticsearch.

Figure 9.8: Retrieval module

The preceding figure illustrates the retrieval module, where user queries are processed into embeddings, enabling efficient semantic search with Elasticsearch.

Reference material: Code examples for all integrations in this chapter (including Jira, Slack, RSS, GDELT, and News API) are provided in the `Chapter-9/Ch09_01_various_integrations.ipynb` Jupyter notebook. Use it to explore working pipelines, test credentials, and adapt the patterns to your own applications.

For semantic search without relying on paid APIs, the sentence-transformers library offers an excellent balance of ease and power. Start with pretrained models such as all-MiniLM-L6-v2 for fast, lightweight embedding generation. These embeddings can be indexed in FAISS or stored in Elasticsearch's dense vector field. Combine this with query embedding on the fly for real-time semantic retrieval. This is ideal for prototypes and production-ready pipelines alike. Try it first locally before scaling:

```
from sentence_transformers import SentenceTransformer
model = SentenceTransformer('all-MiniLM-L6-v2')
embedding = model.encode("What's the latest on semiconductor
stocks?")
```

You'll see how fast and effective local vector search can become.

The expectation is that your retrieval engine should accurately surface the most relevant news articles in response to user queries, with minimal latency. It must handle real-time input effectively, ensuring that responses reflect the freshest, most contextually aligned content available. The system should feel responsive, accurate, and reliable in live usage.

Stretch goal

Upgrade your retrieval pipeline to support hybrid or streaming search. Combine **semantic vector search** with **keyword filtering** (e.g., using BM25 or keyword pre-filtering in Elasticsearch) to balance precision and performance. For near real-time applications, add Kafka or Kinesis Streams to ingest articles as they are published, enabling continuous indexing and immediate availability for search. This architecture prepares your system for dynamic, large-scale use cases such as financial monitoring or crisis alerting.

Step 3: Fine-tune the generative model for summarization

Once the relevant articles are retrieved, you'll need to summarize them concisely. Fine-tune a generative model, such as one from Hugging Face's library, to create summaries that retain key information. Prepare your training data by pairing news articles with high-quality summaries, focusing on maintaining factual accuracy. Use techniques such as extractive summarization as a baseline and gradually incorporate abstractive methods for richer outputs.

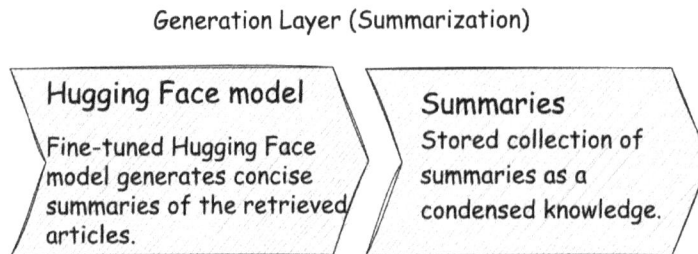

Generation Layer (Summarization)

Hugging Face model
Fine-tuned Hugging Face model generates concise summaries of the retrieved articles.

Summaries
Stored collection of summaries as a condensed knowledge.

Figure 9.9: Summarization module

Figure 9.9 depicts the summarization module, showcasing how retrieved articles are processed by a fine-tuned generative model for concise outputs.

Reference material: All examples related to PDF and HTML parsing, data cleaning with pandas and Beautiful Soup, NER, and hashtag tagging are available in `Chapter-9/Ch09_04_data_parsing_and_organization.ipynb`. This notebook provides a complete, runnable workflow to structure and enrich unstructured documents.

To get started quickly, use open source summarization models such as facebook/ bart-large-cnn or google/pegasus-xsum from Hugging Face. These models offer strong performance out of the box. For real-world use, you can prototype locally or deploy via the Hugging Face Inference API. As you iterate, experiment with prompt tuning or LoRA fine-tuning to match your domain tone. Integrate your summarization step into a modular workflow, triggered after retrieval. If you're using n8n, you can call your summarizer via a FastAPI service or Hugging Face endpoint, letting you build and test workflows without diving deep into orchestration code just yet:

```python
from transformers import pipeline
summarizer = pipeline("summarization", model="facebook/bart-large-cnn")
summary = summarizer("Long article text here", max_length=150,
    min_length=40, do_sample=False)
print(summary[0]['summary_text'])
```

Keep it fast, test with a few news examples, and refine the output style gradually. If latency matters, explore quantization or model distillation to speed things up before going full scale.

After completing this step, your system should include a robust summarization module that delivers clear, concise, and query-relevant summaries of retrieved news content. The model should effectively compress lengthy articles into informative highlights, preserving context and factual integrity. This enables your users to absorb key insights quickly, enhancing usability and relevance in fast-moving, real-time information environments.

Stretch goal

Test your system with ambiguous queries such as "climate updates" or "economic outlook." Explore how well it retrieves and condenses complex, multi-article topics into meaningful summaries.

Package your summarization module as a reusable CLI tool or lightweight web service. Wrap the pipeline (retrieval, summarization, and response formatting) into a single callable interface. Add options to configure model choice, summary length, and query filters. This makes your tool easier to integrate into other workflows or plug into chat interfaces. Bonus: containerize it for fast deployment across environments.

Step 4: Enable real-time updates with dynamic indexing pipelines

Dynamic news aggregation demands a system that updates continuously as new information becomes available. Create a pipeline that ingests new articles periodically, indexes them on the fly, and invalidates outdated content. For this, use cloud storage such as Amazon S3 combined with tools such as Apache Kafka for streaming and Elasticsearch for real-time indexing.

Start with RSS ingestion using n8n or a Python script. Here's how you can extract and clean data from an RSS feed:

```python
import feedparser from bs4 import BeautifulSoup
import pandas as pd

rss_url = "https://news.google.com/rss/search?q=semiconductors"
feed = feedparser.parse(rss_url)
cleaned_articles = []
for entry in feed.entries:
    soup = BeautifulSoup(entry.summary, "html.parser")
    content = soup.get_text()
    cleaned_articles.append({
        "title": entry.title,
        "link": entry.link,
        "summary": content,
        "published": entry.published
    })
df = pd.DataFrame(cleaned_articles)
df.to_csv("/tmp/cleaned_news.csv", index=False)
```

Next, upload cleaned data to Amazon S3:

```
import boto3
s3 = boto3.client('s3')
s3.upload_file('/tmp/cleaned_news.csv', 'your-bucket-name',
    'news/cleaned_news.csv')
```

After that, send metadata to Apache Kafka:

```
from kafka import KafkaProducer
import json

producer = KafkaProducer(bootstrap_servers='localhost:9092',
                         value_serializer=lambda v: json.dumps(v).
encode('utf-8'))

for article in cleaned_articles:
    producer.send("news-stream", article)
```

Consume and index with Elasticsearch:

```
from elasticsearch import Elasticsearch

es = Elasticsearch("http://localhost:9200")
for article in cleaned_articles:
    es.index(index="news", document=article)
```

The expected result is a system that dynamically integrates new articles, keeping the index fresh and responsive to breaking news while maintaining efficient retrieval and summarization.

Step 5: Test and optimize for speed and accuracy

Real-time systems must balance processing speed with the accuracy of results. Test your system by measuring query latency and summarization quality under different loads. Use automated tools such as Apache JMeter to simulate user requests and analyze performance. Experiment with caching mechanisms to handle frequent queries efficiently and improve response times.

Stress-test your system with Apache JMeter

For validating the system's ability to serve real-time summaries under load, you can simulate user requests with Apache JMeter. Here's a minimal walkthrough.

Make sure your summarization endpoint is running locally or deployed:

```
uvicorn summarizer_api:app –reload
```

The preceding command starts a FastAPI app using Uvicorn, a lightning-fast server for Python.

This will start the web service on port 8000 by default.

Create a test plan in JMeter

Open the JMeter GUI, and add a **thread group** with 10–50 concurrent users. Add an **HTTP request sampler** with the following:

- **Method**: POST
- **URL**: http://localhost:8000/summarize
- **Body data**: { "text": "Latest news about quantum computing from Google." }

Then add a **view results tree** listener and run the test, and measure average latency, errors, and throughput. This lets you quantify performance bottlenecks and plan for caching, load-balancing, or asynchronous processing strategies.

Want to make your system more performant?

Quantify -> Diagnose -> Cache -> Scale -> Optimize

The expected result is a responsive and optimized RAG system that consistently retrieves the most relevant news articles and generates concise, high-quality summaries, even when handling frequent updates or operating under peak user demand. The system should demonstrate low latency, minimal errors, and maintain throughput across varying loads, ensuring a smooth user experience and reliability at scale.

> **Stretch goal**
>
> Create a cache layer for popular queries and measure how much it reduces response times for high-frequency user requests. Try the same perf test but use Locust instead of Apache JMeter.

Once you've implemented caching and tested performance with Apache JMeter and Locust, explore horizontal scaling strategies. Deploy multiple instances of your API using a load balancer (e.g., NGINX or AWS ALB) and test system behavior under concurrent user loads. Track how response times and throughput scale with system size. Consider enabling asynchronous processing (e.g., using FastAPI + `asyncio` or a task queue such as Celery) to handle long-running summarization tasks without blocking other requests.

Step 6: Integrate a user-friendly interface

Design a streamlined user experience that operates entirely through chat interfaces. Use **Flask** or **FastAPI** to handle backend logic and integrate your system with platforms such as **Slack** or **Microsoft Teams** using their official APIs. Allow users to submit natural language queries and receive structured results directly in the chat. Enhance the experience by supporting category-based filters (e.g., politics, sports, and tech) and by enabling threaded conversations for deeper follow-up queries. This setup avoids the need for a custom web frontend while supporting real-time, conversational interaction.

A few practical suggestions follow:

- Expose a standard /rag-query endpoint for your custom chat frontend:

```python
from fastapi import FastAPI, Request
from pydantic import BaseModel
app = FastAPI()
class QueryRequest(BaseModel):
    query: str
@app.post("/rag-query")
async def rag_query(payload: QueryRequest):
    result = your_rag_pipeline(payload.query)
    return {"answer": result}
```

- Use the Telegram connector to relay messages from the chat to the RAG endpoint:

```python
import requests
BOT_TOKEN = ""
RAG_API = "http://localhost:8000/rag-query"
URL = f"https://api.telegram.org/bot{BOT_TOKEN}/"
def handle_updates():
    offset = None
    while True:
```

```
                    res = requests.get(URL + "getUpdates",
                        params={"offset": offset}).json()
                for update in res.get("result", []):
                    chat_id = update["message"]["chat"]["id"]
                    text = update["message"]["text"]
                    reply = requests.post(RAG_API,
                        json={"query": text}).json()["answer"]
                    requests.post(URL + "sendMessage",
                        data={"chat_id": chat_id, "text": reply})
                    offset = update["update_id"] + 1
        handle_updates()
```

- Use ngrok during development to expose your local service to platforms such as Slack or Telegram:

  ```
  ngrok http 8000
  ```

By the end of this step, your system should offer a seamless, chat-based interface where users can interact with real-time news content using natural language. Whether integrated into Slack, Teams, or a custom chat endpoint, the experience should feel responsive and effortless, eliminating the need for a traditional frontend.

Takeaway

Building a real-time news aggregator with RAG isn't just a cool project—it's your launchpad into applied AI. Along the way, you've practiced integrating live data, optimizing pipelines, and turning noisy streams into helpful insights.

The key takeaway? You don't have to do everything at once. Start with a small piece: maybe it's parsing RSS feeds, embedding headlines, or summarizing key updates. Then grow it step by step. Each part builds your skills and adds value.

You're now equipped to turn information overload into clarity. Iterate fast, keep learning, and make it yours.

Summary

This chapter was written to ignite your curiosity and inspire you to experiment with RAG systems in creative and practical ways. Through two distinct challenges, building a QA assistant and creating a real-time news summarizer, you've been introduced to the steps, tools, and methods that make RAG a game-changer for solving complex problems. But the goal here isn't just to teach; it's to get you excited about what's possible when you combine data retrieval with generative AI.

In *Challenge 1*, we explored how a QA system can assist engineers by retrieving test cases, debugging steps, and summarizing issues. In *Challenge 2*, we dove into the world of live news aggregation, tackling real-time data ingestion, indexing, and summarization. This chapter was designed to spark your imagination, not limit it. The step-by-step guidance is here to get you started, but the real fun begins when you add your own twists, explore new tools, and push the boundaries of what RAG can do. Every experiment, even the messy ones, is a step toward innovation. So, roll up your sleeves, fire up your favorite APIs, and start building. Who knows? Your next idea might just change the game. Go ahead—break things (safely), learn, and create!

Next up, exploring Mistral on Amazon Bedrock! It's time to experience this pleasant feeling when the infrastructure is handled for you. In the next chapter, we'll see which Mistral models are available on Amazon Bedrock. Let's plug into the cloud and see what enterprise-ready truly looks like.

Join our Discord and Reddit space

You're not the only one navigating fragmented tools, constant updates, and unclear best practices. Join a growing community of professionals exchanging insights that don't make it into documentation.

Stay informed with updates, discussions, and behind-the-scenes insights from our authors. Join our Discord at `https://packt.link/z8ivB` or scan the QR code below:	Connect with peers, share ideas, and discuss real-world GenAI challenges. Follow us on Reddit at `https://packt.link/0rExL` or scan the QR code below:

10

Mistral on AWS Bedrock

Many hands make light work.

—John Heywood

By this point, you're already familiar with the transformative power of LLMs and the challenges they can bring. This chapter is all about helping you get the most out of AWS Bedrock, as it simplifies some of those challenges by offering managed access to advanced models such as Mistral AI. Bedrock takes care of the infrastructure, allowing you to concentrate on building impactful applications that matter.

We'll walk through the theory of how Bedrock works, explore why Mistral is a standout model, and look at how to use them together. Then, we'll jump into a hands-on workshop, covering everything from setting up your environment to integrating Mistral into real-world applications. By the end, you'll have the tools and confidence to make AWS Bedrock and Mistral AI a seamless part of your AI journey.

In a nutshell, the following topics will be covered in this chapter:

- Cloud-based AI models and how Bedrock simplifies scaling
- Securing access with IAM roles and permissions
- Using boto3 to send requests and run inference
- Monitoring activity and trends with CloudWatch logs
- A practical workshop putting Mistral on Bedrock into action

Technical requirements

To follow this workshop, a few essentials will be needed along the way. You will need an AWS account, the **AWS CLI**, and the Python SDK **boto3**. If you already have any of these in place, that's great—you can reuse your existing setup. If not, don't worry – each of these components will be configured step by step as part of the environment setup.

- **AWS account**: Required to access Bedrock services. If you already have a personal account, it can be used. Creating one is part of the guided setup.

- **AWS CLI**: This command-line tool allows interaction with AWS services from your local machine. If it's not installed yet, a setup guide is provided later in the chapter.

- **Python boto3 SDK**: The official AWS SDK for Python, licensed under Apache 2.0. It provides simple programmatic access to Bedrock APIs. We will install it in a clean Python environment, but if you already have it, you can skip the installation step.

All code and references for this chapter are available in the GitHub repository: `https://github.com/PacktPublishing/Learn-Mistral-7B`, under the **Chapter-10** folder. This repository contains scripts aligned with the workshop and will serve as your practical reference.

Problem statement

When working with LLMs, it's easy to find yourself navigating a maze of infrastructure, scaling decisions, and model optimizations. AWS Bedrock aims to simplify this process by offering managed access to powerful models such as Mistral AI, but using it effectively still requires an understanding of the platform and its nuances. For example, how do you set up secure access with IAM roles? How do you fine-tune workflows to get the most out of Mistral while keeping scalability and costs in check?

Let's dive into these questions and more, providing a clear roadmap to mastering AWS Bedrock and Mistral AI. You'll learn how to set up your environment, integrate Mistral into your projects, and scale your applications with confidence. The goal is to streamline your work with LLMs so you can focus on building innovative, high-performing solutions without getting bogged down by technical roadblocks.

Seen in sequence, the upcoming sections form a progression: we start with the *why* of cloud-based AI services, then move to the mechanics of securing access, issuing requests, and finally monitoring activity. Together, these lay the groundwork for the practical workshop later in the chapter.

Cloud-based AI models: Why Bedrock matters

Artificial intelligence has shifted from a complex, infrastructure-heavy endeavor to an accessible, cloud-powered solution. Traditionally, deploying AI requires managing large computing resources, maintaining security updates, and scaling infrastructure manually. These challenges make AI integration costly and time-consuming.

AWS Bedrock removes these barriers by offering pre-trained foundation models through a managed service. Instead of provisioning GPU clusters and handling model updates, developers can access ready-to-use AI via an API. This allows for faster implementation, automatic updates, and seamless security compliance. Bedrock turns AI into a plug-and-play component, removing the burden of managing infrastructure.

Scalability is another major advantage. AI applications often experience fluctuating demand, requiring flexible resource allocation. Serverless AI through Bedrock scales automatically to meet demand, maintaining stable performance whether you're handling a handful of queries or millions—no manual intervention required.

Cost efficiency is also key. Running a self-hosted AI model requires continuous investments in hardware and maintenance. In contrast, Bedrock operates on a pay-as-you-go model, where you only pay for what you use. This makes AI adoption more accessible for start-ups and smaller teams.

By treating AI as a service rather than an infrastructure challenge, Bedrock allows developers to focus on innovation rather than maintenance. Now, at this point, with the *why* established, the next step is understanding how to connect securely—because even with managed infrastructure, access and permissions remain in the developer's control.

Authentication and access control

Before we can interact with AWS Bedrock, we need a structured way to manage access. Every AWS service, including Bedrock, relies on **Identity and Access Management (IAM)** to define who can use resources and what actions they can perform. Without proper authentication and authorization, our applications won't be able to connect to AI models securely.

To enable access, we will configure IAM roles, policies, and access keys. IAM users and roles define who or what can interact with AWS Bedrock, while policies determine their permissions. We will assign necessary privileges to ensure our Bedrock integration functions correctly while keeping security best practices in mind.

To operate with Bedrock, we need specific permissions. The **AmazonBedrockFullAccess** policy provides the ability to list available models, invoke them, and retrieve responses. For logging and monitoring, **CloudWatch** permissions allow us to track API activity. In some cases, temporary **AdministratorAccess** may be used during setup, but granting overly broad permissions should be avoided in real-world applications.

Security best practice

Following the principle of least privilege ensures that only necessary permissions are assigned. Instead of giving full access by default, we will restrict operations to what is required for each component of our setup. This approach enhances security, prevents unintended access, and aligns with AWS best practices.

At this stage, the IAM is properly configured, and we've established the *gatekeeping* layer of our system. Now we're ready to move into the next stage: programmatic interaction with Bedrock using AWS SDKs.

API-driven model interactions

Cloud-based AI services rely on a client-server model, where applications (clients) send requests to AWS Bedrock (the server), which processes them and returns responses. This structured approach enables scalable AI interactions, allowing developers to integrate powerful models without managing complex infrastructure. Instead of manually handling HTTP requests and responses, AWS provides an official **software development kit (SDK)** to simplify communication—**boto3**.

Boto3 is the official AWS SDK for Python, designed to enable seamless interactions with AWS services, including Bedrock. It is open source, released under the Apache 2.0 license, meaning it is free to use and modify. The library abstracts the complexities of authentication, request formatting, and response handling, allowing developers to work with AWS services using familiar Python syntax. Using boto3, applications can interact with Bedrock by listing available foundation models, sending prompts, retrieving AI-generated responses, and managing resources.

A typical request to AWS Bedrock using boto3 involves specifying the model ID, providing structured input parameters, and defining settings such as temperature (which influences response randomness) and max tokens (which limits the length of the output). Bedrock processes these requests and returns structured responses in JSON format, which applications can easily parse and utilize.

This API-driven approach makes it possible to dynamically modify prompts, fine-tune responses, and integrate AI capabilities into various workflows. Since AWS services are designed to scale, boto3 enables AI-driven applications to handle a high volume of requests efficiently.

Boto3 manages communication with AWS services, allowing the focus to stay on meaningful outcomes rather than technical details. This streamlined approach reflects the very purpose of Bedrock: making advanced AI accessible. Before moving into hands-on practice, the last step is ensuring visibility into how these interactions actually unfold.

Observability with CloudWatch Logs

To run AI applications with confidence, observability is non-negotiable. AWS Bedrock integrates with CloudTrail by default, automatically logging key management events such as **InvokeModel**, **ListFoundationModels**, and other API operations. These logs capture details such as request time, parameters, response status, and user identity.

CloudTrail records Bedrock activity behind the scenes, and CloudWatch makes that information useful. By sending logs to CloudWatch, you can track latency, errors, and usage trends in near real time. Dashboards and alerts then help spot issues quickly while also revealing longer-term performance patterns, keeping workloads reliable as demand shifts.

Bedrock takes care of infrastructure, IAM secures access, boto3 manages communication, and CloudWatch ensures observability. Together, these elements form a solid foundation.

The stage is now ready for the practical workshop, where each concept will be applied step by step in a real-world setting.

Practical workshop: Hands-on inference with boto3 and CLI

Artificial intelligence is transforming how we build and interact with technology, and **AWS Bedrock** brings cutting-edge AI models at your fingertips. This workshop is your gateway to mastering AI-driven development, from setting up your environment to making real-time requests with **boto3**. We'll establish a secure connection, send prompts, and retrieve dynamic responses from **Mistral Small**. By the end, you'll have the skills to integrate powerful AI models into real-world applications. Whether you're an AI enthusiast or a developer looking to expand your expertise, this hands-on experience will empower you to create the future.

Step 1: Environment setup

Before we can interact with AWS Bedrock and start working with Mistral Small, we need to ensure our environment is properly set up. This includes accessing reference materials, creating an AWS account, and setting up an IAM user with the necessary permissions. We'll generate access keys, configure the AWS CLI, and request access to the Mistral model. Finally, we'll prepare our development environment in VSCode, ensuring everything is in place for seamless communication with AWS services. Once these steps are complete, you'll be fully prepared to dive into AI-powered development with confidence.

For the workshop setup, you'll need access to the project files hosted on GitHub. Visit the main project repository at `https://github.com/PacktPublishing/Learn-Mistral`. The relevant folder with code is `/Chapter-10`.

These files contain the full solutions we will code in this workshop; they can be used as reference material in case of any issues. Be sure to download or clone the repository before starting!

Create an AWS account

To use AWS Bedrock with Mistral AI, you need an AWS account with the correct permissions. If you already have a personal AWS account and are comfortable navigating the AWS console, you can skip this step. However, avoid using a corporate AWS account unless explicitly approved to prevent billing or compliance conflicts.

1. Visit `https://aws.amazon.com/` and click **Create an AWS Account**.
2. Enter your email address, choose an AWS account name, and set a strong password.
3. Select **Personal Account** unless setting up AWS for a company.
4. Provide billing details (AWS requires a payment method, but free-tier options are available).
5. Complete identity verification and select the Basic Support plan (free).

To access the AWS Console and check Bedrock availability, do the following:

1. Sign in to the AWS Management Console: `https://aws.amazon.com/console/`.
2. AWS Bedrock is only available in select regions, so ensure you're in a supported region. The latest list of Bedrock-supported regions can be found here: `https://docs.aws.amazon.com/general/latest/gr/bedrock.html`.

3. In the AWS console, the selected region is shown in the top-right corner—adjust it if necessary.

Once your account is ready, you can move on to setting up IAM roles and CLI access in the next steps.

Create new IAM user and setup permissions

To interact with AWS Bedrock from the command line, we need a dedicated IAM user with the right permissions. This user, bedrock-cli-user, will be used for secure programmatic access via AWS CLI, allowing us to request and manage foundation models such as **Mistral Small**. We will grant both Bedrock-specific access and full admin privileges to ensure the smooth execution of AWS commands. While full admin access is given for this workshop, in production environments, always follow the principle of least privilege. First, please follow the next steps to create a new IAM user:

1. Sign in to the AWS Management Console at https://aws.amazon.com/console/ and navigate to the **IAM service**.

2. In the left menu, click **Users | Add user**.

3. Enter the username as bedrock-cli-user.

4. Click **Next**.

Figure 10.1 provides an illustration of the user details form:

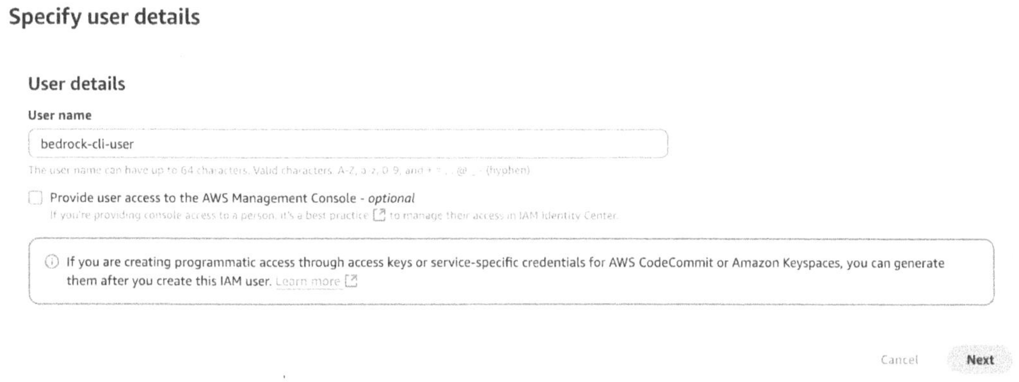

Specify user details

User details

User name

| bedrock-cli-user |

The user name can have up to 64 characters. Valid characters A-Z, a-z, 0-9, and + = , . @ _ - (hyphen)

☐ Provide user access to the AWS Management Console - *optional*
If you're providing console access to a person, it's a best practice ☑ to manage their access in IAM Identity Center.

ⓘ If you are creating programmatic access through access keys or service-specific credentials for AWS CodeCommit or Amazon Keyspaces, you can generate them after you create this IAM user. Learn more ☑

Cancel   **Next**

Figure 10.1: User details

Next, please follow the steps to attach AWS Bedrock permissions:

1. On the **Set permissions** page, select **Attach policies directly**.

2. Search for Bedrock and check the box for the **AmazonBedrockFullAccess** policy.

3. Delete Bedrock from the search bar.

As shown in *Figure 10.2*, the permission list with the Bedrock permission selected appears as follows.

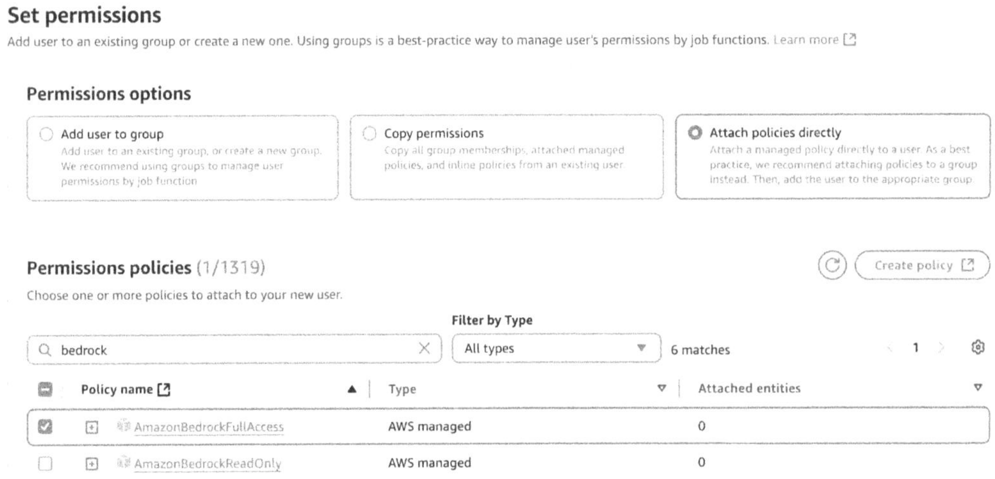

Figure 10.2: Attach Bedrock permissions

The preceding figure demonstrates selecting the appropriate managed policy that grants access to Bedrock services.

Similarly, please follow these steps to attach administrator access permissions:

1. Still on the **Set permissions** page, search for admin.

2. Check the box for **AdministratorAccess** to grant full AWS access.

3. Click **Next**.

See *Figure 10.3* for a depiction of the assignment of admin access.

Set permissions

Add user to an existing group or create a new one. Using groups is a best-practice way to manage user's permissions by job functions. Learn more ☑

Permissions options

Add user to group	Copy permissions	⦿ Attach policies directly
Add user to an existing group, or create a new group. We recommend using groups to manage user permissions by job function.	Copy all group memberships, attached managed policies, and inline policies from an existing user.	Attach a managed policy directly to a user. As a best practice, we recommend attaching policies to a group instead. Then, add the user to the appropriate group.

Permissions policies (2/1319)   ⟳ (Create policy ☑)

Choose one or more policies to attach to your new user.

Filter by Type

🔍 admin ✕	All types ▾	45 matches	1 2 3 > ⚙

☐	Policy name ☑ ▲	Type ▽	Attached entities ▽
☑	⊕ AdministratorAccess	AWS managed - job function	0
☐	⊕ AdministratorAccess-Amplify	AWS managed	1
☐	⊕ AdministratorAccess-AWSElasticBea...	AWS managed	0

Figure 10.3: Attaching AdministratorAccess

This permission set provides full control over AWS resources, including Bedrock, allowing the user to manage services without restrictions. However, it's recommended to apply the principle of least privilege when configuring access.

Next, review and create the user:

1. Review the user details and the attached policies.
2. Click **Create user**.
3. The confirmation screen will display **User details**.

Figure 10.4 demonstrates the layout of the final review and user creation summary.

Review and create

Review your choices. After you create the user, you can view and download the autogenerated password, if enabled.

User details

User name	Console password type	Require password reset
bedrock-cli-user	None	No

Permissions summary   1

Name ☑ ▲	Type ▽	Used as ▽
AdministratorAccess	AWS managed - job function	Permissions policy
AmazonBedrockFullAccess	AWS managed	Permissions policy

Figure 10.4: Review new user summary and create user

We have successfully created **bedrock-cli-user** with the required permissions for AWS Bedrock and administrative access. This ensures we can now securely interact with AWS services from the CLI. Next, we will generate and retrieve access keys for this user, which are essential for authenticating **AWS CLI** commands.

Create an access key for the user

Before we can start issuing AWS commands from our terminal, we need to generate a **secure access key** for **bedrock-cli-user**. This key acts as a unique identifier, allowing the AWS CLI to authenticate our requests. Once created, it must be stored safely, as AWS will not show the secret access key again.

Please follow these steps to create an access key for our user:

1. Click on **bedrock-cli-user** to open its user details page. The structure of the user details is shown in *Figure 10.5*.

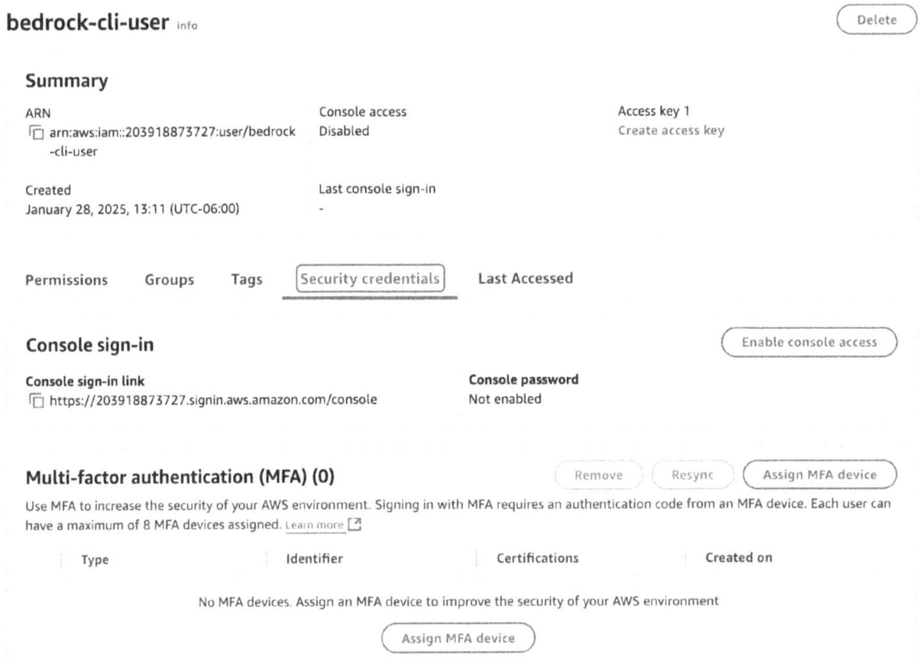

Figure 10.5: User details page

2.   Scroll down to the security credentials tab. Locate the **Access keys** section:

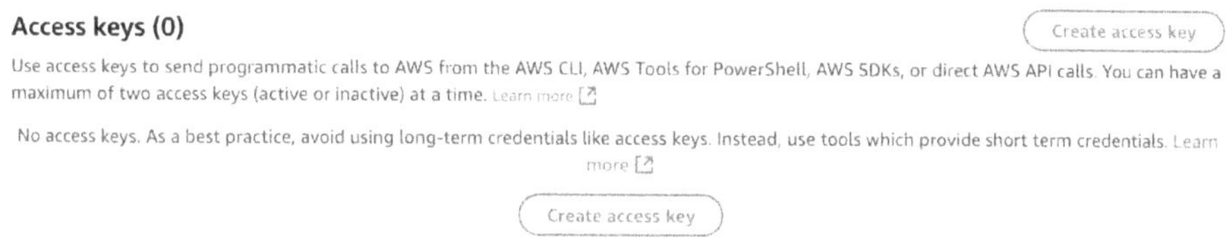

Access keys (0)   (Create access key)

Use access keys to send programmatic calls to AWS from the AWS CLI, AWS Tools for PowerShell, AWS SDKs, or direct AWS API calls. You can have a maximum of two access keys (active or inactive) at a time. Learn more 🗗

No access keys. As a best practice, avoid using long-term credentials like access keys. Instead, use tools which provide short term credentials. Learn more 🗗

(Create access key)

Figure 10.6: AWS IAM user access keys section

3.   Click **Create access key.**

4.   In the **Use case** options, select **Command Line Interface (CLI)** and click **Next.** *Figure 10.7* visualizes the CLI selection of the use case.

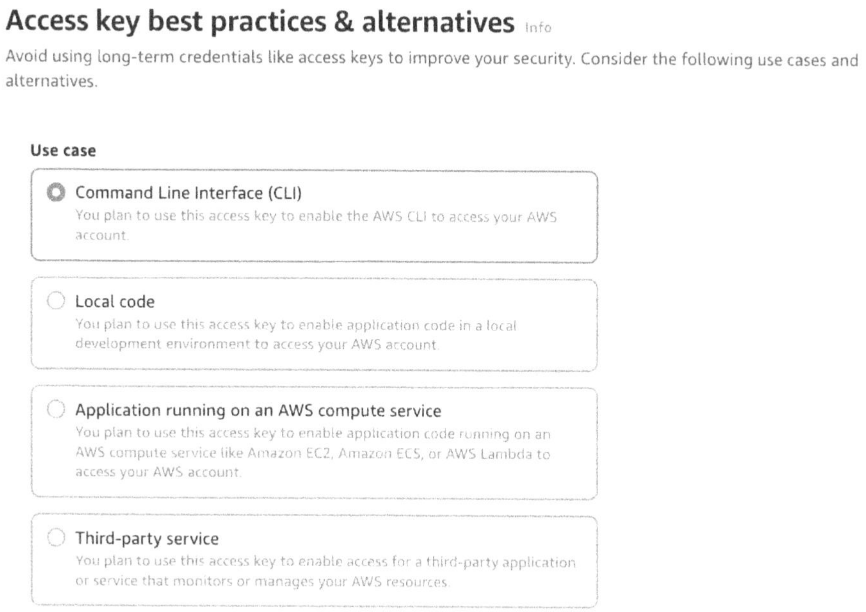

Access key best practices & alternatives Info

Avoid using long-term credentials like access keys to improve your security. Consider the following use cases and alternatives.

Use case

⦿ Command Line Interface (CLI)
    You plan to use this access key to enable the AWS CLI to access your AWS account.

◯ Local code
    You plan to use this access key to enable application code in a local development environment to access your AWS account.

◯ Application running on an AWS compute service
    You plan to use this access key to enable application code running on an AWS compute service like Amazon EC2, Amazon ECS, or AWS Lambda to access your AWS account.

◯ Third-party service
    You plan to use this access key to enable access for a third-party application or service that monitors or manages your AWS resources.

Figure 10.7: Use case selection for the access key

5.   Review the security recommendations and click **Create access key.**

6. The access key ID and secret access key will be displayed. *Figure 10.8* provides an illustration of the generated access key summary.

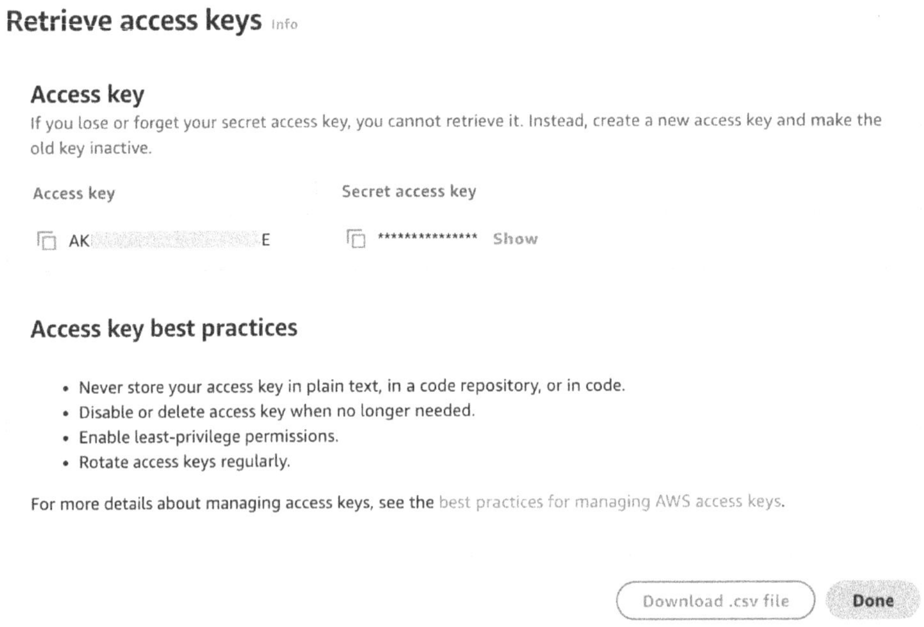

Retrieve access keys Info

Access key
If you lose or forget your secret access key, you cannot retrieve it. Instead, create a new access key and make the old key inactive.

Access key   Secret access key

  🗖 AK███████████████E   🗖 *************** Show

Access key best practices

  • Never store your access key in plain text, in a code repository, or in code.
  • Disable or delete access key when no longer needed.
  • Enable least-privilege permissions.
  • Rotate access keys regularly.

For more details about managing access keys, see the best practices for managing AWS access keys.

(Download .csv file)   **Done**

Figure 10.8: Generated access key

7. Copy both **Access key** and **Secret access key** and store them in a secure location. Alternatively, click **Download.csv file** to save the credentials securely. These credentials will be required for AWS CLI authentication later.

Now that we have successfully created and retrieved our access key, **bedrock-cli-user** is ready for CLI-based authentication. The next step is to configure the AWS CLI V2 client with these credentials, ensuring that our environment is properly set up to interact with AWS Bedrock and access **Mistral Small**.

Configure the AWS CLI V2 client on your computer

Now that we have our access keys, let's configure AWS CLI V2 to authenticate and interact with AWS services. This setup will allow us to issue commands, manage resources, and communicate with AWS Bedrock directly from our terminal.

Please follow these steps to get AWS CLI V2 configured with your access keys:

1. Download and Install AWS CLI V2. Follow the official installation guide for your operating system – AWS CLI V2 installation guide: `https://docs.aws.amazon.com/cli/latest/userguide/getting-started-install.html`.

2. Verify the AWS CLI installation. Open a terminal and run the following:

    ```
    which aws
    ```

    Here's the expected output:

    ```
    /usr/local/bin/aws
    ```

3. Configure AWS CLI with your credentials. Run the following command in the terminal:

    ```
    aws configure
    ```

4. Enter the credentials when prompted, as shown in *Figure 10.9* – use your credentials.

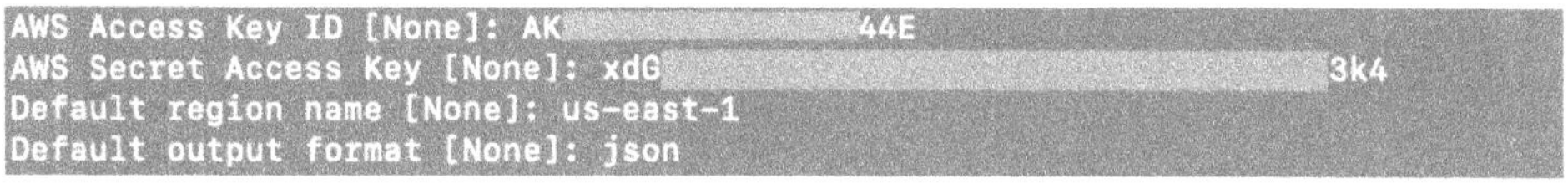

    ```
    AWS Access Key ID [None]: AK            44E
    AWS Secret Access Key [None]: xdG                      3k4
    Default region name [None]: us-east-1
    Default output format [None]: json
    ```

    Figure 10.9: Terminal screen snippet on access key setup

    The text is duplicated here (the secret and the key are masked with stars):

    ```
    AWS Access Key ID [None]: AK**********44E
    AWS Secret Access Key [None]: xdG*****************************3k4
    Default region name [None]: us-east-1
    Default output format [None]: json
    ```

5. Now run the following command to check whether AWS CLI is correctly configured:

    ```
    aws s3 ls
    ```

    If you have any S3 buckets, you should see output similar to the following:

    ```
    2024-09-07 17:04:24 some_s3_bucket
    ```

6. To test AWS Bedrock access, run the following:

```
aws bedrock list-foundation-models
```

Here's the expected JSON output:

```
{
  "modelSummaries": [
    {
      "modelArn":
"arn:aws:bedrock:us-east-1::foundation-model/amazon.titan-tg1-
large",
      "modelId": "amazon.titan-tg1-large",
      "modelName": "Titan Text Large",
      "providerName": "Amazon",
      "inputModalities": ["TEXT"],
      "outputModalities": ["TEXT"]
    },
    ...


  ]
}
```

After configuring AWS CLI V2, you're able to send authenticated requests to AWS services, including Bedrock. Next, we will request access to the Mistral model on Bedrock, ensuring that we have permission to use Mistral Small. Once access is granted, we can start making API calls to the model.

Request access to the Mistral model on Bedrock

Before we can start using Mistral Small, we need to request access through AWS Bedrock. This step ensures that our IAM to Mistral model on Bedrock" user has the necessary permissions to interact with the model. Once access is granted, we will be able to send API requests and integrate Mistral AI into our applications.

Please follow these steps to get access granted:

1. Go back to the AWS Console.

2. In the AWS search bar, type `Bedrock` and select **Amazon Bedrock** from the results.

    See *Figure 10.10* for a depiction of how to navigate to the Amazon Bedrock service.

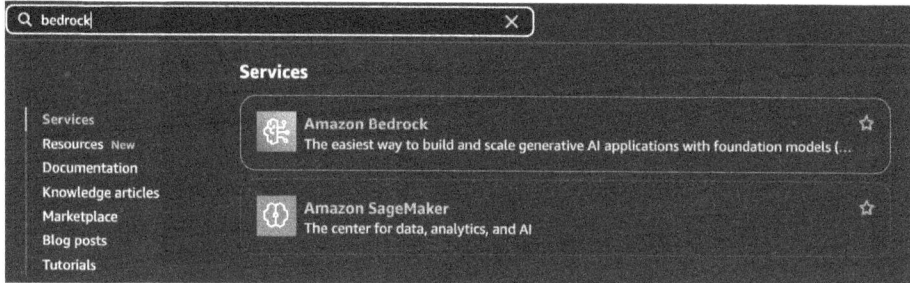

Figure 10.10: Navigate to the Bedrock service

3. In the left-hand side panel, click **Providers**. *Figure 10.11* demonstrates the layout of the left-hand side menu.

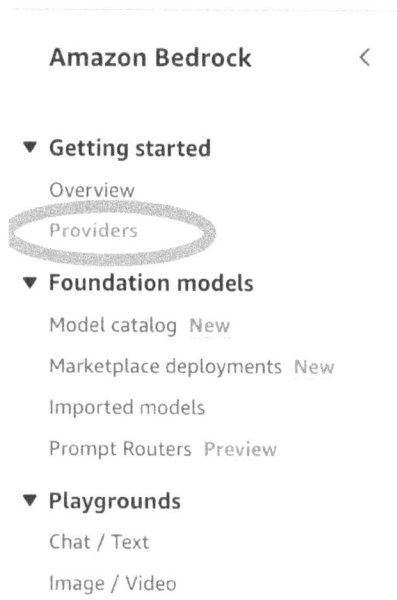

Figure 10.11: Navigate to Providers

4. Locate and to Mistral model on Bedrock" select the Mistral AI provider from the list. Il-
    lustrated in *Figure 10.12* is the relevant part of the **Providers** list.

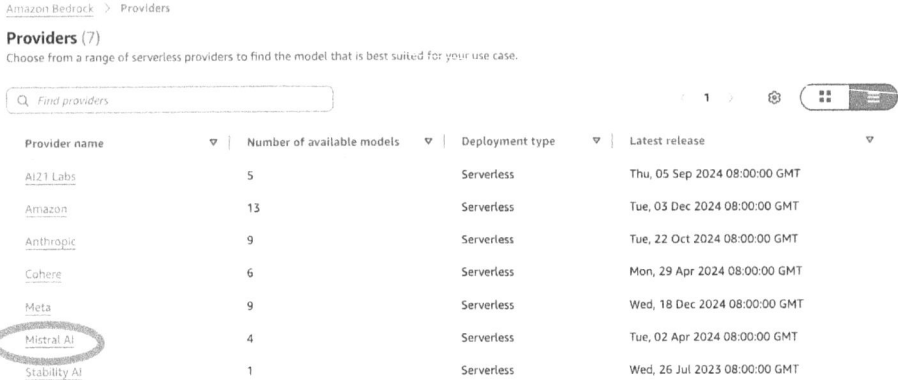

Amazon Bedrock > Providers

Providers (7)
Choose from a range of serverless providers to find the model that is best suited for your use case.

Provider name	Number of available models	Deployment type	Latest release
AI21 Labs	5	Serverless	Thu, 05 Sep 2024 08:00:00 GMT
Amazon	13	Serverless	Tue, 03 Dec 2024 08:00:00 GMT
Anthropic	9	Serverless	Tue, 22 Oct 2024 08:00:00 GMT
Cohere	6	Serverless	Mon, 29 Apr 2024 08:00:00 GMT
Meta	9	Serverless	Wed, 18 Dec 2024 08:00:00 GMT
Mistral AI	4	Serverless	Tue, 02 Apr 2024 08:00:00 GMT
Stability AI	1	Serverless	Wed, 26 Jul 2023 08:00:00 GMT

Figure 10.12: Select Mistral AI provider

5. Find **Mistral Small**, click to Mistral model on Bedrock" the three dots (⋮) menu, and select
    Modify access. *Figure 10.13* visualizes the context menu of the model.

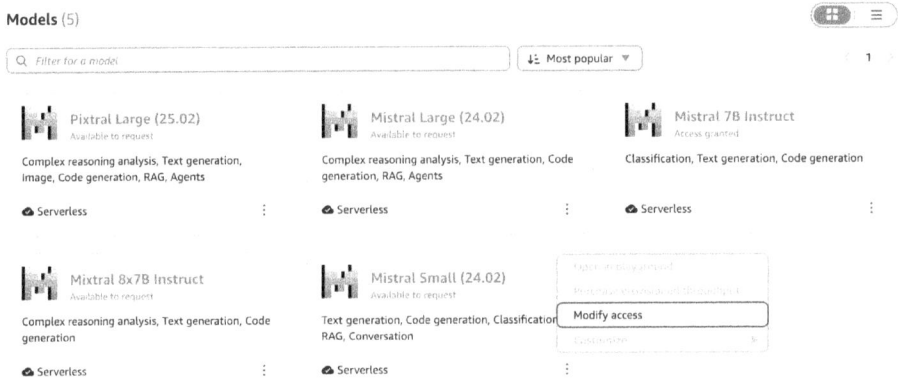

Models (5)

Pixtral Large (25.02) Available to request	**Mistral Large (24.02)** Available to request

Pixtral Large (25.02) — Complex reasoning analysis, Text generation, Image, Code generation, RAG, Agents — ☁ Serverless

Mistral Large (24.02) — Complex reasoning analysis, Text generation, Code generation, RAG, Agents — ☁ Serverless

Mistral 7B Instruct — Classification, Text generation, Code generation — ☁ Serverless

Mixtral 8x7B Instruct — Complex reasoning analysis, Text generation, Code generation — ☁ Serverless

Mistral Small (24.02) — Text generation, Code generation, Classification, RAG, Conversation — ☁ Serverless

Modify access

Figure 10.13: Request Modify access on the relevant model

6. Check the box for **Mistral Small** to request access. See *Figure 10.14* for a depiction of the
    relevant list of the to Mistral model on Bedrock" models to select.

☐ ▼ Mistral AI (5)		1/5 access granted		
Mistral 7B Instruct		⊘ Access granted	Text	EULA
☐ Mixtral 8x7B Instruct		⊝ Available to request	Text	EULA
☐ Mistral Large (24.02)		⊝ Available to request	Text	EULA
☑ Mistral Small (24.02)		⊝ Available to request	Text	EULA
☐ Pixtral Large (25.02) Cross-region inference		⊝ Available to request	Text & Vision	EULA

Figure 10.14: Mark Mistral Small in the list

7. Wait a few moments for AWS to process the request. Then confirm that access has been granted. The model should now be available for use. *Figure 10.15* provides an illustration of the desired access granted rows.

▼ Mistral AI (5)		2/5 access granted		
Mistral 7B Instruct		⊝ Available to request	Text	EULA
Mixtral 8x7B Instruct		⊝ Available to request	Text	EULA
Mistral Large (24.02)		⊝ Available to request	Text	EULA
Mistral Small (24.02)		⊘ Access granted	Text	EULA
Pixtral Large (25.02) Cross-region inference		⊝ Available to request	Text & Vision	EULA

Figure 10.15: Access granted

Now that we have successfully requested and confirmed access to Mistral Small, we are ready to start working with it. The next step is to set up our VSCode project.

Prepare the VSCode project

Now that we have access to Mistral Small, it's time to set up our development environment. In this step, we will prepare a VSCode project, create a Python virtual environment, and install the necessary dependencies. This setup ensures a clean workspace for working with AWS Bedrock using boto3.

Please follow these steps to get the virtual environment ready and boto3 installed on it:

1. Open **VSCode** and create a new project folder.
2. Open a terminal in **VSCode**.
3. Create a virtual environment by running the following:

```
python3 -m venv .venv
```

4. Activate the virtual environment:

    ```
    source .venv/bin/activate
    ```

5. Create a requirements.txt file in the project folder.

6. Add the following dependency to requirements.txt:

    ```
    boto3 >= 1.36
    ```

7. Install the dependencies by running the following:

    ```
    pip install -r requirements.txt
    ```

Once the VSCode project is set up, the environment is fully prepared to interact with AWS Bedrock. Now, we can start using boto3 (AWS SDK for Python) to send API requests, communicate with Mistral Small, and perform AI-driven tasks directly in the AWS cloud. Let's get started!

Step 2: Connect AWS Bedrock with boto3

In this step, we are making our first direct connection from Python to AWS Bedrock. This is a crucial milestone—confirming that our setup is correct and that we can successfully retrieve the list of available foundation models. By running this script, we'll verify our access and identify the correct model ID for Mistral Small, which we will use in the next steps:

1. Open your VSCode project and create a new Python file: ws10_step01_list_models.py.

2. Add the following code:

    ```python
    import boto3

    # Create a Bedrock client in the specified region
    bedrock = boto3.client(service_name='bedrock', region_name='us-
    east-1')

    # Request the list of available foundation models
    response = bedrock.list_foundation_models()
    models = response['modelSummaries']

    # Print provider, model name, and model ID
    for model in models:
        print(model['providerName']
    + " - " + model['modelName']
    + " - " + model['modelId'])
    ```

3. Run the script:

```
python ws10_step01_list_models.py
```

Here's the expected output:

```
...
Mistral AI - Mistral Large (24.02) - mistral.mistral-large-2402-v1:0
Mistral AI - Mistral Small (24.02) - mistral.mistral-small-2402-v1:0
Mistral AI - Pixtral Large (25.02) - mistral.pixtral-large-2502-v1:0
```

If you get an error such as botocore.exceptions.NoCredentialsError: Unable to locate credentials, please return to the AWS CLI configuration and make sure the command line verification step passes.

The script lists all foundation models available in AWS Bedrock, including their provider, name, and model ID. This output confirms that our Python environment is correctly set up and able to communicate with AWS Bedrock.

Among the available models, we will be using the following:

```
Mistral AI - Mistral Small (24.02) - mistral.mistral-small-2402-v1:0
```

This model ID (mistral.mistral-small-2402-v1:0) will be used in the next section to interact with Mistral Small, sending prompts and processing responses.

Now that we've successfully connected to AWS Bedrock and retrieved the model list, we're ready to send our first request to Mistral. The next step will cover how to communicate with the model and retrieve AI-generated responses.

Step 3: Send a prompt to Bedrock and get a stream response

Now that we have everything set up, it's time to send our first API request to Mistral Small through AWS Bedrock. In this step, we will initialize the Bedrock runtime client, construct a request payload, handle potential errors, and extract the model's response. This will allow us to interact with the AI, process text, and verify that our environment is correctly configured.

Follow the steps carefully to ensure smooth communication between Python and AWS Bedrock:

1. To interact with Bedrock at runtime, we use `bedrock-runtime` instead of `bedrock`. The `bedrock-runtime` client is specifically for invoking models, while `bedrock` is used for managing them.

    ```
    client = boto3.client(service_name='bedrock-runtime',
        region_name='us-east-1')
    ```

    > **Bedrock versus bedrock-runtime**
    >
    > AWS provides two distinct clients for working with Bedrock, and it's important to understand their differences.
    >
    > The `bedrock` client is used for administrative tasks. It allows you to list available foundation models, manage access permissions, and configure Bedrock-related settings. In short, it helps you understand what models are available and control who can use them.
    >
    > The `bedrock-runtime` client is dedicated to inference. This is where you send input payloads, execute model calls, and receive AI-generated responses. Anytime you want to actually run prompts against a model, you'll be using this runtime client.

    Since we are requesting a response from Mistral Small, we must use `bedrock-runtime` for this operation.

2. We then need to specify the correct model ID to ensure our request is processed correctly:

    ```
    model_id = ' mistral.mistral-small-2402-v1:0'
    ```

    If an incorrect model ID is used, AWS will return an error message:

    ```
    Exception Type: ValidationException
    Error Message: An error occurred (ValidationException) when calling
    the InvokeModel operation: The provided model identifier is invalid.
    ```

3. The next step is to construct the payload. The payload defines what we want the model to generate. It includes the prompt, response length, and randomness control.

    ```
    payload = {
        "prompt": "Explain the concept of reinforcement learning in
    simple terms.",
    ```

```
        "temperature": 0.7,
        "max_tokens": 300
    }
```

As we already covered in *Chapter 3*, "temperature" controls response creativity, while "max_tokens" limits the response length. Ensure that these values are not wrapped inside a parameters object and that "max_tokens" is correctly spelled.

4. To catch potential issues, we wrap our API call in a try-except block. This block helps troubleshoot issues such as invalid input, API failures, or permission problems. Onwards to send the payload to the model.

```
    try:
        # client invocation happens here
    except Exception as e:
        # Print detailed debug information
        print("Error occurred while invoking the model:")
        print(f"Exception Type: {type(e).__name__}")
        print(f"Error Message: {e}")
        if hasattr(e, 'response'):
            print("AWS Error Response:")
            print(json.dumps(e.response, indent=2))
```

5. Now we invoke the model by passing the payload to the Bedrock runtime client. This sends the request to AWS Bedrock and waits for a response from the model. Next, we will retrieve the response body from the payload.

```
    response = client.invoke_model(
        modelId=model_id,
        body=json.dumps(payload),
        contentType="application/json",
        accept="application/json"
    )
```

6. We then convert the streaming response to a string. AWS Bedrock returns responses in a streaming format, meaning the data comes in chunks rather than all at once. In this step, response["body"].read() reads all available bytes from the stream at once. Since our payload is small, this works instantly.

For larger responses, data may be received in multiple parts, so we would need to handle streaming incrementally by reading chunks of the response as they arrive.

`.decode("utf-8")` converts the byte data into a readable string, and `json.loads(response_body)` parses it into a Python dictionary.

```
response_body = response["body"].read().decode("utf-8")
result = json.loads(response_body)
```

Onwards to retrieve the model's response text.

7. To retrieve the AI-generated text, we extract the "text" field from the JSON response:

```
output_text = result.get("outputs", [{}])[0].get(
        "text",
        "No response received.")
```

If no valid response is received, the script defaults to "No response received." instead of throwing an error. This snippet finalizes the detailed code explanation, and in the next section, we have the full code.

8. The following is the complete script to send a prompt and retrieve the model's response. This script fully automates sending a request to Mistral Small and handling errors. We are ready to run this piece of our work and see the results.

```
import boto3
import json

client = boto3.client(service_name='bedrock-runtime',
    region_name='us-east-1')

model_id = ' mistral.mistral-small-2402-v1:0'

# Payload for Bedrock
payload = {
    "prompt": "Explain the concept of reinforcement learning in
simple terms.",
    "temperature": 0.7,
    "max_tokens": 300
}
```

```
try:
    # Call the Bedrock model
    response = client.invoke_model(
        modelId=model_id,
        body=json.dumps(payload),
        contentType="application/json",
        accept="application/json"
    )

    # Read the response body (convert StreamingBody to string)
    response_body = response["body"].read().decode("utf-8")
    result = json.loads(response_body)

    # Extract the model's output
    output_text = result.get("outputs", [{}])[0].get(
        "text",
        "No response received.")
    print(">>>", payload["prompt"])
    print("<<<", output_text)


except Exception as e:
    # Print detailed debug information
    print("Error occurred while invoking the model:")
    print(f"Exception Type: {type(e).__name__}")
    print(f"Error Message: {e}")
    if hasattr(e, 'response'):
        print("AWS Error Response:")
        print(json.dumps(e.response, indent=2))
```

9.   To test the script, run the following command in your terminal:

```
python3 ./src/ws10_step02_call_model.py
```

If everything is set up correctly, the response will contain AI-generated text from the Mistral Small model.

We have successfully sent our first API request to AWS Bedrock and retrieved a response from Mistral Small. This confirms that our AWS environment is fully operational, and we can now communicate with the model.

Step 4: Check CloudWatch Logs for Bedrock

To review recent AWS Bedrock activity, you can access logs directly in the CloudTrail event history. This helps you verify successful requests and troubleshoot failures without additional setup. Follow these steps to view Bedrock logs:

1. Go to **CloudTrail** in the AWS Console.

2. Open the **Event history** tab.

3. In **Lookup attributes**, filter by **Event source** and enter: `bedrock.amazonaws.com`

Refer to *Figure 10.16* for a visual example of Bedrock logs displayed in the CloudTrail console.

Figure 10.16: Bedrock events

For long-term retention or advanced querying, you can configure CloudTrail to publish these logs to an S3 bucket, where they can be archived or analyzed with services such as Athena or AWS Glue.

This final step completes the workshop and demonstrates AWS Bedrock in action using Mistral Small. Now, let's step back and summarize the key lessons from this chapter before moving on.

Summary

We've successfully built a fully operational AI development environment with AWS Bedrock, enabling seamless interaction with Mistral Small. From setup to executing our first API request, we've transformed an abstract concept into a working AI-powered system with secure IAM authentication and a functional Python workflow using boto3.

The real achievement isn't just connecting to Bedrock—it's the confidence and control you've gained over AI integration. You've structured API calls, handled errors, explored CloudWatch, and gained hands-on experience with cloud infrastructure. This foundation equips you to start integrating AI into real-world applications. Keep experimenting, keep refining, and most importantly, keep creating.

In the next chapter, we explore how to run large language models on Google Cloud using Vertex AI and Model Garden. You'll learn how to work with these models in a fully managed, serverless environment, and we'll introduce optional challenges for those interested in deeper deployment strategies on GCP.

Extracurricular

- **Extend boto3 beyond inference:** Go beyond simple inference calls by connecting boto3 with other AWS services. Store prompts and responses in S3, trigger Lambda functions for automation, or log outputs in DynamoDB to build lightweight retrieval and analysis workflows.

- **Experiment with Bedrock parameters**: Adjust temperature, max tokens, and prompt design to see how outputs change. This exploration highlights how small parameter tweaks can influence creativity, precision, or verbosity, offering deeper insight into model behavior and response control.

- **Build a mini-project:** Apply your skills to a small project, such as creating a chatbot, automating content summarization for S3 documents, or running batch inference. These exercises transform workshop knowledge into practical, real-world problem-solving experience.

- **Automate workflows with n8n and Bedrock**: Use n8n's workflow automation to connect Bedrock with everyday tools. Create pipelines that send prompts from emails or chat apps to Bedrock, then route the responses back automatically, turning AI into a seamless part of daily workflows.

Unlock this book's exclusive benefits now

UNLOCK NOW

Scan this QR code or go to `https://packtpub.com/unlock`, then search for this book by name.

Note: Keep your purchase invoice ready before you start.

11

Harnessing Mistral's Power via Google Cloud Vertex AI

If you want to be happy for a lifetime, plant a garden.

—Chinese Proverb

In this chapter, we'll bring everything together—cloud infrastructure, model APIs, and real-world scripting—to show you how to run and integrate **Large Language Models (LLMs)** using Google Cloud's Vertex AI platform. We'll begin with the theory, covering the key services and components that make up the Vertex AI ecosystem. You'll learn how Model Garden works, what synchronous and streaming inference mean in practice, and how authentication, access control, and configuration all fit into the workflow. Model Garden in Vertex AI offers a curated selection of pre-trained machine learning models and tools, helping you streamline the development, testing, and deployment of AI solutions—without needing to train models from scratch.

Once the concepts are clear, we'll start with a practical workshop where you'll build your own setup from scratch. You'll start in Google Colab Enterprise for quick experimentation, then transition to VS Code with a modular Python environment. You'll configure your project, authenticate using `gcloud`, and make both synchronous and streaming calls to hosted Mistral models. You'll also apply best practices for script structure and environment management.

By the end of this chapter, you'll not only understand how inference works on Vertex AI—you'll have a functioning and reusable code base that mirrors the architecture used in production systems. This is where your LLM integration becomes real.

In a nutshell, the following topics will be covered in this chapter:

- Understanding Vertex AI
- Practical workshop

Technical requirements

This is an **advanced-level workshop** intended for developers and engineers who are comfortable with Python scripting and working in cloud-based environments. While we guide you through each step, some familiarity with CLI tools, project setup, and basic debugging will help you get the most out of the experience.

To follow along and run the code locally, make sure you have the following in place:

- **Google Cloud account**: You must be able to create a new project and link a billing account. A valid credit card is required to enable services such as Vertex AI, even if you're operating within free-tier limits.
- **Google Cloud CLI (gcloud)**: Used to authenticate, configure the active project, and fetch access tokens from the terminal.
- **Python 3.8+ installed locally**: Required for running scripts, managing environments, and interacting with the Vertex AI SDK.
- **VS Code (or any Python-supporting IDE)**: We'll use VS Code throughout the workshop, but any editor that supports Python is fine.
- **Git installed**: You'll need it to clone the workshop repository from GitHub.

You can find all relevant project files for this chapter in the official GitHub repository at `https://github.com/PacktPublishing/Learn-Mistral-7B/tree/main/Chapter-11`.

Understanding Vertex AI

In this section, we will cover the theoretical grounds of Vertex AI. This will help us better understand the course of action and the deployment pipeline used during the practical workshop. While the hands-on steps show how to get things running, the concepts here will explain why those steps matter and how to approach similar challenges in your own projects.

We'll take a closer look at how Vertex AI fits into the broader **Google Cloud Platform** (**GCP**), the purpose of Model Garden, and how model access, pricing, and infrastructure are managed behind the scenes. You'll also learn the differences between synchronous and streaming inference, how requests are structured, and how authentication secures everything in motion.

This section is your foundation for thinking like an AI system builder, not just a user. To begin, let's explore the role of Vertex AI in the GCP ecosystem.

Vertex AI in the GCP ecosystem

Vertex AI is Google Cloud's platform that makes it easy to work with machine learning models—especially large ones like Mistral—without needing to worry about the underlying infrastructure. Instead of setting up your own servers, managing scaling, or configuring load balancers, Vertex AI handles all of that for you. You get an endpoint and can start sending prompts to your model right away.

What's great is how well it plays with the rest of Google Cloud. You can store your data in Cloud Storage, manage access using IAM, and even connect it to Kubernetes if needed. Everything's already wired together, which saves time and reduces setup mistakes. If your goal is to deploy a model and have it running in production—or just accessible for internal tools—Vertex AI gives you the tools to do that fast, without getting buried in DevOps. It's built to let you focus on the model, not the machinery.

Model Garden: Hosted LLMs at your fingertips

Model Garden is the easiest way to start using LLMs on Vertex AI, and it's exactly what we'll use in this workshop. It's a curated library of pre-hosted models such as Mistral, PaLM, and others from Hugging Face, already set up and ready to go. You don't need to build containers or configure hosting environments. Just pick a model, click **Enable**, and it becomes available in your project.

This approach is perfect for getting started quickly and focusing on what matters: sending prompts and handling responses. Pricing is usually based on how many tokens you send and receive, or how long the model runs. You'll need a billing account linked to your GCP project to activate usage, but once that's in place, setup is just a few clicks. For this workshop, Model Garden will be our entry point into deploying Mistral and interacting with it right away—no infrastructure required.

Deploying your own models to Vertex AI

If you're looking for full control over how your model is hosted and served, Vertex AI also supports deploying your own models—including larger variants such as Mistral 7B or your own fine-tuned versions. This is an advanced topic, and while it's not the core focus of this chapter, we touch on it in the *Extracurricular* section for those who want to explore it further.

The process involves building a Docker image, pushing it to Google Artifact Registry, and deploying it to an endpoint that runs on GPU infrastructure. You may also need to request a GPU quota from Google Cloud if your account doesn't already have one. This setup gives you maximum flexibility: you choose the model, the runtime, and how it's exposed.

To help you get started, we've included a sample `docker-compose.yml` file and related setup scripts in the GitHub repository for this book. If you're ready to go beyond pre-hosted models and want full control over the stack, this route gives you the freedom to run Mistral on your own terms.

Inference workflows

Inference is the core interaction with a language model, sending it a prompt and receiving a response. On Vertex AI, you have two main modes of doing this: synchronous and streaming. Each has its use case, and both are easy to implement once your setup is complete.

Synchronous inference gives you the entire response in one go. It's ideal for quick lookups, summarization, or any task where latency isn't a concern. The following example shows a synchronous inference request, where the entire response is returned at once after the prompt is processed:

```
resp = client.chat.complete(
    model=MODEL,
    messages=[{"role": "user", "content": "Summarize today's news."}]
)
print(resp.choices[0].message.content)
```

Streaming inference, on the other hand, returns tokens as they're generated. This is great for chatbots or real-time applications, where you want to start showing results before the full answer is ready. The next code snippet demonstrates streaming inference, where the model returns tokens incrementally so you can display partial results in real time:

```
stream = client.chat.stream(
    model=MODEL,
    messages=[{
```

```
        "role": "user",
        "content": "Tell me a story, one line at a time."}])

  for chunk in stream:
      print(chunk.data.choices[0].delta.content, end="")
```

Both options are supported in the same API, so switching between them is as simple as changing the method call. You'll use both during the workshop to get a feel for how they behave in real scenarios.

Structure of a model request

Every model call is built around a simple but flexible structure that includes the model name, a list of messages, and optional generation parameters. In Vertex AI's chat interface, messages are role-based—usually from the user or the assistant—and the model processes them as a conversation.

Here's the request format you will be using in this chapter's workshop:

```
resp = client.chat.complete(
    model=f"{MODEL}",
    messages=[
        {
            "role": "user",
            "content": "Who is the best French painter? in one short
sentence",
        }
    ],
)
```

In this example, we have the following:

- model specifies which model to use (such as mistral-small-2503)
- messages contain the actual prompt, including the sender role (user) and message content
- Optional parameters such as max_tokens or temperature can be added to control response length and creativity

The **response object (resp)** includes both the generated content and metadata such as token usage, which helps track output size and potential cost. You'll see this structure in every call throughout the workshop in this chapter.

Authentication and access in GCP

Authentication is a core part of working with Vertex AI, ensuring that only authorized users and services can interact with your models and resources. Google Cloud uses OAuth 2.0 under the hood, and for developers, this typically means generating and using access tokens. These tokens are scoped to your Google Cloud project, and permissions are enforced through **Identity and Access Management (IAM) roles**.

For interactive use, the easiest way to authenticate is with the gcloud CLI. Once you've logged in using gcloud auth login, you can retrieve an access token like this:

```
gcloud auth print-access-token
```

> gcloud is Google Cloud's command-line tool. We'll go through the installation and setup steps during the workshop.

This token is then included in the **Authorization** header of your HTTP requests or used within Python scripts. In the workshop, we retrieved the token programmatically using the following:

```python
import subprocess


def get_gcloud_access_token():
    process = subprocess.Popen(
        "gcloud auth print-access-token",
        stdout=subprocess.PIPE,
        stderr=subprocess.PIPE,
        shell=True
    )
    access_token_bytes, _ = process.communicate()
    return access_token_bytes.decode("utf-8").strip()
```

IAM roles determine what that token can do; whether it's allowed to invoke models, read from storage, or deploy new endpoints. Handling tokens securely and knowing when to refresh them is critical in production environments, especially for automation and long-running services.

Choosing the right development flow

Google Colab Enterprise provides a quick, zero-setup environment for working with models in Vertex AI. Because it's already connected to your Google Cloud project, authentication and API access are handled behind the scenes, making it ideal for early exploration, rapid prototyping, or testing model behavior without worrying about configuration.

That said, for more control and long-term development, local tools such as VS Code are essential. They give you full visibility into your code base, access to version control, and the ability to modularize your workflow. You can structure scripts, manage dependencies in virtual environments, debug with precision, and build code that's ready for automation or production.

This workshop supports both flows. You'll begin in Colab for ease of use, then switch to Python scripts in your local environment to build something maintainable, reusable, and real. Understanding when to use each environment helps you balance speed with scalability as your project grows.

Development best practices for AI integration

Building with language models isn't just about getting responses but also about creating maintainable, reusable code that can scale with your project. A good place to start is by modularizing your scripts. Keep your configuration, authentication, and inference logic in separate Python files. This keeps things clean, testable, and easy to change later.

For example, model and project settings should live in a config module:

```
# config.py
MODEL = "mistral-small-2503"
PROJECT_ID = "learnmistral"
LOCATION = "us-central1"
```

Authentication logic should be isolated in a helper:

```
# auth.py
def get_access_token():
    # subprocess call to gcloud token retriever
```

In your primary inference script, you can import the necessary constants and authentication method like this:

```
from config import MODEL, PROJECT_ID, LOCATION
from auth import get_access_token
```

We also strongly recommend using a Python **virtual environment** (**venv**) for this workshop. This keeps your dependencies scoped to the project and avoids cluttering your global Python environment:

```
python3 -m venv ./gcpenv
source ./gcpenv/bin/activate
```

> We will cover venv in more detail during the workshop.

By following these practices (modular code, project-scoped environments, and minimal hard-coding), you'll build AI integrations that are easier to debug, share, and scale over time.

Now that you've got the theory under your belt, it's time to bring it all to life. In this hands-on workshop, you'll spin up a real Vertex AI workflow—from cloud setup to Colab trials to Python-powered inference. Each step builds a modular, maintainable foundation for working confidently with hosted Mistral models in production-like environments.

Practical workshop: Fast-tracking Mistral apps with Vertex AI

Welcome to our workshop on deploying and interacting with Mistral AI models using Vertex AI. Think of this workshop as a guided journey, tailored specifically for developers who want to integrate powerful language models into their applications. We'll start by setting up our environment in Google Cloud, ensuring everything is configured properly. Next, we'll enable critical APIs that allow seamless communication between our application and the **Vertex AI** services.

Once the groundwork is complete, you'll deploy the Mistral model directly from the **Vertex AI Model Garden**, a curated repository of cutting-edge AI models. With your model live, the workshop will guide you through practical exercises in Google Colab Enterprise, offering hands-on experience with authentication, region selection, and project linking. You'll interact with Mistral models directly, using simple yet robust methods for running inference requests and handling responses.

Further along, the workshop explores advanced functionalities, such as streaming requests and leveraging the **Vertex SDK** for Python. We'll create and activate a venv, install the necessary dependencies, and authenticate our requests using Google's cloud **Command-Line Interface** (**CLI**).

Additionally, we'll learn how to structure inference requests programmatically, enhancing our understanding of integrating AI models into real-world software applications.

By the end of this journey, you'll have a clear grasp of deploying Mistral AI models, interacting with them through both interactive notebooks and backend Python scripts, and managing model life cycles in Google Cloud. Key results include a working Vertex AI environment, practical knowledge of API integration, hands-on coding experience with inference requests, and a deeper understanding of how AI models function within your development workflow.

What is needed

Before we start *Step 1*, please ensure you have the following prerequisites in place. You'll need a Google Cloud account; if you do not have one yet, create one at `https://console.cloud.google.com`.

Note that a valid credit card is required to set up a billing account, necessary to enable certain cloud services during our exercises.

Speaking of the code, you'll need access to the project files hosted on GitHub. Visit the main project repository for this chapter at `https://github.com/PacktPublishing/Learn-Mistral-7B/tree/main/Chapter-11`.

These files contain the full solutions we will code up in this workshop. They can be used as reference material in case of any issues. Be sure to download or clone the repository before starting. Add the `Chapter-11` folder to your existing VS Code project.

Step 1: The setup and preparation

In *Step 1*, we'll start by preparing our Google Cloud environment, establishing the foundational setup necessary for using Vertex AI effectively. First, let us create a dedicated project in our Google Cloud account, providing a centralized workspace for our exercises. Next, we'll activate key APIs, including the Vertex AI API, Cloud Resource Manager API, and IAM API, essential components for seamless integration with cloud services. We'll also connect our project to a billing account, enabling full access to all required Google Cloud resources.

Completing these initial setup tasks is critical for ensuring your environment is fully prepared for deploying and interacting with Mistral models.

Creating a Google Cloud project

Before deploying the Mistral model, you'll need a dedicated Google Cloud project. Follow these instructions to create a project named LearnMistral via the Google Cloud console:

1. Go to the Google Cloud console.

2. Click on the project selector field (top bar, left of the search bar). See *Figure 11.1.*

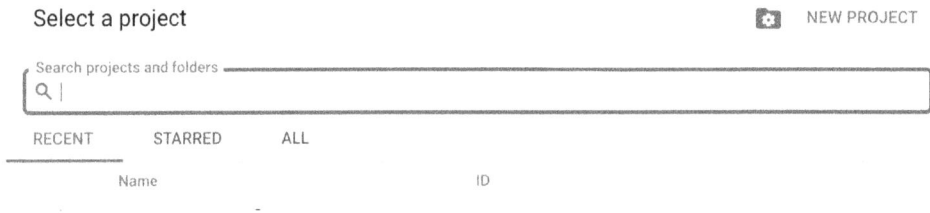

Figure 11.1: Project Selector

3. Click **NEW PROJECT**.

4. Name your project LearnMistral. Refer to *Figure 11.2.*

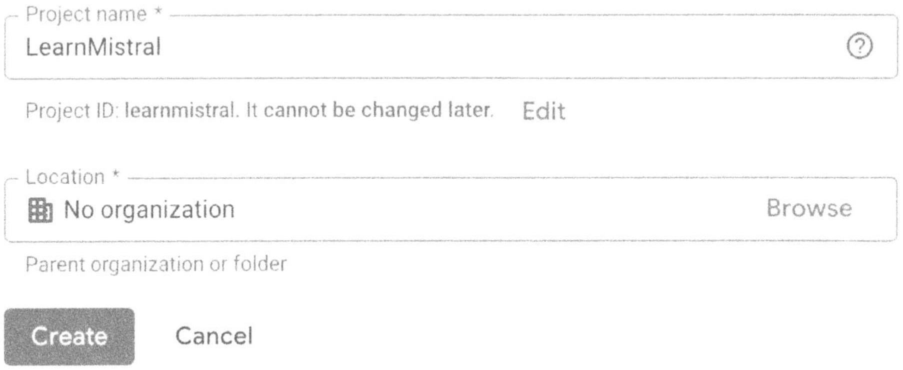

Figure 11.2: New project name

5. Choose a billing account if you have one configured already; if not, we will link it later.

6. Click **Create**.

7. Once created, click **Select Project** to open it.

After a Google Cloud project has been created, next we can enable the required APIs.

Enabling the required APIs

Next, we'll configure essential APIs required for our Google Cloud project to interact effectively with Vertex AI and manage resources. Activating these APIs ensures seamless communication and integration across our Google Cloud services, forming a critical foundation for deploying and using Mistral AI models in the upcoming tasks.

Take the following steps:

1. In the left menu, go to **APIs & Services | Library**.

2. Search for and enable these APIs one by one:

    - **Vertex AI API**

    - **Cloud Resource Manager API**

    - **IAM API**

You can locate APIs by clicking on the APIs card on the dashboard at `https://console.cloud.google.com/apis/dashboard?project=learnmistral`. Please refer to *Figure 11.3*.

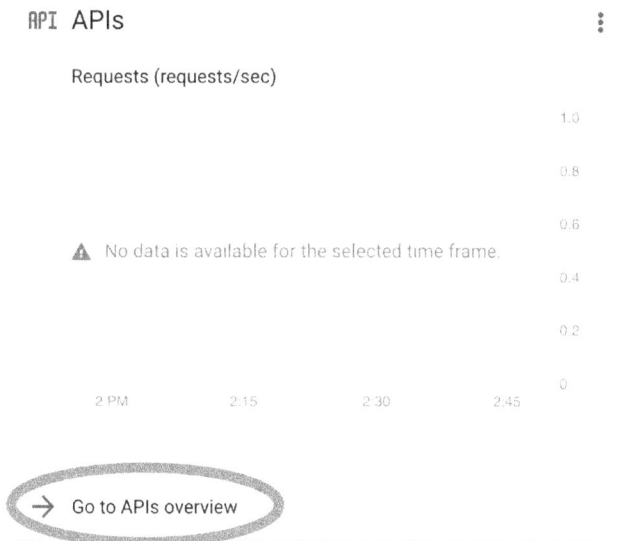

Figure 11.3: APIs card

Alternatively, this can be achieved by visiting the welcome page at `https://console.cloud..google.com/welcome?project=learnmistral` and selecting **APIs & Services**. Please see *Figure 11.4*.

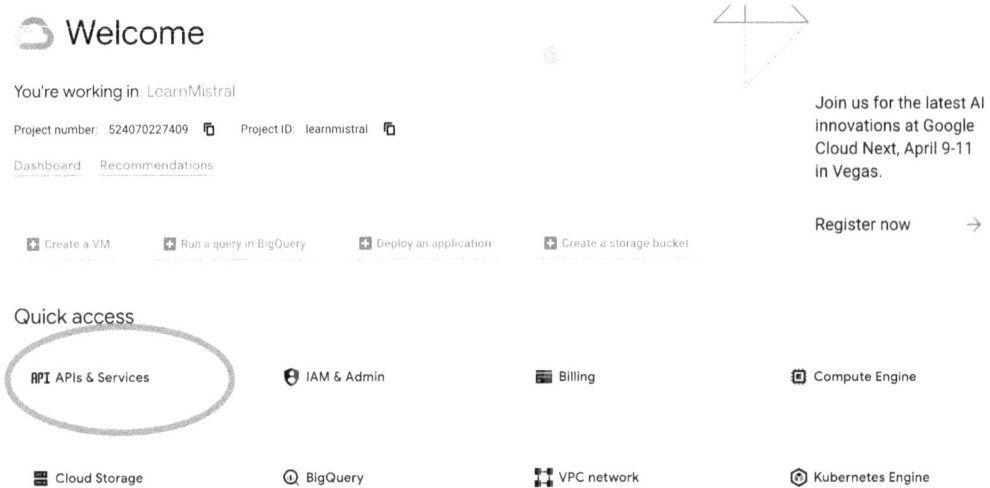

Figure 11.4: Welcome page – quick access

With APIs enabled, your project setup is nearly complete. Next, we will link a billing account, ensuring that all necessary Google Cloud services are accessible and active for the practical exercises ahead. This step is essential to proceed smoothly with model deployment and cloud resource management.

Linking a billing account

The purpose of this step is to link your Google Cloud project to a billing account. This ensures your cloud environment has full access to all of the necessary services, allowing the smooth deployment and management of resources throughout the workshop. Please follow these steps to set up billing in Google Cloud.

Go directly to the billing page at `https://console.cloud.google.com/billing`, as shown in *Figure 11.5*.

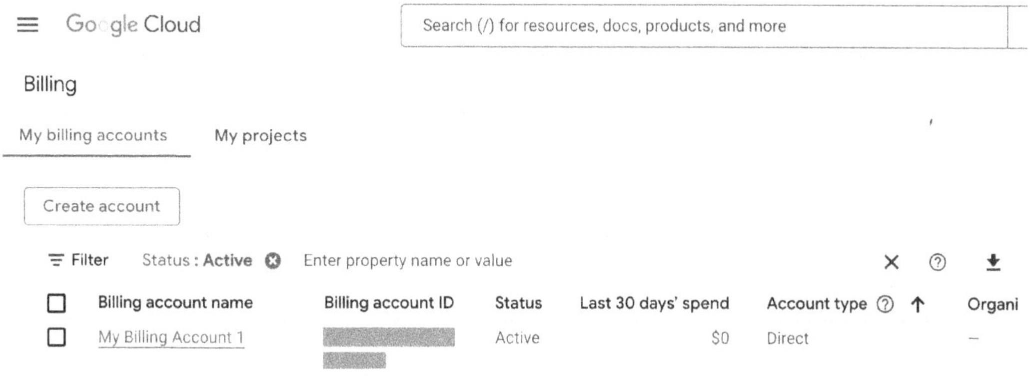

Figure 11.5: My billing accounts

Click **Create account** to set up a billing account if you do not already have one configured. Enter the new billing account name and choose your country, as demonstrated in *Figure 11.6*.

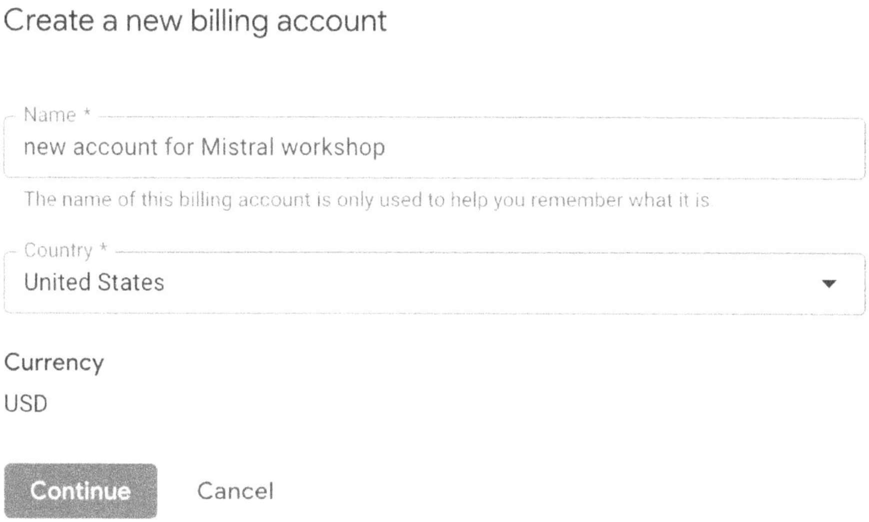

Figure 11.6: Create a new billing account

Next, press **Continue** to provide your payment method details, as illustrated in *Figure 11.7*.

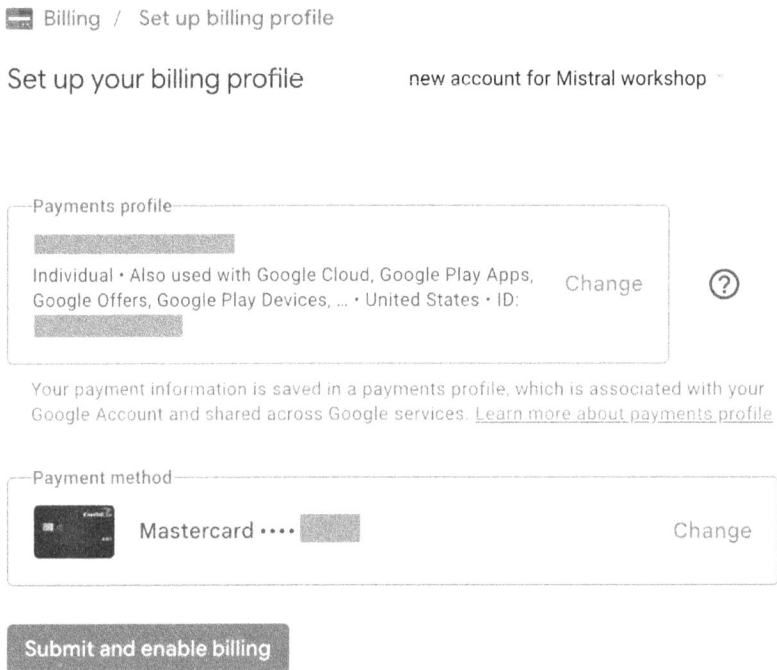

Billing / Set up billing profile

Set up your billing profile   new account for Mistral workshop

Payments profile

Individual · Also used with Google Cloud, Google Play Apps,   Change   ⑦
Google Offers, Google Play Devices, ... · United States · ID:

Your payment information is saved in a payments profile, which is associated with your
Google Account and shared across Google services. Learn more about payments profile

Payment method

Mastercard ····   Change

Submit and enable billing

Figure 11.7: Billing profile summary page

Once the billing account is created and your payment method is confirmed, you are ready to connect this billing account to your specific project. In the next step, we'll walk through how to link your newly created billing account to the LearnMistral project, completing the billing configuration required for using Vertex AI.

Linking a project to a billing account

Now that your billing account is active, the next step is to link it to your project. This connection allows your Google Cloud project to access all paid services, including those needed for Vertex AI and Mistral model deployment.

Begin by navigating to the welcome page of your project at the following URL: `https://console.cloud.google.com/welcome?inv=1&project=learnmistral`. Please refer to *Figure 11.8* to locate the **Billing** section.

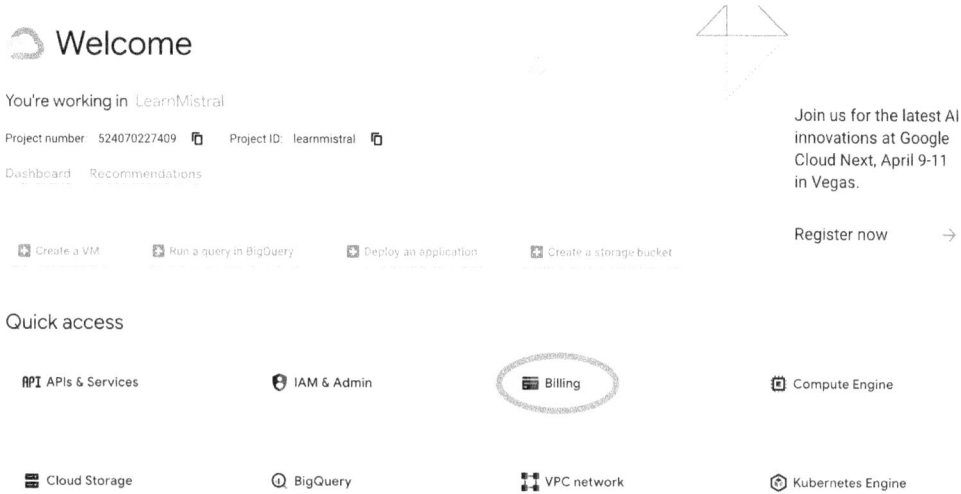

Figure 11.8: Welcome page – quick access to Billing

Click on **Billing** or go directly to the linked billing page at `https://console.cloud.google.com/billing/linkedaccount?project=learnmistral`. See *Figure 11.9* for the linked account view:

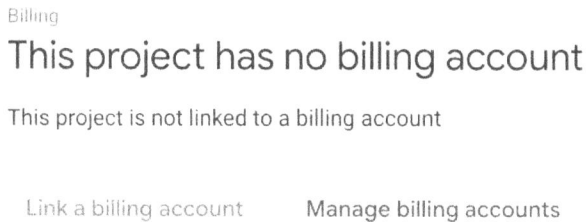

Figure 11.9: Project is initially not linked to a billing account

Once there, hit **Link a billing account**, and you should be taken to the next screen, as illustrated in *Figure 11.10*:

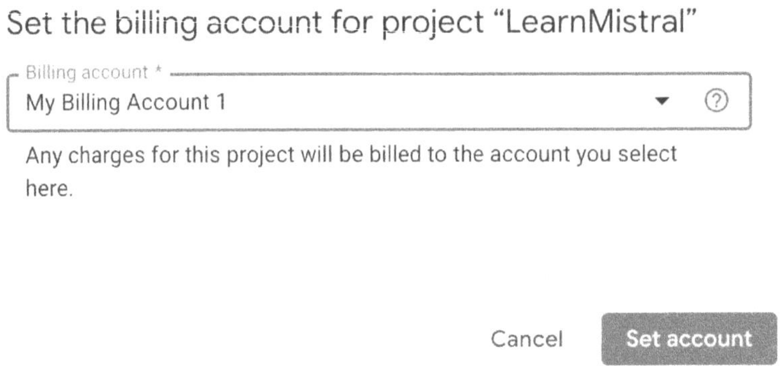

Set the billing account for project "LearnMistral"

Billing account *
My Billing Account 1   ▾   ⓘ

Any charges for this project will be billed to the account you select here.

Cancel   **Set account**

Figure 11.10: Select the billing account for the project

Select your billing account from the list and click **Set account** to confirm the link. This finalizes the billing configuration for your project.

Billing is now properly linked, and it's time to move forward and enable the APIs and services needed to run Mistral models through Vertex AI.

Enabling APIs and services

With your billing account linked, your project is ready to activate the essential APIs that power interactions with Vertex AI. These APIs will allow your application to run models, manage permissions, and access cloud resources—all core components of the Mistral workflow.

Let's walk through enabling them one by one:

1. You can begin by opening the **APIs & Services** console directly at `https://console.cloud.google.com/apis/dashboard?project=learnmistral`. This brings you to the main dashboard where API activity and access permissions are managed. Alternatively, if you're on your project's welcome page (`https://console.cloud.google.com/welcome?inv=1&project=learnmistral`), you can simply click on **APIs & Services** from the **Quick access** area. This will redirect you to the same dashboard.

2. Next, click the **Enable APIs and services** button. This opens the API library, where you can search for and activate the services required. Please refer to *Figure 11.11* for the button location.

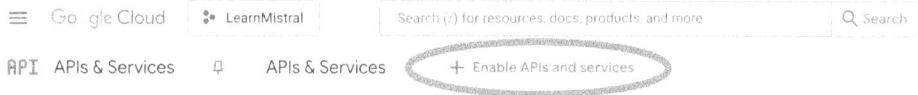

Figure 11.11: APIs & Services – Enable APIs and services

In the search bar, type Vertex AI API, then open its details page. Click **ENABLE** to activate it for your project. This API allows your environment to access and run Mistral models. Please refer to *Figure 11.12* for visual guidance.

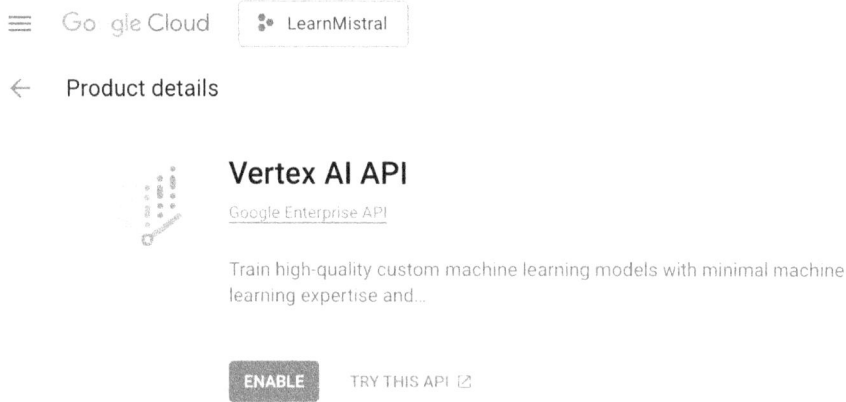

Figure 11.12: Vertex AI API

If you haven't completed the billing setup properly, you may encounter a message prompting you to enable billing. Confirm and select your billing account if requested. See *Figure 11.13* to see how this prompt looks.

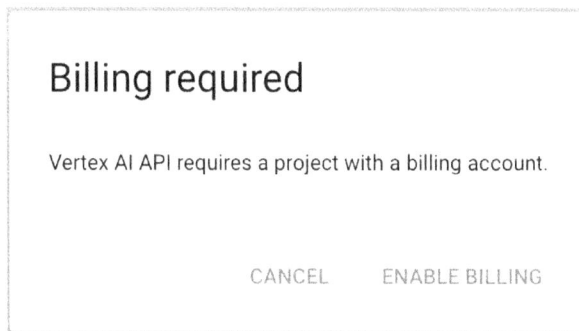

Figure 11.13: Billing required message

3. Now search for Cloud Resource Manager API in the API library. The **Cloud Resource Manager API** is a foundational service in Google Cloud that enables you to programmatically manage the structure and access control of your cloud resources. It allows you to organize projects into folders and organizations, apply IAM policies, and maintain consistent governance. Activating it is essential for working securely and efficiently within GCP. Once the page opens, click **ENABLE**. Refer to *Figure 11.14*.

> The **Cloud Resource Manager API** in GCP helps organize projects and enforce access policies across your cloud resources. Paired with **Identity and Access Management (IAM)**, it controls who can do what. These mirror AWS organizations and AWS IAM, letting you manage project boundaries and permissions at scale across teams and services.

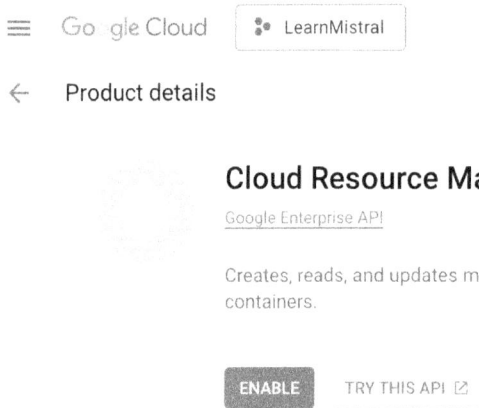

Figure 11.14: Cloud Resource Manager API

4. Lastly, search for the IAM API. This service is essential for managing roles, credentials, and access control to your Vertex AI resources. Once found, click **ENABLE** on its page as well.

After enabling these APIs, your project is fully prepared to interact securely and efficiently with Vertex AI. The next step will take you into **Model Garden**, where you'll deploy the Mistral model directly into your cloud environment.

Deploying Mistral from Model Garden

We are now ready to deploy the Mistral model into the Google Cloud environment. This next step will make the model available for testing and inference through Vertex AI. We'll guide you through locating the model in Model Garden and enabling it for your project. Let's get started:

1. Start by opening the Vertex AI interface in your Google Cloud console at `https://console.cloud.google.com/vertex-ai?project=learnmistral`. From the left-hand menu, navigate to **Vertex AI** | **Model Garden** or use the search bar at the top to search for `Garden` or `Model Garden`. Please refer to *Figure 11.15* for the navigation layout.

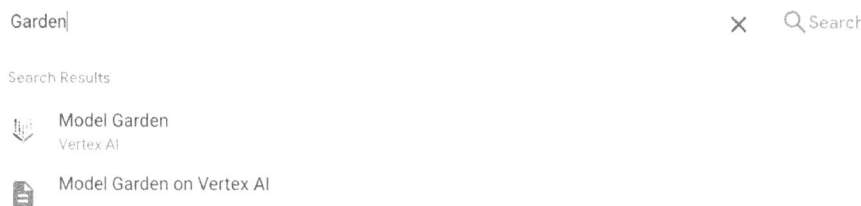

Figure 11.15: Search for "Garden" in the search bar

2. In the search bar within Model Garden, type `Mistral` to locate available models. Look specifically for **Mistral Small 3.1**. This model is optimized for lighter inference use cases and is a great starting point for experimentation. See *Figure 11.16* for the search result view.

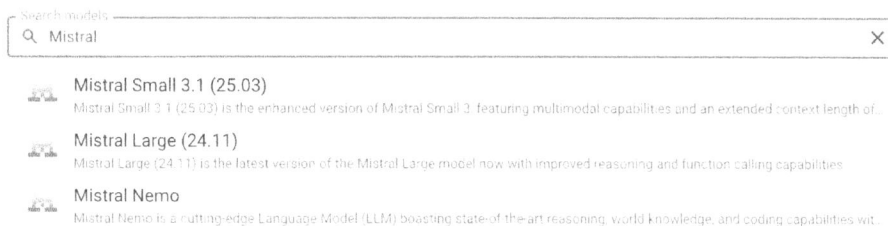

Figure 11.16: Search models

Click on the model card to view its details. The layout of the model card interface is shown in *Figure 11.17*.

Figure 11.17: Model card

3. In the model details page, click the **Enable** button to activate the model for your project. You'll be prompted to review and agree to a purchase order. See *Figure 11.18* for the purchase confirmation screen.

Purchase summary
Agree to the following details and terms to enable this product

Project
LearnMistral
Update a project from the project selector on top navigation bar

Pricing
Usage fee
Usage fee is billed every month

Input Tokens ?

                                                        USD 0.10
                                                        /1M tokens
Output Tokens ?

If you pay in a currency other than USD, the prices listed in your currency on Google Cloud SKUs apply. Please refer to Google Cloud Price List for the latest pricing.

Terms
Terms and agreements

☑ By purchasing, deploying, accessing, or using this product, you acknowledge that Google is the merchant of record and Vendor's reseller with respect to this transaction and you agree to comply with the Google Cloud Marketplace Terms of Service, Mistral AI Terms of Service and the terms of applicable open source software licenses bundled with the product.

AGREE

Figure 11.18: Purchase summary

After accepting the terms, you'll see a confirmation that the model service was successfully activated. Refer to *Figure 11.19* for the success message layout.

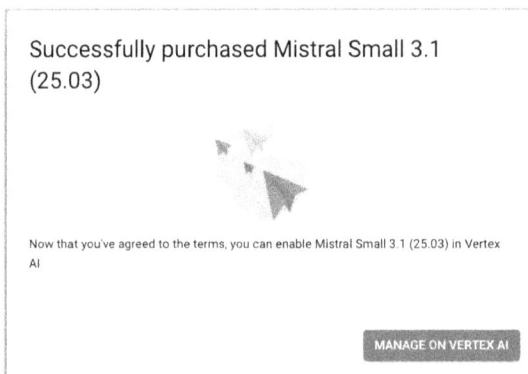

Successfully purchased Mistral Small 3.1 (25.03)

Now that you've agreed to the terms, you can enable Mistral Small 3.1 (25.03) in Vertex AI

MANAGE ON VERTEX AI

Figure 11.19: Success screen

Please note that the cost of using this model is usage-based and calculated by the number of tokens processed. The overall cost for this workshop is expected to be less than $5 USD. For the most accurate and updated pricing, visit the official pricing page at `https://cloud.google.com/vertex-ai/generative-ai/pricing`.

At the time of writing, **Mistral Small** is priced at just a fraction of a dollar per million input tokens and slightly more per million output tokens—making it a highly cost-effective option for experimentation and learning in this workshop setting.

The model is now enabled, and your core environment setup is complete. You've successfully created a project, linked a billing account, enabled the necessary APIs, and deployed a ready-to-use Mistral model into your cloud workspace. This solid foundation will support all the hands-on activities that follow.

Next, you'll move into Google Colab Enterprise to interact directly with the Mistral model.

Step 2: Playing with the model in Google Colab Enterprise

Your cloud environment is now fully prepared, and the Mistral model is live. Let's shift focus to hands-on interaction. In this step, you'll launch a Google Colab Enterprise notebook, tailored to your project and pre-configured with the most recent Mistral models. The walk-through starts with authenticating your session and selecting the model version and region.

As you proceed through the notebook, you'll initialize the runtime environment, then move on to sending your first prompt to the model. You'll also try out a streaming call to experience how responses can be returned in real time. These exercises build a strong foundation for working with LLMs interactively and give you a feel for the model's behavior in action.

Opening a Colab notebook

In this step, you'll access and launch a **Colab Enterprise** notebook directly from the Mistral model card within the **Vertex AI Model Garden**. This notebook is autogenerated by Google based on your selected model and is already tied to your project. If any required APIs are still disabled, you'll be prompted to activate them. Once opened, the notebook provides a fully configured workspace where you can interact with the Mistral model without needing to write setup code or manage dependencies manually.

Take the following steps:

1. From your Vertex AI console, navigate to the model card you enabled earlier in Model Garden. This interface gives you access to the pre-integrated Google Colab Enterprise environment. Refer to *Figure 11.20* to locate the notebook launch option on the model card.

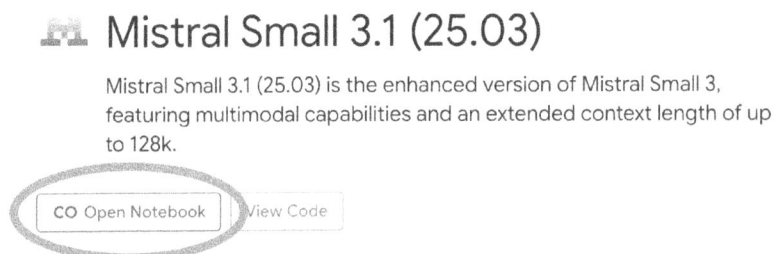

ᴍ Mistral Small 3.1 (25.03)

Mistral Small 3.1 (25.03) is the enhanced version of Mistral Small 3, featuring multimodal capabilities and an extended context length of up to 128k.

CO Open Notebook   View Code

Figure 11.20: Model card – Open Notebook

2. Now, enable missing APIs if prompted. As the notebook initializes, it may prompt you to enable additional APIs that haven't yet been activated. This step ensures your environment has full permissions to execute the code embedded in the notebook. See *Figure 11.21* for how this message appears.

Enable required APIs

ⓘ   To use Colab Enterprise, you need to enable the following APIs.

Vertex AI API ☑ ⑦	✅ Enabled
Dataform API ☑ ⑦	✅ Enabled
Compute Engine API ☑ ⑦	⊙ Not enabled

Send feedback   Cancel   Enable

Figure 11.21: Enable missing APIs

Once launched, the notebook is pre-generated by Google based on the selected Mistral model and your active project. It contains all the setup code, including environment bindings and sample inference calls. Refer to *Figure 11.22* for a preview of this notebook interface.

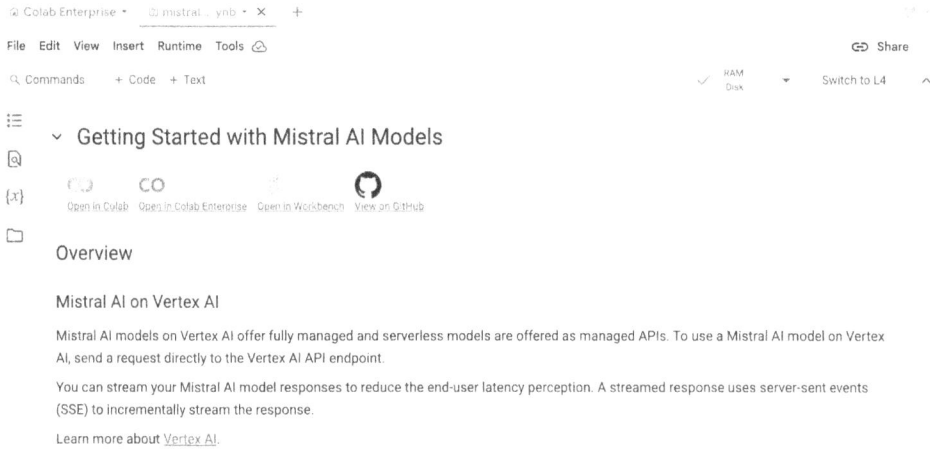

Figure 11.22: Getting Started with Mistral AI Models Colab notebook

> The notebook content itself is not part of our GitHub repository. It is dynamically generated by Google to reflect the latest Mistral model versions available in Model Garden and is already bound to your selected project, saving you manual configuration time.

At this point, your interactive notebook is ready and synced with your Google Cloud project. You've launched a fully equipped environment tailored for your selected Mistral model. This low-friction setup allows you to explore model capabilities without extra installation steps or manual integration work, which is ideal for rapid testing and hands-on learning.

The next step takes you inside the notebook, where you'll authenticate your session. This ensures that your code can securely access Vertex AI services and start communicating with the Mistral model using your cloud credentials.

Running the first step: authenticate user

Once the notebook has fully loaded, scroll to the first executable code cell. This block is designed to authenticate your Colab session with Google Cloud so it can access your Vertex AI resources. You'll see the authentication snippet shown in *Figure 11.23*.

> ∨   Authenticate your notebook environment (Colab only)

```
[1]  import sys

     if "google.colab" in sys.modules:
         from google.colab import auth

     auth.authenticate_user()
```

Figure 11.23: Authentication code block for Colab only

The first two lines of the code check whether the notebook is running in a Google Colab environment. It does this by verifying the presence of "google.colab" in the list of currently loaded Python modules:

```
if "google.colab" in sys.modules:
    from google.colab import auth
```

If this condition is met, it proceeds to import Colab's authentication utility:

```
auth.authenticate_user()
```

In Google Colab Enterprise, authentication is typically handled automatically as part of the workspace context. Running this code may trigger a warning, but it won't interrupt anything. The warning message looks like this:

```
WARNING: google.colab.auth.authenticate_user() is not supported in Colab
Enterprise.
```

You can safely ignore the message. It simply means the notebook is already authenticated through your organizational session, and no manual sign-in is required.

After running the authentication block, your session is now fully authorized to access Vertex AI services behind the scenes. Even if a warning appears, your notebook is ready and connected. No additional manual authentication is needed at this point.

Selecting the Mistral model

Before sending your first prompt, the next step is to select the specific Mistral model and version you want to work with. Choosing the right model ensures your requests are routed correctly and your experiments are consistent with the workshop flow.

Take the following steps:

1. Scroll to the section of the notebook where available Mistral models are listed in a drop-down or variable assignment block. This is where you'll choose which model to work with during the session. Refer to *Figure 11.24* for an overview of the selection interface.

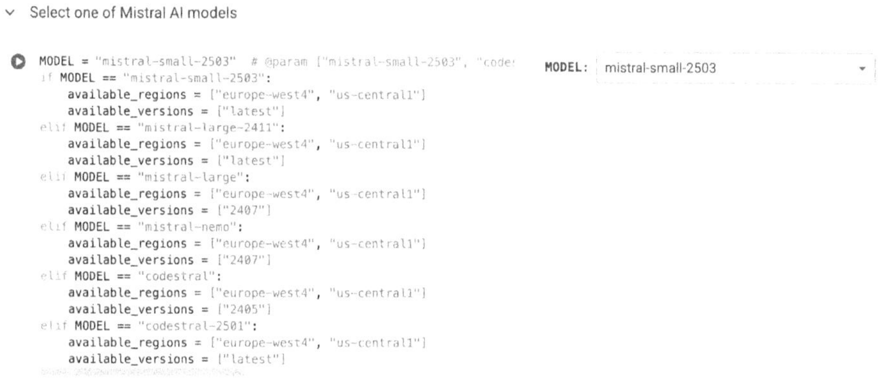

Figure 11.24: Model selection code block and UI

This section of code doesn't carry any functional logic for inference—its main role is to help initialize a few key variables. You could replace this entire block with a simple manual assignment such as the following:

```
MODEL = "mistral-small-2503"
available_regions = ["europe-west4", "us-central1"]
available_versions = ["latest"]
```

However, using the dropdown ensures alignment with what's currently supported in your environment.

2. Among the available options, select **mistral-small-2503** or the latest equivalent listed in your notebook. This is a lightweight, high-performance model suitable for quick inference and experimentation. Depending on version updates, the numeric suffix might differ slightly, but the small variant is generally recommended for workshop use.

3. Once selected, this model will be passed into the notebook's subsequent logic for region matching and inference. You don't need to modify any code manually—simply choosing from the provided interface is enough to set the active model.

Your environment is now linked to a specific Mistral model. This selection determines what version of the model will respond to your prompts during the session. It's a critical step, as different models may offer variations in output style, speed, or cost, depending on your use case.

Running the region selection widget

To complete your configuration, you'll now select a deployment region. This next step introduces a widget that helps you match your model to an available region and version, ensuring proper routing of your inference requests.

Take the following steps:

1. Continue scrolling in the Colab notebook until you reach the section designed to help you choose a deployment region and model version. This section uses interactive widgets to guide your selection. Refer to *Figure 11.25* for the code cell containing the dropdown UI:

```python
import ipywidgets as widgets
from IPython.display import display

dropdown_loc = widgets.Dropdown(
    options=available_regions,
    description="Select a location:",
    font_weight="bold",
    style={"description_width": "initial"},
)
```

Figure 11.25: Region selection block

While this code provides a user-friendly interface, it doesn't perform any logic essential to the workshop's functionality. If needed, you could bypass the widget and assign the values directly using the following:

```python
LOCATION = "us-central1"
MODEL_VERSION = "latest"
```

Running the cell will display two dropdowns: one for selecting the region where your model will be hosted, and another for specifying the model version (if applicable). These choices ensure compatibility between the model variant and the available infrastructure. The widget output is displayed in *Figure 11.26*.

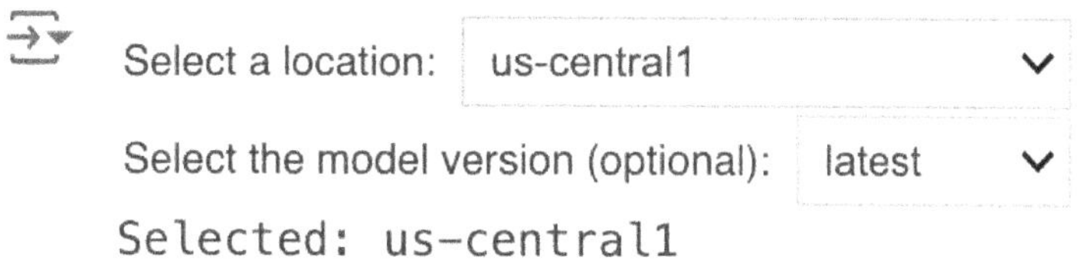

Select a location: us-central1   ⌄

Select the model version (optional):   latest   ⌄

Selected: us-central1

Figure 11.26: UI widget for selection of the location and version

Any region or model version listed in the dropdown should work. The suggested location is typically the one geographically closest to you to reduce latency. The suggested version is the most up-to-date available in Model Garden and is recommended for compatibility and performance.

2. From the dropdowns, choose a supported region—typically **us-central1** or **europe-west4**. For most users, selecting **latest** as the version is sufficient, unless a specific release is required for compatibility or testing.

At this point, you've chosen where your model will run and which version to use. These variables are now ready to be passed into your API calls and will guide the routing of all future inference requests.

Running the project selection widget

In this next step, you'll link your notebook to a specific project by providing its ID. This binds your session to the right billing and model context, unlocking full access to your cloud-hosted Mistral deployment.

Take the following steps:

1. Continue down in the Colab notebook until you reach the section where your Google Cloud project ID is specified. This step is necessary for routing all API calls and billing under the correct cloud environment. The interface allows you to enter your project ID through a form input. Refer to *Figure 11.27* for how the widget appears in the notebook.

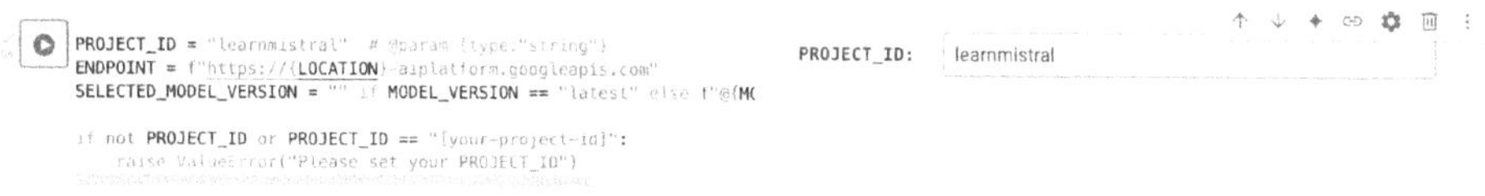

```
PROJECT_ID = "learnmistral"  # @param {type:"string"}              PROJECT_ID:   learnmistral
ENDPOINT = f"https://{LOCATION}-aiplatform.googleapis.com"
SELECTED_MODEL_VERSION = "" if MODEL_VERSION == "latest" else f"@{MC

if not PROJECT_ID or PROJECT_ID == "[your-project-id]":
    raise ValueError("Please set your PROJECT_ID")
```

Figure 11.27: Project selection block

While the cell is designed to dynamically assemble endpoint variables and validate project input, the functionality is straightforward. You could simplify this block with the following three lines of manual initialization:

```
PROJECT_ID = "learnmistral"
ENDPOINT = f"https://{LOCATION}-aiplatform.googleapis.
com"
SELECTED_MODEL_VERSION="""
```

2. The default value shown is `learnmistral`. If you're using a different project, make sure to update it accordingly in the input form. This step guarantees your API requests are authorized and scoped to the correct environment.

3. The cell also includes a basic check: if the project ID is left blank or still set to the place-holder value [`your-project-id`], it will raise `ValueError`. This prevents any accidental misconfiguration before moving forward.

Your Colab notebook is now tied to the correct Google Cloud project. This ensures all future calls to Vertex AI are properly routed, authenticated, and billed. Your environment is now fully defined and ready to interact with the Mistral model through code.

Since the configuration is now out of the way, we can shift focus to executing code. In the next step, you'll import the required libraries that make it possible to send HTTP requests, handle authentication tokens, and manage model responses programmatically.

Importing required libraries

Now that your configuration is complete, it's time to import the essential Python libraries that support your interaction with the model. These libraries handle HTTP communication, token retrieval, and JSON processing—everything you need to interact with Vertex AI from code:

```
import json
import subprocess
import requests
```

These imports are minimal but powerful. `json` is used to structure the payloads you send to the model. `subprocess` helps retrieve your active Google Cloud access token. `requests` is the HTTP client used to send those payloads to the Vertex AI endpoint.

This small block sets the foundation for every request you'll make. Without these imports, the subsequent inference code won't function. Treat this as the backbone of all the logic you're about to run.

All the essential libraries are now in place. You've laid the groundwork for communication between your notebook and the deployed Mistral model via Vertex AI. From here, you can start constructing and sending real prompts. This is where your setup pays off and Mistral begins responding to your input in real time.

Running the inference requests

You'll begin by preparing a simple JSON payload—a structured question the model can understand. Then, you'll send that payload using a cURL command to see how Vertex AI responds in real time. Once that's working, you'll re-run the request using Python to pretty-print the response and make output handling easier. Finally, we'll explore more advanced features, such as streaming, enabling you to experience how Mistral handles conversational flow dynamically and returns results as they're generated.

Preparing the payload

Before you can send a request to the model, you need to define what you're asking it to do. This is done by creating a structured payload—a dictionary that contains the model name, user message, output length, and streaming preference. Once defined, the dictionary is serialized into JSON format, which is the expected structure for Vertex AI API requests:

```
PAYLOAD = {
    "model": MODEL,
    "messages": [{
        "role": "user", "content": "who is the best French painter?"
    }],
    "max_tokens": 100,
    "stream": False,
}

request = json.dumps(PAYLOAD)
```

The "model" key refers to the identifier of your deployed Mistral instance. The "messages" field is an array where each entry mimics a chat message; here, we simulate a single user asking a question. "max_tokens" defines the maximum length of the response, while "stream" set to False means the response will be returned all at once rather than in chunks.

This small block is critical—it's your query wrapper, defining both the content of your prompt and how you expect the model to respond.

You've now created the payload that tells the Mistral model what to do. It includes your question and some configuration parameters, and it's formatted correctly to be sent over the wire.

In the next step, you'll take this payload and use a cURL command to send it directly to the Vertex AI endpoint. This will be your first full round-trip request, where a live response is returned from the Mistral model.

Running the cURL request to the model

Scroll down to the next code cell in your Colab notebook. This section sends the JSON payload you previously prepared directly to the Mistral model hosted in Vertex AI. The command uses cURL—a simple yet powerful tool for making HTTP requests from the terminal or notebook shell:

```
!curl -X POST \
-H "Authorization: Bearer $(gcloud auth print-access-token)" \
-H "Content-Type: application/json" \
{ENDPOINT}/v1/projects/{PROJECT_ID}/locations/{LOCATION}/publishers/
mistralai/models/{MODEL}{MODEL_VERSION}:rawPredict \
-d '{request}'
```

This command constructs a POST request targeting your model's REST endpoint. It includes the proper authorization header (by retrieving your access token through gcloud), sets the content type to JSON, and passes along your serialized request payload. Once executed, the model processes your input and returns a response in JSON format.

You should receive a valid JSON response with no errors. The output contains a generated message under the "content" key, along with metadata such as token usage and response structure. A successful response might look like the following example:

```
{..."content":"Determining the \"best\" French painter can be subjective
and depends on personal preferences, as well as the criteria one uses
to define \"best\" (e.g., historical significance, technical skill,
innovation, etc.). However, several French painters are frequently cited
as among the greatest:\n\n1. **Claude Monet** - Often considered the
father of Impressionism, Monet's work is renowned for its use of light
and color to capture the fleeting effects of the natural world.\n\n2.
**"},...}
```

The response has been shrunk to minimal attributes showing the successful inference.

You've now completed your first live interaction with the Mistral model via Vertex AI. This low-level method is great for understanding how HTTP requests work behind the scenes and gives you full control over how data is passed and returned.

To make results easier to read and handle, you'll now re-run the same request using Python and display the model's response in a more structured, human-friendly format. This is especially helpful when parsing or debugging model output.

Running the request with the response pretty printed

Instead of relying on cURL for inference, this block performs the same request using Python's `requests` library. This approach allows for better error handling, cleaner output, and easier integration into larger code bases. If you're planning to expand or embed model calls into real applications, this method is far more scalable:

```python
# Get the access token
process = subprocess.Popen(
    "gcloud auth print-access-token", stdout=subprocess.PIPE, shell=True)

(access_token_bytes, err) = process.communicate()

access_token = access_token_bytes.decode("utf-8").strip() # Strip newline

# Define query headers
headers = {
    "Authorization": f"Bearer {access_token}",
    "Accept": "application/json",
}

# Replace with your actual values
url = f"{ENDPOINT}/v1/projects/{PROJECT_ID}/locations/{LOCATION}/
publishers/mistralai/models/{MODEL}{SELECTED_MODEL_VERSION}:rawPredict"

data = {
    "model": MODEL,
```

```python
    "messages": [{"role": "user",
        "content": "who is the best French painter?"}],
    "stream": False,
}


# Make the POST request
response = requests.post(url, headers=headers, json=data)


# Check status code and try to parse the response as JSON
if response.status_code == 200:
  try:
    response_dict = response.json()
    print(response_dict["choices"][0]["message"]["content"])
  except json.JSONDecodeError as e:
    print("Error decoding JSON:", e)
    print("Raw response:", response.text)
# Print raw response if parsing fails
else:
    print(f"Request failed with status code: {response.status_code}")
```

The process begins by programmatically retrieving your current access token using gcloud. That token is inserted into the request headers, which are then used to POST the payload to the Vertex AI endpoint. If the request succeeds, it attempts to parse and print only the relevant part of the model's response—just the assistant's message. If anything goes wrong, the script provides helpful output for troubleshooting.

The output from this request will resemble the earlier cURL response but formatted cleanly in your notebook output area. You should see a short paragraph, potentially listing notable French painters such as Monet or Cézanne, based on your original prompt:

```
Determining the "best" French painter can be subjective and depends on
personal preferences, as well as the criteria one uses to define "best"
(e.g., historical significance, technical skill, innovation, or personal
appreciation). However, several French painters are frequently cited for
their significant contributions to art:

1. **Claude Monet**: Known as the founder of French Impressionist ...
2. **Paul Cézanne**: Often referred to as the "father of modern art...
3. **Edgar Degas**: Known for his paintings, sculptures, prints, and
```

```
drawings
4. **Henri Matisse**: Matisse is known for his use of color...
5. **Pablo Picasso**: His work is famous through his co-founding of
Cubism.
6. **Édouard Manet**: Often considered a bridge between Realism and
Impressionism ...
```

> The response has been shrunk in multiple places and serves primarily to show the structure of the message.

This step gives you a more robust and readable way to interact with the model programmatically. Using Python code allows you to go beyond basic prompts and start thinking in terms of building features, testing variations, or integrating responses into more complex workflows.

Next, we'll let you try more advanced interactions—specifically, streaming requests. Instead of waiting for the full response to be generated and returned all at once, you'll see the model stream its output in real time, simulating a more conversational or dynamic user experience.

Playing further with more features

The notebook doesn't stop here—there's plenty more for you to explore on your own. Take a few moments to scroll down and try out some of the additional features included in the demo. You'll find working examples of streaming calls, which return responses in real time, as well as use cases involving Codestral models and **Fill-in-the-Middle (FiM)** prompting. It's a great chance to experiment, tweak parameters, and see how the models behave in different contexts. Don't hesitate to play around—you've already set everything up, so now it's your sandbox.

Now that you've explored the notebook interface and run both standard and streaming inference requests, it's time to take things to the next level.

Step 3: Using Mistral AI's Vertex SDK for Python

You've experienced how powerful and convenient the **Colab Enterprise** environment can be—but now it's time to bring that power to your own machine. In this part of the workshop, we'll leave the notebook behind and shift into a developer-native setup using **VS Code** and the **terminal**.

You'll start by installing the Google Cloud CLI and initializing your environment—just like you might've done before with the AWS CLI. From there, you'll create a clean Python venv, install the required packages, and authenticate your session with gcloud.

Once the setup is complete, we'll define the variables we'll use throughout the workshop—such as MODEL, LOCATION, and PROJECT_ID—and run real inference requests directly from Python. We'll first send a synchronous request and get an immediate response, then follow that with a **streaming request**, which delivers results token by token in real time.

This part of the journey mirrors how real production systems interact with Mistral through Vertex AI, giving you practical tools and workflows to bring back to your projects. Let's move from experimentation to integration.

Setting up the gcloud CLI

Before moving to local Python scripts, you need to set up the gcloud CLI to allow your machine to interact securely with Google Cloud services. In this step, you'll install the CLI tool if needed, authenticate your Google account, and run the gcloud init process to configure your environment. You'll also select the active project you created earlier, making sure that all future API calls and deployments are correctly associated. This setup is essential for managing authentication tokens, interacting with Vertex AI, and running inference requests outside of Colab in a fully controlled environment.

Initial installation of the gcloud CLI

- **Option 1: Choose your installation method based on the OS**

  Before you can interact with Google Cloud from your terminal, you'll need to install the gcloud CLI. This tool provides a command-line interface for initializing your environment, managing projects, and sending API requests. If you're on Windows or Mac, visit the official installation guide and download the appropriate version for your system:

  - For Windows: https://cloud.google.com/sdk/docs/install#windows
  - For macOS: https://cloud.google.com/sdk/docs/install#mac

- **Option 2: Use Homebrew for quick install (Mac only)**

  If you're on macOS and have Homebrew installed, the quickest way to install gcloud is to run the following command in your terminal:

  ```
  brew install --cask google-cloud-sdk
  ```

  This method handles the download and setup for you. Additional documentation on this method is available here: https://formulae.brew.sh/cask/gcloud-cli.

After installation, it's important to restart your terminal shell to ensure the gcloud CLI is properly loaded into your system's path. This allows you to run gcloud commands from any terminal window moving forward.

The gcloud CLI is installed and ready to use on your machine. This tool will be your gateway to authenticating with Google Cloud, selecting projects, and managing Mistral model interactions through the command line.

Now we are ready to authenticate the session and select the active project we'll use throughout the workshop. This step mirrors what we did earlier in the Colab notebook, but this time we'll be doing it locally via the terminal. Let's initialize our CLI environment.

Initializing, authenticating, and selecting an active project

Now that you've moved into your local development environment, it's time to initialize the Google Cloud CLI. Take the following steps:

1. Open your terminal and run the following command:

    ```
    gcloud init
    ```

    This launches an interactive flow that walks you through configuration, authentication, and project selection. Refer to *Figure 11.28* for what this setup prompt looks like.

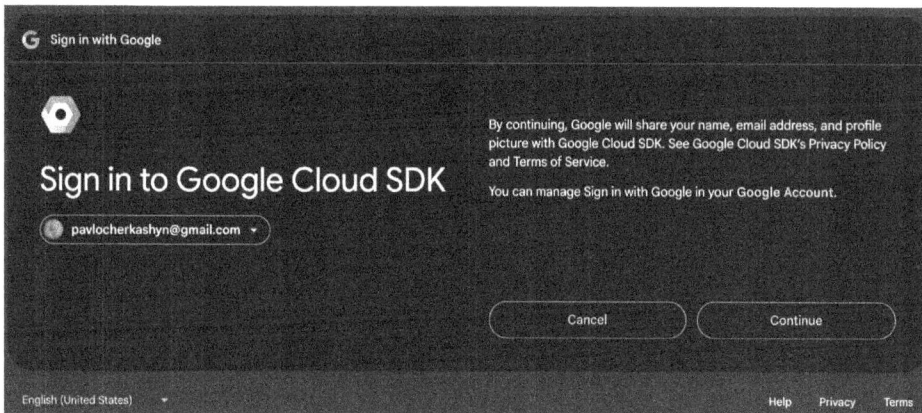

Figure 11.28: Sign in to Google Cloud SDK

2. After the diagnostic check is complete, you'll be prompted to sign in. Google will open a browser window for you to authenticate your identity and allow access to your account. Once redirected, click Continue, as shown in *Figure 11.28*.

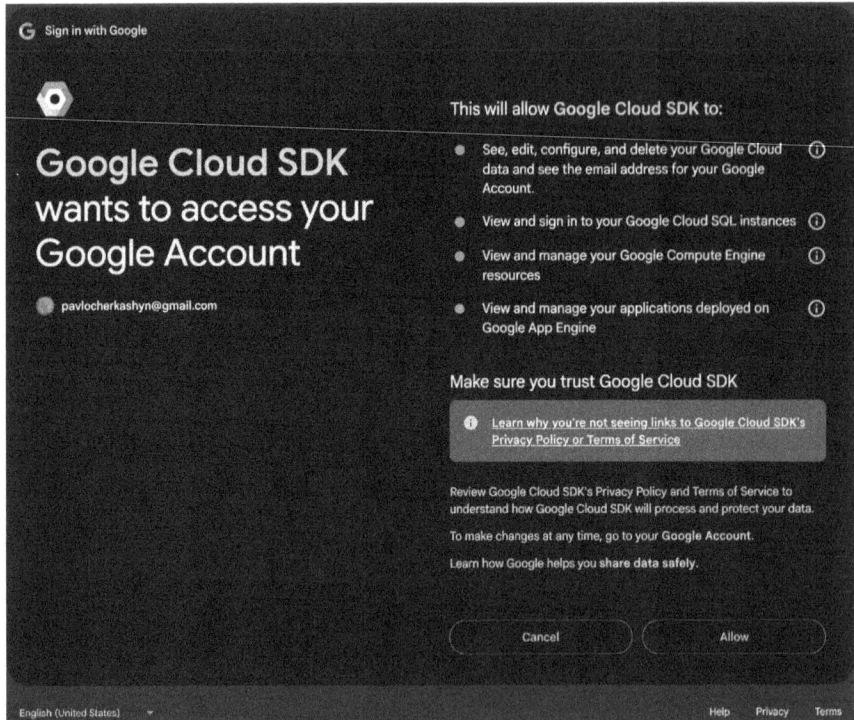

Figure 11.29: Authorization screen

3.   After confirming, you'll be asked to allow the Google Cloud SDK to access your project
     data and credentials. This step completes the authentication process. Refer to *Figure 11.29*
     for the authorization screen.

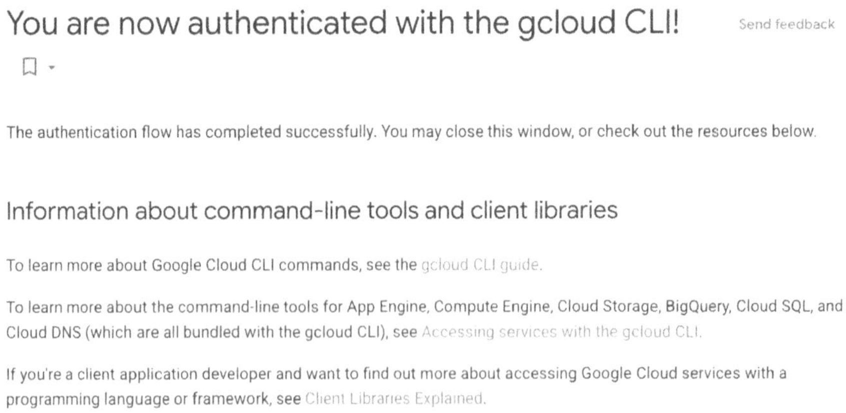

Figure 11.30: gcloud CLI authentication success

4. Once authenticated, the terminal will display a list of projects tied to your account. You can either select an existing project—such as learnmistral—or choose to create a new one. Your current project will be set based on your selection. Here's what the terminal prompt will look like:

```
Pick cloud project to use:

 [1] yourauth-1571888950021
 [2] coffe-cups-agent
 [3] learnmistral
 [4] plasma-creek-454
 [5] Enter a project ID
 [6] Create a new project
```

5. Type the corresponding number (for example, 3) to select your desired project.

> Your list will likely differ and may include only a single project, depending on your account's history.

You've now authenticated your local CLI with Google Cloud and selected your active project. This connection allows your terminal to issue secure commands, manage resources, and run inference directly from your machine—completely outside the Colab interface.

Preparing the virtual environment and requirements

With your environment authenticated and your project configured, the next step is to create a clean Python venv. This isolates your dependencies and ensures your SDK-based code runs predictably, independent of other Python tools installed globally. Let's get your local workspace ready:

1. Start by launching your terminal inside VS Code. Make sure you're inside the Git project directory you checked out earlier—specifically, the folder for this chapter. This ensures all your code and dependencies stay organized in one place. See *Figure 11.31* for the correct terminal view.

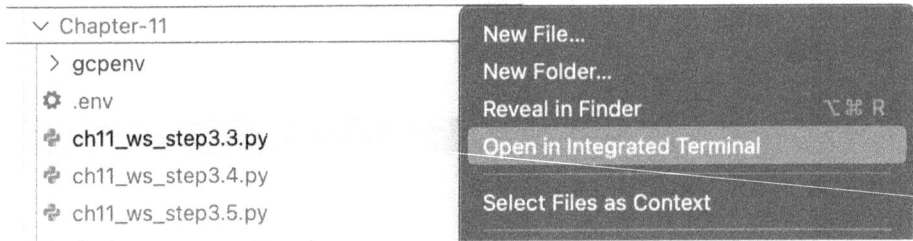

Figure 11.31: VS Code – Open in Integrated Terminal option on the Chapter-11 folder

2. In the terminal, run the following command to create a new Python venv inside your project directory. This environment isolates the packages for this workshop from other Python projects on your system:

```
python3 -m venv ./gcpenv
```

Next, activate the environment:

```
source ./gcpenv/bin/activate
```

3. Once activated, upgrade `pip` to make sure you're using the latest package manager:

```
python3 -m pip install --upgrade pip
```

4. Then, install the `mistralai[gcp]` package, which includes everything needed to work with Mistral on Vertex AI:

```
python3 -m pip install -U -q 'mistralai[gcp]>=1.2.4'
```

5. Finally, install `httpx`, a modern asynchronous HTTP client for Python:

```
python3 -m pip install -U -q httpx
```

Your environment is now fully prepared for secure and clean development. All necessary packages have been installed within an isolated workspace, ensuring reproducibility and minimizing system conflicts. You're now equipped to interact with Mistral directly from your local machine.

Authenticating a session from Python

The next step is to authenticate from within Python. You'll learn how to programmatically retrieve your Google Cloud access token and use it to make secure API requests to the Mistral model, just like we did in the Colab notebook—only this time, entirely through code.

Take the following steps:

1. Authentication is now moving from the terminal into your Python code. You'll use a script located in the Chapter-11 folder to programmatically retrieve your access token from the gcloud CLI. This token will authorize your requests to Vertex AI and enable secure interaction with Mistral models.

    Refer to the function in ./Chapter-11/ch11_ws_step3_3.py:

    ```python
    import subprocess

    def get_gcloud_access_token():
        process = subprocess.Popen(
            "gcloud auth print-access-token",
            stdout=subprocess.PIPE,
            stderr=subprocess.PIPE,
            shell=True
        )
        access_token_bytes, err = process.communicate()

        if process.returncode != 0:
            raise RuntimeError(
                f"Failed to get access token: {err.decode('utf-8').strip()}")

        return access_token_bytes.decode("utf-8").strip()


    # uncomment to test and see the access token
    # print(get_gcloud_access_token())
    ```

2. At the bottom of the script, you'll see a line commented out:

    ```python
    # print(get_gcloud_access_token())
    ```

3. Uncomment it to print the token and confirm that authentication is working. This token will be used in all future inference calls to authenticate your session:

    ```python
    print(get_gcloud_access_token())
    ```

4. Run this command in the built-in VS Code terminal where you prepared the venv:

    ```
    python3 ./ch11_ws_step3_3.py
    ```

If everything is set up correctly, you should see a token printed in your terminal—proof that your Python environment is securely linked to your Google Cloud account.

You've now authenticated directly from Python, completing the bridge between your local environment and Vertex AI. Your script can now interact with Mistral models in the cloud without relying on browser-based flows or notebook environments.

Initializing variables

Now it's time to define your working variables. In this step, you'll initialize model settings such as MODEL, PROJECT_ID, and LOCATION, ensuring your scripts are targeting the correct resources for inference. Take the following steps:

1. Define the key variables your inference script will use. These include the model identifier, the project ID, the region, and the endpoint you'll be sending requests to. Open the file located at ./Chapter-11/ch11_ws_step3_4.py, where all these configurations are centralized and editable:

    ```python
    # please replace with your preferred model if needed
    MODEL = "mistral-small-2503"

    # please replace with your preferred project ID if needed
    PROJECT_ID = "learnmistral"

    # please replace with your preferred location
    LOCATION = "us-central1"

    ENDPOINT = f"https://{LOCATION}-aiplatform.googleapis.com"
    ```

2. This script includes a function named validate_configuration(), which checks whether key variables such as MODEL and PROJECT_ID have been correctly set. If any are missing, it raises a clear and actionable error message to prevent silent failures later in the workflow:

    ```python
    def validate_configuration():
        if not PROJECT_ID:
            raise ValueError("Please set your PROJECT_ID")

        if not MODEL:
            raise ValueError("Please set your MODEL")
    ```

3. Uncomment the line that calls `validate_configuration()` at the bottom of the script and run the file using the following command. This confirms that your environment is correctly configured and ready to make requests:

```
validate_configuration()
```

4. Then, run the script:

```
python3 ./ch11_ws_step3_4.py
```

If everything is set properly, no errors will be raised, and you'll be ready for inference.

You've now defined and validated the essential variables your script will use to interact with the Mistral model.

Now that your configuration is locked in, it's time to trigger your first model call. In the next step, you'll craft an inference request and send it to Vertex AI using the **mistralai SDK**—capturing a real-time response from your deployed Mistral model.

Calling the inference request

Now that all the setup is in place, let's make our first real call to the Mistral model using the Python SDK:

1. Open the `./Chapter-11/ch11_ws_step3_5.py` file. The following is the complete code used to send a prompt and print the model's response:

```python
from mistralai_gcp import MistralGoogleCloud
from ch11_ws_step3_3 import get_gcloud_access_token
from ch11_ws_step3_4 import MODEL, PROJECT_ID, LOCATION

access_token = get_gcloud_access_token()

client = MistralGoogleCloud(
    access_token=access_token,
    region=LOCATION,
    project_id=PROJECT_ID
)

try:
    resp = client.chat.complete(
        model=f"{MODEL}",
```

```
            messages=[
                {
                    "role": "user",
                    "content": "Who is the best French painter? in one
        short sentence",
                }
            ],
        )
        print(resp.choices[0].message.content)

    except Exception as e:
        print(f"An error occurred: {e}")
        print(f"[debug] access_token: {access_token}")
        print(f"[debug] MODEL: {MODEL}")
        print(f"[debug] PROJECT_ID: {PROJECT_ID}")
        print(f"[debug] LOCATION: {LOCATION}")
```

Let's then import the required modules. These lines import the SDK client, your access token helper function, and the environment variables you defined earlier:

```
from mistralai_gcp import MistralGoogleCloud
from ch11_ws_step3_3 import get_gcloud_access_token
from ch11_ws_step3_4 import MODEL, PROJECT_ID, LOCATION
```

We then retrieve the access token. This line uses your helper function to grab the access token from your authenticated Google Cloud session:

```
access_token = get_gcloud_access_token()
```

2. Here, you set up the MistralGoogleCloud client with your token, region, and project ID. This object will be used to communicate with the Vertex AI API:

```
client = MistralGoogleCloud(
    access_token=access_token,
    region=LOCATION,
    project_id=PROJECT_ID
)
```

3. Inside a try block, this code sends a single prompt to the model and prints the response.
    The message format mirrors typical chat-based systems:

```
resp = client.chat.complete(
    model=f"{MODEL}",
    messages=[{
        "role": "user",
        "content": "Who is the best French painter? in one short
    sentence",
    }],
)
print(resp.choices[0].message.content)
```

4. If anything fails—such as an invalid token or misconfigured model—this except block
    prints the error and all key variables to help you debug quickly:

```
except Exception as e:
    print(f"An error occurred: {e}")
    print(f"[debug] access_token: {access_token}")
    print(f"[debug] MODEL: {MODEL}")
    print(f"[debug] PROJECT_ID: {PROJECT_ID}")
    print(f"[debug] LOCATION: {LOCATION}")
```

5. Now execute the script to see the model in action:

```
python3 ./ch11_ws_step3_5.py
```

If configured correctly, this will print a concise answer to your question from the Mistral model.

You've now made a successful synchronous inference call to Mistral using only Python code. The
response returned by Vertex AI confirms that your setup is correct and functional. This workflow mirrors how most production systems would use Mistral for one-off queries or response
generation.

Calling a streaming request

Next, you'll explore streaming responses—where model output is delivered token by token, in
real time. This is ideal for conversational applications or when you want to provide users with
progressive feedback.

Let's dive into streaming interaction:

1. To wrap up this hands-on section of the workshop, we'll test streaming inference. This lets the model return tokens as they are generated, which is ideal for responsive interfaces and conversational flows. Open the ./Chapter-11/ch11_ws_step3_6.py file to begin.

2. We first import the tools we'll need—the Mistral client, the access token function, and the configuration values we defined earlier:

    ```python
    from mistralai_gcp import MistralGoogleCloud
    from ch11_ws_step3_3 import get_gcloud_access_token
    from ch11_ws_step3_4 import MODEL, PROJECT_ID, LOCATION
    ```

3. We then fetch a fresh access token and use it to create an instance of the MistralGoogleCloud client, just like in the synchronous example:

    ```python
    access_token = get_gcloud_access_token()

    client = MistralGoogleCloud(
        access_token=access_token,
        region=LOCATION,
        project_id=PROJECT_ID
    )
    ```

4. Inside the try block, a streaming request is sent to the model. The prompt is the same as before, but the stream() method returns results piece by piece. A for loop iterates over each token chunk and prints them immediately to the terminal:

    ```python
    stream = client.chat.stream(
        model=f"{MODEL}",
        max_tokens=1024,
        messages=[
            {
                "role": "user",
                "content": "Who is the best French painter? One short
    sentence.",
            }
        ],
    )

    for chunk in stream:
        print(chunk.data.choices[0].delta.content)
    ```

5. If something goes wrong—such as an expired token or unreachable endpoint—the exception is caught and the error is printed:

```
except Exception as e:
    print(f"An error occurred: {e}")
    print(f"[debug] access_token: {access_token}")
    print(f"[debug] MODEL: {MODEL}")
    print(f"[debug] PROJECT_ID: {PROJECT_ID}")
    print(f"[debug] LOCATION: {LOCATION}")
```

6. To see the streaming response in action, run the script in your terminal:

```
python3 ./ch11_ws_step3_6.py
```

You should see the response appear gradually, simulating a real-time output stream from the model.

You've now implemented both synchronous and streaming inference requests from your own environment using Python and the Vertex AI SDK. This brings your workshop journey to a close from a practical standpoint—and sets you up to build interactive, scalable AI-driven applications by yourself.

Summary

You've just completed an impressive, hands-on journey—one that transformed Mistral from a concept into a working part of your own development environment. Starting with Google Cloud setup and API configuration, you built a solid foundation, then stepped confidently into Colab for quick experimentation.

But the true highlight of this chapter was your work in VS Code. You set up a dedicated Python environment, authenticated with the Google Cloud CLI, and wrote clean, modular code to run both synchronous and streaming inference requests. Each script you created brought you closer to the kind of workflows used in real production systems. You handled credentials, structured payloads, managed errors, and watched as Mistral generated responses on demand—all from your terminal.

This wasn't just a guided demo; it was a build-your-own-toolkit experience. You now have re-usable components, tested workflows, and a deeper understanding of how to bring language models into your projects with purpose and precision.

Whether you continue with advanced features or jump straight into applying these skills in your own apps, you've earned this confidence. You're not just capable of using AI—you're ready to build with it, shape it, and scale it. And that's a powerful place to be.

Extracurricular

Now that you've completed the core workshop, you're in a perfect position to push further. Whether you're curious about more powerful models or looking to self-host with full control, the following extracurricular activities will challenge your skills and unlock new possibilities with Mistral on Vertex AI and beyond:

1. Explore advanced features with Mistral Large

    If you're ready to experiment with a more capable model, go back to Model Garden and enable Mistral Large instead of the small variant. Once enabled, scroll through the autogenerated Google Colab notebook linked from the model card. It includes extended features such as the following:

    - Code generation
    - FiM prompt handling
    - Function calling with structured inputs and schema-aware outputs

These sections showcase Mistral's enhanced reasoning and structuring capabilities and give you a chance to interact with more nuanced prompts and scenarios. The notebook is pre-bound to your project, so you can jump straight into experimenting.

2. Deploy Mistral 7B or 8B on **Text Generation Inference (TGI)**

For users seeking a self-hosted setup, attempt to deploy Mistral 7B Instruct or Ministral 8B Instruct using **Text Generation Inference (TGI)**—through either Google Cloud or Hugging Face's infrastructure. This is an advanced workflow and includes the following:

- Preparing a `docker-compose.yml` file to run the TGI server (samples are provided in GitHub)
- Uploading the model to Google Artifact Registry or another accessible storage location
- Creating and exposing an endpoint for your model
- Launching the service on a GPU-enabled VM (you may need to request a GPU quota from Google Cloud beforehand)

Ensure your Hugging Face API token is active, and your account is approved to use the selected Mistral model. This token will allow Google Cloud to pull the model image from Hugging Face during deployment.

These optional challenges are ideal for developers who want to go deeper—whether to explore production hosting, benchmark performance, or unlock features reserved for larger models. Each path offers a different perspective on how Mistral can be used in real-world systems. Treat this as your open field for experimentation and growth.

Subscribe for a Free eBook

New frameworks, evolving architectures, research drops, production breakdowns—*AI_Distilled* filters the noise into a weekly briefing for engineers and researchers working hands-on with LLMs and GenAI systems. Subscribe now and receive a free eBook, along with weekly insights that help you stay focused and informed.

Subscribe at `https://packt.link/TR05B` or scan the QR code below.

<packt>

packtpub.com

Subscribe to our online digital library for full access to over 7,000 books and videos, as well as industry leading tools to help you plan your personal development and advance your career. For more information, please visit our website.

Why subscribe?

- Spend less time learning and more time coding with practical eBooks and Videos from over 4,000 industry professionals
- Improve your learning with Skill Plans built especially for you
- Get a free eBook or video every month
- Fully searchable for easy access to vital information
- Copy and paste, print, and bookmark content

At www.packtpub.com, you can also read a collection of free technical articles, sign up for a range of free newsletters, and receive exclusive discounts and offers on Packt books and eBooks.

Other Books You May Enjoy

If you enjoyed this book, you may be interested in these other books by Packt:

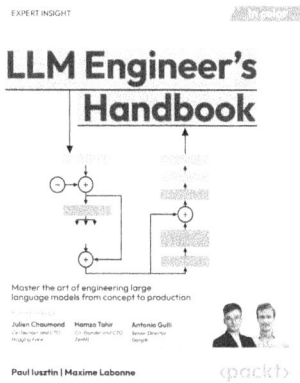

EXPERT INSIGHT

LLM Engineer's Handbook

Master the art of engineering large language models from concept to production

Julien Chaumond
Hamza Tahir
Antonio Gulli

Paul Iusztin | Maxime Labonne

<packt>

LLM Engineer's Handbook

Paul Iusztin, Maxime Labonne

ISBN: 978-1-83620-007-9

- Implement robust data pipelines and manage LLM training cycles
- Create your own LLM and refine it with the help of hands-on examples
- Get started with LLMOps by diving into core MLOps principles such as orchestrators and prompt monitoring
- Perform supervised fine-tuning and LLM evaluation
- Deploy end-to-end LLM solutions using AWS and other tools
- Design scalable and modularLLM systems
- Learn about RAG applications by building a feature and inference pipeline

Building Agentic AI Systems

Create intelligent, autonomous AI agents that can reason, plan, and adapt

Forewords by
Matthew R. Scott Chief Technology Officer, Minori at
Dr. Alex Arora member of the National Academy of Engineering, IEEE Fellow

Anjanava Biswas | Wrick Talukdar   ⟨packt⟩

Building Agentic AI Systems

Anjanava Biswas, Wrick Talukdar

ISBN: 978-1-80323-875-3

- Master the core principles of GenAI and agentic systems
- Understand how AI agents operate, reason, and adapt in dynamic environments
- Enable AI agents to analyze their own actions and improvise
- Implement systems where AI agents can leverage external tools and plan complex tasks
- Apply methods to enhance transparency, accountability, and reliability in AI
- Explore real-world implementations of AI agents across industries

Packt is searching for authors like you

If you're interested in becoming an author for Packt, please visit authors.packtpub.com and apply today. We have worked with thousands of developers and tech professionals, just like you, to help them share their insight with the global tech community. You can make a general application, apply for a specific hot topic that we are recruiting an author for, or submit your own idea.

Share your thoughts

Now you've finished *Learn Mistral*, we'd love to hear your thoughts! Scan the QR code below to go straight to the Amazon review page for this book and share your feedback or leave a review on the site that you purchased it from.

https://packt.link/r/1835888658

Your review is important to us and the tech community and will help us make sure we're delivering excellent quality content.

Index

A

abstractive summarization 3

actions 151

adaptive indexing 385

agentic systems
  building blocks 151, 152

agent performance testing 189
  agent-specific functions, defining 194
  customer service system wrapper and
      queries 195
  error handling 192
  final metrics calculation and
      persistence 193
  performance runs, executing 195, 196
  process time-measured agent call 192
  research agent wrapper and
      queries 194, 195
  result initialization 191
  summary of metrics, printing 193
  tester class, defining 190
  tester, creating 194
  tests loop 191

agents 22, 148, 149
  defining, in AI systems 147
  features 152-154
  versus traditional automation 150

AI systems
  agents, defining 147
  automation, shortcomings 147, 148

alert prioritization 348

AmazonBedrockFullAccess policy 406

Amazon S3 384

AMD's Strix Halo 62

API-driven model interactions 406

atomic sub-queries 279
  environment preparation 280
  indexing 281
  retrieval 281
  summarized response, generating 285-287

attention masking 80

Authorization header 434

average true range (ATR) 213

AWS Bedrock 404
  authentication and access control 405
  CloudWatch Logs, checking for 426
  connecting, with boto3 420, 421
  features 405
  prompt, sending to 421-425

AWS CLI V2 client
  configuring 414-416

B

bedrock
  versus bedrock-runtime 422

BMO Chatbot 44

Bootstrap RAG implementation 248
  environment preparation 248
  generation 255
  indexing 251
  retrieval 254, 255

boto3 407
  AWS Bedrock, creating with 420, 421

building blocks, agentic systems
  actions 151
  environment 151
  memory 151
  policies 151
  reasoning loops 151
  tools 151

C

**challenge implementation, semantic search
      and document classification 19-21**
  ambiguity 21
  context loss 21
  false positives 21

ChatMistralAI model 307

classification prompts 72

Cloud Resource Manager API 446

cloud security
  analysis 357-362

CloudWatch Logs
  checking, for AWS Bedrock 426
  using, for observability 407

code and cloud security, with Mistral
  practical workshop 356-369

Codestral, in VS Code 311
  application, running 321
  changes, applying to workspace 321
  code, running 326
  endpoint, testing 326
  environment, preparing 311
  errors, troubleshooting 329, 330
  FiM technique, using 331-333
  final code, reviewing 325
  first code, generating 318-320

fix, verifying 331
  generated code, enhancing 321-323
  learn from code 333, 334
  suggested changes, applying 324
  web page, creating 327, 328
  web page, testing 328, 329

Codestral model 311

coding prompts 76
  code reusability 78
  exception handling, improvements 77
  initial scaffolding 76
  unit test creation 76

Command-Line Interface (CLI) 436

context analysis 123
  future neighbor words, in Mistral 124, 125
  role of previous words, in Mistral 123

contextual understanding 4
  context handling, in long conversations 4
  context sensitivity and personalization 5
  limitations 5
  task adaptation, across domains 4

Continue extension
  installing 313, 314
  turning up 316-318

convolutional neural networks (CNNs) 8

**Cross-Site Scripting (XSS)
      vulnerabilities 366-369**

D

DDoS traffic
  spotting 344, 345

detailed sub-queries 264

Docker Desktop
  reference link 52

document classification

LLMs, for automatic sorting and categorization 16, 17

domain-specific embeddings 382

dynamic caching strategies 385

E

embedding generation 121

context analysis 123

for single line 122

embeddings, practical use cases 141

document classification service 142

job description and candidate matching service 142

news analysis 142

recommendation systems 142

stock prices, correlating to 142

embeddings, visualizing 111

heatmaps 114, 115

PCA 112

PSA, versus t-SNE 113

t-SNE 111, 112

environment, Codestral in VS Code

Continue extension, installing 313, 314

Continue extension, turning up 316-318

Flask, setting up 314, 315

logging, into GitHub 312

new project, preparing 318

preparing 311

Python extension, installing 314

Python virtual environment, setting up 314, 315

VS Code, installing 312

environment preparation, Bootstrap RAG implementation 248, 249

environment variables, initializing 250

required libraries, preparing 249

user prompts, preparing 250

environment preparation, multi-query approach 266

user prompts, preparing 267, 268

environment setup, inference with boto3 and CLI 408

AWS account, creating 408

AWS CLI V2 client, configuring 414-416

IAM user, creating 409-412

permissions, setting up 409-412

request access, to Mistral model on Bedrock 416-418

user access key, creating 412-414

VSCode project, preparing 419, 420

environment setup, semantic search system 116

draft notebook, uploading 118

Google Colab 116

recommended GPU runtime, setting up 117

workshop repository, cloning 116

error analysis dashboard 384

evaluation prompts 73

explainable AI (XAI) 8

extractive summarization 3

F

FastAPI 399

few-shot learning scenarios 382

Fill-in-the-Middle (FiM) 298, 461

using 331-333

finite element methods (FEM) 8

firewall logs analysis 343
  alert prioritization 348
  anomalous traffic detection 344-346
  geolocation-based analysis 346, 347
  zero-day threat detection 349-351

Flask 399
  setting up 314, 315

G

gcloud CLI
  active project, authenticating 463-465
  active project, initializing 463, 464
  active project, selecting 463, 464
  initial installation 462
  setting up 462

GCP ecosystem
  Vertex AI 431

generated output
  refining 81

generation, Bootstrap RAG implementation
  chain, invoking to answer specific
     question 258, 259
  chain on multiple questions,
     testing 259, 260
  ChatMistralAI 263, 264
  LLM, initializing 257
  prompt template,
     initializing for generator 255, 256
  prompt template, using from LangChain
     Hub 256, 257
  RunnableSequence TRACE 261
  simple chain, initializing 257, 258
  VectorStoreRetriever 262

generation, RAG architecture 243
  chain, creating 245
  chain, invoking 245
  LLM, preparing 244
  prompt, preparing 244

generification approach 287, 288
  environment preparation 288
  indexing 289
  retrieval 289
  summarized response 293-295

geolocation-based analysis 346, 347

Google Cloud account
  reference link 437

Google Cloud Platform (GCP) 431

Google Colab 116

Google Colab Enterprise
  Colab notebook, opening 449-451
  inference requests, running 457
  Mistral model, selecting 452-454
  model, playing with 449
  project selection widget, running 455, 456
  region selection widget, running 454, 455
  required libraries, importing 456, 457
  user, authenticating 451, 452

Google News HTTP request
  adding 216

Google News nodes
  Attach Symbol 217
  Parse RSS 218, 219
  two Code nodes, connecting after 217

graph databases (Graph DBs) 237

H

hardware configurations 60, 61
   powerful hardware configuration 62-64
   single-user 61
heatmaps 114
   features 115
HTTP request node
   adding 204, 205
   configuring 205
HTTP request sampler 398
hybrid search approach 380

I

Identity and Access Management
      (IAM) 405, 446
   roles 434
impersonation techniques 74
indexed data
   graph databases (Graph DBs) 237
   Lucene indexes 238
   persistent binary trees and distributed
         caches 238
   relational databases (RDBs) 238
   types 237
   vector stores 237
indexing 305
indexing, Bootstrap RAG
      implementation 251
   text, grinding to vectors 253, 254
   text, loading from URL 251, 252
   text, sending to vector store 253, 254
   text, splitting into chunks 252

indexing, RAG architecture
   embeddings 240
   indexed data 237
   initial document loading 239
   text, slicing 239, 240
inference requests, running
   cURL request, running to model 458, 459
   payload, preparing 457, 458
   with response printed 459-461
interactive demo interface setup 177
   chat interface workflow, building 182-185
   interface class, creating 178
   query submission, handling 185-187
   UI components, importing 178
   widgets, creating 179-182
interactive demo launch 188
   interface, creating 188, 189
   interface, displaying 188, 189
   usage instructions 188
InvokeModel 407

J

JMeter
   test plan, creating 398

K

Kullback-Leibler divergence 113

L

LangChain 301
LangChain Hub
   prompt templates, using 256, 257
LangSmith 249

LangSmith metrics
  ChatMistralAI 278
  overview 276, 277
  VectorStoreRetriever 277, 278

large language models (LLMs) 1, 146, 429
  contextual understanding 4
  predictive accuracy 5
  versus traditional algorithms 7

ListFoundationModels 407

LlamaIndex 142

LLMs for automatic sorting and
        categorization
  example use cases 17, 18

local Mistral model
  integration, with web UI 51
  using, in note-taking 50, 51

local Mistral model customization 37
  custom model, interacting with 42, 43
  manifest, creating 41, 42
  Modelfile, drafting 40, 41
  moderation, with system prompts 38, 39

local Mistral model exposure, to users
  customizing 37
  integration, with Obsidian 44-49
  integration, with web UI 51
  Ollama, installing 30-36
  Ollama, running 30-36
  playing with 36, 37
  powerful hardware configuration 29

local Mistral model integration, with
        Obsidian 44-49

local Mistral model integration
        with webUI 52
  Docker pull 52-57
  users, governing 58-60

logits 80
  sorting, by probability 96

Lucene indexes 238

M

macOS
  reference link 57

manifest 41

market data
  data, sorting 208, 209
  deduplicating 208, 209
  duplicates, removing 208
  processing script 209-212
  streams, merging 207
  workflow, rerunning 212, 213

max_tokens parameter 91
  command-line example 92

memory 151

Merge block
  setting up 220-222

Microsoft Teams 399

Milvus 384

min_p function 89, 90
  implementing 98, 99

Mistral
  supported parameters 94, 95

Mistral 8B 1
  shared idea with different faces 23, 24
  use cases 9

Mistral 8B, use cases
  adaptive models,
        for user personalization 10
  codestral and coding assistant 11
  data summarization and extraction 10
  multilingual support 10

Mistral AI client

client object, initializing 118, 119

dry run, performing 118, 119

initializing 118

mistralai package, installing 118

Mistral API key, setting up 119-121

Mistral API keys

preparing 156

**Mistral apps, fast tracking
with Vertex AI 436, 437**

interacting, in Google Colab Enterprise 449

prerequisites 437

setup and preparation 437

Mistral prompt

building 223-225

Mistral Small 407-409, 449

Modelfile

defining 40, 41

Model Garden 431

model performance, evaluation 18

accuracy 19

speed considerations 19

multi-agent answering service 154

agent loop, refining 159-161

agent performance testing 189

connection, testing 156, 157

interactive demo interface setup 177

interactive demo, launching 188

Mistral API keys, preparing 156, 157

research agent, creating with
multiple tools 166

safe calculator tool, creating 157-159

shared ReAct prompt, using 159-161

specialized customer service
agents 169, 174-177

stage, setting up 155

web search tool, building 161

web search tool, implementing 162-164

web search tool, testing 165

multi-query approach 265, 266

environment preparation 266

indexing 268

LangSmith metrics 276

summarized response, generating 273-276

multi-query generation 264

N

n8n

Visual AI agents, using with 196

natural language processing (NLP) 2

NLP tasks, LLMs

summarization 3

O

observability

with CloudWatch Logs 407

Obsidian

reference link 44

Ollama

installing 30-34

reference link 35

running 30-34

open, high, low, close, volume (OHLCV) 213

P

personalization prompts 73

Pinecone DB 131

pipeline

attention masking 80

context window 81

input length 81
logits 80
overview 69, 70
positional encoding 80
sequential token processing 79
system prompts 71
tokenization 79
weighting 80

Pixtraill 7

policies 151

port scanning attempts
identifying 345

positional encoding 80

predictive accuracy, limitations
bias and ethical concerns 7
complex multimodal data 7
lack of generalization 6
overfitting 6
real-time decision-making 6
unforeseen situations, handling 6

presence penalty 93
command-line example 94

Principal Component Analysis (PCA) 114
global picture, capturing 112

problem statement 340

prompts 71
classification prompts 72
coding prompts 76
evaluation prompts 73
personalization prompts 73
summarization prompts 72

Python extension
installing 314

Python Package Index (PyPI) 132

Python virtual environment
setting up 314, 315

Q

query expansion module 380

R

RAG architecture 234-236
challenges and trade-offs 247, 248
generation 243
indexing 236, 237
interaction, between retrieval and
generation models 246, 247
retrieval 241

RAG-powered assistant 299
API keys, initializing 300
chat conversation capabilities,
adding 308, 309
chat infrastructure, constructing 307
chat, preparing 307, 308
code chunks, indexing 304-307
data, loading from files 301, 303
documents, splitting into chunks 303, 304
environment, preparing 299
GitHub repo source code, indexing 300
interaction, with chat system 310
remote repository, cloning 301
required libraries preparing 299, 300

real-time decision-making, limitations 6

real-time log processing 354

real-time news summarizer, with RAG
building 388-390
generative model, fine-tuning for
summarization 394, 395
live news feeds and public APIs
integration 390, 391

real-time updates, enabling with dynamic indexing pipelines 396, 397

retrieval system, building for relevant articles 392, 393

speed and accuracy, optimizing 397

speed and accuracy, testing 397

system, stress-testing with Apache JMeter 398

test plan, creating in JMeter 398

user-friendly interface, integrating 399, 400

real-world QA test suite 384

reasoning loops 151

relational databases (RDBs) 238

repetition penalty 92, 93

command-line example 93

research agent class

defining 166, 167

research agents

creating, with multiple tools 166

research methods, adding 167, 168

testing 168, 169

response generation workflow

generated output 70

logits calculation 70

max_tokens 70

neural network processing 70

penalties 70

selected token 70

softmax function 70

temperature scaling 70

tokenization 70

top_k 70

top_p 70

user input 70

response object (resp) 433

retrieval, atomic sub-queries 281

detailed questions, generating 283, 284

drill-down prompt template, initializing 282, 283

init retriever 281

unique union, preparing 284, 285

retrieval-augmented generation (RAG) 2, 11, 12, 62

retrieval, generification approach

init retriever 289

step-back prompt, initializing 290, 291

step-back questions, generating 292, 293

retrieval, multi-query approach 268

drill-down prompt template, initializing 269, 270

rephrased questions, generating 271, 272

retrieval chain, calling 272, 273

retrieval chain, initializing 272, 273

retriever, initializing 269

retrieval, RAG architecture 241

documents, retrieving from vector store 242, 243

retriever, preparing 241, 242

rule compliance auditing 341-343

S

sampling functions

testing 99-101

scipy.spatial.distance module 128

secure access key 412

security applications 340

firewall logs analysis 343

other applications 354-356

rule compliance auditing 341-343

stateful firewall logs 351

semantic match of user input, with existing
        options 127, 128
    array dimension incompatibility,
        resolving 129
    distances, calculating 128, 129
    relevant dish match, displaying 130
    relevant dish match, finding 129

semantic search 12
    context role, in query interpretation 13, 14
    example use cases 14-16
    intent beyond keywords 12

semantic search system, with Mistral and
        Pinecone 116
    comparison embedding 125, 126
    demo retrospective 131
    embeddings, generating 121
    environment setup 116
    Mistral AI client, initializing 118
    user input, reading 126, 127
    user input, with existing options 127, 128

semantic search, with Pinecone DB 131
    closest match, finding 134, 135
    embeddings, upserting
        to Pinecone 133, 134
    Pinecone client, initializing 132
    Pinecone index, creating 132, 133

semantic similarity
    with heatmap visualization 135-138
    with t-SNE visualization 138-140

sequential token processing 79

setup and preparation, for deployment of
        Mistral apps with Vertex AI 447-449
    APIs and services, enabling 444-446
    APIs, enabling 439, 440
    billing account, linking 440-442
    Google Cloud project, creating 438
    project, linking to billing account 442-444

single-user hardware configuration
    AMD's Strix Halo 62
    Apple devices 61
    Windows/Linux, with discrete GPUs 61, 62

Slack 399

Smart PDF Loader 142

softmax function 82
    applying 83
    implementing 96
    initial code 85-87
    logit, exponentiating 84
    probabilities, calculating 84, 85
    sum of exponentiated logits 84

software development kit (SDK) 406

software QA 373

software QA revolutionizing, with RAG
        testing 373
    optimization 384, 385
    outputs, validating 383, 384
    QA RAG system scope, defining 375, 376
    QA workflows, integrating 385-387
    RAG system, fine-tuning 380-382
    relevant data sources ingestion 376-378
    retrieval process design 378-380
    scaling 384, 385

specialized customer service agents 169
    base specialized agent, defining 170, 171
    incoming inquiries in role, handling 171
    incoming role inquiries, handling 171, 172
    role-specific agents, implementing 172-174

SQL injection detection 363-365

stateful firewall logs 351
    protocol misuse 352, 353
    session tracking 351, 352

step-back generification 264

stress testing scenarios 384

summarization prompts 72

system prompts 29, 71
example 74, 75
impersonation techniques 74, 75

T

t-Distributed Stochastic Neighbor
Embedding (t-SNE) 111-113
local clusters, revealing 111, 112

techniques, for classification accuracy
multi-label classification 17
supervised fine-tuning 17
zero-shot classification 17

temperature parameter 87, 88

terminal 461

thread group 398

tokenization 79

tools 151

top-k filtering 97

top_k function 89
implementing 97

top_p function 89
implementing 98

traditional automation
versus agents 150

U

unauthorized access attempts
addressing 346

V

vector 106-108
comparison 108
databases 109-111
examples 108

Vertex AI 431
authentication and access, in GCP 434
development flow, selecting 435
inference workflows 432
in GCP ecosystem 431
integration, development
best practices 435, 436
Model Garden 431
model request, structure 433
models, deploying to 432
used, for fast tracking Mistral apps 436, 437

Vertex AI Model Garden 436

Vertex SDK 436

Vertex SDK for Python, Mistral AI 461
gcloud CLI, setting up 462
inference request, calling 469-471
session authentication,
from Python 466-468
streaming request, calling 471-473
variables, initializing 468, 469
virtual environment and requirements,
preparing 465, 466

virtual environment (venv) 436

visual AI agents, with n8n 196
chat for notifications, configuring 199-203
code nodes, wiring after
Google News 217-219
connections, making 219, 220
first HTTP request node, adding 204, 205
free data sources, setting up 196-199
Google News HTTP request, adding 216
HTTP request node, configuring 205
HTTP requests, configuring 203
HTTP requests, duplicating for gainers and
losers 206, 207
manual trigger, adding 203
Merge block, setting up 220-222
Mistral prompt, building 223-225

prompt, delivering to Telegram 226-229

prompt, sending to Mistral 226-229

request body, declaring 225

run, verifying 219, 220

system prompt, declaring 225

Telegram bot, configuring 199-201

workflow, rerunning 220

Yahoo Finance, configuring 213-215

VS Code 461

installing 312

VSCode project

preparing 419, 420

W

Weaviate 384

WebBaseLoader 239

web search tool

building 161

implementing 162-164

testing 165

web UI

Mistral model, integrating with 51, 52

weighting 80

Y

Yahoo Finance

configuring 213-215

Z

zero-day threat detection 349

examples 349-351

zero-shot learning scenarios 382

z-scores 213

www.ingramcontent.com/pod-product-compliance
Lightning Source LLC
Chambersburg PA
CBHW072007230326
41598CB00082B/6817